A WORLD ON THE WANE

C. LÉVI-STRAUSS

A WORLD
ON THE WANE

Translated by
JOHN RUSSELL

CRITERION BOOKS · NEW YORK

English translation © Hutchinson & Co. (*Publishers*) Ltd., London, 1961

Library of Congress Catalog Card Number: 61–7203

Originally published in France under the title
Tristes Tropiques by Librairie Plon, Paris, 1955: Chapters
XIV, XV, XVI and XXXIX of the French
edition are omitted in this translation.

This text is identical with that first published in
America in 1961 by Criterion Books, Inc., New
York, under the title TRISTES TROPIQUES, and all the
black-and-white illustrations have been retained.

MANUFACTURED IN THE UNITED STATES OF AMERICA

FOR LAURENT

Nec minus ergo ante haec quam tu cecidere, cadentque.

Lucretius, *De Rerum Natura*, III, 969

Contents

Illustrations

THE TUPI-KAWAHIB

LINE DRAWINGS

PART I

Destinations

1 *Departure*

TRAVEL and travellers are two things I loathe—and yet here I am, all set to tell the story of my expeditions. But at least I've taken a long while to make up my mind to it: fifteen years have passed since I left Brazil for the last time and often, during those years, I've planned to write this book, but I've always been held back by a sort of shame and disgust. So much would have to be said that has no possible interest: insipid details, incidents of no significance. Anthropology is a profession in which adventure plays no part; merely one of its bondages, it represents no more than a dead weight of weeks or months wasted en route; hours spent in idleness when one's informant has given one the slip; hunger, exhaustion, illness as like as not; and those thousand and one routine duties which eat up most of our days to no purpose and reduce our 'perilous existence' in the virgin forest to a simulacrum of military service. . . . That the object of our studies should be attainable only by continual struggle and vain expenditures does not mean that we should set any store by what we should rather consider as the negative aspect of our profession. The truths that we travel so far to seek are of value only when we have scraped them clean of all this fungus. It may be that we shall have spent six months of travel, privation, and sickening physical weariness merely in order to record—in a few days, it may be, or even a few hours—an unpublished myth, a new marriage-rule, or a complete list of names of clans. But that does not justify my taking up my pen in order to rake over memory's trash-cans: 'At 5.30 a.m. we dropped anchor off Recife while the seagulls skirled around us and a flotilla of small boats put out from the shore with exotic fruits for sale. . . .'

And yet that sort of book enjoys a great and, to me, inexplicable popularity. Amazonia, Africa, and Tibet have invaded all our book-stalls. Travel-books, expeditionary records, and photograph-albums abound; and as they are written or compiled with an eye mainly for effect the reader has no means of estimating their value. His critical sense once lulled to sleep, he asks only to be given 'more of the same' and ends by devouring it in unlimited quantity. Exploration has become a profession; not, as one might suppose, that it's a matter of unearthing new facts in the course of several years' laborious study —not at all! Mere mileage is the thing; and anyone who has been far enough, and collected the right number of pictures (still or moving, but for preference in colour), will be able to lecture to packed houses for several days running. Platitudes take shape as revelations once the audience is assured that the speaker has sanctified them by travelling to the other side of the globe.

For what do these books, these lectures, amount to? A luggage-list, a story or two about the misdemeanours of the ship's dog, and a few scraps of information—scraps that have done a century's service in every handbook to the region. Only the speaker's impudence and the ignorance and naivety of his hearers could cause them to pass as an 'eye-witness account' or even, for all I know, as 'an original discovery'. Doubtless there are exceptions; every age has its authentic travellers, and among those who today enjoy the public's favours I could point to one or two who deserve the name. My aim, however, is neither to expose the one nor to authenticate the other, but rather to understand a moral and social phenomenon which is peculiar to France and is, even there, of recent origin.

Not many people travelled professionally in the 1930s, and those who returned to tell their tales could count not on five or six full houses at the Salle Pleyel, but on a single session in the little, dark, cold, and dilapidated amphitheatre that stood in a pavilion at the far end of the Jardin des Plantes. Once a week the Society of Friends of the Museum organized—and may still organize, for all I know—a lecture on the natural sciences. 'Lantern lectures', they were; but as the screen was too large for the projector, and the lamp too weak for the size of the hall, the images thrown were intelligible neither to the lecturer, who had his nose immediately beneath them, nor to the audience, who could with difficulty distinguish them from the huge patches of damp that disfigured the walls. A quarter of an hour before the appointed time there was always doubt as to whether anyone would come to the lecture, apart from the handful of habitués who could be picked out here and there in the gloom. Just when the lecturer was losing all hope, the body of the hall would half fill with children, each accompanied by mother or nanny, some delighted by the prospect of a free change of scene, others merely craving relief from the dust and noise of the gardens outside. This mixture of moth-eaten phantoms and impatient youngsters was our reward for long months of struggle and hardship; to them we unloaded our treasured recollections. A session of this sort was enough to sever us for ever from such memories; as we talked on in the half-light we felt them dropping away from us, one by one, like pebbles down a well.

If this, our return, had its funereal side, as much could have been said of our departure, which was signalized by a banquet held by the Franco-American Committee in a disused private house in what is now the Avenue Franklin Roosevelt. A caterer, hired for the occasion, had arrived two hours earlier and set up his apparatus of hot-plates and china and table-silver: too late, however, for a hasty 'airing' to blow away the stench of desolation.

No less unfamiliar to us than the solemnity of our surroundings was the aroma of fusty tedium with which they were permeated. There had been just time, quite clearly, to sweep clean the centre of the enormous saloon in which we were to dine, and it was at the table—dwarfed, like ourselves, by its environment—that we made one another's acquaintance for the first time. Most of us were young teachers who had only just begun work in provincial *lycées*; there had stretched before us a damp winter, with lodgings in a second-rate hotel in a market-town and an all-pervading smell of grog, cellars, and stale wine. And now, George Dumas' slightly perverse whimsies were to whisk us away from all that and set us down in luxury-liners headed for the tropical seas: an experience which was to bear only the most distant resemblance to the stock notions of travel which were already forming within us.

I had been one of Georges Dumas' students at the time of the Traité de Psychologie. Once a week—Thursday or Sunday morning, I can't remember which—the philosophy students would go and hear him in one of the lecture-halls at the Hôpital Sainte-Anne. The walls facing the windows were covered with hilarious paintings by madmen; these set, from the very beginning, a peculiarly exotic note. Dumas was robustly built, with a body like a billhook and a great battered head that looked like a huge root which had been whitened and pared down by a sojourn on the sea-bed. He had a waxy complexion that unified his whole face with the white hair that he wore very short and *en brosse* and the little beard, also white, that grew in all directions at once. A curious fragment of vegetable matter, one would have said, with its rootlets still adhering to it, had not the coal-black gaze affirmed that it was beyond doubt a human being. The antiphony of black and white recurred in the contrast between the white shirt, with its starched and downturned collar, and the large-brimmed black hat, the black tie with its flowing knot, and the unvarying black suit.

We never learnt much from his lectures. He never 'got them up' in advance, because he knew that he never failed to cast a spell over his hearers. His lips, though deformed by a continual rictus, were marvellously expressive; but it was above all the hoarse and melodious voice that did the trick. It was a veritable siren's voice, with strange inflections that took us back not only to his native Languedoc but to certain ancient modes of speech, musical variants that went beyond all regional considerations and partook of the quintessential music of spoken French. In voice, as in looks, Dumas evoked a particular style, at once rustic and incisive: the style of the French humanists of the sixteenth century—the doctors and philosophers of whom he seemed to be the mental and bodily perpetuation.

A second hour, and sometimes a third, was devoted to the presentation of individual 'cases'. Often they were veterans who knew exactly what was wanted of them, and we would then witness astonishing displays of virtuosity in which they and the lecturer would vie with one another in cunning and guile. Some would produce their symptoms at exactly the right moment; others would offer just enough resistance to call for a display of bravura from the lecturer. The audience, though not taken in by these demonstrations, found them entirely fascinating. Those who won the maestro's particular favour were allowed a private interview with one or other of the patients. And never, in all my experience of primitive Indian tribes, was I as intimidated as I was by the morning I spent with an old woman who told me, from within her enveloping shawls, that she likened herself to a rotten herring buried deep in a block of ice: intact to all appearances, that is to say, but menaced with disintegration should the protective cover turn to water.

Dumas was not above mystification; and the general syntheses of which he was the sponsor had, for all their ample design, a substructure of critical positivism which I found rather disappointing. And yet, as was to be proved later, he was a man of great nobility. Just after the armistice of 1940, and not long before his death, when he was almost blind and in retirement in his native village of Ledignan, he made a point of writing me a discreet and considerate letter, with no other object than to put himself firmly on the side of those who had been the first to suffer from the turn of events.

I have always regretted not knowing him in his first youth, when the scientific perspectives opened up by nineteenth-century psychology had sent him off, wild with excitement and bronzed as a conquistador, to make the spiritual conquest of the New World. Between Dumas and Brazilian society it was to be a case of love at first sight: a mysterious phenomenon, in which two fragments of a four-hundred-year-old Europe met and recognized one another and were all but joined together again. Certain essential elements had remained intact in both cases: in a southern Protestant family, on the one hand, and on the other in a fastidious, slightly decadent bourgeois society that was turning over at half speed in the tropics. George Dumas' mistake was that he never grasped the authentically archaeological character of this conjunction. The Brazil that he wooed and won was only one of the possible Brazils, although it later seemed, when it came momentarily to power, to be the 'real' one. In Dumas' Brazil the ground landlords were steadily moving their capital into industrial holdings financed from abroad; seeking for an ideological cover of some sort, they settled for a right-thinking parliamentarianism. Our students, meanwhile, were the offspring of recent immigrants or squireens who lived by the land and had been ruined by fluctuations in world prices; to them, Dumas' friends were the *grao fino*—a bitter phrase that meant 'the smart set'. Oddly enough, the foundation of the University of São Paulo, which was Georges Dumas' greatest achievement, made it possible for people of modest station to begin to climb up the ladder by obtaining the diplomas which allowed them access to the civil service. Our academic mission did, in fact, help to form a new élite. But neither Dumas nor, later, the Quai d'Orsay would realize that this élite was a very valuable creation. As a consequence it drew steadily clear of our influence. It aimed, of course, to do away with the feudal structure which we had introduced into Brazil; but we had, after all, introduced it partly as a surety for good behaviour, and partly as a way of passing the time.

But, on that evening of the Franco-American dinner, neither my colleagues nor I—and that goes, of course, for our wives, who were to accompany us—had any idea of the role which we were to play, however involuntarily, in the evolution of Brazilian society. We were too busy taking stock of one another and avoiding, in so far as we could, the fatality of social error. Georges Dumas had just warned us that we must be prepared to lead the same life as our new masters: the life, that is to say, of Automobile Club, casino, and race-course. This seemed quite extraordinary to young teachers who had been earning twenty-six thousand francs a year; more recently—so few were those who applied to go abroad—our salaries had been tripled.

'Above all,' Dumas had said, 'you *must* be well dressed.' And as he wanted to reassure us he added, with rather touching candour, that it could be done at no great expense, not far from the Halles, at an establishment called À La Croix de Jeannette, where they had fitted him out very acceptably when he had been a young medical student in Paris.

2 *On Board Ship*

W<small>E HAD</small> no idea, in any case, that for the next four or five years our little group would constitute—with a few rare exceptions—the entire complement of first-class passengers on the Compagnie des Transports Maritimes' passenger-and-cargo steamers which plied between France and South America. We had a choice of either second-class on the only luxury-liner which worked this route, or first-class on the humbler sort of vessel. The intriguers went by luxury-liner, paid the difference out of their own pockets, and hoped by so doing to rub shoulders with an Ambassador or two and in some way profit thereby. We others chose the *bateau mixte*; it took six days longer, but we were its masters and, what is more, it made many stops en route.

How I wish today that I had realized twenty years ago the full value of what we were given! The unbelievable luxury, that is to say: the royal privilege of sharing with eight or ten others exclusive rights over the first-class deck, cabins, smoking-room, and dining-room on a ship built to carry a hundred or a hundred and fifty passengers. We were nineteen days at sea; our province was rendered almost illimitable by the lack of other passengers; our appanage went everywhere with us. After our second or third crossing we came back to 'our' ships, 'our' own way of life; and we knew by name, even before we got aboard, those sterling stewards from Marseilles, with their moustaches and their heavy-soled shoes, who overpowered us with their garlicky smell as they bent over us with *suprême de poularde* or *filet de turbot*. The meals, planned in any case on a Rabelaisian scale, became even more so from the fact that there were so few of us to sit down to them.

That one civilization is ending and another beginning; that our world has suddenly found itself to be too small for the people who live in it: these are facts which became real to me, not because of figures or statistics or revolutions but because I happened, a few weeks ago, to make a certain telephone call. I had been playing with the idea of retrieving my youth by a return visit, after fifteen years, to Brazil. The answer was that I should need to book my cabin four months in advance.

And I had imagined that, since the establishment of regular air-services between France and South America, the sea route was the preserve of a few eccentrics! It is, alas, a mistake to suppose that because one element has been invaded the other has been set free.

But in between the marvellous voyages of 1935 or thereabouts and the one to which I returned an immediate 'No' there was one, in 1941, which was charged with symbolic meaning for the years to come. Shortly after the armistice I was invited to the New School for Social Research in New York. (This I owed in part to the friendly interest which had been taken in my work by Robert H. Lowie and Alfred Metraux, in part to the vigilance of relations of mine long settled in the U.S.A., and, finally, to the Rockefeller Foundation's scheme for the rescue of European scholars who might find themselves menaced by the German occupation.) The problem was: how to get there? My first idea was that I should pretend to be returning to Brazil in order to continue my pre-war researches there. I went to the ground-floor rooms in Vichy, where the Brazilian Embassy had set up its temporary home, and asked to have my visa renewed. The interview was cruelly brief. I was well known to the Ambassador, Luis de Souza-Dantas, and he would, in any case, have behaved in the same way had I not known him. He was just raising his hand to stamp my passport when one of his staff reminded him, in tones of chilling respect, that under the new regulations he could no longer renew visas. For several seconds his arm remained poised, and there was a look almost of entreaty in his eyes as he tried to make his junior turn aside for a moment. My passport once stamped, I could at least have left France, even if I could not get into Brazil. But he wouldn't; and at length the Ambassador had to let fall his hand wide of my passport. No visa for me; he handed me back my passport with a gesture of distress.

I went back to my house in the Cevennes—not far from where, at Montpellier in fact, I had been demobilized—and began to hang about Marseilles harbour. Eventually I heard a rumour that a ship would soon be sailing for Martinique, and, after a great deal of to-ing and fro-ing from quayside to office and back again, I discovered that this ship belonged to that same Compagnie des Transports Maritimes which had found such a faithful and exclusive clientele among the members of our academic mission to Brazil. The winter bise was blowing keenly when, in February 1941, I walked into the company's unheated and three-quarters-closed offices. The official was one who had been wont to come and greet us on the company's behalf. Yes, the ship did exist; yes, it would shortly be leaving. But I couldn't possibly go on it. Why not? Well, I didn't realize how things were; he couldn't explain, but it wouldn't be at all what it used to be. How, then? Oh, it would be endless, and so uncomfortable! He couldn't imagine my putting up with it.

The poor man still saw me as a small-bore ambassador of French culture, but *I* saw myself as marked down for a concentration camp. Moreover, I had spent the previous two years, first in the virgin forests of Brazil, and later in one improvised billet after another in the course of a disorderly retreat that had taken me from the Maginot Line to Béziers by way of the Sarthe, the Corrèze, and the Aveyron: cattle-trains on the one hand and sheepfolds on the other: so that my inter-locutor's scruples seemed to me out of place. I saw myself going back to my wandering life—but on the oceans this time, sharing the labours and the frugal repasts of a handful of seamen, sailing hither and yon on a clandestine vessel, sleeping on deck, and gaining in health and strength from the day-long nearness of the sea.

I did at last get a ticket for the *Capitaine Paul Lemerle*. When the time came to embark the quayside was cordoned off. Helmeted *gardes-mobiles*, with automatic pistols at the ready, severed all contact between passengers and the relatives or friends who had come to see them off. Good-byes were cut short by a blow or a curse. This was not the solitary adventure I had had in mind; it was more like the departure of a convict-ship. If I had been amazed by the way in which we were treated, I was dumbfounded by our numbers. Somehow or other we were to be three hundred and fifty on board a little steamer which —as I lost no time in discovering—could boast only two cabins, with in all seven couchettes. One of these cabins had been allotted to three ladies, and the other was shared between four men, of whom I was one. This favour I owed—and may I thank him here and now—to M.B., who felt that it was out of the question for one of his former first-class passengers to be quartered like a cow or a pig. And, indeed, all the other passengers—men, women, and children—had to pile into the dark and airless hold, where the ship's carpenters had made a rough scaffolding of beds, one on top of another, with pallets of straw for bedding. Of the four fortunate males, one was an Austrian, travelling in metals, who doubtless knew what he had paid for the privilege; the second was a young 'béké', a rich creole, who had been cut off from his native Martinique by the war; he deserved special treatment in that he was the only person on board who was not presumed to be either a Jew, a foreigner, or an anarchist. The third was a mysterious North African who claimed to be going to New York 'for just a few days' (in itself an extravagant notion, since we were to be three months en route), had a Degas in his luggage, and, although as Jewish as I myself, appeared to be persona grata with the police, immigration, and security authorities of every colony and protectorate that we touched upon: an astonishing and mysterious state of affairs, at that juncture, and one which I never managed to fathom.

The scum, as the gendarmes described us, included among others André Breton and Victor Serge. Breton, by no means at his ease in such a situation, would amble up and down the rare empty spaces on deck, looking like a blue bear in his velvety jacket. We were to become firm friends in the course of an exchange of letters which we kept up throughout our interminable journey; their subject was the relation between aesthetic beauty and absolute originality.

As for Victor Serge, the fact that he had been an associate of Lenin was all the more intimidating, because it was difficult to reconcile it with his looks, which were those of a maiden lady of high principles. The smooth and delicate features, piping voice, and stilted, hesitant manner added up to the almost asexual character that I was later to encounter among Buddhist monks on the frontiers of Burma; they were remote, certainly, from the superabundant vitality and positive temperament which French tradition accords to the so-called 'subversive' agent. The point is that certain cultural types occur in all societies, because they result from straightforward antitheses; but their social function may differ widely from society to society. In Russia Serge's particular type had been able to make contact with reality in the course of a revolutionary career; elsewhere it might have found a very different outlet. The relations between any two societies would no doubt become very much easier if it were possible to establish, by the use of a sort of grille, a system of equivalences between the ways in which each would employ analogous human types in quite different social functions. Instead of confining ourselves, as we do now, to confrontations within certain professional groups (doctors with doctors,

teachers with teachers, industrialists with industrialists) we might come
to realize that there exist certain subtler correspondences between
individuals and the roles they play.

In addition to its human beings the ship was clearly carrying some
sort of secret cargo. We spent an unconscionable amount of time both
in the Mediterranean and on the west coast of Africa in putting into
port after port—seeking refuge, it appeared, from inspection by the
Royal Navy. Holders of French passports were sometimes allowed to
go ashore; the others had to stay parked in the few inches available to
them. As we got steadily nearer to the tropics the heat made the hold
more and more unbearable, and turned the deck into a mixture of
dining-room, dormitory, nursery, wash-house, and solarium. But most
unpleasant of all were the circumstances of what is sometimes called
'personal hygiene'. The crew had erected on either side of the ship,
port for the men and starboard for the women, two pairs of wooden
cubicles. These had neither light nor air. The one had two or three
douches which could be used for a short while each day; they were
filled each morning. The other had in it a long wooden trench, roughly
lined with zinc, which gave directly on to the ocean; you can guess its
purpose. Not everyone likes promiscuity in such matters, and in any
case the ship's rolling made it an unsteady business to squat in company:
the only way round this problem was to get there betimes, with the
result that the more fastidious passengers began to vie with one
another, until in the end it was only at about three o'clock in the
morning that one could hope for some degree of privacy. People
simply gave up going to bed. Two hours later the same situation arose
in respect of the douches: once again modesty played its role and, in
addition, the press soon grew so great that the water, insufficient from
the start, was as if vaporized by contact with so many moist bodies and
seemed no longer to get through to the skin. In both cases we all made
haste to get on and get out. The unventilated huts were made of planks
of green and resinous fir-wood; these planks, impregnated with filthy
water, urine, and sea air, would ferment in the sun and give off a warm,
sweet, and altogether nauseating smell, which, when mingled with
other smells, soon became intolerable, more especially if a swell was
running.

After a month at sea we suddenly glimpsed, in the middle of the
night, the lighthouse of Fort de France. And the hope which filled all
our hearts was not that of enjoying, at long last, an eatable meal, a bed
with real sheets, or a night's unbroken rest. No: these people who had

been used, on land, to what the English call the 'amenities of civilization' had suffered more from the unavoidable filth of these conditions
—aggravated as these were by great heat—than from hunger, or
fatigue, or sleeplessness, or promiscuity, or others' contempt. There
were young and pretty women on board, and there had been the
beginnings of flirtations. It was not simply from coquetry that these
women wanted to 'make the most of themselves' before all went their
separate ways: it was rather an obligation, a debt to be honoured, a
proof that they were not altogether unworthy of the attentions which
they considered—and with what charming delicacy!—to have been
theirs by token only. So that when the traditional cry of 'Land, land!'
was replaced by a unanimous shout of 'A bath, at last! A bath!' there
was something pathetic in it, as well as much that was comical. And
everyone set about searching for the last morsel of soap, the undirtied
towel, the clean blouse that had been held in reserve for this great
occasion.

Bathrooms are not all that common in Fort de France, and in our
dreams of hydrotherapy we took, it may be, an unduly optimistic view
of the effect of four centuries of colonization upon that island. We
very soon learnt, in any case, that our filthy and overloaded ship was a
floating Eden in comparison with the welcome that we were to
receive. Hardly had we dropped anchor in the roads when The Military
came aboard, in a state of cerebral derangement which would have
offered a rewarding field of study, had I not needed all my intellectual
capacities for the struggle to avoid disaster at their hands.

Most French people had lived through the 'phoney' war in ways
which deserved that adjective: none more so, however, than the
officers who formed the garrison on Martinique. Their sole duty was
to guard the Bank of France's gold; but this had gradually foundered
in a waking nightmare for which over-indulgence in rum punch was
only partly responsible. No less fundamental to it, and perhaps even
more insidious, were the position of the island, its remoteness from the
homeland, and a rich local tradition of piracy. The one-eyed peg-legs
of legend, with their golden ear-rings, had been replaced by phantoms
born of inspection by the U.S. Navy and the secret activities of
the German submarine fleet. Gradually there had spread among the
garrison an obsessional fever amounting almost to madness; and this
had gained ground in spite of the fact that never had a shot been fired
in anger or an enemy been sighted in the light of day. As for the
islanders, their talk revealed similar preoccupations, although they put

them in more prosaic terms: 'Island's done for, if you ask me—no more cod, they say,' and so forth. Others held that Hitler was none other than Jesus Christ returned to earth to punish the white race for having neglected his teaching.

When the armistice was announced all ranks sided with Vichy rather than with Free France. They hoped to remain at a safe distance from events; physically and morally their resistance was at its minimum, and such fighting spirit as they had ever had had long been dissipated. It was a comfort for them to replace the real enemy—one so distant that it had become for them a kind of abstraction—by an imaginary foe that had the advantage of being near at hand and readily visible. They exchanged, that is to say, America for Germany. Two ships of the U.S. Navy kept a constant watch outside the harbour; an ingenious member of the French C.-in-C.'s staff took luncheon on board one of them every day, while his superior busied himself with teaching his men to loathe and despise the Anglo-Saxons.

To these people we were well-assorted specimens of The Enemy, on whom they could work off the aggression which they had been accumulating for months. We could also be held responsible for a defeat which seemed to them quite foreign to themselves, since they had taken no part in the fighting, but of which, in another sense, they felt themselves confusedly guilty. Had they not exemplified and carried to its farthest point the nonchalance, the power of self-delusion, and the lassitude to which France, or a part of France, had fallen a victim? It was a little as if the Vichy authorities, in allowing us to take ship for Martinique, had marked us out as a cargo of scapegoats on whom these gentlemen could work off their spleen. They installed themselves —steel-helmeted, guns at the ready, wearing tropical shorts—in the captain's cabin; and when we appeared before them, one by one, it was not for the normal interview with the immigration authorities, but rather for an exercise in invective in which our role was to sit silent and listen. Those who were not French were treated as enemies of France; those who *were* French, on the other hand, had their Frenchness called grossly in question and were at the same time reproached for their cowardly abandonment of the motherland . . . reproaches, contradictory in themselves, which rang particularly oddly in the mouths of men who, since the day war was declared, had to all intents and purposes been living under the protection of the Monroe Doctrine.

So it was good-bye to our baths! The authorities decided to intern the whole lot of us in a camp called the Lazaret on the other side of the bay. Only three of us were allowed to go ashore: the 'béké', who had been ruled out of court, the mysterious Tunisian, who had had only to show certain of his papers, and myself. The captain of our ship had been second officer on one of the ships I had sailed in before the war; we had met, therefore, as old acquaintances, and he had induced the naval authorities to make an exception in my case

3 The Antilles

WHEN the clocks struck two in the afternoon
Fort de France was a dead town. There was no sign of life in the
hovel-bordered 'main square', which was planted with palm-trees and
overrun with rampant weeds—a patch of dead ground, one would
have thought, in which someone had left behind a statue of Josephine
Tascher de la Pagerie, later Beauharnais. No sooner had the Tunisian
and I checked into the deserted hotel than, still shaken by the events
of the morning, we hired a car and set off towards the Lazaret, with the
intention of comforting our companions and, more especially, two
young German women who had led us to believe, during the voyage
out, that they would be unfaithful to their husbands just as soon as
they could get properly cleaned up. From this point of view the
business of the Lazaret was yet another disappointment to us.

As the old Ford stumbled up and down the rough tracks in first
gear I had the pleasure of rediscovering many vegetable species which
had been familiar to me in Amazonia. Here they had new names,
however: caimite for *fruta do conde*—an artichoke in shape, with the
taste of a pear—corrosol for *graviola*, papaye for *mammão*, sapotille for
mangabeira. Meanwhile I went over in my mind the morning's painful
scenes and tried to relate them to others of the same sort. For my
companions, who had for the most part been hurled into their present
adventure after a lifetime of tranquillity, the soldiers' mixture of imbecility and spite appeared as a unique, exceptional, hardly credible
phenomenon: they and their jailers were in the grip, they thought, of
an international catastrophe such as had never before occurred. But I
had seen much of the world in the preceding years, and the incident
was of a kind with which I was not entirely unfamiliar. I knew that,
slowly and steadily, humanity was breeding such situations as a sick
body breeds pus. It was as if our race was no longer able to cope with

31

its own numbers and with the problems—greater every day—that resulted from this. Facility of communication exacerbated these feelings alike on the material and the intellectual plane. And, in the French territory in question, war and defeat had accelerated a universal process, and facilitated the establishment of an infection that would never again disappear completely from the face of the world. No sooner would it have vanished in one place than it would appear in another. Not for the first time, I was experiencing those manifestations of stupidity, hatred, and credulity which all social groups secrete within themselves when history comes too close to them.

Only a short while before, for instance, on my way home to France—it was a few months before the outbreak of war—I went for a walk in the upper section of Bahia. As I went from one church to another—there are said to be three hundred and sixty-five in all, one for each day of the year, and varying in their architectural and decorative style as if to fit the day and the season—and photographed such architectural details as took my eye, I was pursued by a gang of half-naked 'little nigger boys' who kept begging me to '*Tira o retrato! Tira o retrato!* Take a picture of us!' I found it touching that they should beg for a photograph that they would never see, rather than for a coin or two, and in the end I agreed to do as they asked. I hadn't gone another hundred yards when two plain-clothes policemen tapped me on the shoulder. They had kept me company since the outset of my walk; and now, they informed me, I had been caught in an act hostile to Brazil. My photograph, if put to use in Europe, would confirm the legend that some Brazilians have black skins, and that children in Bahia go barefoot. I was arrested—not for long, happily, because the ship was about to sail.

That ship brought me bad luck, undoubtedly. Something of the same kind had happened to me a few days before—when I was embarking, this time, and the ship was still at the quayside in Santos harbour. Hardly was I on board when I was arrested and confined to my cabin by a senior officer of the Brazilian Navy in full-dress uniform and two marines with fixed bayonets. *That* mystery took four or five hours to unravel: the Franco-Brazilian expedition of which I had been in charge for a year had been subject to the rule by which all 'finds' were to be shared between the two countries. The sharing was to be done under the supervision of the National Museum in Rio de Janeiro, and this museum had notified every port in Brazil that if I were to attempt to leave the country with more bows, arrows, and feather head-dresses than had been allotted to France I must be put under immediate and close arrest. Subsequently the museum had changed its mind and decided to make over Brazil's share of the finds to a scientific institute in São Paulo; consequently our French share had to be despatched from Santos, and not from Rio. Meanwhile the previous instructions had been forgotten and not, therefore, countermanded; with the result that, in the eyes of the port authorities, I had committed a crime.

Luckily, however, there still slumbered within every Brazilian official at that time a tradition of anarchy. Tags from Voltaire and Anatole France kept this tradition alive and had somehow been incorporated, even in the depths of the forest, as elements of Brazilian culture. (Once when I was in the interior I was forcibly embraced by an old man who, doubtless, had never seen a Frenchman before. 'Ah, monsieur, a Frenchman!' he cried, almost in delirium. 'Ah, France! Anatole, Anatole!') I'd met enough Brazilians to know that I must first show all possible deference to the Brazilian State, as a whole, and more especially to its maritime authorities. Next I tried to strike a note of deep feeling: and not without success, for after several hours spent in a cold sweat—I was leaving Brazil for good, our collections had been packed away with my library and my furniture, and I was haunted by visions of my possessions lying in pieces on the quayside as the ship drew out to sea—I was able to dictate to my interlocutor the exact terms of his report. In this he took upon himself the glory of having averted an international incident, and in consequence a humiliation for Brazil, by allowing me to sail with my baggage intact.

Perhaps I should have been less audacious had it been still possible for me to take the South American police system quite seriously. But something had happened, two months previously, to make this out of the question. I had had to change aeroplanes in a large village in Lower Bolivia. When the connection failed to arrive, my companion, Dr J. A. Vellard, and myself were held up there for several days. Flying in 1938 was very different from what it is now. In the remoter South American regions it had jumped several stages of 'progress' and offered itself as a sort of mechanical pick-a-back for villagers who, hitherto, for lack of decent roads, had had to reckon on a four or five days' journey, on foot or horseback, to their nearest market-town. And now it had suddenly become possible for them to get their hens and ducks to market in a matter of a few minutes' flying time—though with, as often as not, a delay in departure of a week or more. The little aeroplanes were crammed with barefooted peasants, farmyard animals, and cases too cumbrous to be dragged through the forest; and in the midst of all this was oneself, squat-legged on the floor.

We were killing time in the streets of Santa Cruz de la Sierra when suddenly a police patrol, seeing strangers, put us under arrest. We were conducted, pending interrogation, to a room in the former palace of the Provincial Governor. An air of old-fashioned high comfort clung to the panelled saloon, with its glass-fronted bookcases, its rows of richly bound volumes, and the astonishing handwritten notice— framed and glazed, likewise—which I here transcribe from the Spanish: 'On pain of severe sanctions it is strictly forbidden to tear out pages from the archives for personal or hygienic purposes. All persons infringing this order will be punished.'

I must own that if my situation in Martinique took a turn for the better, it was thanks to the intervention of a high official of the Ponts et Chaussées whose opinions, though concealed beneath an appearance of frigid reserve, were very different from those current in official circles; perhaps I also owed something to my frequent visits to the offices of a religious review, where the Fathers of some Order or other had accumulated box upon box of archaeological remains, dating back to the Indian occupation. I spent my leisure hours in making an inventory of these

One day I went into the Assize Courts, which were then in session. It was my first, and only, visit to a trial. The accused was a peasant who had bitten off a part of another peasant's ear in the course of a quarrel. Accused, plaintiff, and witnesses expressed themselves in a flood of creole eloquence which seemed almost supernatural, in such a place, by reason of its crystalline freshness. All this had to be translated to the three judges, whose robes, scarlet in colour and trimmed with fur, had wilted in the heat and hung about them like bloodstained bandages. In five minutes exactly the irascible negro was condemned to eight years' imprisonment. Justice had been, and is still, associated in my mind with the notions of doubt, and scruple, and respect. I was stupefied to find that a human life could be disposed of so quickly and with such nonchalance. I could hardly believe that it had really happened. Even today no dream, however fantastic or grotesque, can leave me so entirely incredulous.

My travelling companions owed their release, meanwhile, to a difference of opinion between the maritime authorities and the Chamber of Commerce. To the one, they were spies and traitors; the other saw them as a source of income which could not be exploited while they were locked up in the Lazaret. The shopkeepers got their way, in the end, and for a fortnight one and all were free to get rid of their last French francs. The police kept a close watch on all this and did their best to involve all the passengers, and more especially the women, in a network of temptation, provocation, seduction, and reprisal. The Dominican Consulate was besieged with requests for visas, and every day brought new rumours of hypothetical ships which were on their way to take us all a stage farther. A new situation developed when the villages of the interior grew jealous of the harbour-town and intimated that they too had the right to a share in the refugees. And, from one day to the next, the entire company was moved to the interior and told to stay there. I was exempt from this, once again, but in my anxiety to visit my lady-friends in their new residence at the foot of the Mont Pelé I came to cover on foot an unfamiliar and unforgettable part of the island. Thanks, in fact, to the machinations of the police I came to experience a form of exoticism more classical than that to be found on the mainland of South America: dark tree-agate, surrounded by a halo of beaches where the black sand was speckled with silver; valleys deep in a milk-white mist where a continual drip-drip allowed one to hear, rather than see, the enormous, soft, and feathery leafage of the tree-ferns as it foamed up from the living fossils of the trunks.

Hitherto I had been luckier than my companions. I was pre-occupied, none the less, with a problem which, if not satisfactorily solved, would have made it impossible for this book to be written. I had left France with a trunkful of material brought back from my expeditions: linguistic and technological files, travel-journals, field-notes, maps, plans, photographic negatives, thousands of sheets of paper, filing-cards, and rolls of film. It had already been very dangerous for the *passeur* to get this heavy load across the line of demarcation, and it was clear to me from our welcome in Martinique that I must not allow Customs, police, or naval security authorities to get at my possessions. The vocabularies would certainly strike them as an elaborate system of codes, and the maps, plans, and photographs they would interpret as pieces of military information. I therefore declared the trunk 'luggage in transit' and it was sealed up and left at the Customs. Later I managed to effect a compromise by which the trunk, if put directly aboard a foreign ship, need not be opened by the Customs. And so it was that I set sail for Porto Rico on board a

Swedish banana-boat. For four days on this dazzlingly white vessel I found myself back in pre-war conditions; the voyage was uneventful and there were only seven other passengers on board.

I did well to make the most of it. For when I disembarked at Porto Rico two things became clear. One was that the U.S. immigration laws had changed during the two months that had elapsed since I left Marseilles. The documents I had received from the New School for Social Research no longer sufficed for admission. Second, and above all, the American police, when faced with my load of anthropological material, had their full share of the suspicions which I had feared to meet with in Martinique. In Fort de France I had been treated as a Jew and a Freemason who was probably in the pay of the Americans. Here, in Porto Rico, I was taken for an emissary of Vichy —if not, indeed, of the Germans. I telegraphed to the New School to get me out of it, if they could, and the F.B.I. was asked to send a French-speaking specialist to examine my papers. (I trembled to think how long it would take to find a specialist who could decipher my notes, since these mostly related to the almost entirely unknown dialects of central Brazil.) Meanwhile I was interned, at the shipping company's expense, in an austere hotel in the Spanish style, where I was fed on boiled beef and chick-peas, while two filthy and ill-shaven native policemen took it in turns, night and day, to guard my door.

So it was at Porto Rico that I made my first contact with the U.S.A. For the first time I smelt the lukewarm varnish and the wintergreen tea—olfactory extremes between which is stretched the whole gamut of American comfort—from motor-car to lavatory, by way of radio-set, pastry-shop, and toothpaste—and I tried to find out what thoughts lay behind the farded masks of the young ladies in the drug-stores, with their mauve dresses and their chestnut hair. There too, in the rather special environment of the Grandes Antilles, I had my first glimpse of certain characteristics of American urban life. The flimsiness of the buildings, their preoccupation with effect, and their desire to catch the eye—all were reminiscent of a Great Exhibition that had not been pulled down; at Porto Rico one seemed to have strayed into the Spanish section.

Ambiguities of this kind often confront the traveller. The fact of having passed my first weeks on American territory in Porto Rico made me feel, later, that Spain itself was Americanized. Similarly, the fact that my first glimpse of British University life was in the neo-Gothic precincts of the University of Dacca in eastern Bengal has since made me regard Oxford as a part of India that has got its mud, its humidity, and its superabundant vegetation under surprisingly good control.

The F.B.I. inspector arrived three weeks after I came ashore at San Juan. I ran to the Customs house and threw open my trunk. A solemn moment! He was a well-mannered young man, but when he took up a card at random his face clouded over and he spat out the words: 'This is in German!' It was, in effect, a note drawn from the classic work of von den Steinen, my illustrious and distant forerunner in the Mato Grosso: *Unter den Naturvölkern Zentral-Braziliens*, Berlin, 1894. The long-expected 'specialist' was reassured to hear of this, and before long he lost all interest in my concerns, and I found myself free to enter the U.S.A.

But that's quite enough. Each one of these trifling adventures calls forth another from my memory; and I could summon up others, more recent, if I drew upon my travels in Asia during the post-war years. My charming inquisitor from the F.B.I. might not be so easily satisfied today. The atmosphere thickens, everywhere.

4 *The Quest for Power*

I ALWAYS remember the first occasion on which I had some indication of the disturbances which lay below the surface of pre-war life. The incident was a ridiculous one; and yet, like a doubtful smell or a sudden shift in the wind, it was a portent of worse things to come.

I had refused to renew my contract with the University of São Paulo, preferring to make an extended foray into the interior, and with this in view I left France some weeks earlier than the rest of my colleagues. For the first time in four years I was the only academic figure on board and, likewise for the first time, there were a great many passengers. Some were foreign business men, but most were members of a military mission on its way to Paraguay. The familiar shipboard scene was rendered unrecognizable by their presence; nothing remained of its old tranquillity. Officers and wives alike seemed to mistake the transatlantic voyage for a colonial expedition; and although they were to act as instructors to what was, after all, an army of no great pretensions, they behaved as if they were about to occupy a conquered country. And they made ready for this—morally, at any rate—by transforming the boat-deck into a barrack-square, with the civilian passengers enlisted as temporary 'natives'. So blatant and so gross was the insolence involved that the other passengers did not know where to go to be free from it; even the ship's officers felt uneasy. The mission's commanding officer was very different from his subordinates, and he and his wife were discreet and considerate in their behaviour; one day they sought me out in the quiet corner to which I had made my escape and, while showing a kindly interest in my activities, past and future, they gave me a clear hint that their role in the whole affair was that of witnesses who deplored the goings-on but could do nothing to prevent them. There was something mysterious in it all; three or four years later I happened on the senior officer's name in a newspaper and realized that his personal situation had, in effect, something of paradox about it.

It was then that I learnt, perhaps for the first time, how thoroughly the notion of travel has become corrupted by the notion of power. No longer can travel yield up its treasures intact: the islands of the South Seas, for instance, have become stationary aircraft-carriers; the whole of Asia has been taken sick; shanty-towns disfigure Africa; commercial and military aircraft roar across the still 'virgin' but no longer unspoilt forests of South America and Melanesia. . . . Travel, in such circumstances, can only bring us face to face with our historical existence in its unhappiest aspects. The great civilization of the West has given birth to many marvels; but at what a cost! As has happened in the case of the most famous of their creations, that atomic pile in which have been built structures of a complexity hitherto unknown, the order and harmony of the West depend upon the elimination of that prodigious quantity of maleficent by-products which now pollutes the earth. What travel has now to show us is the filth, *our* filth, that we have thrown in the face of humanity.

I understand how it is that people delight in travel-books and ask only to be misled by them. Such books preserve the illusion of something that no longer exists, but yet must be assumed to exist if we are to escape from the appalling indictment that has been piling up against us through twenty thousand years of history. There's nothing to be done about it: civilization is no longer a fragile flower, to be carefully preserved and reared with great difficulty here and there in sheltered corners of a territory rich in natural resources: too rich, almost, for there was an element of menace in their very vitality; yet they allowed us to put fresh life and variety into our cultivations. All that is over: humanity has taken to monoculture, once and for all, and is preparing to produce civilization in bulk, as if it were sugar-beet. The same dish will be served to us every day.

People used to risk their lives in India and America for the sake of returns which now seem to us derisory: redwood (*bois de braise*, from which comes the name of Brazil); red dye, or pepper, for which there was such a craze at the court of Henri IV that people carried a grain or two with them everywhere, in *bonbonnières*; such things gave an extra stimulus to sight and smell and taste, and extended, as it were, the sensory keyboard of a civilization which had not recognized its own insipidity. Are we to draw a parallel with the Marco Polos of our own day who bring back from those same territories—in the form, this time, of photographs—the heightened sensations which grow ever more indispensable to our society as it founders deeper and deeper in its own boredom?

Another parallel seems to me more significant. The 'red peppers' of our own day are falsified, whether intentionally or not. This is not because their character is purely psychological; but because, however honest the traveller may be, he cannot, or can no longer, present them to us in their authentic form. Before we consent to accept them they must be sorted and sieved; and, by a process which in the case of the more sincere travellers is merely unconscious, the stereotype is substituted for the real. I open one of these 'traveller's tales': the author describes a certain tribe as 'savage' and lightly sketches in a caricature of the habits which, according to him, have been preserved among them since the beginnings of time; but it happens that, when I was a student, I spent several years in the study of the books, some of them fifty years old, some quite recent, which men of science devoted to that same tribe before it was reduced, by contact with the whites and the epidemics that resulted from this, to a handful of uprooted wretches. Another group has been 'discovered' and, in the space of forty-eight hours, 'studied' by a traveller, a mere boy, who glimpsed them while they were being moved out of their territory. In his simplicity he mistook their temporary camp for a permanent village. Nor was anything said of the available means of approach to the area: the missionary post which for twenty years has maintained unbroken contact with the natives, and the little motor-boat line which runs deep into the interior. To an experienced eye this latter is instantly revealed by certain small details in the 'explorer's' photographs; the trimmer has left in some of the rusted cans which show where these 'unknown' people have set up their kitchen.

If we examine the vanity of these pretensions, the naive credulity which not only welcomes them but calls them forth, and the talent which goes into these pointless activities (pointful they may be however, if they extend further the deterioration which, outwardly, they do their best to conceal); if we examine all these, we shall find that they appear to correspond to powerful psychological demands, alike in the performers and in their public; and the study of certain primitive institutions may help us to analyse the nature of these demands. Anthropology must help us, in short, to understand the fashion which has attracted in our direction so many auxiliaries who do us nothing but harm.

Among many North American tribes the social prestige of any particular individual is determined by the nature of the ordeal to which he has submitted himself in adolescence. Some have themselves cast off alone, on a raft, without food; others seek the isolation of the mountainside, where they are exposed to rain, and cold, and wild beasts. For days, weeks, months even in some cases, they go without cooked food; eating only raw stuffs, or fasting altogether for long periods, they accentuate their bodily dilapidation by the use of emetics. They do everything possible to break through to the world beyond: prolonged immersion in ice-cold baths, the voluntary amputation of one or more fingertips, and the tearing of the aponeuroses. (In this last instance wooden pins are thrust beneath the muscles of the back; to these pins are attached lengths of string, and on the end of each string is a heavy weight which the victim must haul along as best he can.) Not all go quite so far; but at the very least they must exhaust themselves in some pointless activity, plucking the hairs one by one from their bodies, or picking away at fir-branches until not a spine remains, or hollowing out a huge block of stone.

Lassitude, weakness, and delirium result; and they hope, while in this state, to enter into communication with the supernatural world. Their prayers, and the intensity of their sufferings, will be rewarded; a magic animal will present itself to them, and in a vision there will be revealed to them both the spirit who will henceforth be their guardian and the particular power, derived from that spirit, which will define their rank, and the number of their privileges, within their social group.

Could one say of these natives that Society has nothing to offer them? It is as if their customs and institutions seemed to them to function mechanically: luck, chance, and talent are of no avail, and the man who wishes to wrest something from Destiny must venture into that perilous margin-country where the norms of Society count for nothing and the demands and guarantees of the group are no longer valid. He must travel to where the police have no sway, to the limits of physical resistance and the far point of physical and moral suffering. Once in this unpredictable borderland a man may vanish, never to return; or he may acquire for himself, from among the immense repertory of unexploited forces which surrounds any well-regulated society, some personal provision of power; and when this happens an otherwise inflexible social order may be cancelled in favour of the man who has risked everything.

This would be, none the less, a superficial interpretation. The

question among these North American tribes is not one of the antithesis between individual convictions and the doctrines of Society. The
dialectic springs directly from the customs and the philosophy of the
group. From the group the individual learns his lesson; the belief in
guardian spirits is the creation of the group, and Society as a whole
teaches its members that their only hope of salvation, within the
established social order, lies in an absurd and despairing attempt to get
free of that order.

Quite clearly the relationship between the French public of today
and its favourite explorers is a naive variant of this ancient convention.
Our adolescents, like those of the North American Indians, are encouraged to get clear, by one means or another, of civilization. Some
climb mountains; some go far below ground; others escape horizontally and penetrate some distant land. Or it may be that the sought-
after extremity lies in the moral sphere; some choose to be put in
situations so difficult that, as far as we can now tell, they cannot
possibly survive them.

Society is completely indifferent to the rational consequences, if one
may so describe them, of these adventures. Scientific discovery plays
no part in them. Nor can they be considered to enrich the 'literature of
the imagination'; for very often they are abominably written. It's the
attempt that counts, and not its object. Once again the parallel is very
close: any young man who isolates himself for a few weeks or months
from the group and exposes himself to an extreme situation of any sort
may count on being invested, on his return, with a kind of magic
power. (Some of our contemporaries are men of sincere conviction,
some are sly and calculating; these same distinctions occur in primitive
societies also.) In our world the power comes out in newspaper articles,
best-selling books, and lectures with not an empty seat in the hall. Its
magic character is evident in the process of auto-mystification of the
group and by the group which is, in every case, the basis of the
phenomenon. Lofty and lucrative are the 'revelations' which these
young men draw from those enemies of Society—savages, snowbound
peaks, bottomless caves, and impenetrable forests—which Society
conspires to ennoble at the very moment at which it has robbed them
of their power to harm. 'Noble' they are today, but when they were
really the adversaries of Society they inspired only terror and disgust.
Today the savages of the Amazonian forests are caught, like game-
birds, in the trap of our mechanistic civilization. I can accept as
inevitable the destruction of these vulnerable and powerless beings;

what I will not be deceived by, on the other hand, is the 'black magic', more paltry even than their own, which brandishes before an eager public an album in 'full colour'. Now that the Indians' masks have been destroyed, these albums have taken their place. Perhaps our readers hope, by the intermediacy of these colour-plates, to take on something of the Indian's charms? To have destroyed the Indians is not enough—the public may, indeed, not realize that the destruction has taken place—and what the reader wants is to satisfy, in some sort, the cannibal-instincts of the historical process to which the Indians have already succumbed.

Myself the already-grey predecessor of these 'explorers', I may well be the only white traveller to have brought back nothing but ashes from my journeys. Perhaps my voice alone will be heard to say that travel no longer offers an escape? Like the Indian in the legend, I have been to the world's end and there asked questions of people, and of things; and like him I was disappointed with what I heard. 'And he stood there, in tears; praying and groaning aloud. And he heard no mysterious sounds; nor did he fall asleep, to be carried away while sleeping to the temple of the magic animals. He could doubt no longer; no power, from any source, had been given to him. . . .'

Missionaries used to speak of dreams as 'the savage's god', but through my hands, at any rate, they have always slipped like mercury. Where did I sense some small part, some glittering particle of their power? At Cuiaba, where the earth once yielded gold by the nugget? At Ubatuba, the now-deserted port where two centuries ago the great galleons put in to load? Flying over the Arabian desert, pink-and-green-streaked like the mother-of-pearly ear-shell? In America or in Asia? On the Newfoundland banks, the plateaux of Bolivia, or the hills on the frontiers of Burma? I choose at random a name still charged with the authority of legend: Lahore.

A landing-ground, vaguely in the suburbs; interminable avenues, tree-lined, villa-bordered; and then, in an enclosure, an hotel reminiscent of a Normandy stud-farm, where a number of identical buildings, with doors opening directly on to the road, were laid out like so many diminutive stables. Each door opened on to a uniform apartment: sitting-room, bedroom, bathroom. Half a mile or more away, along the avenue, was a little square, such as one finds in a French market-town, and at considerable intervals along the avenues that stretched out, star-wise, from that square there were three or four shops: chemist, photographer, bookseller, watchmaker. A captive in these unmeaningful

expanses, I felt my objective slipping beyond reach. Where could
it be, the old, the authentic Lahore? To get to it, at the far end
of the badly laid-out and already decrepit suburbia, one had to
cross a lengthy bazaar-area, in which were to be found cosmetics,
medicines, imported plastic materials, and shoddy jewellery—made,
this last, by the operation of a mechanical saw on gold the thickness of
white lead. As I sought for the 'real Lahore' at the end of those shaded
alleys I had constantly to flatten myself against the wall: flocks of sheep
were passing—sheep with pink and blue lights in their wool—or
buffaloes, each as big as three cows, or, most often, lorries. Perhaps the
secret lay with the wooden buildings that were falling to pieces from
sheer old age? I could have appreciated the lacy, finely chiselled working
of the wood had I not been kept at a distance by the metallic spider's
web of primitive electric wiring that crossed and criss-crossed from one
wall to the next. From time to time, too, and for the space of two or
three paces, an image or an echo would rise up from the recesses of
time: in the little street of the beaters of silver and gold, for instance,
there was a clear, unhurried tinkling, as if a djinn with a thousand arms
was absent-mindedly practising on a xylophone. No sooner was I out
of this labyrinth than I came to the area where huge avenues have been
sketched out among the ruins (due, these, to the riots of the recent
years) of houses five hundred years old. So often, however, have these
houses been destroyed and patched together again, so absolute is their
decrepitude, that the notion of period has no meaning in their context.
And that is how I see myself: traveller, archaeologist of space, trying
in vain to repiece together the idea of the exotic with the help of a
particle here and a fragment of debris there.

At this point Illusion begins to set its insidious traps. I should have
liked to live in the age of *real* travel, when the spectacle on offer had
not yet been blemished, contaminated, and confounded; then I could
have seen Lahore not as I saw it, but as it appeared to Bernier,
Tavernier, Manucci. . . . There's no end, of course, to such conjectures.
When was the right moment to see India? At what period would the
study of the Brazilian savage have yielded the purest satisfaction and
the savage himself been at his peak? Would it have been better to have
arrived at Rio in the eighteenth century, with Bougainville, or in
the sixteenth, with Léry and Thevet? With every decade that we
travelled further back in time, I could have saved another costume,
witnessed another festivity, and come to understand another system of
belief. But I'm too familiar with the texts not to know that this back-

ward movement would also deprive me of much information, many curious facts and objects, that would enrich my meditations. The paradox is irresoluble: the less one culture communicates with another, the less likely they are to be corrupted, one by the other; but, on the other hand, the less likely it is, in such conditions, that the respective emissaries of these cultures will be able to seize the richness and significance of their diversity. The alternative is inescapable: either I am a traveller in ancient times, and faced with a prodigious spectacle which would be almost entirely unintelligible to me and might, indeed, provoke me to mockery or disgust; or I am a traveller of our own day, hastening in search of a vanished reality. In either case I am the loser —and more heavily than one might suppose; for today, as I go groaning among the shadows, I miss, inevitably, the spectacle that is now taking shape. My eyes, or perhaps my degree of humanity, do not equip me to witness that spectacle; and in the centuries to come, when another traveller revisits this same place, he too may groan aloud at the disappearance of much that I should have set down, but cannot. I am the victim of a double infirmity: what I see is an affliction to me; and what I do not see, a reproach.

For a long time I was paralysed by this dilemma, but now it seems to me that the cloudy liquid is beginning to clear. To what is this due, if not to the passage of time? Forgetfulness has done its work among my recollections, but it has not merely worn them thin, not merely buried them. It has made of these fragments a construction in depth that offers firmer ground beneath the feet and a clearer outline for the eye. One order has been substituted for another. Two cliffs mark the distance between my eye and its object; in the middle ground Time, which eats away at those cliffs, has begun to heap up the debris. The high ridges begin to fall away, piece by considerable piece; Time and Place come into opposition, blend oddly with one another, or become reversed, like sediment shaken clear by the trembling of a withered skin. Sometimes an ancient and infinitesimal detail will come away like a whole headland; and sometimes a complete layer of my past will vanish without trace. Unrelated events, rooted in the most disparate of regions and periods, suddenly come into contact with one another and take shape as a crusader castle which owes its architecture not to my private history but to some altogether wiser designer. As Chateaubriand wrote in his *Voyage en Italie:* 'Every man carries within himself a world made up of all that he has seen and loved; and it is to this world that he returns incessantly, though he may pass through, and

seem to inhabit, a world quite foreign to it.' Henceforth I can pass
from one of these worlds to the other. Between life and myself, Time
has laid its isthmus; and it is a longer one than I had expected. Twenty
years' forgetfulness has enabled me to elucidate an old experience: one
that I had pursued to the ends of the earth without managing either to
decipher its meaning or to remain on intimate terms with it.

PART II

From a Log-book

5 A Backward Glance

M<small>Y</small> CAREER was initiated one Sunday morning in the autumn of 1934. At nine o'clock the telephone rang. It was Célestin Bouglé, who was then the Director of the École Normale Supérieure. For several years he had taken a kindly interest in my affairs; and if that interest had hitherto been rather distant, and that kindness entirely inactive, it was first because I was not a Normalien, and above all because, even if I had been one of his former students, I should not have been a member of the group whom Bouglé held in exclusive esteem. No doubt he had turned to me as a last resort. 'D'you still want to do ethnography?' he asked without preamble. 'Why, of course!' 'Then apply at once for the post of Professor of Sociology at São Paulo University. The outskirts are full of Indians and you can spend your week-ends studying them. But you must give Georges Dumas a definite answer before twelve this morning.'

Neither Brazil nor South America meant much to me at that time. But I can still see, in every detail, the images which formed in my mind in response to this unexpected suggestion. Tropical countries, as it seemed to me, must be the exact opposite of our own, and the name of Antipodes had for me a sense at once richer and more ingenuous than its literal derivation. I should have been astonished to hear it said that any species, whether animal or vegetable, could have the same appearance on both sides of the globe. Every animal, every tree, every blade of grass, must be completely different and give immediate notice, as it were, of its tropical character. I imagined Brazil as a tangled mass of palm-leaves, with glimpses of strange architecture in the middle distance, and an all-permeating smell of burning perfume. This latter olfactory detail I owe, I think, to an unconscious awareness of the assonance between the words '*Brésil*' (Brazil) and '*grésiller*' (sizzle). No

49

amount of later experience, in any case, can prevent me from still
thinking of Brazil in terms of burning scent.

Now that I look back on them, these images no longer seem to me
so arbitrary. I have learnt that the truth of any given situation does
not yield so much to day-to-day observation as to that patient and
fractionated distillation which the equivocal notion of burning scent
was perhaps already inviting me to put into practice. The scent brought
with it, it may be, a symbolic lesson which I was not yet able to
formulate clearly. Exploration is not so much a matter of covering the
ground as of digging beneath the surface: chance fragments of landscape, momentary snatches of life, reflections caught on the wing—
such are the things that alone make it possible for us to understand and
interpret horizons which would otherwise have nothing to offer us.

Quite other problems, meanwhile, resided in the wild promise
which Bouglé had made me. How could he have come to suppose that
São Paulo, or its outskirts, comprised a native settlement? Doubtless he
was confusing it with Mexico City or Tegucigalpa. The philosopher
who had written a book on the caste regime in India without wonder-
ing for one moment if it would not be better to go there and see for
himself (What was the lofty phrase he had used in his preface of 1927?
That 'in the flux of events it is institutions that float free') was not the
man to suppose that the condition of the Brazilian native could yield
serious ethnographical results. Nor was he the only one of the 'official'
sociologists to profess this indifference: others of the breed are still
with us.

Be that as it may, I was too innocent not to welcome an illusion
that so happily seconded my intentions. Georges Dumas, as it happened,
was equally ill-informed: he had known southern Brazil at a time when
the extermination of the native population was not yet concluded; and,
moreover, he had enjoyed the society, unenlightening in that respect,
of dictators, feudal lords, and Maecenases.

I was therefore very much surprised to hear, at a luncheon-party
to which Victor Margueritte had taken me, the official point of view in
such matters. The speaker was the Brazilian Ambassador in Paris:
'Indians?' he said. 'Alas, my dear sir, the Indians have all been dead and
gone for many a year. It's a sad page—yes, and a shameful one—in the
history of my country. But the Portuguese colonists in the sixteenth
century were a brutal, money-grubbing lot. Who are we to reproach
them if they behaved as everyone else behaved at that time? They used
to grab hold of the Indians, tie them to the cannons' mouth, and blow

them to pieces. That's how they went, every man Jack of them. There'll be plenty to interest you, as a sociologist, in Brazil—but as for the Indians, you'd better forget about them, because you'll never find a single one. . . .'

Today it seems to me incredible that even a *grão fino*, and even in 1934, should have talked in this way. But at that time—things are different now, I'm glad to say—the Brazilian upper classes could not bear to hear the natives mentioned. The primitive conditions which existed in the interior of Brazil were likewise taboo, unless it were a question of admitting—or even suggesting—that an Indian great-grandmother might have been responsible for a certain barely per-ceptible exoticism of feature. There was never any mention of those drops, or rather those pints, of black blood on which their ancestors of the Imperial era had prided themselves, but which they now preferred to forget. And yet it was undeniable, for instance, that Luis de Souza-Dantas was of predominantly Indian descent; he could, indeed, have afforded to boast of it. But he was an 'export Brazilian', and France had been his adopted country ever since his adolescence. He had lost all contact with the real Brazil, preferring to substitute for it a lay-figure of officialdom and high breeding. Certain things he could hardly have forgotten: but no doubt he found it more convenient to blow upon the memory of the Brazilians of the sixteenth century than to tell his hearers of the way in which the men of his parents' generation—and even, in some cases, those of his own—had amused themselves. Their favourite pastime had been to call at the hospital for the clothes left behind by those who had died of small-pox: these they would then strew, together with other presents, along the lanes still used by the natives. This brought about the following brilliant result: that whereas in 1918 two-thirds of the State of São Paulo (as big as France, by the way) was marked on the map as 'unexplored territory, inhabited only by Indians', not one single native Indian was left at the time of my arrival in 1935—with the exception of a few isolated families on the coast, who sold so-called 'curiosities' every Sunday on the beaches of Santos. So that there were no Indians in the outskirts of São Paulo; but luckily they were still to be found some two thousand miles away, in the interior.

I cannot pass over this period without kindly mention of a quite different world. It was Victor Margueritte—the same who introduced me to the Brazilian Ambassador—who made it possible for me to glimpse it. I had been his secretary for a short while during my last years as a student, and he remained kindly disposed towards me. My task had been to help to launch one of his books—*La Patrie Humaine*—by taking round to some five score Parisian 'personalities' a copy which the Master (for so he liked to be called) had himself inscribed for them. I had also to draft reviews and paragraphs of 'inside gossip' which might lighten the critics' work and generally set them on the right road. If I still remember Victor Margueritte, it is not only because he always treated me so well, but because (as is the case with all that makes a lasting impression upon me) of the contradiction which existed between himself and his work. Margueritte himself was as memorable as his work was over-simplified and, for all its warmth of nature, disagreeable of access. His features had the grace of a Gothic angel, and something of that angel's femininity, and there was something so noble and so natural about his manner that even his failings, of which vanity was not the least, did not shock or irritate but seemed rather as auxiliary evidence of some privilege either of blood or of intellect.

He lived over towards the 17th arrondissement in a large old-fashioned middle-class apartment. He was nearly blind, and his wife took all possible care of him. As a young woman she had probably been admired for a certain piquancy of looks and manner; but with age, which renders impossible the confusion of moral with merely physical characteristics, this piquancy had been broken down into ugliness, on the one hand, and over-animation on the other.

He entertained hardly at all—not only because he supposed himself to be largely unknown among the younger generation but, above all, because he had set himself upon a pedestal so lofty that it was becoming difficult for him to find people good enough for himself to talk to. Wittingly or not (that I could never judge) he had banded together with a few others to found an international brotherhood of supermen, five or six in number: himself, Keyserling, Ladislas Reymond, Romain Rolland, and—I believe, for a time—Einstein. The basis of the system was that whenever any member of the group published a book the others, though scattered all over the world, would hurry to salute it as one of the highest manifestations of human genius.

But what was really touching about Victor Margueritte was the simplicity with which he wished to sum up, in his own person, the whole history of French literature. This was all the easier for him in that he came of literary stock: his mother was a first cousin of Mallarmé: anecdote and reminiscence could always be called in to support his affectations. Zola, the Goncourts, Balzac, and Hugo were talked of at the Marguerittes' as if they were uncles and grandparents whose appointed trustee he was. 'They say I've no style!' he would cry. 'But when did Balzac have style, after all?' And you would have thought yourself in the presence of one who, himself descended from ruling monarchs, would explain away his outbursts by allusion to the imperious temperament of some royal forbear. A legendary temperament, this, which the common run of mortals would speak of, not as a characteristic that they might share, but as the accepted explanation of some great upheaval in contemporary history. It was with a shiver, but a shiver of pleasure, that they would see it reborn in Monsieur Margueritte. Other writers have had more talent; but few, I think, have forged for themselves so graceful, and above all so aristocratic, a conception of their profession.

6 *How I became an Anthropologist*

I was reading for a philosophy degree—not because I had any true vocation for philosophy, but because I had sampled other branches of learning and detested them, one and all. I had begun my philosophy classes with a vague liking for a form of rationalistic monism. This I meant to justify and reinforce, and to this end I pulled every string to get put up to the teacher who was reputedly the most 'advanced' in his views. Gustave Rodrigues was, as a matter of fact, an active member of the S.F.I.O.; but as far as philosophy was concerned his mixture of Bergsonism and neo-Kantianism was a sad disappointment to me. Arid and dogmatic as he was, he advanced his views with great fervour from the first lecture to the last, gesticulating the while like a man possessed. Never have I seen such skimpy intellectual processes put forward with such ingenuous conviction. He killed himself in 1940 when the Germans entered Paris.

It was then that I began to learn how any problem, whether grave or trivial, can be resolved. The method never varies. First you establish the traditional 'two views' of the question. You then put forward a commonsense justification of the one, only to refute it by the other. Finally you send them both packing by the use of a third interpretation, in which both the others are shown to be equally unsatisfactory. Certain verbal manœuvres enable you, that is, to line up the traditional 'antitheses' as complementary aspects of a single reality: form and substance, content and container, appearance and reality, essence and existence, continuity and discontinuity, and so on. Before long the exercise becomes the merest verbalizing, reflection gives place to a kind of superior punning, and the 'accomplished philosopher' may be recognized by the ingenuity with which he makes ever-bolder play with assonance, ambiguity, and the use of those words which sound alike and yet bear quite different meanings.

54

Five years at the Sorbonne taught me little but this form of mental gymnastics. Its dangers are, of course, self-evident: the mechanism is so simple, for one thing, that there is no such thing as a problem which cannot be tackled. When we were working for our examinations and, above all, for that supreme ordeal, the *leçon* (in which the candidate draws a subject by lot, and is given only six hours in which to prepare a comprehensive survey of it), we used to set one another the bizarrest imaginable themes. I brought myself to the point at which, given ten minutes' preparation, I could lecture for an hour on the respective merits of the tramway and the omnibus and miss not one of the arguments for either side. The method, universal in its application, encouraged the student to overlook the many possible forms and variants of thought, devoting himself to one particular unchanging instrument. Certain elementary adjustments were all that he needed: it was as if music could be reduced to one single tune, as soon as he realized that it was played sometimes in G Major and sometimes in F. From this point of view philosophy, as taught at the Sorbonne, exercised the intelligence but left the spirit high and dry.

It seems to me even more dangerous to confuse the advance of knowledge with the growing complexity of intellectual organization. We were invited to bring into being a dynamic synthesis in which we would start from the least adequate of philosophical systems and end by appraising the subtlest among them. But at the same time (and because all our teachers were obsessed with the notion of historical development) we had to explain how the latter had gradually grown out of the former. Philosophy was not *ancilla scientiarum*, the handmaid and auxiliary of scientific exploration: it was a kind of aesthetic contemplation of consciousness by consciousness. We watched self-consciousness in its progress through the ages—elaborating constructions ever lighter and more audacious, resolving problems of balance and implication, inventing refinements of logic; and the more absolute the technical perfection, the more complete the internal coherence, the 'greater' was the system in question. It was as if the student of art-history had been taught that Gothic was necessarily better than Romanesque, and flamboyant Gothic better than primitive Gothic, without stopping to wonder what was beautiful and what was not. The signification was what mattered, not the thing signified: nobody connected the one with the other. Know-how had taken the place of the passion for truth. After spending several years on exercises of this sort I found myself still falling back, when alone, on unsophisticated convictions which I had held, more or less, since I was a boy of fourteen. I was better able, perhaps, to see where they fell short of my needs; but at least they were instruments adapted to my purpose, and I was in no danger either of being deluded by their internal complication or of forgetting, in the excitement of watching the marvellous machinery go round, that it was meant to serve practical ends.

I also had my own personal reasons for turning away in disgust from professional philosophy and looking to anthropology for my salvation. My first year as a teacher at the Lycée de Mont-de-Marsan had been a happy one, for I had been able to work out the syllabus of my courses as I went along. At the beginning of the next year I went to Laon, where I had been transferred, and was horrified to find that for the rest of my life I should have to go on giving the same lectures. Now, my mind has the particularity—and it may well be an infirmity—that I find it difficult to concentrate twice on the same subject. Most people consider their University finals as an inhuman ordeal by which, whether they like it or not, they earn the right to relax for the rest of their lives. For me it was just the opposite. Though the youngest in my year, I had got through at my first attempt, steeplechasing at my ease through doctrines, theories, and hypotheses. My ordeal began later: it proved physically impossible for me to address my students if I were not delivering an entirely new series of lectures. This incapacity proved an even greater embarrassment when I had to appear in the role of examiner; I would take questions at random from the examination-schedule and find that I no longer knew even what answers the candidates should have given. Even the fatuous among them seemed to me to say all that there was to be said. It was as if the subjects dissolved before me from the mere fact of my once having applied my mind to them.

Today I sometimes wonder if I was not attracted to anthropology, however unwittingly, by a structural affinity between the civilizations which are its subject and my own thought-processes. My intelligence is neolithic: I have not the gift of regular sowing and reaping, year by year, in one particular field. Like a brush-fire, my mind burns its way into territory which may sometimes prove unexplored; sometimes these excursions prove fertile, and I snatch at a harvest or two, leaving devastation behind me. But, at the time of which I am writing, I knew nothing of these deep-lying motives. I knew nothing of ethnology, and had never studied it systematically; when Sir James Frazer paid his last visit to the Sorbonne and gave a memorable lecture there—in 1928, I think—it never entered my head to go and hear him.

I had, as matter of fact, been making a collection of exotica since my early childhood. But I did this purely as an antiquarian, and an antiquarian in search of a field he could afford. When I reached adolescence I was so far from having shown any one particular bent that the first person who tried to plumb the matter—my philosophy teacher at school: André Cresson was his name—considered that I was temperamentally best suited to the study of law. I have always been very grateful for the half-truth which underlay his mistake.

I therefore gave up the idea of the École Normale, and put my name down for law school. I went on reading for a philosophy degree, none the less, because it looked so easy. A curious fatality hangs over the teaching of law. Sandwiched between theology, with which it had certain intellectual affinities at that time, and journalism, towards which recent reforms have sent it swerving, it seems unable to find firm and objective ground on which to take its stand. The firmer it is, the less objective: and vice versa. Himself a subject for serious study, the jurist is, to me, like an animal trying to explain to a zoologist the workings of a magic lantern. At that time, as luck would have it, law examinations could be got up in a fortnight, if one learnt certain *aides-mémoire* by heart. And if law study was sterile, the law student was himself a repulsive creature. Whether the distinction is still valid, I can't say, but in 1928 or thereabouts first-year students could be divided into two species—two races, I might almost say—law and medicine on the one hand, letters and natural sciences on the other.

Little as I care for the terms 'extrovert' and 'introvert', they are doubtless the best way of defining the antithesis. On the one hand, 'youth' (in the sense in which traditional folklore employs the word to designate a certain age-class): noisy, aggressive, out to make itself felt by no matter what vulgar means, politically (at that time) drawn to the extreme right; and, on the other side, adolescents already middle-aged, solitary, untalkative, in general Left-minded, and hard at work making their way among the grown-ups whom they were schooling themselves to resemble.

This difference is quite easily explained. The apprentice doctors and lawyers had a profession ahead of them. Their behaviour reflected their delight in having left school behind and assumed a sure place in the social system. Midway between the undifferentiated mass of the *lycée* and the specialized activity which lay before them, they felt themselves in, as it were, the margin of life and claimed the contradictory privileges of the schoolboy and of the professional man alike.

Where letters and the sciences are concerned, on the other hand, the usual outlets—teaching, research-work, and a variety of ill-defined 'careers'—are of quite a different character. The student who chooses them does not say good-bye to the world of childhood: on the contrary —he hopes to remain behind in it. Teaching is, after all, the only way in which grown-ups can stay on at school. Those who read letters or the sciences are characterized by resistance to the demands of the group. Like members, almost, of some monastic order they tend to turn more and more in upon themselves, absorbed in the study, preservation, and transmission of a patrimony independent of their own time: as for the future savant, his task will last as long as the universe itself. So that nothing is more false than to persuade them that they are committed; even if they believe that they are committing themselves the commitment does not consist in accepting a given role, identifying themselves with one of its functions, and accepting its ups and downs and the risks in which it may involve them. They still judge it from outside, and as if they were not themselves part of it. Their commitment is, in fact, a particular way of remaining uncommitted. Teaching and research have nothing in common, as they see it, with apprenticeship to a profession. Their splendours reside, as do also their miseries, in their being a refuge, on the one hand, or a mission, on the other.

An antinomy, therefore, in which we have a profession on the one hand, and on the other an ambiguous enterprise, oscillating between a mission and a refuge, bearing within itself elements of both and yet always recognizably one rather than the other. Anthropology has in all this an especially favoured place. It represents the second alternative in its most extreme form. The ethnographer, while in no wise abdicating his own humanity, strives to know and estimate his fellow-men from a lofty and distant point of vantage: only thus can he abstract them from the contingencies particular to this or that civilization. The conditions of his life and work cut him off from his own group for long periods together; and he himself acquires a kind of chronic uprootedness from the sheer brutality of the environmental changes to which he is exposed. Never can he feel himself 'at home' anywhere: he will always be, psychologically speaking, an amputated man. Anthropology is, with music and mathematics, one of the few true vocations; and the anthropologist may become aware of it within himself before ever he has been taught it.

Personal particularities and one's attitude to Society may be decisive, therefore, but motives of a purely intellectual character must also be considered. The period of 1920–30 was marked in France by widespread diffusion of the theories of psycho-analysis. These taught me that the static antinomies around which we were encouraged to build our philosophical essays (and, eventually, our examination answers)—rational and irrational, intellectual and affective, logical and pre-logical—were no more than meaningless games. In the first place there existed beyond the rational a category at once more important and more valid: that of the meaningful. The meaningful is the highest form of the rational, but our masters (more concerned, no doubt, with the perusal of the *Essai sur les données immédiates de la conscience* than with F. de Saussure's *Cours de linguistique générale*) never so much as mentioned its name. Freud's works then made it clear to me that our antitheses were not real antitheses, since those actions which seem most purely affective, those results which seem least logical, and those demonstrations which we call pre-logical, are in point of fact precisely those which are meaningful in the highest degree. 'Acts of faith' and Bergsonian question-begging were used to reduce people and things to pap-form—the better, of course, to body forth their ineffable essence; but I became convinced that, on the contrary, people and things could be apprehended in essence without losing that sharpness of outline which serves to distinguish one from the other and gives to each a decipherable structure. Knowledge was not founded upon sacrifice or barter: it consisted in the choice of those aspects of a subject which were *true*—which coincided, that is to say, with the properties of my own thought. Not at all, as the neo-Kantians claim, because my thought inevitably exerted a certain constraint on the object under study: but rather because my thought was itself such an object. Being 'of this world', it partook of the same nature as that world.

Much of these intellectual processes I shared with other men of my generation, but they bore, in my case, a particular colour by virtue of the intense curiosity which had drawn me, ever since childhood, to the study of geology. One of the memories dearest to me is not so much that of my excursions into the unknown centre of Brazil as that of the search, on a limestone plateau in Languedoc, for the line of contact between two geological strata. It's a very different thing from just taking a walk, or even from the straightforward exploration of a given area: what seems mere incoherent groping to an uninformed observer is to me the very image of knowledge-in-action, with the difficulties that it may encounter and the satisfactions it may hope to enjoy.

Every landscape offers, at first glance, an immense disorder which

may be sorted out howsoever we please. We may sketch out the history
of its cultivation, plot the accidents of geography which have befallen
it, and ponder the ups and downs of history and prehistory: but the
most august of investigations is surely that which reveals what came
before, dictated, and in large measure explains all the others. From that
pale broken line, that often imperceptible difference in the form and
consistency of the jumbled rocks, I can detect that, where there is now
nothing but an arid waste, one ocean once followed another. The
investigator who establishes, trace by trace, the evidence of their
millenary stagnation may not seem to make much sense as, indifferent
alike to footpath and barrier, he negotiates the obstacles—landslips,
cliff-faces, stretches of bush, farmland—that stand in his way. But his
contrariness springs from a determination to find the master-key to the
landscape; baffling this may well be, but in comparison with it all others
are deformed or incomplete.

And sometimes the miracle happens. On one side and the other of a
hidden crevice we find two green plants of different species. Each has
chosen the soil which suits it; and we realize that within the rock are
two ammonites, one of which has involutions less complex than the
other's. We glimpse, that is to say, a difference of many thousands of
years; time and space suddenly commingle; the living diversity of that
moment juxtaposes one age and the other and perpetuates them.
Thought and sensibility take on a new dimension, in which every
drop of sweat, every movement of muscle, every quick-drawn breath
becomes the symbol of a story; and, as my body reproduces the
particular gait of that story, so does my mind embrace its meaning. I
feel myself luxuriating in a state of heightened perception, in which
Place and Period make themselves known to one another and have at
last a common language in which to communicate.

When I first read Freud his theories seemed to me to represent
quite naturally the application to individual human beings of a method
of which geology had established the canon. In both cases the investigator starts with apparently impenetrable phenomena; and in both he
needs a fundamental delicacy of perception—sensibility, flair, taste:
all are involved—if he is to detail and assess the complexities of the
situation. And yet there is nothing contingent, nothing arbitrary, in
the order which he introduces into the incoherent-seeming collection
of facts. Unlike the history of the historians, history as the geologist and
the psycho-analyst see it is intended to body forth in time—rather in
the manner of a *tableau vivant*—certain fundamental properties of the

physical or psychical universe. A *tableau vivant*, I said: and, in effect, the acting-out of proverbs does provide a crude parallel to the activities of geologist and psycho-analyst. These consist, after all, in the interpretation of each act as the unfolding in time of certain non-temporal truths. Proverbs are an attempt to pin down these truths on the moral plane, but in other domains they are just called 'laws'. In every case our aesthetic curiosity acts as a springboard and we find ourselves immediately in a state of cognizance.

When I was about seventeen I was initiated into Marxism by a young Belgian socialist whom I had met on holiday. (He is today one of his country's Ambassadors abroad.) Reading Marx was for me all the more enthralling in that I was making my first contact, by way of that great thinker, with the philosophical current that runs from Kant to Hegel. A whole world was opened to me. My excitement has never cooled: and rarely do I tackle a problem in sociology or ethnology without having first set my mind in motion by reperusal of a page or two from the *18 Brumaire of Louis Bonaparte* or the *Critique of Political Economy*. Whether Marx accurately foretold this or that historical development is not the point. Marx followed Rousseau in saying—and saying once and for all, as far as I can see—that social science is no more based upon events than physics is based upon sense-perceptions. Our object is to construct a model, examine its properties and the way in which it reacts to laboratory tests, and then apply our observations to the interpretation of empirical happenings: these may turn out very differently from what we had expected.

At a different level of reality, Marxism seemed to me to proceed in the same way as geology and psycho-analysis (in the sense in which its founder understood it). All three showed that understanding consists in the reduction of one type of reality to another; that true reality is never the most obvious of realities, and that its nature is already apparent in the care which it takes to evade our detection. In all these cases the problem is the same: the relation, that is to say, between reason and sense-perception; and the goal we are looking for is also the same: a sort of *super-rationalism* in which sense-perceptions will be integrated into reasoning and yet lose none of their properties.

And so I stood out against the new tendencies in metaphysical thinking which were then beginning to take shape. Phenomenology I found unacceptable, in so far as it postulated a continuity between experience and reality. That the one enveloped and explained the other I was quite willing to agree, but I had learnt from my three mistresses

that there is no continuity in the passage between the two and that to
reach reality we must first repudiate experience, even though we may
later reintegrate it in an objective synthesis in which sentimentality
plays no part. As for the trend of thought which was to find fulfilment
in existentialism, it seemed to me to be the exact opposite of true
thought, by reason of its indulgent attitude towards the illusions
of subjectivity. To promote private preoccupations to the rank of
philosophical problems is dangerous, and may end in a kind of shop-
girl's philosophy—excusable as an element in teaching procedure, but
perilous in the extreme if it leads the philosopher to turn his back on his
mission. That mission (he holds it only until science is strong enough to
take over from philosophy) is to understand Being in relation to itself,
and not in relation to oneself. Phenomenology and existentialism did
not abolish metaphysics: they merely introduced new ways of finding
alibis for metaphysics.

Marxism and psycho-analysis are human sciences whose perspectives are social in the one case, and individual in the other. Geology
is a physical science, but it is also the mother and wet-nurse of history,
alike in its methods and in its aims. Between these is the kingdom that
ethnography has spontaneously marked out for itself. For humanity,
which we imagine to have no limitations other than those of space, puts
quite a different complexion on the transformations of the terrestrial
globe which geological history has bequeathed us. This history is an
indissoluble activity which has gone forward from one millennium to the
next, in the work of societies as anonymous as telluric forces and the
work of individuals, each one of whom, to the psycho-analyst, represents a particular case. Anthropology affords me an intellectual satisfaction: it rejoins at one extreme the history of the world, and at the
other the history of myself, and it unveils the shared motivation of one
and the other at the same moment. In suggesting Man as the object of
my studies, anthropology dispelled all my doubts: for the differences
and changes which we ethnographers deal in are those which matter to
all mankind, as opposed to those which are exclusive to one particular
civilization and would not exist if we chose to live outside it. Anthropology set at rest, what is more, the anxious and destructive curiosity
of which I have written above: I was guaranteed, that is to say, a more
or less inexhaustible supply of matter for reflection, in the diversity of
human manners, customs, and institutions. My life and my character
were reconciled.

This being so, it may seem strange that I should so long have remained deaf to a message which had after all been transmitted for me, ever since I first began to read philosophy, by the masters of the French school of sociology. The revelation did not come to me, as a matter of fact, till 1933 or 1934 when I came upon a book which was already by no means new: Robert H. Lowie's *Primitive Society*. But instead of notions borrowed from books and at once metamorphosed into philosophical concepts I was confronted with an account of first-hand experience. The observer, moreover, had been so committed as to keep intact the full meaning of his experience. My mind escaped from the closed circuit which was what the practice of academic philosophy amounted to: made free of the open air, it breathed deeply and took on new strength. Like a townsman let loose in the mountains, I made myself drunk with the open spaces and my astonished eye could hardly take in the wealth and variety of the scene.

Thus began my long intimacy with Anglo-American anthropology. Nurtured at a distance by reading, and later reinforced by personal contacts, this was to be the cause of serious misunderstandings. In Brazil, to begin with, the University faculty had expected me to contribute to the teaching of a sociology derived from Durkheim. The positivist tradition is very strong in South America, and they were also anxious to give a philosophical basis to the moderate liberalism which is the oligarchy's usual safeguard against excessive personal power. I arrived as an avowed anti-Durkheimian and the enemy of any attempt to put sociology to metaphysical uses. I was certainly not going to help to rebuild those derelict walls at the very moment when I was trying with all my strength to broaden my horizons. I have been reproached since then for being, as people suppose, in fief to Anglo-Saxon thought. What an imbecility! Quite apart from the fact that I am probably at this moment nearer than any of my colleagues to the Durkheimian tradition—and the fact has not passed unnoticed abroad—the authors to whom I gladly acknowledge my debt—Lowie, Kroeber, Boas— seem to me to stand at the furthest possible remove from that American philosophy which derives from William James and Dewey (and now from the so-called logical positivists) and has long been out of date. European by origin, and themselves educated in Europe, or by European masters, they stand for something quite different: a synthesis reflecting, where knowledge is in question, the synthesis for which Columbus provided the objective opportunity four centuries ago; they applied vigorous scientific methods to that unique field of experiment, the New World, and they did it at a time when libraries were already improving and it was possible to leave one's University and enter primitive territory with no more difficulty than we encounter in leaving Paris for the Basque country or the Mediterranean. It is to a historical situation, not an intellectual tradition, that I am paying homage. The reader must imagine to himself the privilege of making contact with primitive societies which were more or less intact and had never before been studied seriously. Just how recently, as luck would have it, the whites had set out to destroy them will be clear from the following story: the Californian tribes had still been quite wild at the time of their extermination, and it happened that one Indian escaped, as if by a miracle, from the holocaust. For years he lived unknown and unobserved only a dozen miles from the great centres of population, and kept himself alive with his bow and the sharp-pointed arrows whose stone heads he carved himself. Gradually there was less and less for him to shoot, and finally he was found, naked and starving, on the outskirts of a city suburb. He ended his days in peace as a college porter in the University of California.

7 Sunset

It was on a February morning in 1934 that I arrived in Marseilles to embark on the ship that was to take me to Santos. It was to be the first of many such departure-mornings, and they have merged in my memory, leaving an impression of, above all, the gaiety that is peculiar to the south of France in winter-time; the clear blue sky even more immaterial than usual, and a bite in the air that was almost painfully pleasant—like a glass of iced soda-water drunk too quickly when one is parched with thirst. Over-heated, by contrast, was our ship as it lay motionless by the quay; and in its corridors the smells hung heavy—sea-smells, some of them, mixed in with fresh paint and an overflow from the kitchen. And I remember with what satisfaction, what stillness of spirit, what tranquil happiness, almost, I listened in the middle of the night to the muffled throbbing of the engines and the susurration of the sea as it rushed along the hull's flanks. It was as if the ship's movement related to an idea of stability that not even immobility itself could approach; a ship's stillness—when it puts into an anchorage by night, for instance—has often, indeed, the contrary effect, and provokes a feeling of insecurity and uneasiness, and an impatience, too, that the 'natural course of things', as we have learnt to regard it, should have been interrupted.

Our ships put in at many ports. The first week of our passage was, in fact, spent almost entirely on shore, as far as we were concerned, because the ship travelled at night and spent the day loading and unloading its cargoes. Each morning we woke to find ourselves in a new port: Barcelona, Tarragona, Valencia, Alicante, Malaga, sometimes Cadiz; or Algiers, Oran, and Gibraltar, and then the longer hops that took us first to Casablanca and then to Dakar. Only then did the passage proper begin, either direct to Rio or Santos, or, less often, with a further bout of harbour-hopping along the Brazilian coast, with stops at Recife, Bahia, and Victoria. The air grew steadily warmer, the Spanish sierras filed by on the horizon, and mirages of cliffs, or sand-hills, kept the spectacle in being for several more days, though we were by now steaming alongside the African coastline which at that stage was too flat and marshy to be visible. It was the opposite of 'travel', in that the ship seemed to us not so much a means of transport as a place of residence—a home, in fact, before which Nature put on a new show each morning.

I was, as yet, so little of an anthropologist that I never thought to take advantage of these opportunities. I've learnt, since, that these brief glimpses of a town, a region, or a way of life, offer us a school of attention. Sometimes—so great is the concentration required of us in the few moments at our disposal—they may even reveal to us characteristics which in other circumstances might have long remained hidden. But other things attracted me more; and it was with the ingenuousness of a beginner that I stood on the empty deck and watched, each day at sunrise and again at sunset, the supernatural cataclysms which were played out in full, as it seemed to me, with beginnings, development, and end, across the four corners of a sky vaster than any I had as yet seen. I felt that if I could find the right words to describe these ever-changing phenomena, if I could communicate to others the character of an event which was never twice the same, then I should have penetrated—or so I felt—to the inmost secrets of my profession: bizarre and peculiar as might be the experiences to which I should be subject in my career as an anthropologist, I could be sure of putting them, and their implications, at the disposal of the common reader.

Many years have passed, and I don't know if I could recapture that early state of grace. Could I re-live those moments of fever when, notebook in hand, I would jot down, second by second, phrases evocative of the evanescent and constantly renewed forms before me? It's a gamble that still fascinates, and I'm often tempted to begin it all over again.

Shipboard notes
To the scholars, dawn and twilight are one and the same phenomenon; and the Greeks thought the same, since they used the same word for both, qualifying it differently according to whether morning or evening was in question. This confusion is an excellent illustration of our tendency to put theory first and take no account of the practical

aspect of the matter. That a given point on the earth should shift its position in an indivisible movement between the zone of incidence of the sun's rays and the zone in which the light vanishes or returns to it is perfectly possible. But in reality no two things could be more different than morning and evening. Daybreak is a prelude, and nightfall an overture—but an overture which comes at the end, and not, as in most operas, at the beginning. The look of the sun foretells what the next hours will bring; dark and livid, that's to say, if we are in for a wet morning, and pink, frothy, and insubstantial if the weather is to be fine. But as to the rest of the day, the dawn makes no promises. It simply sets the meteorological stage and adds a direction: 'Fine' or 'Wet'. The sunset, on the other hand, is a complete performance, with a beginning, a middle, and an end: a synopsis of all that has happened during the previous twelve hours. Dawn is simply the day's beginning; sunset the day run through again, but fifty times as fast.

That is why people pay more attention to sunset than to sunrise. Dawn merely adds a footnote to what they have already learnt from barometer and thermometer or, in the case of the less 'civilized', from the phases of the moon, the flight of birds, and the oscillations of the tide. Whereas a sunset reunites within its mysterious configurations the twists and turns of wind and rain, heat and cold, to which their physical being has been exposed. Much else may be read into those fleecy constellations. When the sky is first lit up by the setting sun (just as, in the theatre, the sudden blaze of the footlights indicates that the play is about to begin) the peasant stops dead in his tracks, the fisherman ties up his boat, and the savage winks an eye as he sits by a fire that grows pale. Remembrance is a source of profound pleasure—though not to the extent that it is complete, for few would wish to 'live over again', literally, sufferings and exhaustions which are, none the less, a pleasure to look back upon. Remembrance is life itself, but it has another quality. And so it is that when the sun lowers itself towards the polished surface of a flat calm at sea, like a coin thrown down by a miser in the heavens, or when its disc outlines the mountain-tops like a metal sheet at once hard and lacy, then Man has a brief vision—a hallucination, one might say—of the indecipherable forces, the vapours and fulgurations whose obscure conflicts he has glimpsed vaguely, within the depths of himself, from time to time during the day.

These inner spiritual struggles must have been sinister indeed, for the day had not been marked by any outward event that might have justified an atmospheric upheaval. It had, indeed, been featureless.

Around four in the afternoon—just at that moment when the sun is half-way through its run and is becoming less distinct, though not, as yet, less brilliant, and the thick golden light pours down as if to mask certain preliminaries—the *Mendoza* had changed her course. A light swell had set her rolling, and with each oscillation the heat had become more apparent, but the change of course was so small that one might have mistaken the change of direction for a slight increase in the ship's rolling. Nobody had paid any attention to it, for nothing is so much like a transfer in geometry as a passage on the high seas. There is no landscape to point up the transition from one latitude to the next, or the crossing of an isotherm or a pluviometric curve. Thirty miles on dry land can make us feel that we have changed planets, but to the inexperienced eye each of the three thousand miles at sea is much like the last. The passengers were preoccupied neither with our position, nor with the route we had to follow, nor with the nature of the countries which lay out of sight behind the horizon. It seemed to them that if they were shut up in a confined space, for a number of days that had been decided in advance, it was not because a distance had to be covered but because they had to expiate the privilege of being carried from one side of the world to the other without making, themselves, the smallest exertion. They'd gone soft: lie-abed mornings, to begin with, and indolent meals which had long ceased to be a pleasure and were now merely a device (and one that had to be made to last as long as possible) for getting through the day.

Nowhere on the ship was there any visible sign of the efforts which, somewhere and on someone's part, were being made. The men who were actually running the ship did not want to see the passengers any more than the passengers wanted to see them. (The officers, too, had no wish for the two groups to mingle.) All that we could do was to drag ourselves round the great carcase of the ship; a sailor retouching the paintwork, or a steward in blue overalls swabbing down the first-class corridors—these are much as we saw, or would ever see, in token of the thousands of miles that we were covering.

At twenty to six in the evening the sky in the west seemed encumbered with a complicated edifice, horizontal at its base, which was so exactly like the sea that one would have thought it had been sucked up out of it in some incomprehensible way, or that a thick and invisible layer of crystal had been inserted between the two. Attached to its summit—suspended, as it were, to the very top of the sky as if by some heaviness in reverse—were flimsy scaffoldings, bloated pyramids, vapours arrested in the act of boiling—not clouds, one would have said, but sculptured imitations of clouds; and yet clouds have themselves that same quality, the polished and rounded look of wood that has been carved and gilded. The whole mass masked the sun and was dark, with occasional highlights, except towards the summit, where it was beginning to break into little flames.

Higher still in the sky were mottled shapes that came apart in insubstantial and fugacious wisps and curls: pure light, they seemed, in texture.

Following the horizon round towards the north one could see the main edifice grow thinner and vanish in a complication of clouds behind which, in the far distance, a lofty strip of vapour could be discerned; it was effervescent along its top, and on the side nearest the still-invisible sun the light gave its outline a heavily modelled hem. Farther to the north the element of modelling disappeared and nothing remained but the strip itself, flat and lustreless, as it merged with the sea.

To the south this same strip re-emerged, this time with great massive blocks of cloud above it that stood like cosmological dolmens on the smoky crests of their understructure.

When one turned one's back on the sun and gazed eastwards there could be seen two long thin superimposed groups of cloud that stood out as if in their own light against a background of ramparts: battlements heavy-breasted and yet ethereal, pearly and soft with reflections of pink and silver and mauve.

Meanwhile the sun was gradually coming into view behind the celestial reefs that blocked the view to the west; as it progressed downwards inch by inch its rays would disperse the mists or force their way through, throwing into relief as they did so whatever had stood in their way, and dissipating it in a mass of circular fragments, each with a size and a luminous intensity all its own. Sometimes the light would gather together, as one might clench one's fist, and through the sleeve-end would appear, at most, two or three stiff and glittering fingers. Or else an incandescent octopus would come forward momentarily from the vaporous grottoes.

Every sunset has two distinct phases. At the beginning the sun plays the role of architect. Later, when its rays no longer shine directly and are merely reflections, it turns into a painter. As soon as it disappears behind the horizon the light weakens and the complexity of the planes becomes ever greater and greater. Broad daylight is the enemy of perspective, but, between day and night, there is a moment of

transition at which the architecture of the skies is as fantastic as it is
ephemeral. When darkness comes, everything flattens down again, like
some marvellously coloured Japanese toy.

At exactly a quarter to six the first phase began. The sun was already
low, but had not yet touched the horizon. At the moment when it
appeared beneath the cloud-structure, it seemed to break open like the
yolk of an egg and its light spilled over the forms to which it was still
attached. This burst of bright light was soon followed by a withdrawal;
the sun's surroundings lost all brilliance and in the empty space that
marked off the topmost limit of the sea from the bottom of the cloud-
structure there could be seen a cordillera of vapours, which had but
lately been so dazzling as to be indecipherable and was now darkened
and sharp-pointed. At the same time it began to belly out, where
originally it had been quite flat. These small objects, black and solid,
moved to and fro, lazy-bodied migrants, across a large patch of
reddening sky which marked the beginning of the colour-phase and
was slowly mounting upwards from the horizon.

Gradually the evening's constructions-in-depth began to dismantle
themselves. The mass which had stood all day in the sky to the west
seemed to have been beaten flat like a metal leaf, and behind it was a
fire first golden, then vermilion, then cerise. This fire was beginning
to work on the elaborate clouds—melting, disintegrating, and finally
volatilizing them in a whirlwind of tiny particles.

Network after network of fine vapours rose high in the sky; they
seemed to stretch in all directions—horizontal, oblique, perpendicular,
even spiral. As the sun's rays went down (like a bow that must be tilted
this way or that, according to which string we seek to use) they caught
one after another of these and sent them flying in a gamut of colour
which one would have thought to be the exclusive and arbitrary
property of each one in turn. When it appeared, each network seemed
as exact, as precise, and as rigid in its fragility as fine-spun glass, but
gradually they all dissolved, as if their substance had been over-heated
by exposure in a sky which was everywhere in flames; their colour lost
its brightness and their outline its individuality, until finally each
vanished from the scene, giving place to a new network, and one
freshly spun. In the end it was difficult to distinguish one colour from
the next—just as liquids of different colour and density will at first seem
to keep their individuality when they are poured into the same glass,
only to mingle later for all their apparent independence.

After that it became difficult to follow a spectacle which seemed to be repeating itself in distant parts of the sky, at intervals sometimes of several minutes, sometimes of a second or two. When the sun's disc cut down into the western horizon we suddenly saw, very high up in the east, clouds acid-mauve in tonality which had hitherto been invisible. After a rapid efflorescence and enrichment these apparitions vanished slowly, from right to left, at their moment of greatest subtlety, just as if someone were wiping them away firmly and unhurriedly with a piece of cloth. After a few seconds nothing remained but the cleaned slate of the sky above the nebulous cloud-rampart. And this rampart was turning to white and grey while the rest of the sky went rose-pink.

Over towards the sun the old strip of cloud had receded into a shapeless block of cement, and behind it a new long strip was flaming in its turn; when its rednesses turned pale the mottled patches at the zenith, whose turn had not yet come, began to take on weight. Below there was a great burst of gold; above, where the summit had glittered, it turned first to chestnut, then to violet. At the same time we seemed to be scrutinizing its texture through a microscope; and it turned out to be made up of a thousand little filaments, each supporting, like a skeleton, its plump little forms.

The sun no longer shone directly. The colour-range of the sky was pink and yellow; shrimp-pink, salmon-pink, flax-yellow, straw-yellow; and this unemphatic richness was, in its turn, disappearing, as the celestial landscape re-formed in a gamut of white and blue and green. Yet a few corners of the horizon were still enjoying a brief independence. To the left, the atmosphere was suddenly veiled—a whim, one would have thought, on the part of a mysterious combination of greens. And these greens merged progressively into a group of reds—intense to begin with, then darker, then tinged with violet, then smudged with coal, and evolving at the very end into the tracery of a stick of charcoal on granulated paper. The sky behind was an Alpine yellow-green and the strip of cloud, still firmly outlined, remained opaque. In the westerly sky little horizontal stripes of gold glimmered for an instant, but to the north it was almost dark; the full-breasted rampart had dwindled to a series of whitish swellings beneath a chalky sky.

Nothing is more mysterious than the ensemble of procedures, always identical and never predictable, by which night succeeds day. The first portent of these procedures is always a matter for doubt and anxiety. No one can tell what forms will be adopted, on this one particular occasion, by the night's insurrection. Impenetrable is the alchemy by which each colour transforms itself into its complementary colour, whereas, on the palette, as we all know, we should have to open another tube of paint to achieve this same result. Where night is concerned there is no limit to the minglings and comminglings which may be achieved; for night comes to us as a deceiver. The sky turns from pink to green; but it does so because I have failed to notice that certain clouds have turned bright red and, in doing so, make the sky look green by contrast. The sky *had*, in effect, been pink; but a pink so pale that it could no longer struggle against the very high-keyed red; and yet I had not seen that red come into being, since a modulation from gold to red is less startling to the eye than a modulation from pink to green. It was by a trick, therefore, that night made its entrance into the sky.

And so night began to deny the sky its golds and purples; warmth of tone gave place to whites and greys. The set stage of night began to reveal a sea landscape above the sea: an immense screen of clouds filing by like an archipelago of long thin islands in front of an ocean-wide sky; or like a flat sandy shore as it might look to a traveller in an aeroplane flying low on its side with one wing almost in the sea. The illusion was all the stronger for the fact that the last glimmers of day fell obliquely on these cloud-forms and gave them, in high relief, the air of solid rocks—rocks too, at other times, are as if sculpted from light and shadow—and it was as if the sun, no longer able to exercise its etching-needle on granite and porphyry, was lavishing its day-time skills on these vaporous and insubstantial subjects.

The cloud background, therefore, was like the edge of an unnamed coast. And as the sky cleared we could see beaches, lagoons, islets by the hundred, and sandbanks overrun by the inactive ocean of the sky. Fjords and inland lakes appeared where all had been flat and smooth. And because the sky which surrounded these arrowy shapes was like an ocean, and because the sea normally reflects the colours of the sky, the scene was like the reconstruction of some distant landscape in which the sun was setting all over again. We had only to look at the real sea, far below, to escape from the mirage; that real sea had no longer either the white-hot flatness of noonday or the curling prettiness of after-dinner. No longer did the all-but-horizontal rays of daylight illuminate the tops of the little waves that looked towards them, leaving the rest in darkness. The water, too, was now seen in relief, and its precise and heavy shadows were as if cast in steel. All transparency had gone.

And so, by a process at once unvarying and imperceptible, evening gave place to night. All was changed. The sky on the horizon was opaque, and above it the last clouds that had been brought into being by the day's end were scattering across a ground that was livid yellow at its base and turned blue towards its zenith. Soon they were but lean and weakly shadows, like scenery-frames seen without stage-lights; the performance over, we see them for what they are—poor, fragile, ephemeral—and owing the illusion of reality which they had helped to create not so much to their own nature as to some trickery of lighting or perspective. Only a few moments earlier they had been alive and in continual transformation; now they seem set fast in a form as sad as it is unalterable, in the middle of a sky which will soon merge them within its gathering darkness.

PART III

The New World

8   *The Doldrums*

W̶E SAID good-bye to the Old World at Dakar and proceeded, without any glimpse of the Cape Verde Islands, to the fateful 7° North. Here it was that, in 1498, Columbus on his third voyage changed course towards the north-west. But for this he would have done as he intended and discovered Brazil; as it was, it was by a miracle that he did not miss, fifteen days later, Trinidad and the Venezuelan coast.

As we drew towards the doldrums, so much dreaded by navigators in ancient times, the winds proper to both hemispheres dropped away; we were entering the zone where sails hang idle for weeks on end. So still is the air that one would think oneself in an enclosed space rather than in the middle of the ocean. The dark clouds, with never a breeze to disturb them, respond to gravity alone as they lumber slowly down towards sea-level; if their inertia were not so great they would sweep clean the polished surface of the water as they trail their fringes along it. The ocean, lit indirectly by the rays of an invisible sun, offers an oily and unvarying reflection that reverses the normal light-values of air and water. (Look at it upside-down and you will see a more orthodox 'sea-picture', with sky and ocean each impersonating the other.) There's a strange intimacy about the passive, half-lit horizon; and the area between the sea and its cloud-ceiling seems even narrower for the little funnels of cloud which idle their way across from one side to the other. The ship slithers anxiously between the two surfaces, as if it had none too much time to avoid being stifled. Sometimes a cloud comes near, loses its shape, bellies out all round us and whips across the deck with damp finger-ends. Then it re-forms on the far side of the ship; but it can no longer be heard.

All life had gone from the sea. No longer did dolphins cut gracefully through the white waves ahead of us; nothing spouted on the

77

horizon; and we had lost the spectacle of the pink-and-mauve-veiled nautiluses.

Should we find, on the far side of the deep, the marvels vouched for by the navigators of old? When they moved into unknown regions they were more anxious to verify the ancient history of the Old World than to discover a new one. Adam and Ulysses were authenticated by what they saw. When Columbus, on his first journey, stumbled on the Antilles, he thought that they might be Japan; but he preferred to think of them as the Terrestrial Paradise. Four centuries have elapsed since then, but they can't quite obliterate the twist of circumstance by which the New World was spared the agitations of 'history' for some ten or twenty millennia. Something of this must remain, even if on another level. I soon found out that even if South America was no longer Eden before the Fall, it was still, thanks to that mysterious circumstance, in a position to offer a Golden Age to anyone with a bit of money. Its good fortune was melting like snow in the sun. How much of it is left today? Already the rich alone had access to its remnants, and now its very nature has been transformed and is historical, where once it was eternal, and social, where once it was metaphysical. The earthly paradise which Columbus glimpsed was at once perpetuated and destroyed in the ideal of 'good living' which only the rich could enjoy.

The charcoal skies and louring atmosphere of the doldrums summarize the state of mind in which the Old World first came upon the new one. This lugubrious frontier-area, this lull before the storm in which the forces of evil alone seem to flourish, is the last barrier between what were once—quite recently—two planets so different from one another that our first explorers could not believe that they were inhabited by members of the same race. The one, hardly touched by mankind, lay open to men whose greed could no longer be satisfied in the other. A second Fall was about to bring everything into question: God, morality, and the law. Procedures at once simultaneous and contradictory were to confirm these things, in fact, and refute them in law. The Garden of Eden was found to be true, for instance; likewise the ancients' Golden Age, the Fountain of Youth, Atlantis, the Gardens of the Hesperides, the pastoral poems, and the Fortunate Islands. But the spectacle of a humanity both purer and happier than our own (in reality, of course, it was neither of these, but a secret remorse made it seem so) made the European sceptical of the existing notions of revelation, salvation, morality, and law. Never had the human race been faced with such a terrible ordeal; nor will one such ever recur, unless there should one day be revealed to us another earth, many millions of miles distant, with thinking beings upon it. And we know, even then, that those distances can, in theory at any rate, be covered, whereas the early navigators were afraid that an enormous nothingness might lie before them.

Certain incidents will remind us of how absolute, complete, and intransigent were the dilemmas which confronted our predecessors in the sixteenth century. Take, for instance, what they called Hispaniola: the Haiti and San Domingo of our day. In 1492 there were about a hundred thousand people on those islands. They were to dwindle in the next hundred years to a mere two hundred; horror and disgust at European civilization were to kill them off quite as effectively as disease and ill treatment. The colonists couldn't make these people out, and commission after commission was sent to enquire into their nature. If they were really men, were they perhaps the descendants of the ten lost tribes of Israel? Or Mongols who had ridden over on elephants? Or Scotsmen, brought over some centuries earlier by Prince Modoc? Had they always been pagans, or were they lapsed Catholics who had once been baptized by St Thomas? That they were really men, and not animals or creatures of the devil, was not regarded as certain. In 1512, for instance, King Ferdinand authorized the importation of white women as slaves into the West Indies, with the object of preventing the Spaniards from marrying the native women 'who are far from being rational creatures'. And when Las Casas tried to put an end to forced labour in the islands, the colonists were not so much indignant as incredulous. 'What?' they said. 'Does he want to stop us using our beasts of burden?'

The most famous of the commissions is, quite rightly, that of the monks of the Order of St Jerome in 1517. The story is worth recalling, both for the light it sheds on the mental attitudes of the time and for the marks of a scrupulosity which was to be well and truly banished from colonialism. The enquiry was held on the most up-to-date psycho-sociological lines, and in the course of it the colonists were asked whether, in their estimation, the Indians were capable of running their own society, 'like the Castilian peasantry'. A unanimous 'No' was the answer. 'Their grandchildren just *might* be up to it, but they're so profoundly anti-social that you couldn't be sure. Take an instance: they dodge the Spaniards when they can, and you can't get them to work for nothing—and yet sometimes you'll find them giving all their belongings away. And when we cut the ears off one of them they all stick by him, just the same.' And, with one voice: 'The Indian is better off as a slave, among men, than as an animal on his own.'

Ten years later Ortiz spoke up as follows before the Council of the Indies: 'They eat human flesh and they've no notion of justice; they go about naked and eat spiders and worms and lice, all raw. . . . They've no beard, and if one of them happens to start one he makes haste to pull it out, hair by hair. . . .'

At this same time, so Oviedo tells us, the Indians in the neighbour-ing island of Porto Rico used to kill off any captured Europeans by drowning. Then they would mount guard for weeks round the dead men to see whether or not they were subject to putrefaction. We can draw two conclusions from the differences between the two methods of enquiry: the white men invoked the social, and the Indians the natural, sciences; and whereas the white men took the Indians for animals, the Indians were content to suspect the white men of being gods. One was as ignorant as the other, but the second of the two did more honour to the human race.

To these moral disturbances were added ordeals of a more intel-lectual order. Our predecessors were baffled at every turn: Pierre d'Ailly's *Imago Mundi* speaks of a newly discovered race of supremely happy beings, *gens beatissima*, made up of pygmies, and headless creatures, and people who lived for ever. Peter Martyr described monsters of many sorts: snakes in the likeness of crocodiles; ox-bodied creatures with tusks as big as an elephant's; ox-headed fish, each with four legs and a long shell on its back, like a tortoise covered with warts; and man-eating tyburons. What he meant, of course, were boa-constrictors, tapirs, sea-cows or hippopotamuses, and sharks (*tubarão*, in Portuguese). Conversely things genuinely mysterious were taken as quite natural. When Columbus wanted to justify the abrupt change of course which cost him Brazil, he put into his official report an account of extravagances such as have never been reported since, above all in that zone of perennial humidity: a blazing heat which made it impossible to set foot in the hold, with the result that his casks of wine and water exploded, his grain caught fire, and his lard and dried meat roasted for a week on end; the sun was such that his crew thought they were being burnt alive. O happy age, when all was possible!

Surely it was here, or hereabouts, that Columbus sighted the sirens? Actually he saw them in the Caribbean, on the first of his voyages, but they would not have been out of place off the Amazonian delta. 'The three sirens,' he tells us, 'lifted their bodies above the surface of the ocean, and although they were not as beautiful as the painters have made them their round faces were distinctly human in form.' Sea-cows have round heads and carry their udders on their chests; as the females feed their young by clutching them to their breasts there is nothing very surprising in Columbus' interpretation—especially in an age when people were ready to describe the cotton plant (and even to draw a picture of it) as a 'sheep-tree': a tree that bore whole sheep, where others bore fruit; dangling by their backs, so that they could be shorn by any passer-by.

Rabelais must have worked from narratives of this sort in the Fourth Book of Pantagruel. In offering us our earliest caricature of what anthropologists now call a system of relationships he embroidered freely upon the skimpy original; the system can barely be conceived, surely, in which an old man could address a young girl as 'Father'. The sixteenth century lacked, in any case, an element more essential even than knowledge itself: a quality indispensable to scientific reflec-tion. The men of that time had no feeling for the style of the universe—just as, today, where the fine arts are in question, an uninstructed person who had picked up some of the surface-characteristics of Italian art, or of primitive African sculpture, would be unable to distinguish a faked Botticelli from a real one or a Pahouin figure from a mass-produced imitation. Sirens and sheep-trees are something different from, and more than, failings of objectivity; on the intellectual level they should rather be called faults of taste; they illustrate the falling short of minds which, despite elements of genius and a rare refinement in other domains, left much to be desired where observation was concerned. Not that I mean this by way of censure: rather should we revere those men the more for the results which they achieved in spite of their shortcomings.

Anyone who, in our own day, wants to rewrite the *Prière sur l'Acropole* should choose, not the Acropolis, but the deck of a steamer bound for the Americas. It's not to the anaemic goddess of old, the headmistress of our ingrown civilization, that I for one should offer homage. And higher even than those heroes—navigators, explorers, conquerors of the New World—who risked the only total adventure yet offered to mankind (the journey to the moon will one day replace it), I would set the survivors of that rearguard which paid so cruelly for the honour of holding the doors open: the Indians whose example, as transmitted to us by Montaigne, Rousseau, Diderot, and Voltaire, so enriched the substance of what I learnt at school. Hurons, Iroquois, Caribs, Tupis—it is to you that I would pay homage!

When Columbus saw a glimmer of light along the horizon by night he took it for the coast of America; but it was merely a marine variety of glow-worm which produces its eggs between sunset and moonrise. These I, too, saw during a night which I spent watchfully on deck in readiness for my first sight of the New World.

That world had been present to us since the previous day: not in sight, though, for despite a change of course which took us more and more to the south we were to steam parallel to the coast from Cape São Agostino to Rio. For two days at least, and maybe for three, we were to keep company with an unseen America. No longer was it the great sea-birds which gave us warning that the voyage was nearly over: the strident tropic birds, or the tyrannical petrels which swoop down on gannets in flight and force them to disgorge their prey. Both of these, as Columbus learnt to his cost, travel far from land; he had sighted them with joy when he had still half the Atlantic to cross. The flying-fish, too, had become, if anything, less common for the last few days. It is by its scent that the New World first makes itself known to the traveller; and it is difficult to describe that scent to anyone who has not experienced it.

At first it seemed as if the sea-smells of the previous weeks were no longer circulating freely; somewhere they had come up against an invisible wall; immobilized, they had no longer any claim upon our attention, which was free to sample quite other smells—smells to which experience had as yet given us no guide; it was as if forest breezes alternated with the smells of the hot-house, quintessences of the vegetable kingdom any one of which would have intoxicated us by its intensity had we savoured it in isolation; but, as it was, they were spaced out as if in an arpeggio, isolated and yet commingled, with each strong scent following fast upon its predecessor. To understand what all that is like, you must first have plunged your nose deep into a freshly crushed tropical pepper; and before that you must know what it is like to walk into a *botequin* in the Brazilian interior and smell the honeyed black coils of the *fumo de rolo*, which is made of fermented tobacco-leaves rolled into lengths several yards long. In the union of those two smells you will recapture the America which, for many a thousand years, alone held their secret.

But when the visible image of the New World first presents itself, at four o'clock the following morning, it seems worthy of its smells.

For two days and two nights the ship steams past an enormous cordillera: enormous not in its height but because it goes on repeating itself exactly, with never an identifiable beginning or end in the disordered succession of its crests. Several hundred yards above the sea we could see, continuously, mountain-tops of polished stone: there was an element of wild absurdity in their outline, of the kind one sees in sand-castles that the waves have washed half away; I should not have believed it possible for such shapes to exist, on such a scale, anywhere on our planet.

This impression of immensity is, of course, characteristic of America. I have experienced it on the plateaux of central Brazil, in the Bolivian Andes and in the Rocky Mountains of Colorado, in the outskirts of Rio and the suburbs of Chicago. . . . The initial shock is the same in every case: the streets remain streets, the mountains mountains, and the rivers rivers—and yet one feels at a loss before them, simply because their scale is such that the normal adjustment of man-to-environment becomes impossible. Later one gets used to America and comes to make, quite naturally, the necessary adaptations; a momentary change of gear in one's mind, as the aeroplane comes down, and 'normal functioning' continues. But our judgments are, none the less, permeated and deformed by this difference of scale. Those who call New York ugly, for instance, have simply failed to make the necessary change of registration. Objectively, no doubt, New York is a city, and can be judged as one; but the spectacle which it offers to a European sensibility is of a different order of magnitude: that of European landscape; whereas American landscape offers us, in its turn, an altogether more monumental scheme of things, and one for which we have no equivalent. The beauty of New York, is not, therefore, an urban beauty. It results from the creation of a new kind of city: an artificial landscape in which the principles of urbanism no longer operate. And our eye will adapt itself at once, if we do not inhibit it, to this new landscape, in which the values that count are those of the velvety light, the sharpness of the far distances, the sublimity of the skyscraper and the shaded valleys in which the many-coloured motor-cars lie strewn like flowers.

· This makes it all the more embarrassing for me to have to say that I do not respond at all to the renowned 'beauty' of the bay of Rio de Janeiro. How shall I put it? Simply that the landscape of Rio is not built to the scale of its own proportions. The Sugar Loaf mountain, the Corcovado, and the other all-too-famous points of beauty seemed

to me, as I arrived by sea, like stumps left at random in the four corners
of a toothless mouth. Geographical accidents, lost for the greater part
of the time in the brown mists of the tropics, they are too small to
furnish adequately the colossal horizon. The bay is best seen in reverse:
if you stand on the heights, that is to say, and look down towards the
sea you will feel as if you were looking down into an enormous
builder's yard. Nature, in short, will give you the feeling that mankind
has given you in New York.

The bay's various landmarks give no real impression of its proportions; but as the ship creeps into the harbour, changing course this
way and that to avoid the islands, cool scented breezes blow down upon
us from the wooded hillocks and we establish a sort of preliminary
contact with flowers and rocks which, though they have not as yet
any individual existence for us, are the prefiguration of the whole
continent. Once again Columbus comes to mind:

> 'The trees were so high that they seemed to touch the sky; and,
> if I understood aright, they never lose their leaves; for they were
> as fresh and as green in November as ours are in the month of May;
> some were even in flower, and others were bearing fruit. . . . And
> wherever I turned the nightingales were singing, accompanied by
> thousands of other birds of one sort and another.'

That's America: the continent makes itself felt at once. It is made up
of all the presences which enliven, at the end of the day, the misted
horizon of the bay; but to the newcomer these shapes, these movements, these patches of light do not stand for provinces, or towns, or
hamlets; he will not say to himself: 'There's a forest' (or a stretch of
open country, or a valley, or a 'view'); nor will he see them in terms of
the activity of individuals, each enclosed within his own family and
his own occupation and knowing nothing of his neighbours. No: it
all strikes him as an entity, unique and all-comprehending. What
surrounded me on every side, what overwhelmed me, was not the
inexhaustible diversity of people and things, but that one single and
redoubtable entity: the New World.

9 *Guanabara*

THE bay of Rio has bitten Rio itself right to the heart; and when the traveller disembarks in the centre of the city, it is as if the other half, the Ys of our day, had foundered beneath the waves. And, in a certain sense, it *has* so foundered: the first city of Rio, a simple fort, stood on the rocky islet which our ship had just negotiated. It still bears the name of the founder of the city: Villegaignon.

Once ashore, I ambled along the Avenida Rio Branco, where once the Tupinamba villages stood; in my pocket was that breviary of the anthropologist, Jean de Léry. He had arrived in Rio three hundred and seventy-eight years previously, almost to the day. With him were ten other Genevese, Protestants to a man, sent by Calvin to seek out Villegaignon, his friend of student days, who had gone over to Protestantism barely a year after his arrival in the bay of Guanabara. Villegaignon was a strange figure, who had turned his hand to more or less everything and taken part in all the quarrels that were going. He had, for instance, fought the Turks, the Arabs, the Italians, the Scots (he had abducted Mary Stuart in order to facilitate her marriage to François II), and the English. He had turned up at Malta, at Algiers, at the battle of Cérisoles. Just when he was almost at the end of his adventurous career, and appeared to be settling down as a military architect, he suffered a professional disappointment and decided to go off to Brazil, with intentions cut to the pattern of his restless and ambitious mind. He aimed to found a colony that was more than a colony: an empire, in fact. And his immediate objective was to establish a place of refuge for Protestants who were being persecuted in Europe. A Catholic himself, and possibly a free thinker, he secured the patronage of Coligny and the Cardinal of Lorraine. After a brisk recruiting campaign among the faithful of both beliefs, and a diversionary drive among debauchees and runaway slaves, he managed to get six hundred people aboard his two ships, on July 12th, 1555: pioneers drawn from every rank of Society, with an admixture of convicts among them. The only things he forgot were women and food.

There was trouble at the start: twice the ships put back to Dieppe, and when they finally got away on August 14th there was trouble again: fighting broke out when they reached the Canaries, the ship's water became polluted, and there was an outbreak of scurvy. On November 10th, however, Villegaignon dropped anchor in the bay of Guanabara, where the French and the Portuguese had been in competition, for several years past, for the natives' favours.

France's privileged position on the Brazilian coast dated back at least to the beginning of the century. We know of many French travellers who were in Brazil at that time—notably Gonneville, who returned to France with a Brazilian son-in-law; and it was, of course, in 1500 that Cabral discovered Santa Cruz. There may even be something in the tradition, so long current in Dieppe, that Jean Cousin discovered Brazil four years before Columbus' first voyage. The French did, after all, immediately call the new country *Brésil*, which had been the name given in secret, since the twelfth century at least, to the mythical continent whence wooden dyes were obtained. And the French language incorporated directly within itself—and with no intermediary passage by way of the Iberian languages—a great many items from the natives' vocabulary: *ananas*, for instance, and *manioc*, and *tamandua*, and *tapir*, and *jaguar*, and *sagouin*, and *agouti*, and *ara*, and *caiman*, and *toucan*, and *coati*, and *acajou*. . . . Cousin had a man called Pinzon among his crew, and it was the Pinzons who gave Columbus fresh courage at Palos, when he seemed ready to turn back; and it was a Pinzon, yet again, who commanded the *Pinta* on Columbus' first voyage: Columbus discussed every change of course with him. And if, finally, Columbus had not gone off the course which was to be followed, a year later, by yet another Pinzon, he would have pushed on as far as Cabo São Agostino. Columbus, not Pinzon, would have had the honour of the first 'official' discovery of Brazil.

Only a miracle will ever resolve this mystery, since the archives of Dieppe, with Cousin's narrative among them, were lost in the fire started by an English bombardment in the seventeenth century. But when I first set foot on Brazilian soil I could not but remember the incidents, some tragic and some grotesque, which witnessed to the

intimacy of Franco-Indian relations four centuries earlier. The interpreters from Normandy who 'went native', married Indian women,
and took to cannibalism; and the unhappy Hans Staden who for years
expected to be eaten and was saved every day by some fresh accident.
He it was who tried to pass himself off as a Frenchman by growing a
red beard, by no means Iberian in colour, and drew from King
Quoniam Bébé the remark: 'I've already captured and eaten five
Portuguese. They all pretended to be French, the liars!' And what an
intimacy can we read into the fact that in 1531 the frigate *La Pélérine*
brought back to France, along with three thousand leopard-skins and
three hundred monkeys, 'six hundred parrots that already know a few
words of French'!

Villegaignon founded Fort Coligny on an island in the middle of
the bay. The Indians built it and supplied the little colony with food;
but before long, weary of always giving and never getting anything in
return, they ran away and left their villages deserted. Famine and
sickness broke out in the fort. Villegaignon's tyrannical side soon
showed itself; and when the convicts rebelled against him he had them
massacred to a man. The epidemic soon reached the mainland, and the
few Indians who had remained faithful to the mission caught the
contagion: eight hundred died of it.

Villegaignon began to disdain the crises of this world; a crisis of
the spirit took all his time. Contact with Protestants led him to go over
to their beliefs, and he appealed to Calvin to send out missionaries who
would have more to teach him in the matter. And that is how, in 1556,
Léry came to arrive in Rio.

The story then takes so curious a turn that I am amazed no novelist
or scenario-writer has seized upon it. What a film it would make!
A handful of Frenchmen, isolated on an unknown continent—an
unknown planet could hardly have been stranger—where Nature and
mankind were alike unfamiliar to them; incapable of growing anything with which to keep themselves alive, racked with illness, and
dependent for all their needs on an unintelligible population which had
taken an intense dislike to them: and caught, what was more, in their
own trap. For, although they had left Europe to found a community
in which Catholic and Protestant could co-exist in amity, they soon
began to try to convert one another. Where they should have been
working to keep themselves alive, they spent week after week in
insane discussions: How should one interpret the Last Supper? Should
water be mixed with wine for the Consecration? The Eucharist and

the problems of baptism gave rise to veritable theological tournaments at the end of which Villegaignon would veer now to one side, now to the other.

They went so far as to send an emissary to Europe to ask Calvin to adjudicate on certain knotty points. Meanwhile their disputes grew steadily worse. Villegaignon's faculties began to give way; Léry tells us that they could judge, from the colour of his clothes, how he was likely to behave and in what field his excesses would lie. When finally he turned against the Protestants, and tried to starve them out, they left the community, crossed over to the mainland, and threw in their lot with the Indians. The idyll which resulted is described in that master-piece of anthropological literature, the *Voyage faict en la Terre de du Brésil* by Jean de Léry. The adventure ended sadly: the Genevese embarked with great difficulty on a French boat. On the outward voyage they had been strong enough to pillage every ship that crossed their path; now things were very different, and famine reigned on board. They ate the monkeys, and they ate the parrots—though these were so valuable that an Indian woman, a friend of Léry's, refused to give hers up until she was given a cannon in exchange. The rats and mice from the hold were eaten in their turn, and sold for as much as four *écus* each. The water gave out. In 1558 the ship's company arrived in Brittany, half dead from hunger.

On the island, the colony disintegrated. Terror reigned, and executions were frequent. Loathed by all, regarded by one party as a traitor and by the other as a renegade, an object of dread to the Indians, and himself terrified by the Portuguese, Villegaignon said farewell to his dream. Fort Coligny, commanded at the time by his nephew, Bois-le-Comte, fell to the Portuguese in 1560.

Now that I was free to explore Rio on foot, I began by looking about for some lingering vestige of this adventure. I was to find one, eventually, in the course of an archaeological excursion to the far side of the bay. On the swampy beach where the motor-boat had deposited our party I suddenly saw an old rusted hulk. Doubtless it did not date back to the sixteenth century; but it introduced the element of historical perspective into a region otherwise unequipped to illustrate the passage of time. The clouds hung low and fine rain had fallen continuously since daybreak. Nothing could be seen of the city. The black mud was alive with crabs; there were mangroves—is it a mark of growth, or of decay, that they swell up to such an extraordinary size? —and, beyond where a few ageless straw huts stood out against the forest, the lower slopes of the mountains were swathed in pale mists. Over towards the trees was the goal of our expedition: a sand-pit where peasants had lately brought to light some fragments of pottery. I ran my hand over one of them: the white slip, bordered with red, proved that they were of Tupi origin, and the lacy black markings seemed to form a labyrinth—destined, so people say, to deter those evil spirits which would otherwise have sought out the bones that were once preserved in these urns. I was told that we could have motored the thirty-odd miles that separated us from the centre of Rio, had it not been that the rain might well have flooded the tracks and cut us off for a week. This isolation would at least have brought me nearer to Léry, who may have whiled away the months of waiting by watching the manufacture of just such a pot as I had, in fragments, before me. He describes, at any rate, how the natives would take up a thin rod, dip it in black varnish, and describe 'charming and amusing patterns by the thousand'.

Quite different was my first contact with Rio. For the first time in my life I was on the other side of the Equator, in the tropics, and in the New World. By what master-token should I recognize this triple transformation? What voice would confirm it for me, what never-yet-heard note ring out in my ear? Flippancies first: Rio seemed to me like one huge drawing-room.

Running off the main avenue are any number of narrow, winding, shadowy alleyways, each faced with black and white mosaic. When I came to explore them I found that they had an atmosphere all their own. The transition from house to street was less clearly marked than it is in Europe. No matter how smart the shop-front, the goods have a way of spilling over into the street, so that you hardly notice whether you are, or are not, 'inside' the shop. The street is a place to be lived in, not a place to pass through. It is at once tranquil and animated—more lively, and yet more sheltered, than our streets at home. Or, more exactly, what happens is this: the change of hemisphere, continent, and climate has made it unnecessary for the Brazilians to erect the thin glass roof which, in Europe, creates artificially something of the same sort. It is as if Rio had taken the Gallerias in Milan, the Amsterdam Galerij, or the Passage des Panoramas or the hall of the Gare St Lazare in Paris, and reconstituted them in the open air.

People generally think of travel in terms of displacement in space, but a long journey exists simultaneously in space, in time, and in the social hierarchy. Our impressions must be related to each of these three

before we can define them properly; and as space alone has three
dimensions all to itself we should need at least five to establish an
adequate notion of travel. This I sensed as soon as I went ashore in
Brazil. That I had crossed the Atlantic and the Equator and was near
the tropics I knew from several infallible signs: among them, the easy-
going damp heat which emancipated my body from its normal layer
of woollens and abolished the distinction (which I recognized, in
retrospect, as one of the marks of our civilization) between 'indoors'
and 'outdoors'. I soon found out that for this distinction the Brazilians
had substituted another (that between mankind and the jungle) which
does not exist in our entirely humanized landscapes. And then there
were the palm-trees, the unfamiliar flowers, and in front of each café
the heap of green coconuts which, when cut open, offered a cool
sweet liquid that smelt of the cellar.

Other changes struck me. I, who had been poor, was now rich. My
material condition had changed, to begin with; and then the prices of
local produce were incredibly low—one franc for a pineapple, two
francs a huge bunch of bananas, four francs for the chicken that the
Italian shopkeeper would roast for me on a spit. Quite magical, all this:
and to it was added the slight recklessness which always attaches to a
brief visit to somewhere new. The fact that one feels bound to profit by
opportunities of this kind introduces, moreover, an element of
ambiguity, which may well provoke the traveller to throw caution
aside and embark upon the traditional bout of prodigality. Travel can,
of course, have exactly the opposite effect—this I was to experience
when I arrived in New York after the armistice without a penny in my
pockets—but, generally speaking, it can hardly ever fail to wreak a
transformation of some sort, great or small, and for better or for worse,
in the situation of the traveller. He may go up in the world, or he may
go down; and the feeling and flavour of the places he visits will be
inseparable in his mind from the exact position in the social scale
which he will have occupied there.

There was a time when travel confronted the traveller with
civilizations radically different from his own. It was their strangeness,
above all, which impressed him. But these opportunities have been
getting rarer and rarer for a very long time. Be it in India or in
America, the traveller of our day finds things more familiar than he
will admit. The aims and itineraries which we devise for ourselves are,
above all, ways of being free to choose at what date we shall penetrate
a given society. Our mechanistic civilization is overcoming all others,

but we can at least choose the speed at which it will be effecting its conquests. The search for the exotic will always bring us back to the same conclusion, but we can choose between an early or a late stage of its development. The traveller becomes a kind of dealer in antiques— one who, having given up his gallery of primitive art for lack of stock, falls back on fusty souvenirs brought back from the flea-markets of the inhabited world.

These differences can already be detected within any large city. Just as each plant flowers at a particular season, so does each quarter of a great city bear the mark of the centuries which witnessed its growth, its apogee, and its decline. In Paris the Marais was at its zenith in the seventeenth century and is now far gone in decay. The 9th arrondissement flowered later, under the Second Empire, but it has now 'gone off' considerably and its shabbified mansions have been given over to a lower-middle-class horde. As for the 17th arrondissement, it has remained set in its bygone luxury like a huge chrysanthemum whose long-dead head remains proudly erect. Only yesterday the 16th arrondissement was one long bedazzlement; today its blooms are giving way to an undergrowth of apartment-houses that is making it merge more and more into the suburbs.

Where the comparison is between cities remote from one another both historically and geographically, certain rhythmic differences are added to the varying speeds of the cycle in question. The centre of Rio is very 1900–10 in character, but elsewhere you will find yourself in quiet streets and among long avenues bordered with palm-trees, mangoes, and clipped Brazilian rosewood-trees, where old-fashioned villas stand in gardens of their own. I was reminded (as I was, later, in the residential areas of Calcutta) of Nice or Biarritz in the time of Napoleon III. The tropics are not so much exotic as out of date. It's not the vegetation which confirms that you are 'really there', but certain trifling architectural details and the hint of a way of life which would suggest that you had gone backwards in time rather than forwards across a great part of the earth's surface.

Rio de Janeiro is not built like an ordinary city. Originally built on the flat and swampy area which borders the bay, it later pushed up into the gloomy escarpments which glower down on every side. Like fingers in a glove too small for them, the city's tentacles—some of them fifteen or twenty miles long—run up to the foot of granitic formations so steep that nothing can take root in them. (Just occasionally an isolated fragment of forest has grown up on a lonely terrace or deep

shaft in the rock; virgin it will remain, although sometimes from an
aeroplane we seem almost to brush against its branches, as we skim
along the cool and solemn corridor that runs between sumptuous rock
tapestries.) Rio, so rich in hills, treats them with a scorn which does
much to explain the shortage of water in its higher regions. It is, in this
respect, the opposite of Chittagong, which lies on marshy ground in
the Bay of Bengal; in Chittagong the rich set themselves apart alike
from the oppressive heat and from the horrors of lower-class life by
living in lonely bungalows set high on grassy hillocks of orange-
coloured clay. In Rio, on the other hand, such is the reverberation of
the heat on those strange granite skull-caps that the cool breezes below
never get a chance to rise. The urbanists may have resolved the problem
by now, but in 1935 the altimeter was also an unfailing index of social
position; the higher you lived, the less important you were. Poverty
perched on the hill-tops, where the black population lived in rags; only
at carnival-time would they come swarming down into the city
proper, there to sweep all before them with the tunes they had picked
out, on high, on their guitars.

Distance counts in Rio, just as height does. Follow any one of the
tracks that lead up into the foothills and you will at once find yourself
in a suburb. Botafogo, at the far end of the Avenue Rio Branco, was
still a smart section; but after Flamengo you might think yourself in
Neuilly, and towards the Copacabana tunnel you came, twenty-five
years ago, upon St Denis and Le Bourget, plus a certain element of
rustication, such as the suburbs of Paris must have had before the war
of 1914. In Copacabana, which today bristles with skyscrapers, I saw
merely a small provincial town.

When I was leaving Rio for good, I went to an hotel on the flank
of the Corcovado to call on some American colleagues. To get there,
you took a rough-and-ready funicular which had been erected on the
site of a landslide in a style half garage and half mountaineers' cabin,
with command-posts manned by attentive stewards: a sort of Luna
Park. All this just to get to the top: the car was hauled up over patch
after patch of chaotic mountainside—almost vertical, often enough—
until in the end we got to a little residence of the Imperial era, a *terrea*
house: single-storeyed, that is to say, stuccoed and painted ochre. We
dined out, on a platform that had been turned into a terrace, and looked
out across an incoherent mixture of concrete houses, shanties, and
'built-up areas' of one sort or another. In the far distance, where one
would have expected factory chimneys to round off the heterogeneous

scene, there was a shining, satiny, tropical sea and, above it, an overblown full moon.

I went back on board. The ship got under way, ablaze with light, and as it set the sea atremble with its passing the reflected lights looked like a street of ill fame on the move. Later it blew up for a storm and the open sea gleamed like the belly of some enormous animal. Meanwhile the moon was masked by scurrying clouds that the wind formed and reformed as zigzags, triangles, and crosses. These strange shapes were lit up, as if from within: as if an Aurora Borealis adapted to tropical usage were being projected on to the dark background of the sky. From time to time these smoky apparitions would allow us a glimpse of a reddish moon that looked, on its intermittent appearances, like a disquieted lantern wandering somewhere aloft.

10 *Into the Tropics*

THE coastline from Rio to Santos still offers us the tropical landscape of our dreams. The mountains, at one point well over six thousand feet, run down steeply into the sea. Creeks and islets abound; and although there is beach after beach of fine sand, with coconut-trees and steamy forests overgrown with orchids, each is accessible only from the sea, so abrupt is the wall of sandstone or basalt behind them. Every fifty or sixty miles there's a little harbour where eighteenth-century houses, now in ruins, were built for the captains and vice-governors of times gone by. Fishermen live in them now; but Angra dos Reis, Ubatuba, Parati, São Sebastião, and Villa Bella all served in their time as points of embarkation for diamonds, topazes, and chrysolites from the Minas Geraes, or 'general mines', of the kingdom. It took weeks to bring them down by mule-back through the mountains. But if today we search for mule-tracks along the tops of those mountains it seems incredible that the traffic was once so abundant that men could make a living by collecting the shoes lost by mules en route.

Bougainville has described with what precautions the extraction and transport of these precious stones was surrounded. No sooner were they found than they had to be handed over to one of the company's depots: Rio des Morts, Sabara, Serro Frio—each had one. There the royal percentage was exacted, and whatever remained for the individual miner was given to him in bars marked with their weight, title, and value, and also with the royal arms. Half-way between the mines and the coast there was a second control-point. A lieutenant and fifty men were charged with the collection of the ritual twenty per cent and of the tolls payable both for animals and for men. These taxes were shared between the King and the soldiers concerned; and so it's not

94

surprising that every party bound for the coast was searched 'very thoroughly indeed'.

Private traders then took their bars of gold to the Mint in Rio de Janeiro, where they were exchanged for official currency—demi-doubloons worth eight Spanish piastres, on each of which the King had a profit of one piastre on account of the alloyage and the tax on money. Bougainville adds that 'the Mint is one of the finest in existence; and it has all the equipment which it needs to work as quickly as possible. As the gold comes down from the mines just as the fleet arrives from Portugal there is no time to be lost in the striking of the money. This is, indeed, carried out with astonishing speed.'

Where diamonds are concerned the system was even more rigorous, and Bougainville tells us that individual entrepreneurs were compelled to give up every single stone that they found. These were then consigned to a triple-locked box which, in its turn, was locked within two other boxes, each sealed by a high official. Not till the whole consignment was safely in Lisbon was it allowed to be opened, and then only in the presence of the King himself, who took such diamonds as he wanted himself and paid for them according to a fixed tariff.

Of all the intense activity which, in the year 1762 alone, resulted in the transport, supervision, striking, and despatch of more than a ton and a half of gold, nothing now remains along a coastline that has reverted to its paradisal beginnings: nothing, that is to say, save here and there a lonely and majestic house-front at the far end of a creek, with the sea still beating against the high walls where once the galleons moored. We would gladly believe that a few barefooted natives have alone had the run of those grandiose forests, those unblemished bights, those steep rock-faces; but it was there, on the high plateaux above the sea, that two centuries ago the destiny of the modern world was forged in Portuguese workshops.

The world, gorged with gold, began to hunger after sugar; and sugar took a lot of slaves. When the mines were exhausted—and, with them, the forests which had to be torn down to provide fuel for the crucibles—and slavery had been abolished, there arose an ever-greater demand for coffee. São Paulo and Santos, its port, were sensitive to this, and their gold, which had been first yellow, and then white, became black. But although Santos was to become a centre of international commerce its site has never quite lost its secret beauty; it was there, as the boat nosed its way slowly through the islands, that I made my first direct contact with the tropics. Green leaves pressed all around us. We could almost have reached out and touched the vegetation which, in Rio, is kept at a distance in high-lying greenhouses.

The country behind Santos is made up of inundated flatlands: a network of swamps and rivers and canals and lagoons, with a mother-of-pearly exhalation to smudge every contour. It looks as the earth must have looked on the day of creation. The banana-plantations are the freshest and most tender of imaginable greens; they are sharper in key than the greeny-gold of the jute-fields in the Brahmaputra delta, and where the jute-fields have a tranquil sumptuosity the Santos hinterland has a delicacy of nuance and an uneasy charm that relates us to a primordial state of things. For half an hour the motor runs between the banana-trees—mastodon vegetables, rather than dwarf-trees—with sap-laden trunks, a great quantity of elastic leaves, and beneath many of those leaves a hundred-fingered hand emerging from a huge and pink-and-chestnut lotus. Then the road climbs to two thousand five hundred feet: the summit of the serra. As everywhere along the coast, the steep slopes have kept the forests free of our humankind, with the result that they are not merely 'virgin', but of a luxuriance for which you would have to go several thousand miles north—near the basin of the Amazon, in fact—to find the equal. As we crawled up the unending spiral of the road, layer upon layer of plants and trees was laid out for inspection, as if in a museum.

The forest differs from our own by reason of the contrast between trunks and foliage. The leafage is darker and its nuances of green seem related rather to the mineral than to the vegetable world, and among minerals nearer to jade and tourmalin than to emerald and chrysolite. On the other hand, the trunks, white or grey in tone, stand out like dried bones against the dark background of the leaves. Too near to grasp the forest as a whole, I concentrated on details. Plants were more abundant than those we know in Europe. Leaves and stalks seemed to have been cut out of sheet metal, so majestic was their bearing, so impervious, as it seemed, the splendid development of their forms. Seen from outside, it was as if Nature in those regions was of a different order from the Nature we know: more absolute in its presence and its permanence. As in the exotic landscapes of the Douanier Rousseau, beings attained the dignity of objects.

Once before I had experienced something of the same sort: during a first holiday in Provence, after several years' vacationing in Normandy and Brittany. It was rather as if I had been whisked from a village of no interest to a site where every stone was of archaeological

1 Virgin forest in Parana

THE CADUVEO

2 The Pantanal

3 Nalike, capital of the Caduveo country

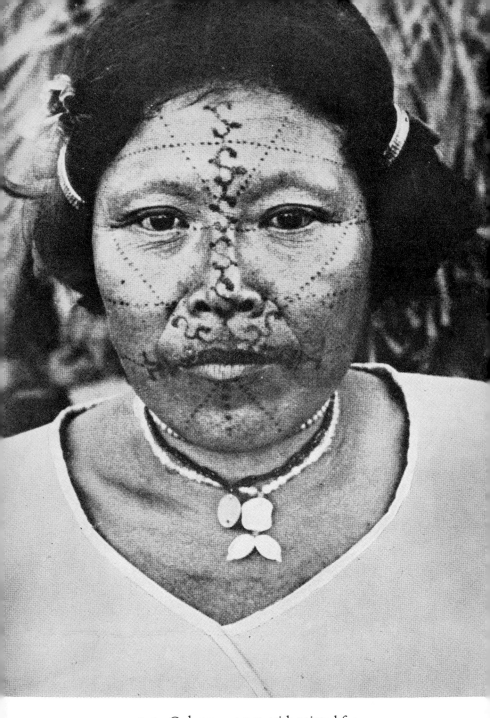

4-5 Caduveo women with painted faces

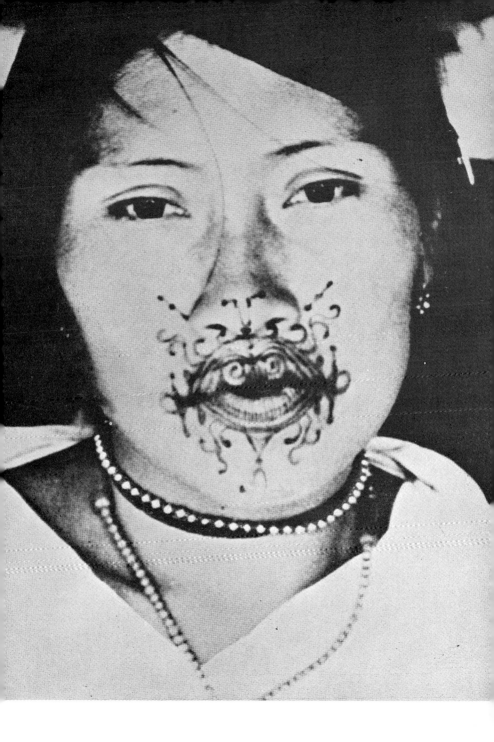

6   A Caduveo belle in 1895 (after Boggiani)

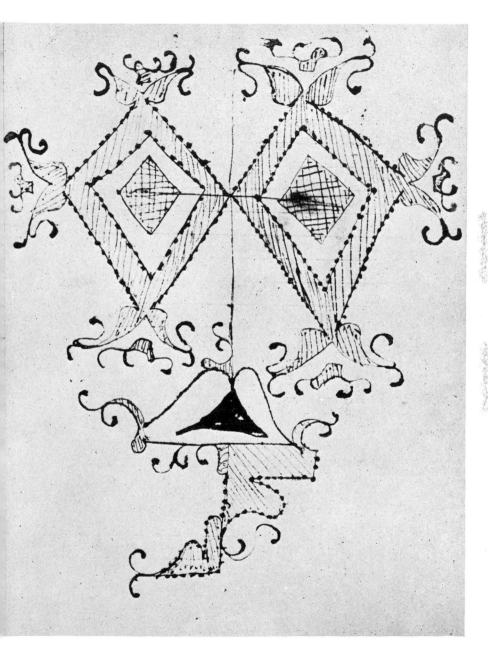

7   Face-painting; an original drawing by a Caduveo woman

8   Another face-painting, drawn by a native

9   Another face-painting, drawn by a native

10   A Caduveo girl dressed and painted for the rites of puberty

THE BORORO

12   A Bororo couple

13　The author's best informant in full regalia

15   Funeral dance

16   Dance of the Paiwe clan

17 Preparations for the *mariddo* dance

18 Funeral ceremony. (Photograph by René Silz)

19 The Nambikwara tribe on the move

THE NAMBIKWARA

20 Resting

21   A leaf shelter in the dry season

22 Little girl with a monkey

23 Building a hut for the rainy season

24　Two Nambikwara men. Note the cigarette rolled in a leaf and tucked through the bracelet on the upper arm

25　Sabané the sorcerer

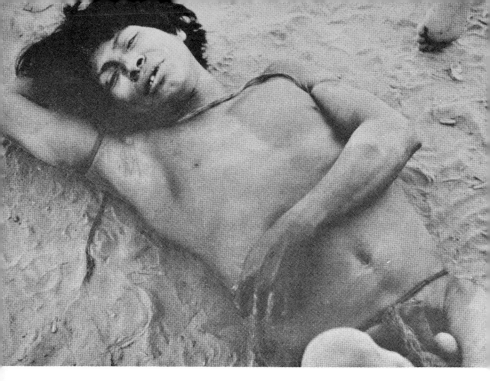

26　Chief Wakletoçu

27　Preparing curare

28 The Nambikwara position of the right hand in drawing the bow: the so-called secondary position. Cf. plate 52

29 A Nambikwara woman piercing mother-of-pearl from the river for ear-rings

30 The Nambikwara at work: grading pearls, threading them, and, in the background, weaving

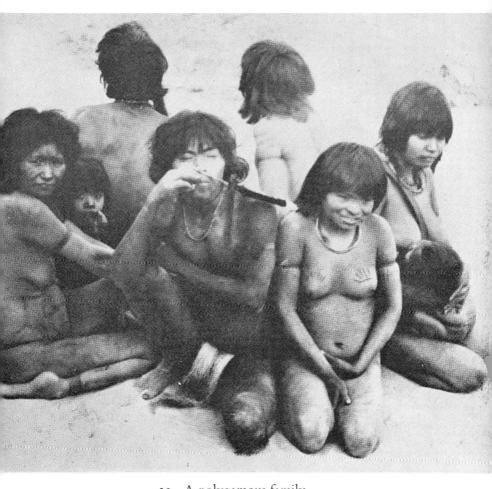

31   A polygamous family

32   A woman suckling her child in the native manner

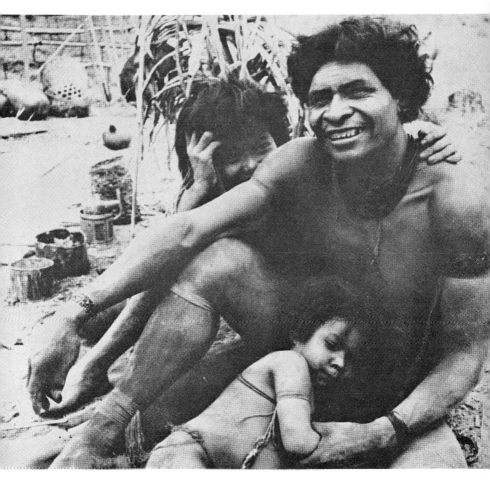

33   A Nambikwara family

34   Siesta

35   Conjugal felicity

36 Affectionate frolics

37 . . . and struggles meant only in fun

38   Looking for lice

39   Young woman with a monkey

40   Pregnant woman dozing

41   Carrying a child

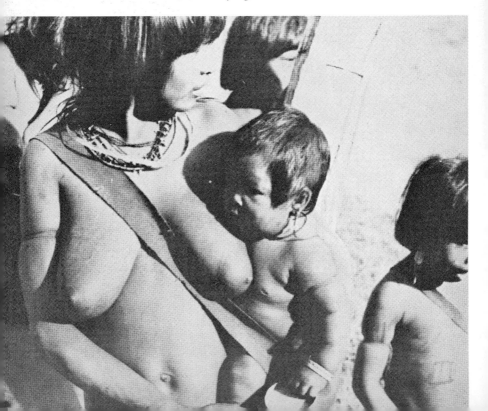

42 The spinner interrupted

43   The sorcerer's two wives in conversation

44   Nambikwara youth with a nasal ornament and a stiff fibre lip-plug

45   The day-dreamer

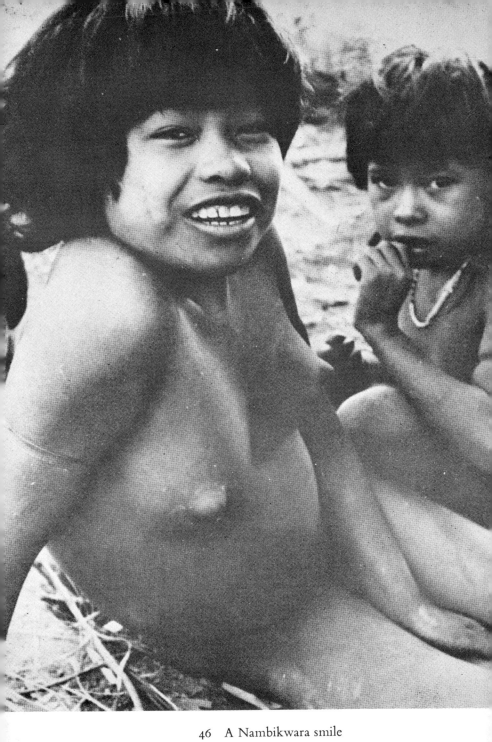

46 A Nambikwara smile

47   Going up the Rio Pimenta Bueno

THE TUPI-KAWAHIB

48   The Mundé village amidst its plantations

49 The Mundé village square

50 A Mundé man with lip-plugs of hardened resin

51   The dome of a Mundé hut seen from inside

52   Mundé archer; note the position of the right hand (the 'Mediterranean release') which differs from that adopted by the Bororo and Nambikwara, most often found in America. Cf. plate 28

53 Two young Mundé mothers

54   A Mundé woman and her child whose eyebrows are coated with wax
ready for plucking

55 Sharing camp with the Tu
Kawahib on the edge of the
Machado

56 Lucinda

57 A Tupi-Kawahib man skinning a monkey. Note the belt, a recent gift, and the penis-sheath

58   Taperahi, chief of the Tupi-Kawahib

59 Kunhatsin, chief wife of Taperahi, with her child

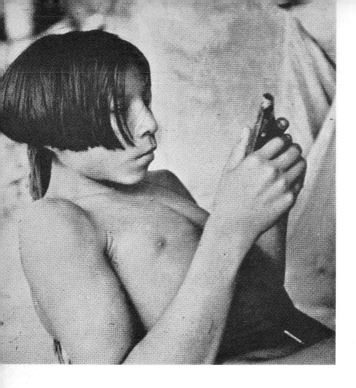

60 Pwereza,
Taperahi's son

61 Penhana, the
young wife of the
two brothers

62   Maruabai, co-wife (with her daughter Kunhatsin) of Chief Taperahi

63   Carrying canoes to by-pass rapids on the Rio Gi-Parana

importance: a witness, and not merely part of a house. I ran about the countryside in high excitement, telling myself over and over again that the growing things before me were called thyme, rosemary, basil, laurel, lavender, marjoram, and arbutus, and that each had a nobility all its own. The heavy resinous smells convinced me that I was in the presence of a superior order of vegetable things. What the flora of Provence proved to me by their smells, the flora of the tropics proved by their forms. Provence was a living herbal, as rich in receipts as in superstitions; but in the tropics the vegetable troupe took on another guise—that of a corps de ballet of great dancers, each of whom had paused at her moment of highest advantage, as it to make manifest a Grand Design the more evident for having no longer anything to fear of life; a ballet of no motion, with nothing now to disturb it but certain mineral agitations of the springs far below.

Once at the top, all is changed again. Gone are the damp heat of the tropics and the heroic entanglements of rock-face and liana. Instead of the enormous self-reflecting panorama that stretches from the serra to the sea we survey, in the opposite direction, an accidented and disgarnished plateau where crest succeeds ravine, and ravine crest, beneath an undependable sky. A Breton drizzle falls over all. For we are at nearly three thousand feet, although the sea is not far distant. At this point there begin the uplands proper—a continual ascent in which the coastal chain is the first and steepest step. To the north, these uplands gradually fall away towards the basin of the Amazon where, two thousand miles away, they fall abruptly to sea-level. Twice, however, their descent is interrupted by a line of cliffs: Serra de Botucatu, some three hundred miles from the coast, and Chapada de Mato Grosso, a further seven hundred and fifty miles onwards. I was to negotiate them both before coming upon a forest comparable to this one. Most of Brazil, with the Atlantic, the Amazon, and Paraguay as its boundaries, is like a sloping table-top with a high rim at the edge of the sea: or a crinkled springboard of bush surrounded by a damp circle of jungle and swamp.

Erosion had done much to ravage the country before me; but above all Man was responsible for its chaotic appearance. Originally it had been dug and cultivated; but after a few years continual rain and the exhaustion of the soil made it impossible to keep the coffee-plantations in being. They were therefore moved to an area where the soil was fresher and more fertile. The relationship between Man and the siol had never been marked by that reciprocity of attentions which, in the

Old World, has existed for thousands of years and been the basis of our prosperity. Here in Brazil the soil had been first violated, then destroyed. Agriculture had been a matter of looting for quick profits. Within a hundred years, in fact, the pioneers had worked their way like a slow fire across the State of São Paulo, eating into virgin territory on the one side, leaving nothing but exhausted fallow land on the other. Begun in the middle of the nineteenth century by *mineiros* who had exhausted their seams, this form of 'agriculture' had proceeded from east to west; and before long I was to meet it on the far side of the Parana river, where confusion reigned, with felled trunks on the one hand and uprooted families on the other.

The road from Santos to São Paulo runs through one of the first territories to be exploited by the colonists. It has, therefore, the air of an archaeological site in which a vanished agriculture may be studied. Once-wooded hills offer their bone-structure for our inspection with, at most, a thin covering of sickly grass upon it. We can make out here and there earthworks which mark where a coffee-plantation once stood; they jut out like atrophied breasts through the grassy embankments. In the valleys the region has, as it were, gone back to Nature; but not to the noble architecture of the primeval forest. The *capoeira*, or secondary forest, is a mere wretched entanglement of half-hearted trees. Sometimes, too, we glimpsed the dwelling of some Japanese emigrant who was trying, by some archaic method, to regenerate a patch of land and set up a market garden there.

To the European traveller, this is a disconcerting, because an unclassifiable, landscape. We know nothing of untamed Nature, because our own landscape is entirely subject to our needs and desires. If it sometimes strikes us as untamed, it is either because—in our forests, for instance—its changes operate to a slower rhythm; or because —as in the mountains—the problems were of such complexity that Man has tackled them in detail rather than in one systematic assault. Such coherence as has resulted from these innumerable individual initiatives now seems to share the original primitive character of the mountain-world, whereas in fact it is due to an interlocking chain of decisions and enterprises, each of which seemed at the time to be independent of the others.

Yet even the wildest of European landscapes has something of order and proportion about it. (Poussin was the incomparable interpreter of this.) Walk among our mountains and you will notice the contrast between forest and bare slope, the relation between the forest and the meadows below it: and the variety of expression which comes about as first one kind of vegetation, and then another, dominates the scene. . . . Travel in America, and you will realize that this sublime harmony, far from being the spontaneous expression of Nature herself, is the result of agreements long sought for between mankind and the site in question. What causes us to gape, in all simplicity, are the traces of our bygone enterprise.

In inhabited America—and this applies to the north as well as to the south, with the exception of more thickly populated areas like Mexico, central America, and the plateaux of the Andes, where something approaching a European situation has come about—we have only two alternatives before us. The one is a Nature so ruthlessly put to work in our service that the result is more like an open-air factory than a landscape (I am thinking now of the cane-fields in the Antilles, and the maize-fields in the corn-belt). The other is of the kind that I shall be considering in a moment or two—an area where Man has presided for long enough to ruin the scene, but not for so long that a slow and continuous process of accommodation has re-raised it to the level of 'a landscape'. In the outskirts of São Paulo, as later in the State of New York, in Connecticut, and even in the Rocky Mountains, I became familiar with a Nature which, though more savage than our own, because less populated and less under cultivation, had yet lost all its original freshness: Nature not so much 'wild' as degraded.

These patches of dead ground—as big as counties, maybe—were once owned, and once briefly worked, by Man. Then he went off somewhere else and left behind him a battleground strewn with the relics of his brief tenure. And over the area which, for a decade or two, he had striven to convert to his uses, there has arisen a new, disorderly, and monotonous vegetation. Its disorder is the more deceptive because, beneath its look of innocence, it has preserved intact the memory and the outline of the struggles of long ago.

11 *São Paulo*

THE cities of the New World have one character-
istic in common: that they pass from first youth to decrepitude with
no intermediary stage. One of my Brazilian girl-students returned in
tears from her first visit to France: whiteness and cleanness were the
criteria by which she judged a city, and Paris, with its blackened
buildings, had seemed to her filthy and repugnant. But American
cities never offer that holiday-state, outside of time, to which great
monuments can transport us; nor do they transcend the primary urban
function and become objects of contemplation and reflection. What
struck me about New York, or Chicago, or their southerly counterpart
São Paulo, was not the absence of 'ancient remains'; this is, on the
contrary, a positive element in their significance. So far from joining
those European tourists who go into sulks because they cannot add
another thirteenth-century cathedral to their collection, I am delighted
to adapt myself to a system that has no backward dimension in time;
and I enjoy having a different form of civilization to interpret. If I err,
it is in the opposite sense: as these are new cities, and cities whose
newness is their whole being and their justification, I find it difficult
to forgive them for not staying new for ever. The older a European
city is, the more highly we regard it; in America, every year brings
with it an element of disgrace. For they are not merely 'newly built';
they are built for renewal, and the sooner the better. When a new
quarter is run up it doesn't look like a city, as we understand the word;
it's too brilliant, too new, too high-spirited. It reminds us more of our
fairgrounds and temporary international exhibitions. But these are
buildings that stay up long after our exhibitions would have closed,
and they don't last well: façades begin to peel off, rain and soot leave
their marks, the style goes out of fashion, and the original lay-out is

ruined when someone loses patience and tears down the buildings next door. It is not a case of new cities contrasted with old, but rather of cities whose cycle of evolution is very rapid as against others whose cycle of evolution is slow. Certain European cities are dying off slowly and peacefully; the cities of the New World have a perpetual high temperature, a chronic illness which prevents them, for all their everlasting youthfulness, from ever being entirely well.

What astonished me in São Paulo in 1935, and in New York and Chicago in 1941, was not their newness, but the rapidity with which time's ravages had set in. I knew that these cities had started ten centuries behind our own, but I had not realized, somehow, that large areas in them were already fifty years old and were not ashamed to let it be seen. For their only ornament was their youth, and youth is as fugitive for a city as for the people who live in it. Old ironwork, trams red as fire-engines, mahogany bars with balustrades of polished brass; brickyards in deserted alleys where the wind was the only street-cleaner; countrified parish churches next door to office buildings and stock exchanges built in the likeness of cathedrals; apartment-houses green with age that overhung canyons criss-crossed with fire-escapes, swing-bridges, and the like; a city that pushed continually upwards as new buildings were built on the ruins of their predecessors: such was Chicago, image of the Americas, and it isn't surprising that the New World should cherish in Chicago the memory of the 1880s, for this modest perspective, less than a century in extent, is all that antiquity can mean in those parts. To our millenary cities it would hardly serve even as a unit of judgment, but in Chicago, where people do not think in terms of time, it already offers scope for nostalgia.

In 1935 the people of São Paulo liked to boast that their city was expanding at the rate of a house every hour. Villas they were, at that date; but I'm told that the rate remains the same, though the figures now apply to office or apartment buildings. São Paulo is growing so fast that you can't buy a map of it; there'd have to be a new edition every week. And if you take a taxi to an address that you fixed on several weeks ahead, you run the risk of getting there the day before the house has gone up. That being so, my recollections of a quarter of a century ago can be of, at most, documentary interest: I offer them to the municipal archives.

São Paulo was thought ugly at that time. The big buildings in the centre were pompous and outmoded, and their ornamentation was as shoddy in execution as it was pretentious and vapid in design. Statues and reliefs were in plaster, not stone, and a hasty coat of yellow paint did little to conceal the fact. Where real stone is in question, the extravagances of the 1890 style may be excused, in part, by the sheer heaviness and density of the material; but in São Paulo the improvisations had the air of an architectural leprosy, or a dream city run up for the cinema.

Yet I never found it an ugly city, for all the faked colours that heightened the shadows and the too-narrow streets where the air could not circulate. It was an untamed city—as are all American cities save, perhaps, Washington, D.C., which is like a captive dying of boredom in the star-shaped avenue-cage devised for it by L'Enfant. São Paulo at that time was running quite wild. Originally it was built on a spur-shaped terrace that faced north, at the point where two little rivers meet —the Anhangabahu and the Tamanduatehy—these later joined the Rio Tiete, a tributary of the Parana. Its function was simply to 'get the Indians under control': it was a missionary centre at which, from the sixteenth century onwards, Portuguese Jesuits did their best to round up the natives and initiate them into the blessings of civilization. There were still, even in 1935, a few rusticated alleyways up on the spit of land that drops down towards the Tamanduatehy and dominated the popular quarters of the Braz and the Penha. There were also a few *largos*: grass-grown squares surrounded by low tile-roofed houses with small grilled windows. The houses were painted with chalk and beside them was an austere parish church with no other decoration than the double accolade that cut out a baroque pediment on the upper part of the façade. In the distance to the north the Tiete's silvery meanderings began to widen out into marshlands, and from marshlands into centres of population, each surrounded by an irregular circle of suburbs and plots of land. Immediately behind these was the commercial centre of the city which, in style and aspirations, had remained faithful to the Exposition Universelle of 1889: the Praça da Sé, Place de la Cathédrale, midway between the builder's yard and complete ruin. Then the famous Triangle, as dear to São Paulo as the Loop is to Chicago—a business area formed by the intersection of the Rues Direita, São Bento, and 15-Novembre. These were streets filled with trade-signs, where the busy dark-suited men of affairs proclaimed not only their allegiance to European or North American ways but their pride in the two thousand five hundred feet above sea-level which raised them high above the torpors of the tropics.

The tropics made themselves felt, none the less. In January, for instance, the rains do not 'arrive'; they grow spontaneously from the dampness that pervades the city. It's as if the omnipresent steam had materialized itself into pearly drops of water that were yet arrested, as they fell, by their affinity with the surrounding atmosphere. The rain does not fall straight, as in Europe; it's more like a pale scintillation, a multitude of tiny water-globes that mingle with the dampness in the air. A waterfall, one might say, of clear soup with tapioca in it. Nor does the rain stop when the clouds blow over: it stops when the atmosphere has been disembarrassed of a certain surplus humidity by the very passage of the rain. The sky lightens, at such times, and a very pale blue can be glimpsed between the blond clouds, and torrents like mountain streams come coursing down the street.

At the northern corner of the terrace a vast workshop came into view: the Avenida São João, several miles in length, which was being built parallel to the Tiete along the route of the old North Road towards Ytu, Sorocaba, and the rich Campinas plantations. To the right, it passed the Rue Florencio-de-Abreu which led off to the station, between the Syrian bazaars, purveyors of heterogeneous rubbish to the entire interior, and the tranquil workshops where weavers and leather-workers were still (but for how much longer?) producing high saddles of tooled leather, horse-blankets of tufted cotton, and harnesses embellished with chased silver, all for the use of the planters and peons who lived in the nearby bush. Then the Avenue passed São Paulo's only—at that time—skyscraper, the pink and still-unfinished Predio Martinelli; crossed the Campos Élyseos, once the preserve of the rich, where painted wooden villas were going to rot in gardens of mango- and eucalyptus-trees; and then the working-class Santa Ifigenia, on the edge of which was a brothel quarter where the girls solicited from their windows. On the far edge of the city were the petit-bourgeois smallholdings of Perdizes and Agua Branca; to the south-west these merged into the shady and more aristocratic hillside of Pacaembu.

Towards the south, the terrace rose steadily in height; and along its backbone, as it were, ran the Avenida Paulista, where the millionaires of half a century earlier had built their once-luxurious residences in a style half casino, half spa. But the millionaires had moved on since then, and in concert with the general expansion of the city had gone down the hill to the south. And there, in undisturbed suburbs with winding roads, they had built themselves houses Californian in style, with micaceous cement and wrought-iron balustrades; these could be

glimpsed, at most, in among the thick woods that came ready-made
with the building plots.

Certain privileged parts of the city seemed to combine all its
elements. At the point, for instance, where two roads diverge on their
way towards the sea, you found yourself on the edge of the Rio
Anhangabahu ravine, which is crossed by a bridge that is one of the
city's main arteries. Below was a park designed on English lines: lawns
embellished with statues and kiosks; and at the point where the two
slopes rose up were the city's principal buildings—the municipal
theatre, the Hotel Esplanada, the Automobile Club, and the offices
of the Canadian company which provided the city with lighting and
public transport.

Here, among these massive but transitional erections, the élite of
São Paulo was to be found. In many ways these people were strikingly
like their favourite orchids; botanists tell us, for instance, that whereas
tropical species are much more numerous than those of more temperate
zones, each species may consist of only a small number of individuals.
The local *grão fino* had brought this to a point of extreme development.

The available roles had been allotted among a society that was none
too numerous for them. Every occupation, every taste, every form of
curiosity allowed by modern civilization could be found in São Paulo,
but each was represented by a single person. Our friends were not so
much people as functions, and the role assigned to them was theirs not
because of its intrinsic importance but because it happened to be free.
There were, for instance, the Catholic, the Liberal, the Legitimist,
and the Communist; on another level there were the Gourmet, the
Bibliophile, the Lover of the Thoroughbred (horse, or dog), or of the
Old Masters, or Modern Art; and the local Savant, Musicologist,
Artist, and Surrealist Poet. Not that any of these people wished to carry
their studies very far: vacant possession was what counted, and if any
two people turned out to overlap in any way, they set about destroying
one another with a ferocity and a persistence that were quite remarkable. There were, on the other hand, any number of 'intellectual
exchanges' and a general desire, not merely to stand up for one's own
preoccupation, but to perfect the collective execution of what seemed
to be an inexhaustibly enjoyable sociological minuet.

Certain roles were played with tremendous dash. Inherited means,
innate charm, and an acquired mastery of polite deception made the
salons of São Paulo as amusing as they were, in the end, frustrating. The
necessity of presenting a complete, if small-scale, model of the great

world obliged the players to admit of certain paradoxes: the Communist, for instance, was also the richest of the heirs to the local feudal system, and the avant-garde poet was allowed to introduce his young mistress into even the most prudish of local drawing-rooms.

This high degree of specialization was combined with an encyclopaedic appetite for knowledge. Cultivated Brazilians took an immense delight in popular manuals of all kinds. Instead of preening themselves on the high standing (which at that time had no rival) of our country abroad, our ministers would have done better to understand what it was based on; it was inspired not by our declining activities in the field of creative science, but by the skill with which our men of learning could make accessible to everyone the solutions and discoveries to which they had made some modest contribution. If France was loved in South America it was because the South Americans, like ourselves, were at heart inclined rather to consume, and to make it easy for others to consume, than to produce. The names held in honour in South America were names from the past: Pasteur, Curie, Durkheim. Admittedly that past was near enough for us to draw a substantial credit from it: but our clients—again like ourselves—preferred to dilapidate that credit, rather than to reinvest it. And we spared them the trouble of making 'discoveries' of their own.

It is sad to have to realize that France is no longer in a position to act as the 'public relations officer' of the mind. We seem to have stuck fast in the nineteenth-century conception of science, according to which anyone with the traditional French qualities of general cultivation, vivacity, and lucidity of mind, a gift for logic, and the ability to write, could turn to any field in science, rethink it for himself in isolation, and produce a valid synthesis. Modern science has no place for that sort of thing. Where once a single specialist could render his country famous, we now need an army of them; and we haven't got it. Creative science has become a collective, almost an anonymous, activity, and one for which we could not be worse prepared. We still have our old-style virtuosi; but no amount of style in the playing can go on concealing the absence of the score.

Countries younger than ours have learnt this lesson; Brazil had had outstanding men, but they had been few in number: Euclides da Cunha, Oswaldo Cruz, Chagas, Villa Lobos. Culture had been the preserve of a few rich people; and it was to create an informed public—and one that would owe nothing to the traditional influence of Army and Church—that the University of São Paulo was founded.

When I arrived in Brazil to teach in this new University I took pity on my Brazilian colleagues. Wretchedly paid, they could exist only by taking on extra work of some humble sort. I was proud to belong to a country where the exercise of a liberal profession had had its prestige and its privileges for many generations. What I did not foresee was that twenty years later my poverty-stricken students would be occupying University Chairs more numerous and often better equipped than our own, with libraries at their disposition such as few of us can count on in France.

The students who crowded into our lecture-rooms were of all ages and had come from far and wide, not without certain misgivings, to study with us. There were young people hungry for the jobs which our diplomas would equip them for; people already established in life —lawyers, politicians, engineers—who feared that unless they, too, got a University degree they would be ill able to compete with their graduate rivals. They were one and all would-be men of the world with a passion for disparagement. This was inspired in part by that concept of nineteenth-century Parisian life which originated with Meilhac and Halévy and was being carried on by one or two Brazilians; but their main inspiration was something as evident in the Paris of a hundred years ago as in the São Paulo or Rio de Janeiro of 1930: the need of the new-fledged metropolitan to prove that he had really got clear of country ways. The despised image of rustic simplicity was symbolized for our students by the *caipira*—the country bumpkin, that is to say— just as in our *théâtre du boulevard* the native of Arpajon or Charentonneau was the butt of one and all. One instance of this dubious 'humour' comes back to me as I write.

The Italian colony had erected a statue of Augustus in the middle of those unending countrified streets that stretch for several miles from the centre of the city. It was a reproduction in bronze, life-size, of an ancient marble statue. No great shakes as a work of art, it was at least deserving of some respect in a city where it alone evoked a period earlier than the nineteenth century. The people of São Paulo decided, however, that the Emperor's uplifted arm indicated that 'Carlito lives here'; Carlos Pereira de Souza, a prominent Brazilian politician, was in effect the owner, in that very direction, of a large villa, now considerably dilapidated, whose rosettes and volutes were meant to hark back to the luxuries of the colonial era.

It was also agreed that Augustus was wearing shorts; humour played only a half-share in this, for most of the population had never seen a toga before and had no idea what it was. These jests went all over São Paulo an hour after the unveiling and were repeated, with many a thump in the back, at the 'exclusive' performance of that evening at the Odeon cinema. Thus did the bourgeoisie of São Paulo avenge themselves on the Italian immigrants who, from having arrived in the city fifty years earlier as pedlars, had worked their way up to become the owners of the most ostentatious villas on the 'Avenidas' and the donors of the statue in question.

Our students wanted to know everything: but only the newest theory seemed to them worth bothering with. Knowing nothing of the intellectual achievements of the past, they kept fresh and intact their enthusiasm for 'the latest thing'. Fashion dominated their interests: they valued ideas not for themselves but for the prestige that they could wring from them. That prestige vanished as soon as the idea passed from their exclusive possession; there was great competition, therefore, for the magazines and handbooks and 'popular' studies that would empower them to get a lead over their fellows, and my colleagues and I suffered much from this. Ourselves trained to respect only those ideas which had been fully matured, we were besieged by students who knew nothing at all of the past but were always a month or two ahead of us in the novelties of the day. Learning was something for which they had neither the taste nor the methods; yet they felt bound to include in their essays, no matter what their nominal subject might be, a survey of human evolution from the anthropoid apes to the present day. Quotations from Plato, Aristotle, and Auguste Comte would be followed by a peroration paraphrased from some egregious hack— the obscurer the better, for their purpose—since their rivals would be the less likely to have happened upon him.

Our students regarded the University as a tempting, but also a poisonous, fruit. These young people had seen nothing of the world, and most of them were too poor to have any hopes of travelling to Europe. To many, we were suspect as representatives of the ruling class and beneficiaries of a cosmopolitanism which cut across the life and the national aspirations of Brazil. Yet we bore in our hands the apples of knowledge; and therefore our students wooed and rebuffed us, by turns. We came to judge of our influence by the size and quality of the little groups which grew up around us, each anxious to outdo the other. *Homenajes*—manifestations in honour of the preferred teacher—took the form of luncheon- or tea-parties which we found the more touching because they must have meant real privation for our hosts. Our personal standing, and the standing of the methods we taught, would go up and down like stock-market quotations according to the prestige of the establishment concerned, the number of people involved, and the social or official position of the 'personalities' who had consented to attend. As each of the major nations had its 'embassy' in São-Paulo—the English tea-room, the French or Viennese confectioners', and the German brasserie—the choice of meeting-place had many a serpentine implication.

If these lines should come to the notice of any of those who, once delightful students, are now my respected colleagues I must ask them not to resent what I say. When I think of you it is by your Christian names, according to your custom: rich and strange they are, to a European ear, and proof of how your fathers were still free to range over the whole of human history to find just the name that would suit your own fragrant beginnings. Anita, you were called, and Corina, and Zenaide, and Lavinia, and Thais, and Gioconda, and Gilda, and Oneide, and Lucilia, and Zenith, and Cecilia. And you others were called Egon, and Mario-Wagner, and Nicanor, and Ruy, and Livio, and James, and Azor, and Achilles, and Decio, and Euclides, and Milton. It is not in irony that I recall those first hesitant days. Quite the contrary: for they taught me how precarious are the advantages conferred by time. I think of what Europe was then, and of what it is now; I realize that you have made intellectual advances, in the last thirty years, of a kind which one might expect to take several generations; and I see how one society dies and another comes into being. I see, too, that the great upheavals which seem, from the history-books, to result from the play of nameless forces in the heart of darkness, may also be brought about, in an instant of lucidity, by the virility and set purpose of a handful of gifted young people.

PART IV

A Land and its People

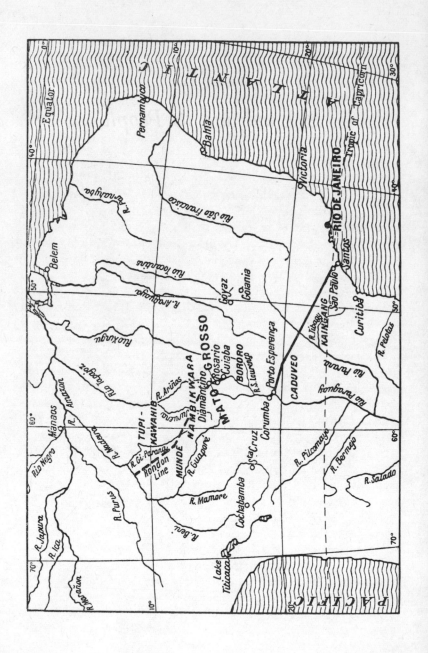

12 *Town and Country*

THERE was a certain amount of Sunday-anthropologizing to be done in São Paulo. But it was not among the 'Indians in the suburbs' whom I had been so misleadingly promised; the suburbs were either Syrian or Italian. The nearest ethnological curiosity was to be found some ten miles away, in a primitive village whose tatterdemalion inhabitants bore, in their fair hair and blue eyes, the marks of a recent Germanic ancestry. It was, in fact, around the year 1820 that groups of German colonists had come over to settle in the least-tropical parts of the country. Around São Paulo they were to a large degree dispersed among the near-destitute local peasantry; but farther south, in the State of Santa Catarina, the little towns of Joinville and Blumenau had kept intact, beneath the araucarias, a nineteenth-century décor. The streets, lined by steep-roofed houses, had German names; German was the only language spoken. On the café terraces old men with moustaches and whiskers could be seen smoking long pipes with bowls made of porcelain.

There were also many Japanese in the region round São Paulo. These were less easily approached. Their immigration was systematized: they travelled free, they were guaranteed a temporary lodging on arrival, and eventually they were distributed among farms, in the interior, which were half village, half military-camp in character. Every aspect of life was catered for: schools, workshops, infirmary, shops, entertainment—all were available on the spot. The emigrants remained there for long periods in virtual isolation. The organizing company naturally did all it could to encourage this, and the emigrants meanwhile paid off the money owed to the company and salted away their earnings in its coffers. The company undertook to ship them home in due time, so that they could die in the country of their ancestors; and if the malaria got the better of them while they were still in Brazil, then their bodies, at least, were repatriated. Everything possible was done to persuade the emigrants that during the entire course of this great adventure they were always, as it were, in Japan. The organizers' motives may not, however, have been exclusively financial, economic, or humanitarian. Close study of the map seems to suggest that strategy also may have prompted the location of certain farms. It was very difficult to get inside the offices of the Kaigai-Iju-Kumiai and the Brazil-Takahoka-Kumiai, and harder still to penetrate the almost clandestine network of hotels, hospitals, brickyards, and saw-mills to which the emigrants owed their self-sufficiency. In all this, and in the choice of the areas for cultivation, certain devious designs could be glimpsed. The segregation of the colonists in areas ingeniously chosen, and the pursuit of such archaeological studies as could be combined with the work of agriculture (the detection, for instance, of analogies between Japanese neolithic artifacts and those of pre-Colombian Brazil) —these may well have been merely the visible extremities of a tortuous and subterranean policy.

In the heart of São Paulo several of the markets in the poorer quarters were run by coloured people. But perhaps the word 'coloured' has little meaning in a country where a great diversity of racial strains and—in the past, at any rate—an almost complete lack of colour-prejudice has led to every kind of cross-breeding. Let us rather say that the visitor could train himself to distinguish the *mestiços* (black crossed with white), the *caboclos* (white crossed with Indian), and the *cafusos* (black crossed with Indian). The goods on offer displayed, by contrast, an unmixed ancestry.

There was, for instance, the *peneiras*, or sieve for manioc flour. This was of characteristic Indian design, and composed of a rough trellis-work of split bamboo-stalks held in place by a circular batten. And the *abanicos*, with which the Indians fanned their flames. These were also of traditional design, and it was amusing to study them closely. Palm-leaves are by nature tousled and pervious, and to plait them in such a way that they formed a single hard smooth surface and could be used to set the air in motion was a considerable technical feat. As there were several sorts of palm-leaf—and many ways, too, of plaiting them—the fans took on every conceivable shape: each illustrating, as it were, the solution of a particular technical theorem.

There are two main species of palm-leaf. In the one, the folioles are distributed symmetrically on either side of a central stalk; in the other, they fan out from their base. In the first case, two methods suggest

FIG. I.   A *figa* found at Pompeii
(the tip of the thumb has
been broken)

themselves: either you fold all the folioles over on one side of the stalk
and plait them together, or you plait each group individually, folding
the folioles at right angles to one another and inserting the bottom of
one into the top of the other, and vice versa. You then have two sorts
of fan: one wing-shaped, the other like a butterfly. The butterfly type
offers many possibilities: and these are always, in varying degree, a
combination of two others. The final result, whether shaped like a
spoon, a palette, or a rosette, reminds one of a sort of big flattened
chignon.

Another very attractive speciality of the São Paulo markets was the
figa, or fig. This was an ancient Mediterranean talisman in the shape of
a fore-arm ending in a clenched fist; the thumb peeped out between the
first joints of the second and third fingers. Doubtless this was probably
a symbol of sexual intercourse. The *figas* to be seen in São Paulo were
either trinkets of silver or ebony, or objects as big as street-signs, naive
in design and brilliantly coloured. I used to hang them in hilarious
groups from the ceiling of my house—a villa painted ochre, in the
'Rome, 1900' style, and situated in the upper part of the town. The
entrance was overhung with jasmine and to the rear there was a little
old-fashioned garden in which I had asked my landlord to plant a
banana-tree by way of assurance that I was really in the tropics. After a
few years this symbolic banana-tree turned into a small forest and
provided me with great quantities of fruit.

A certain amount of work could also be done, in the outskirts of São Paulo, on surviving tribal customs: May-day festivities where the village was hung with green palm-leaves; commemorative contests between *mouros* and *cristãos*, in which Portuguese tradition was faithfully observed; the procession of the *nau catarineta*, with a cardboard boat decked out with paper sails. And there was the pilgrimage to certain distant leper-protecting parishes: here the foul-smelling *pinga* would circulate (*pinga* is an alcoholic drink made from cane-sugar, though not at all like rum: it is drunk either neat or mixed with the juice of a lemon). Half-caste bards—high-booted, dressed with a strange gaudy fancy, drunk beyond redemption, and urged on by the beating of the drums—would strive to outdo one another in tournaments of satirical song.

There were also beliefs and superstitions to be tabulated: that a stye should be cured, for instance, by laying a gold ring on the eye; that all ailments were divided into two incompatible groups—*comida quente* and *comida fria*, hot food and cold food. And other maleficent combinations: fish and meat, mango with any alcoholic drink, bananas and milk.

But what was still more interesting was to get out into the hinterland and examine, not the last traces of Mediterranean tradition, but the strange devices of a society as yet hardly in being. The subject was the same—past and present were still in question—but whereas in classical anthropology the past serves to explain the present I was faced with a situation in which the present harked back to certain very early stages in the evolution of Europe. As in Merovingian times in France, the beginnings of urban and communal organizations were taking shape against a background of latifundia.

The agglomerations then coming into being were not like the towns of today. There was none of that ever-more-complete uniformity in which administrative distinctions alone differentiate one city from another and all trace of origins has been worn away. No: these towns could be examined as a botanist examines his plants. And by the name, the look, or the structure of each town one could trace their affiliations with one or other branch of that urban kingdom which Man has added to Nature.

During the last hundred and fifty years the 'pioneering fringe' has moved slowly from east to west and from south to north. Around 1836 it was only in the Norte, that is to say the region between Rio and São Paulo, that the colonists had any firm hold, but there was great progress in the central area of the State. Twenty years later the colonists were eating into the north-east, on the Mogiana and the Paulista; in 1886 inroads were being made into the Araraquara, the Alta Sorocabana, and the Noroeste. Even in 1935, in those two latter zones, the increase in population ran parallel with the increase in the production of coffee, whereas, in the older territories of the Norte, it took more than fifty years for the decline of the one to be reflected in the collapse of the other. As early as 1854, that is to say, the exhausted plantations began to fall into disuse, but it was not until 1920 that any sharp fall in population was noted.

The use and disuse of these territories corresponded to a historical evolution whose visible marks came and went in much the same way. Only in the two big cities on the coast—Rio and São Paulo—was expansion so massive as to seem irreversible. São Paulo had two hundred and forty thousand inhabitants in 1900, five hundred and eighty thousand in 1920, a million or more in 1928, and more than double that number today. But in the interior towns of a sort would come into being, only to find the surrounding countryside suddenly deserted. The population moved from one region to another, did not increase in numbers, and changed constantly in social type, with the result that fossil-towns could be observed side by side with towns in embryo; and in a very short space of time the anthropologist could scrutinize transformations as striking as those revealed to the palaeontologist who studied the history of anatomical organization over a period of millions of years.

Once away from the coast it was essential to remember that in the previous hundred years Brazil had changed much more than it had developed.

In Imperial times the human population, though small in numbers, was relatively well laid out. The towns on or near the coast were tiny by today's standards, but those in the interior had a vitality now lost to them. We too often forget that paradox of history by which it is the poorest who stand to profit by any general insufficiency of communications. When riding is the only means of transport, a journey measured in months, rather than in weeks or days, is somehow less distasteful and a mule-track less forbidding. The Brazilian hinterland had an existence which, though slow, was unbroken; the river-boats worked to a fixed schedule, even if it took months to complete one's journey, stage by tiny stage; and tracks since completely forgotten, like that from Cuiaba to Goyaz, were in full use in the 1830s, with caravans of up to two hundred mules to be met with en route.

Central Brazil was more or less completely abandoned at the beginning of the twentieth century—not because it was undeveloped, but because a price had had to be paid for the modernization of life in the coastal areas and the consequent movement of the population in that direction. In the interior, on the other hand, it was difficult to make real headway; the wise thing would have been to accept and allow for a slower rhythm of development, but instead of this the whole area went steadily to pot. Steam navigation, by accelerating the whole rhythm of sea travel, has killed off many places which were once famous ports of call; the aeroplane may well do the same. Mechanical progress pays many dividends, and not the least of them may be the measure of solitude and oblivion which it has given us in return for that intimacy with the world which we may no longer enjoy.

The interior of the State of São Paulo and its neighbours illustrated these transformations on a smaller scale. There was no longer any trace, admittedly, of those fortified towns which had once guaranteed the ownership of a province. Many towns on the coast, or on a river-bank, owe their origins to this practice: Rio de Janeiro, Victoria, Florianopolis on its island, Bahia and Fortaleza on the cape, Manaus, Obidos on the banks of the Amazon, or Villa Bella de Mato Grosso, whose ruins near the Guaporé are invaded from time to time by the Nambikwara Indians; this was once the renowned garrison-city of a *capitão do mato* (bush-captain) on the Bolivian frontier—on the line, that is to say, by which Pope Alexander VI had partitioned the still-undiscovered New World, in 1493, between the rival kingdoms of Spain and Portugal.

To the north and east were to be found a few deserted mining-towns, now in the last stages of decay, where flamboyant baroque churches of the eighteenth century contrasted with the desolation around them. Once they hummed with activity: and in their fantastic architecture they seem to have striven to preserve some particle of that wealth which was to be their undoing. For the mines brought devastation to the country around them—to the forests, above all, whose timber kept the foundries going—and the mining-towns died out, like so many fires, as soon as they had consumed their own substance.

The State of São Paulo calls to mind other incidents in history: the struggle, for instance, which from the sixteenth century onwards was to rage between the planters and the Jesuits as to what form of social organization should be followed. The Jesuits would have liked to take the Indians in hand and get them organized in some form of communal

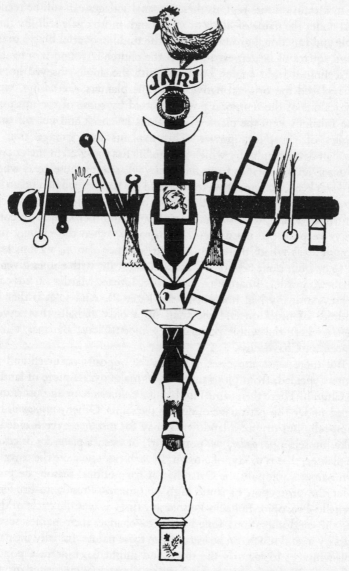

FIG. 2. A rustic calvary in the interior of the State of São Paulo decorated with various objects representing the instruments of the Passion

life. In certain remote regions these original villages can still be recognized under the name of *aldeia* or *missãs* and, more easily still, by their ample and functional ground-plan: in the middle, overlooking a grass-grown square of beaten earth, stands the church. Around it are roads intersecting at right angles, bordered with the single-storeyed houses that replaced the original native huts. The planters, *fazendeiros*, were very jealous of the temporal power exerted by some of the missions: these missions kept the planters' exactions in check and cut off their supplies of cheap manpower. This explains that strange trait in Brazilian demography by which village life has survived in the poorest regions as an inheritance from the *aldeia*, whereas in those areas where there was keener competition for the land the natives had no choice but to group themselves around the house of their master. Their shacks, uniform in design, were of straw or of mud, and their employer could always keep an eye upon them. Even today, when the railway runs through areas where there are no centres of population, stations have had to be built quite arbitrarily, at fixed intervals, with names given in alphabetical order: Buarquina, Felicidade, Limao, Marilia (in 1935 the Paulista company had just got to the letter P). And so it is that for hundreds of miles on end the train stops only at halts that serve a *fazenda* where the whole population gathers: Chave Bananal, Chave Conceição, Chave Elisa. . . .

But there were also cases in which the opposite occurred and the planters decided, from pious motives, to make over a piece of land to the Church. There then came into being a *patrimonio*, or agglomeration placed under the patronage of one of the saints. Other *patrimonios* had a non-religious origin: a landowner may for instance have decided to make himself a *povoador*, or 'populator', or even a *plantador de cidade*: the planter, that is to say, of a town. In such cases he gave the town his own name: Paulopolis, or Orlandia; or for political reasons he put it under the protection of some high personage—Presidente-Prudente, Cornelio-Procopio, Epitacio-Pessoa. . . . Brief as was the cycle of their life, the agglomerations found time to change their names several times over, and much can be learnt from these names. Initially the name served merely to identify the town and might be, indeed, a popular nickname: 'Batatas', or potatoes, for a small patch of cultivated ground in the bush; or 'Feijão-Cru', raw beans, for a place where no fuel was on hand to heat the saucepan. Or, if the place was simply a very long way off, and provisions normally ran short, it might be called 'Arroz-sem-Sal' or rice-without-salt. And then one day a 'Colonel'—such was the generic title given to all big landowners or political agents—with a concession of several thousand acres would aim to become a person of influence. He'd take on labour in a big way, begin to build, and create a town where once there was only a floating population. Raw beans would turn into Leopoldina or Ferdinandopolis. Later the city which his ambition, or his caprice, had brought into being would peter out and disappear; nothing would be left but the name, a hut or two, and the remnants of a population eaten away by malaria and ankylostomiasis. Or else the city would flourish: its new-found civic consciousness will resent the fact that it was once the instrument, if not the plaything, of a single man. A population newly arrived from Italy, Germany, and half a dozen other sources will want to have roots of its own; it will then hunt through the dictionary for an indigenous name, generally of Tupi derivation, which will suggest that it has come to live in a city of pre-Colombian origins: Tanabi, or Votuparanga, or Tupão, or Aymoré. . . .

The staging-points along the river had been killed off by the railway, but there were still to be seen, here and there, traces illustrative of a cycle broken in mid-course: sheds and a rude lodging at the water's edge, to allow the boatmen to get a night's rest without being ambushed by the Indians; then the *portos de lenha*, every twenty miles or so, where the slender-funnelled paddle-steamers could put in for wood; the water-terminus at either end of the navigable stretch; and the transfer-points wherever rapids or a waterfall made it impossible to proceed direct.

In 1935 there were two sorts of town which, though strictly traditional in appearance, were still full of life. These were the *pousos*, or crossroad villages, and the *boccas do sertão*, or 'mouths of the bush', which stood at the head of a track leading into the interior. Already the lorry was taking the place of the mule-train and the ox-cart; taking the same tracks, however, making much the same speed as it crawled in first or second gear for hundreds of miles on end, stopping at the same halts, where the drivers in their oil-stained overalls would drink side by side with the leather-girt *tropeiros*.

The tracks were not all that one would have liked them to be. Mostly they were the old caravan routes that had served to bring coffee, sugar, and cane-alcohol in one direction and salt, flour, and dried foods in the other. These would be interrupted from time to time, in the middle of the bush, by a *registro*: a wooden barrier surrounded by a hut or two. Here a tatterdemalion peasant, the representative of some

FIG. 3.   Ox-cart axle

problematical authority, would demand a toll. This led to the establishment of other, more clandestine networks: the *estradas francanas*, which aimed to avoid paying those tolls; there were also the *estradas muladas*, mule-tracks, and the *estradas boiadas*, or ox-tracks. On these latter could be heard, for two or three hours at a time, the coming and going of the sound that nearly drove a new arrival demented: the squeaking axle of an ox-cart. These were built to a model imported from the Mediterranean in the sixteenth century. Unchanged in essence since proto-historic times, it brought the heavy body into direct contact with the axle, with the result that it was as difficult for the oxen to get the cart into motion at all as for them to haul the entire load.

Animals, carts, and lorries had forced their way along these tracks, more or less in the same direction, according to the prevailing circumstances of weather and vegetation. Such levelling as had taken place was largely accidental, and the traveller had to do as best he could with the ravines and the steep slopes stripped of all living matter that would suddenly present themselves. Sometimes the track would widen until it was like a boulevard, a hundred yards across, in the very middle of the bush; sometimes it would divide itself into a score of indistinguishable paths, leading in every direction at once, with nothing to show which was the true *fil d'Ariane* that would lead one out of the labyrinth. At such times one could easily take the wrong one, toil for many hours over a stretch of some twenty dangerous miles, only to find oneself bogged down, at the end, in sand or marshlands. In the rainy season the track would turn into a canal of greasy mud and could not be used at all; and later, when the first lorry managed to get through, it would leave deep ruts that dried quickly and hardened within three days to the consistency of cement. The vehicles that came later had to fit into these as best they could, and many there were who had to travel for hundreds of miles with a dangerous list, or found themselves repeatedly marooned on crests that had to be cut away with a spade.

I well remember a trip on which Jean Maugüé, René Courtin, and myself had set off with the object of travelling as far as Courtin's brand-new Ford would take us. We got as far as the banks of the Araguaya, about a thousand miles from São Paulo, and there visited a family of Karaja Indians. On the way back the front suspension broke and we went for some sixty miles with the engine resting directly on the front axle and for another four hundred with the engine propped up on an iron bar that had been run up for us by a village blacksmith. I remember especially the anxious hours we spent after nightfall in the unpopulated hinterland of the States of São Paulo and Goyaz—never knowing how soon the furrows that we had chosen from among a dozen others would betray us. Suddenly the *pouso* came into view beneath the half-hearted stars; the sound of the generator that kept its electric lamps alight had probably been audible for hours, but we had not distinguished it from the other night-noises of the bush. The inn offered us a choice of hammocks or iron bedsteads, and at dawn we were off along the main street of the little town, with its houses and its all-purpose shops, and its main square where *regatões* and *mascates* held sway: hawkers, itinerant doctors, dentists, and even lawyers.

On market-days the scene was one of great animation. Peasants by the hundred had left their lonely hutments and travelled for days on end with their entire families, for the sake of the annual transaction by which they sold a calf, a mule, a tapir's or a puma's skin, or a few sacks of rice, maize, or coffee and received in exchange a length of cotton, some salt, some petroleum for their lamp, and some ammunition.

In the background is the plateau: brushwood, with a tree or two here and there. It had lost most of its vegetation half a century earlier, and the beginnings of erosion could be seen—as if someone had made a first few tentative strokes with an adze. Terrace formations were marked off by a drop of a few yards in the level of the ground: later these would turn into ravines. There was a broad but shallow stretch of water—not so much a river-bed as a piece of spasmodic flooding—and not far from this two or three avenues ran parallel along the borders of a luxuriant property: a mud-walled rancho, roofed with tiles, and dazzlingly white where the sun shone on its coating of chalk. The shutters were framed in chestnut-brown and there were purple shadows on the ground. As soon as the first dwelling-houses appeared —they were like big covered markets, with unglazed window-spaces, wide open for the most part, in the walls—meadows of rough grass sprang up beside them, and this grass was kept down to its very roots by the cattle. The organizers of the fair had laid in special stores of fodder: hay made from sugar-cane or pressed young palm-leaves. The visitors camped out between the big square heaps of fodder, and the heavy wheels of their carts were studded on the outside with huge nails. Walls freshly made of wicker and a roof of rawhide roped into place had protected the travellers on their journey and a screen of palm-leaves or a tent-like strip of white cotton had hung out over the rear of the cart. Rice, black beans, and dried meat were cooked in the open, and naked children ran in and out between the feet of the oxen as they chewed their sugar-canes; the soft stalks hanging down, meanwhile, like fountains of greenery.

A day or two later, not a soul remained. The company had vanished once again into the bush. The *pouso* drowsed in the sun, excitements over for the rest of the year; save only the weekly opening of the *villas do Domingo*, the Sunday rendezvous where horsemen would find, at the crossroads, a drink-shop and a handful of huts.

13   *The Pioneer Zone*

Scenes of this sort can be repeated ad infinitum in the interior of Brazil once you get away from the coast and head north or west. The bush extends in those directions as far as the marshes of Paraguay or the forest-bordered tributaries of the Amazon.

If you travel southwards, on the other hand, towards the State of Parana, other landscapes and other modes of life come into view; the ground stands higher, you draw farther and farther away from the tropics, and the subsoil becomes volcanic. The visitor finds, side by side, the remains of tribal society and the most up-to-date varieties of colonial practice. It was therefore in the Norte-Parana that I made my first expeditions.

It took hardly more than twenty-four hours to get to that farther bank of the river Parana which marked the frontier of the State of São Paulo. There lay the great damp forest of conifers, vast in size and temperate in climate, which had for so long resisted the planters' efforts to penetrate it. Till 1930 or thereabouts it was more or less virgin territory, known only to the bands of Indians who wandered freely within it and to a few isolated pioneers—poor peasants, for the most part—who worked on their tiny plantations of maize.

At the time of my arrival in Brazil the region was beginning to be opened up. A British company had secured from the government a concession of nearly four million acres in return for an undertaking to build roads and a railway. The British intended to re-sell the land, plot by plot, to emigrants, mostly from central and eastern Europe, and to keep the railway for themselves. By 1935 the experiment was well under way: the railway was biting deeper and deeper into the forest— thirty-odd miles at the beginning of 1930, eighty and more by the end of that year, one hundred and thirty in 1932, one hundred and seventy-five in 1936. . . . Every ten miles or so a station would be built, and a space about a kilometre square would be cleared all round it: here a town was to come into being. These towns were built up slowly but surely: at the head of the line stood Londrina, the senior, with already three thousand inhabitants. Next came Nova Dantzig with ninety, Rolandia with sixty, and so on; the newest of all was Arapongas, which in 1935 could boast only one house and one inhabitant: a Frenchman, already in middle life, who went prospecting in the desert in military leggings dating from the war of 1914-18 and a yachting-cap. Fifteen years later the population of Arapongas was ten thousand.

Riding or motoring along the new roads (like those of ancient Gaul, these kept to the high ground) there was no way of knowing that the country was alive. The lots ran down from the road to the river at the bottom of the valley, and it was at the farther end, by the water, that things had begun to move. The clearance work began below and crept gradually up the slope, so that the road, the symbol of civilization, was still deep in the forest which, for months or even years to come, would still crown the top of the slopes. Down below, on the other hand, the first harvests—always on a prodigious scale in this *terra roxa*, this untouched violet earth—pushed their way between the great fallen trees. The winter rains would soon turn these remains into a fertile humus, which would be swept and driven along the slopes, in company with that other humus that had for so long nourished the now-destroyed forest. It would not take long, we thought—perhaps ten, twenty, thirty years—for this land of Canaan to turn into an arid and devastated waste.

For the moment the emigrants had merely the problems of superabundance to cope with. The Pomeranian and Ukrainian settlers had not even had time to build themselves houses—they still lodged with their animals in wooden hutments beside the stream—so urgent was the need to curb the ardour of this magnificent soil and 'break it in' like a wild stallion. Had this not been done their maize and cotton would have run amok in over-luxuriant vegetation instead of coming to orderly fruition. We saw German farmers weep for joy as they showed us how a whole grove of lemon-trees had sprung from a cutting or two. For what astounded the men from the north was not only the fertility: it was the strangeness of these crops that they had known of only through fairy-tales. As the area is on the frontier between the tropical and the temperate zones, a difference of even a few feet in altitude could bring about a marked difference in climate. European and South American specialities could be grown side by side, and the settlers delighted in exploiting this fact—setting wheat next to cane-sugar and coffee next to flax. . . .

The new cities were entirely nordic in character; like those who, a century earlier, had grouped themselves in the south of the State, around Curitiba, the new arrivals were Germans, Poles, Russians, and, to a lesser extent, Italians. Houses built of planks, or from squared-off tree-trunks, called to mind central and eastern Europe. Long carts, each with four spoked wheels and horses between the shafts, replaced the Iberian ox-carts. There were unexpected survivals from the past, of course, but what I found more interesting was the rapidity with which the future was taking shape. Faceless areas would seem to acquire an urban structure overnight; and just as an embryo forms itself into cells, each of which becomes part of a particular group and has a function all its own, so did each of the new towns acquire a character peculiar to itself. Londrina was already well organized, with a main street, a business centre, an artisans' quarter, and a residential section. But what mysterious formative powers were at work in the patch of dead ground which was all that Rolandia, and still more Arapongas, as yet amounted to? What authority was parking out one set of citizens here, and another there, and giving each sector of the new town an inescapable function? Each town was initially a rectangular clearing in the forest, with every street at right angles to every other street: they were depersonalized tracings, geometrical outlines—nothing more. Yet some were in the centre, and some on the periphery; some parallel to the road or the railway, some at right angles to them. Some, therefore, 'went with' the stream of traffic, while the others cut across it. Business and commerce tended to string themselves out along the first group; private houses and certain public services either chose the second group or were forced into it. The two antitheses (central/peripheral, parallel/perpendicular) immediately established four different modes of urban life; and over the future inhabitants of the city there already hung a fatality—success and failure, discouragement and initial advantage derived automatically from the accidents of the grid. And more: there would be two main types of inhabitant—those who craved human company and would gravitate naturally to the sectors which were more heavily urbanized, and those who preferred isolation and liberty. Thus would come into being a further contrapuntal element.

And then there was that strange element in the evolution of so many towns: the drive to the west which so often leaves the eastern part of the town in poverty and dereliction. It may be merely the expression of that cosmic rhythm which has possessed mankind from the earliest times and springs from the unconscious realization that to move with the sun is positive, and to move against it negative; the one stands for order, the other for disorder. It's a long time since we ceased to worship the sun; and with our Euclidean turn of mind we jib at the notion of space as qualitative. But it is independently of ourselves that the great phenomena of astronomy or meteorology have their effect—an effect as discreet as it is ineluctable—in every part of the globe. We all associate the direction east-to-west with achievement, just as every inhabitant of the temperate zone of the southern hemisphere associates the north with darkness and cold and the south with warmth and light. None of all this comes out, of course, in our considered behaviour. But urban life offers a strange contrast. It represents civilization at its most complex and in its highest state of refinement; but by the sheer human concentration which it represents within a limited space, it precipitates and sets in motion a number of unconscious attitudes. Infinitesimal as these are in themselves, they can produce a considerable effect when a large number of people are reacting to them at the same time and in the same manner. Thus it is that every town is affected by the westward drive, with wealth gravitating to one side and poverty to the other. What is at first sight unintelligible becomes clear if we realize that every town has the privilege (though some would see in it rather a form of servitude) of bringing to our notice, as if under a microscope, the incessant and insect-like activity of our ancestral and still-far-from-extinct superstitions.

And can they really be called superstitions? I see these predilections as a form of wisdom which primitive peoples put spontaneously into practice; the madness lies rather in our modern wish to go against them. These primitive peoples attained quickly and easily to a peace of mind which we strive for at the cost of innumerable rebuffs and irritations. We should do better to accept the true conditions of our human experience and realize that it is not within our power to emancipate ourselves completely from either its structure or its natural rhythms. Space has values peculiar to itself, just as sounds and scents have their colours and feelings their weight. The search for correspondences of this sort is not a poets' game or a department of mystification, as people have dared to say of Rimbaud's *sonnet des voyelles*: that sonnet is now indispensable to the student of language who knows the basis, not of the colour of phenomena, for this varies with each individual, but of the relation which unites one phenomenon to another and comprises a limited gamut of possibilities. These correspondences offer the scholar an entirely new terrain, and one which may still have rich yields to offer. If fish can make an aesthetic distinction between smells in terms of light and dark, and bees classify the strength of light in terms of weight—darkness is heavy, to them, and bright light light—just so should the work of the painter, the poet, and the composer and the myths and symbols of primitive Man seem to us: if not as a superior form of knowledge, at any rate as the most fundamental form of knowledge, and the only one that we all have in common; knowledge in the scientific sense is merely the sharpened edge of this other knowledge. More penetrating it may be, because its edge has been sharpened on the hard stone of fact, but this penetration has been acquired at the price of a great loss of substance; and it is only efficacious in so far as it can penetrate far enough for the whole bulk of the instrument to follow the sharpened point.

The sociologist has his part to play in the elaboration of this world-wide, concrete humanism. For the great manifestations of Society have this in common with the work of art: that they originate at the level of unconscious existence—*because* they are collective, in the first case, and *although* they are individual, in the second; but the difference is not of real importance—is, indeed, no more than apparent—because the first is produced *by*, and the second *for*, the public; and the public supplies them both with their common denominator and determines the conditions in which they shall be created.

Cities have often been likened to symphonies and poems, and the comparison seems to me a perfectly natural one: they are, in fact, objects of the same kind. The city may even be rated higher, since it stands at the point where Nature and artifice meet. A city is a congregation of animals whose biological history is enclosed within its boundaries; and yet every conscious and rational act on the part of these creatures helps to shape the city's eventual character. By its form, as by the manner of its birth, the city has elements at once of biological procreation, organic evolution, and aesthetic creation. It is both natural object and a thing to be cultivated; individual and group; something lived and something dreamed; it is *the* human invention, *par excellence*.

In the synthetic towns of southern Brazil one could detect in the lay-out of the houses, the specialized use to which each street was put, and the beginnings of individual style in each quarter of the town, the workings of a clandestine and enormously obstinate will. And this seemed all the more significant in that it ran contrary to (though it also prolonged) the fancies which had brought the towns into being. Londrina, Nova Dantzig, Rolandia, and Arapongas had been born of the decisions of a group of engineers and financiers, but already they were reverting to the authentic diversity of urban life, just as Curitiba had reverted a century ago and Goiania may be reverting today.

Curitiba, the capital of the State of Parana, appeared on the map on the day the government decided that a town should be built: the territory which had been bought from its former owner was cut up into lots and sold at a price cheap enough to attract an immediate influx of population. The same system was later used to endow the State of Minas with its capital, Bello Horizonte. With Goiania a greater risk was taken, because the original plan was to build up from nothing at all the future federal capital of Brazil.

About a third of the way, as the crow flies, from the south coast to the line of the Amazon there are enormous plateaux which we have left untouched for the last two hundred years. In the days when the caravans were in constant use and there were boats on the river they could be crossed in a few weeks, if you were making your way northwards from the mines; and once on the banks of the Araguaya you could take a boat to Belem. The only remaining witness to all this, when I arrived, was the little town of Goyaz, capital of the State which had taken its name, which eked out a sleepy existence some seven hundred miles from the coast, from which it was virtually cut off. It stood among a mass of greenery and was dominated by an erratic skyline of palm-topped hills. Streets of low houses ran down the hillsides green with gardens. Horses passed to and fro in front of the ornamented façades of churches that were half barn, half bell-towered mansion. The colonnades, the use of stucco, the sumptuous porticos freshly painted in white or pink or ochre or blue—all reminded me of Spanish country-town baroque. On either side of the river were moss-grown quays that had caved in, here and there, under the weight of the lianas, the banana-trees, and palm-trees that had run wild among the unoccupied properties; but this superabundant vegetation did not so much underline the decrepitude of those properties as add a note of silence and dignity to their dilapidated façades.

Whether it was a matter for outrage or for rejoicing I'm not quite sure—but the administration had decided to forget about Goyaz, and its countryside, and its pebble-paved streets, and its unfashionable graces. It was all too old and too small. They needed a clean slate before they could get on with the enormous undertaking that they had in mind. This was to be found sixty-odd miles to the east, on a plateau where nothing grew but rough grass and thorny shrubs, as if some plague had swept across it and destroyed all living creatures and all other vegetation. No railway led to it, and there were no roads: cart-tracks, merely. This was the region, sixty miles square, which had been marked out on the map as the site of the federal district in which the capital of the future was to be built. Its architects, untempted by any natural advantages, could proceed as if on a drawing-board. The town-plan was marked out on the site; the outer boundaries were fixed and, within them, each zone was clearly prescribed: residential, admin-istrative, commercial, industrial. Pleasure, likewise, had its allotted space, for there was no denying its importance in a pioneer city. When the town of Marilia was built in the 1920s in much the same way some fifteen per cent of the six hundred houses were brothels. Most of their inmates were *Francesinhas* of the sort which, in the nineteenth century, formed with the more orthodox sisters of mercy the twin spearheads of French civilization abroad: so much so, indeed, that even in 1939 the French Foreign Office devoted a substantial part of its clandestine credits to their furtherance. It would be only fair to add that the foundation of the University of Rio Grande do Sul, in Brazil's most southerly State, and the predominance of French studies there, were due to the passion for French literature and French liberty which a future dictator learned, in his Paris student days, from a French lady of easy virtue.

Suddenly every newspaper was full of the news. The city of Goiania was to be founded: and along with the town-plan, which could not have been more complete if Goiania had been already a hundred years old, there was a list of the advantages to be enjoyed by its inhabitants: modern roads, a railway, running water, up-to-date drains, and the cinema. I even seem to remember that at one time land was offered at a premium to anyone who would pay the legal fees: lawyers and speculators were the earliest citizens of Goiania.

I visited Goiania in 1937. Among endless flatlands—half dead ground, half battlefield—with telegraph poles and surveyors' stakes all over the place, a hundred or so brand-new houses could be seen at the four corners of the horizon. The biggest of these was the hotel, a square box of cement, with the look of an air-terminus or a miniature fort; one might have called it the 'bastion of civilization' in a literal, and, therefore, a strangely ironical sense. For nothing could be more barbarous, more essentially inhuman, than this way of grabbing at the desert. This graceless erection was the contrary of Goyaz. It had no history. It had neither lived long enough nor acquired any of the associations which might have concealed its emptiness or softened its awkward outlines. One felt as one feels in a station or a hospital: always in transit. Only the fear of some catastrophe could have justified the erection of this square white fortress. And indeed that catastrophe had occurred: silence and stillness served only to heighten its menaces. Cadmus the civilizer had sown the dragon's teeth. The earth had been torn up and burnt away by the dragon's breath: Man would be the next crop.

PART V

The Caduveo

14 *Parana*

CAMPERS, camp in Parana! Or rather—don't! Keep your greasy papers, your empty beer-bottles, and your discarded tins for Europe's last-remaining sites. There is the place for your tents. But, once beyond the pioneer zone, and until the day, now all too imminent, when they will be ruined once and for all—leave the torrents to foam undisturbed down terraces cut into hillsides violet with basalt. Keep your hands off the volcanic mosses, so sharp and cool to the touch; tread no farther when you come to the first of the uninhabited prairies, and to the great steamy conifer-forest, where the trees that rise above the entangled bracken and liana and thrust up into the sky are the exact opposite, in shape, of our European conifers: not cone-shaped, that is to say, and tapering towards the summit, but on the contrary so designed that their branches stand out in hexagonal platforms, growing always wider and wider, until at the very top they spread out like an immense umbrella, as if to prove Baudelaire's contention that it is by its irregularity that the vegetable contrasts with the mineral kingdom.

It was a landscape intact and unchanged for millions of years past: carboniferous majesty personified. High-lying, and far enough from the tropics to have escaped the confusion of the Amazonian basin, it had preserved a solemn dignity and sense of unblemished order which seemed explicable only by the workings of a race wiser and more powerful than our own. It is apparently to the disappearance of this race that we owe the opportunity of exploring these sublime parklands, now given over to silence and abandonment.

My first contacts with a primitive people were made on this high ground, some three thousand feet above sea-level, in the area which stands above both banks of the Rio Tibagy. I was travelling with one

of the district commissioners of the Indians' Protection Service on one
of his tours of inspection.

At the time when we Europeans discovered it the whole of southern
Brazil was inhabited by tribes related to one another both in language
and in culture. We grouped them under the collective name of Gé.
They would seem to have been pushed back, not many centuries before,
by Tupi-speaking invaders who were already in occupation of the
entire coastal strip; the struggle against them was still going on. The
Gé of southern Brazil had fallen back into regions difficult of access; and,
whereas the coastal Tupi had quickly been mopped up by the colonists,
the Gé had survived for several centuries. Certain small bands had even
survived into the twentieth century in the forests of the southern States
of Parana and Santa Catarina. One or two may even have kept going
until 1935, for they had learnt from the ferocious persecutions of the
previous hundred years to keep themselves entirely hidden from the
outer world. But for the most part they had been rounded up towards
the year 1914, and the Brazilian government had corralled them with
the object of 'integrating them into modern life'. In the village, for
instance, of São Jeronymo, which was my own particular base, there
had been a locksmith's shop, a chemist's, a school, and a saw-mill.
Axes, knives, and nails were sent up at regular intervals, and clothes
and blankets were made available to all. Twenty years later this experiment had been abandoned. The Protection Service left the Indians to
their own devices, and in so doing revealed to what an extent it had
itself been deserted by the authorities (it has since regained a little
ground); and the Service was compelled, quite involuntarily, to try
another method—that of inciting the natives to take things into their
hands, once again, and follow their own bent.

All that remained to the natives of their brief experience of
civilization were their Brazilian clothes and the use of the axe, the knife,
and the needle and thread. In other respects the failure was complete.
Houses had been built for them, and they preferred to live in the open.
Efforts had been made to install them in villages, and they were still
nomads. They had broken up their beds for firewood and gone back
to sleeping on the ground. The herds of cows sent by the government
had been left to roam off as they pleased, since neither their milk nor
their meat was acceptable to the Indians. The mechanical pestle made of
wood (it was worked by leverage) stood rotting and seemed never to
have been used: the meal was still ground by hand.

It was a great disappointment to me to find that the Tibagy Indians were neither 'true Indians' nor, for that matter, 'true savages'. But, in so far as they disabused me of the ingenuous and poetical notion of what is in store for us that is common to all novices in anthropology, those Indians taught me a lesson in prudence and objectivity. Not only were they less 'intact' than I had hoped: they also had secrets that I could not have guessed on first acquaintance. They were a perfect example of that sociological predicament which is becoming ever more widespread in the second half of the twentieth century: they were 'former savages', that is to say, on whom civilization had been abruptly forced; and, as soon as they were no longer 'a danger to Society', civilization took no further interest in them. Their culture was made up for the most part of ancient traditions (such as the practice, still common among them, of filing down and inlaying their teeth) which had held out against the influence of the whites. But it also included certain borrowings from the civilization of our own day, and the combination, though not rich in the accepted elements of the picturesque, was nevertheless an original field of study, and one quite as instructive as that offered by the uncontaminated natives with whom I was to have to do later.

Now that these Indians were thrown back upon their own resources, there could be noted a strange reversal of the apparent equilibrium between 'modern' and 'primitive' cultures. Old ways of life and traditional techniques reappeared; the 'past' to which they belonged was, after all, neither dead nor distant. How else could one account for the admirably polished stone pestles which stood side by side, in the Indians' houses, with the enamelled metal plates, the cheap mass-produced spoons, and—in more than one instance—the skeletal remains of a sewing-machine? Perhaps the pestles had been acquired by barter, in the depths of the forests, with those unsubdued and ferocious populations against whom, in certain parts of the Parana, the small-holders had never made any headway? To know for certain one would have to retrace, stage by stage, the odyssey of the elderly Indian *bravo* who was spending his years of retirement on government territory.

These mysterious and haunting relics related to the times when the Indian had neither house, nor clothes, nor metal utensils of any sort. And the ancient techniques survived, likewise, in the half-conscious memories of these people. They knew of matches, for instance; but as these were expensive and hard to come by the Indians preferred to make fire by the rotation or rubbing together of two soft pieces of palmito wood. The government had distributed rifles and pistols, at one time, but these were mostly to be found hanging in the long-abandoned houses; the Indians went hunting with bows and arrows fashioned with the traditional skills of a people that had never seen firearms. And so the old ways of life would reassert themselves after the brief period of official obsolescence, just as slowly and as surely as the Indians would file along the tiny forest paths, while in the deserted villages roof after roof would crumble in dust.

For a fortnight on end we rode forward on horseback through the forest. Often the distances were so vast, and the tracks so sketchy, that it was far into the night before we arrived at our staging-point. It astonished me that our horses should never put a foot wrong in the impenetrable darkness: this was made the more impenetrable by the ceiling of foliage that closed down, a hundred feet above our heads. But they kept up the same jerky motion, hour after hour; sometimes the track would lurch abruptly downhill and we would have to reach quickly for the tall pommel of our peasant saddles; sometimes a sudden coolness from below us and the squelch of water would show that we were crossing a stream. And then our mounts would scramble up the farther bank with movements so frantic as to suggest that their one wish was to be rid of both saddle and rider. Once on flat ground again, we had only to remain alert and profit by that strange awareness which allows one, as often as not, to duck in time to avoid the low branch which one has sensed but not seen.

And then suddenly an identifiable sound comes to us from somewhere ahead: not the jaguar's roar which we heard for a moment at nightfall, but the barking of a dog. Our night's lodging is not far distant. A few minutes later our guide swings off the main track and we follow him into a little enclosure where rough tree-trunk barriers mark out a cattle-pen and the solitary hut is roofed with straw. Our white-clad hosts are in hospitable commotion: the husband is often of Portuguese origin, his wife Indian. With the aid of a wick soaked in kerosene, we make a rapid inventory: floor of beaten earth, a table, a plank bed, a few packing-cases to serve as chairs, and on the baked-clay hearth a collection of old cans and tins: our hosts' *batterie de cuisine*. We hastily sling our hammocks through the interstices of the openwork wall of juxtaposed palm-trunks; sometimes we go and sleep outside, under the canopy that protects the garnered maize from the rain. Surprising as it may seem, it's deliciously comfortable to lie on a heap of maize; the long ears, with the leaves still wrapped around them, form themselves into a compact mass that adapts itself perfectly to one's body and there is something marvellously soothing about their sweet grassy smell. But at dawn the cold and the damp put an end to sleep; a milk-white mist rises from the clearing; we make haste to go inside the hut, where the glow from the hearth relieves the perpetual semi-darkness. (There are no windows, of course, but the light penetrates the insterstices in the walls.) Our host brews the blackest of black coffee with plenty of sugar at the bottom of it and *pipoca* (popcorn), mixed with pieces of larding bacon. Our horses are brought up and saddled, and we are off; a few moments, and the watery forest closes down again and the hut is lost and forgotten.

The São Jeronymo reserve covers about a quarter of a million acres and is inhabited by about four hundred and fifty Indians, grouped in some five or six villages. I was able before leaving to examine the statistics and get an idea of the harm done by malaria, tuberculosis, and alcoholism. In the previous ten years there had not been more than one hundred and seventy births, and infantile mortality alone had accounted for one hundred and forty of them.

We visited the wooden houses which the federal government had built. They were grouped in villages of from five to six fires, with water nearby; we also saw the more isolated houses which the Indians occasionally built for themselves; these consisted of a square palisade of palmito-trunks, bound together with liana, and a roof made of leaves and hung on to the walls by its four corners. And we also examined those branch-hung awnings beneath which whole families would often live, leaving the adjacent house unoccupied.

The inhabitants, in such cases, would be assembled round a fire that was kept burning night and day. The men generally wore the ragged remains of a shirt and an old pair of trousers, and the women either a cotton dress, worn next the skin, or a blanket rolled under their armpits. The children went naked. All wore, as did we ourselves while travelling, large hats of straw; the making of these was, indeed, their only activity and their only way of making money. Both men and women bore, at every age, the marks of the Mongolian type: lightly built, with broad flat faces, prominent cheekbones, yellow skin, narrow eyes, black straight hair—worn either long or short, in the case of the women—and the body almost or entirely hairless. They live in one room. They eat, at no matter what time of the day, the sweet potatoes that lie roasting in the ashes, picking them out with long pincers of bamboo. They sleep on either a thin layer of bracken or a pallet of maize-straw. Each lies with his feet nearest the fire. The few remaining embers and the screen of tree-trunks roughly thrown together make a poor protection, in the middle of the night, against the intense cold that comes down at an altitude of over three thousand feet.

The houses built by the Indians themselves amount to this one same room, just as in the houses built by the government only one room is ever put to use. All the Indian's worldly goods are to be found there, laid out on the ground in a degree of disorder that scandalized our guides. It was difficult to distinguish the objects that were Brazilian in origin from those made near at hand. Brazilian, in general, were axes, knives, enamelled plates and metal receptacles, rags, needle and thread, bottles and, on rare occasions, an umbrella. The furniture was of the rudest: a few low wooden stools of *guarani* origin; baskets of all sizes and for every purpose, in which was to be found the technique of

FIG. 4.   Kaingang pottery

'twilled plaiting' which is so common in South America; a sieve for flour, a wooden mortar, a pestle of wood or stone, a pot or two; and, finally, an immense number of receptacles of every sort and size, constructed from the *abobra*, a gourd emptied of its contents and dried. It was very difficult indeed for us to get hold of one of these pathetic objects: often a preliminary and wholesale distribution of rings, necklaces, and glass brooches would have failed to establish the friendly contact without which nothing could be done. Even the offer of milreis, in a quantity vastly in excess of the intrinsic value of the coveted object, would leave its owner indifferent. 'He just can't. If he'd made it himself he'd give it gladly. But he got it a long time ago from an old woman who alone knew the secret of its manufacture, and if he gave it away he could never get another.' The old woman is, of course, never at hand. She is: 'I don't know where . . . somewhere in the forest.'

Besides, what good are our milreis to an elderly Indian, trembling with fever, who lives sixty miles from the nearest white man's shop? One would be ashamed to wrest from these people, who already have so few possessions, something that, for them, would represent an irreparable loss.

But often it's a very different story. The Indian woman in question would be delighted to sell the pot. But unfortunately it's not hers to dispose of. Whose is it, then? Silence. Her husband's? No. Her brother's? No. Her son's? No. It's her little daughter's. The little daughter invariably turns out to own all the things that we would like to buy. Aged perhaps three or four, she's squatting beside the fire, entirely absorbed in the little ring that I slipped on her finger a while ago. And there follow endless negotiations with the young lady: negotiations in which the parents take no part. A ring and five hundred reis do not tempt her, but she is won over by a brooch and four hundred reis.

The Kaingang are not great cultivators. Fishing, hunting, and collecting are their main activities. Their fishing equipment is such a wretched imitation of our own that one can hardly believe they ever catch anything: a supple branch, a Brazilian hook attached with a little resin to the end of the line, sometimes a piece of ordinary rag in the guise of a net. Hunting and collecting dominate their nomadic life in the forest, where for weeks on end whole families disappear from view and nobody can find them out in their secret lairs or follow their complicated itineraries. Sometimes we come on the little troop at the moment when they happen to cross our path; instantly they duck back into the forest. The men lead the party, with *bodoque* in hand—a form of pellet-bow used in the hunt for birds—and over their shoulders the quiver, made of basketwork, in which is kept their ammunition: pellets of dried clay. Next come the women, with all their worldly goods either wrapped in a woven scarf or supported in a basket by a strap of bark wound round their foreheads. Children and household objects were both carried by this means. A few words might be exchanged, as we reined in our horses and they slackened their pace for a moment: and then the forest would fall silent again. We knew only that the next house, like so many others, would be empty. For how long?

This nomadic life can go on for weeks or months. The hunting season, like the season for fruit—*jaboticaba*, orange, *lima*—sees the entire population on the move. Where do they find shelter in the depths of the forest? From what secret hiding-places do they retrieve their bows and arrows? (We ourselves found, at most, a specimen or two that had been forgotten in some corner of a deserted house.) And what are the traditions, the rites, the beliefs that prompt them to go back to the forest?

Gardening comes last in the Indians' economy. Sometimes a patch of cultivated ground can be glimpsed in the forest: between high ramparts of trees, a few poor square yards of greenstuff—bananas, sweet potatoes, manioc, maize. The grain is first dried by the fire, and then pounded with the mortar by women working singly or in couples. Flour is eaten as it is or made up with fat into a firm cake. To this diet black beans are added; and as far as meat is concerned there may be either game or the semi-domestic pig. These are invariably impaled on a stick and roasted above a fire.

Nor should I forget the *koro*, a whitish worm that pullulates in the trunks of certain trees when they begin to rot. The Indians now refuse to admit that they enjoy eating these creatures: such is the effect of the white man's continual teasing. But if you go into the forest you are sure to come upon the phantom of a great tree, a *pinheiro* sixty or eighty feet high that has been blown down in a storm and torn to pieces by the *koro*-fanciers. And if you enter an Indian house unannounced you can often see—just for a second, before they have time to whip it away—a cup in which the favourite worms are wriggling by the score.

All this makes it difficult actually to watch the *koro*-extractors at their work. We spent a considerable time plotting and planning how best to achieve it. One old fever-stricken Indian whom we found, all by himself in an abandoned village, seemed just the man to help us; we put an axe in his hand and tried to push or prod him into action. But to no avail: he feigned not to know what we were after. As a last inducement we told him that we were ourselves longing to taste *koro*. Eventually we got him to a suitable trunk, and with one blow of the axe he cut down to where, deep in the hollow of the tree, a network of canals lay waiting. In each was a fat white creature, not unlike a silk-worm. Now it was up to us; and the Indian looked on impassively while I cut off the head of the worm. The body oozed a whitish substance which I tasted, not without some hesitation. It had the smoothness and the consistency of butter and the flavour of coconut-milk.

15 *Pantanal*

Thus baptized, I was ready for real adventures. An opportunity for these was to present itself during the period of University vacation. This runs, in Brazil, from November to March, and has the disadvantage of also being the rainy season. I planned, in spite of this, to make contact with two groups of natives. The one, never as yet the object of serious study, had perhaps already very largely disappeared: the Caduveo on the Paraguayan frontier. The other group was better known, but still promised much: the Bororo in the central Mato Grosso. In addition the National Museum in Rio de Janeiro suggested that I should go and identify an archaeological site which lay on my route. No one, as yet, had had a chance to investigate this, although it had long figured in the archives.

I've often travelled, since then, between São Paulo and the Mato Grosso, sometimes by aeroplane, sometimes by lorry, and sometimes by train and boat. It was this last means that I used in 1935-6; the site in question lay, in fact, near the railway and not far from the end of the line at Porto Esperança, on the left bank of the Rio Paraguay.

It was a tedious journey, with not much to be said about it; the Noroeste railway company took you first to Bauru, in the middle of the pioneering zone; from there you took the Mato Grosso 'night-train' which ran across the southern part of the State. A three days' journey, in all, in a train that proceeded slowly, used wood for fuel, and stopped long and often for fresh loads of logs. The carriages were also of wood, and none too well put together; the traveller awoke to find his face covered with a film of stiffened clay—so thoroughly had the red fine dust of the *sertão* made its way into every fold and every pore. The restaurant-car had already adopted the gastronomic manners of the interior: meat, fresh or dried, as opportunity offered, and rice or black beans with *farinha* (poached corn) to absorb the juice. (*Farinha*

141

consists of the pulp of maize or fresh manioc, dehydrated by great heat and pounded down into a coarse powder.) Next came the eternal Brazilian dessert—a slice of quince or guava jelly, with cheese to go with it. At every station boys would offer us, for a penny or two, juicy yellow-fleshed pineapples; these were delightfully refreshing.

The State of Mato Grosso begins just before the station of Tres Lagoas, where the train crosses the Rio Parana, a river so wide that even when the rainy season has already begun you can still see the dry bed in many places. Then began the landscape which was to become at once familiar, insupportable and indispensable during the years that I travelled in the interior. It is typical of central Brazil, from the Parana to the Amazonian basin: featureless, or at most gently rolling plateaux, distant horizons, a tangle of brushwood, and occasionally a troop of zebus that scattered as the train went by. Many travellers make the mistake of translating Mato Grosso as 'big forest': the word forest is rendered rather by the feminine 'mata', whereas the masculine 'mato' stands for the complementary element in South American landscape. Mato Grosso means, in fact, 'big bush': and one could devise no better name for this part of the world. Wild and forlorn as it is, its very monotony is somehow grandiose and stirring.

Admittedly I also translate *sertão* as 'bush'. But the word has a slightly different connotation. Mato relates objectively to the bush as an element in the landscape which contrasts with the forest. *Sertão*, on the other hand, has a subjective significance: landscape, in this case, is considered in relation to human beings, and *sertão* means 'the bush', as opposed to land that is inhabited and cultivated—a region, that is to say, where man has not yet contrived to set up his home. French Colonial slang has an equivalent in the word 'bled'.

Sometimes the plateau is interrupted and there comes into view instead a wooded, overgrown valley: a 'happy valley', almost, beneath the unmenacing sky. Between Campo Grande and Aquidauana a deeper ravine allows us to glimpse the blazing cliffs of the Maracaju serra; over there in the gorges, at Corrientes, there is already to be found a *garimpo*—a centre, that is to say, of diamond-hunters. And suddenly the whole landscape changes: once past Aquidauana, the traveller enters the *pantanal*: the world's greatest marshland, which occupies the middle basin of the Rio Paraguay.

Seen from the air, this region, with river after river snaking across the flat ground, seems to be made up of arcs and meanders where the water lies stagnant. Even the line of the river-bed seems marked with innumerable *pentimenti*, as if Nature had hesitated before giving it its present and temporary course. At ground-level, the *pantanal* becomes a dream landscape. The zebu-troops take refuge there, as if on an ark poised on the top of a submerged hill; and in the marshlands proper the big birds—flamingoes, egrets, herons—band together to form compact islands, pink and white in colour, though not so feathery as the fantail foliage of the caranda-palms which secrete a valuable wax in their leaves; these are the palm-trees whose scattered groves alone disturb the misleadingly pleasant perspectives of this watery desert.

Lugubrious and ill-named Porto Esperança remains in my memory as the oddest site to be found anywhere on the globe. Its only possible rival in this respect is Fire Island in the State of New York; and it amuses me to put the two side by side, for they have at least one thing in common: that each, in its different key, offers within itself the wildest contradictions. Geographically and humanly speaking an identical absurdity finds outlet in them: comic in the one case, sinister in the other.

Perhaps it was Swift who invented Fire Island? It's a long strip of sand on which nothing grows, and it runs to seaward of Long Island. It has length, but not breadth: fifty-odd miles in one direction, two or three hundred yards in the other. On the ocean side the sea runs freely, and with such violence that people dare not bathe there. To landward a flat calm prevails, and the water is so shallow that it's as much as you can do to get wet. People amuse themselves by catching the inedible fish of the region; and in order that these should not decay notices are posted at regular intervals along the beach, ordering the fishermen to bury their catch as soon as they have it out of the water. The dunes of Fire Island are so unstable, and so precarious is their ascendancy, that another series of notices has been put up: 'Keep Off The Dunes,' this says, for they may suddenly subside into the waters below. It's Venice back-to-front, with earth that turns to water and canals that hold firm: the inhabitants of Cherry Grove, the hamlet which stands at the half-way point of the island, can move about only on a network of wooden gangplanks that has been put up on stilts.

The picture is completed by the fact that Cherry Grove is mainly inhabited by homosexual couples—doubtless drawn to the area by its wholesale inversion of the normal conditions of life. As nothing grows in the sand, save large clumps of poison ivy, there's daily revictualling at the island's only shop. This stands at the landing-stage; and as each sterile couple clambers back up towards the cabins that line the slender alleys above the dunes. it pushes before it a pram: no other form of vehicle can negotiate the narrow 'streets'. Empty they are, none the less, but for the week-end bottles of milk that no nurslings are waiting to drink.

Fire Island has an element of high-spirited farce; its equivalent at Porto Esperança is adapted, one would say, to a population more thoroughly damned. Nothing justifies the existence of this town; it's simply that the railway-track pulls up at this point against the river, and a line a thousand miles long, which runs through uninhabited territory for three-quarters of its length, comes to a halt. Thenceforward it's by boat alone that the traveller can penetrate the interior; the line peters out on the muddy river-marge, where a ramshackle construction of planks serves as a landing-stage for the little river-steamers.

The railway employees form the entire population; their homes, the entire town. Wooden huts, they are, built directly on the marshes, and accessible only by the decrepit gangways which mark out the inhabited area. The company had put at our disposition a 'chalet': a cubiform box, that is to say, that stood on tall stilts and was reached by a ladder. The door opened into space above a railway-siding, and we were aroused at dawn by the whistle of the tall-framed locomotive that was to serve us as our private limousine. The nights were very disagreeable; everything combined to make sleep impossible—the damp heat, the big marsh-mosquitoes that moved in to the attack, and even our mosquito-nets whose design, all too carefully studied before departure, turned out to be far from satisfactory. At five o'clock in the morning, when the steam from our locomotive came hissing up through the flimsy floor, the day had already developed its full heat. There was no mist, in spite of the damp, but the sky was like lead and the atmosphere seemed weighted down, as if by some supplementary element that had made it impossible to breathe. Luckily the locomotive got up a good speed and as we sat in the breeze with our legs dangling over the guard-irons we gradually shook off the night's languor.

The single track (it's used by two trains a week) had been laid across the marshes in rough-and-ready style. It was no more than a flimsy gangplank that the locomotive seemed constantly disposed to jump aside from. On either side of the line there was water: dirty, disgusting, stale, and foul in smell. Yet this was to be, for weeks, our drinking-water.

To left and right were clumps of shrubs, spaced out as if in an orchard; at a distance they formed into dark masses, while the sky, reflected in the water, projected here and there its own likeness beneath the branches. Everything seemed to be simmering at a low heat: it was a stew that would take a long time to mature. If it were possible to linger for many thousands of years in this prehistoric landscape, and to follow its evolution closely, we should no doubt witness the trans- formation of organic matter into peat, or coal, or petrol. I even thought that I saw some petrol rising to the surface, staining the water with its delicate iridiscence; this intrigued our engine-crew, who had refused to believe that we should give ourselves, and them, so much trouble for the sake of a few shards; and they were encouraged by our pith helmets, symbol of the 'engineer', to believe that archaeology was merely a pretext for prospecting of a more lucrative sort.

Sometimes the silence was broken by creatures who were not frightened by us: a *veado*, or astonished and white-tailed roebuck; or a troop of emu (small ostriches); or the white flash of the egret as it skimmed along the surface.

As we went along, workmen would often hail the locomotive and clamber up beside us. Then came a halt: Kilometre 12; the branch-line gave out at that point and we had to do the rest of the journey on foot. We could already see our destination in the distance, with its typical look of the *capão*.

The waters of the pantanal are not stagnant, as they would seem to be; they drag along with them a quantity of shells and alluvium, which piles up at points where vegetation has taken root. This is how the pantanal comes to be strewn with spiky tufts of verdure—*capões*, they are called—where once the Indians set up their camps. Traces of their passage may still be found.

And so we would go off every day to our particular *capão*, which we reached by a wooded track that we had built up with sleepers taken from the side of the line. These were very disagreeable days, for it was difficult to breathe, and our 'drinking-water', taken direct from the marshes, was hot from the sun. At the end of the day the locomotive came to fetch us; or sometimes it was one of the 'devils', as they were called—open trucks pushed along by workmen who stood, one in each corner, and shoved away with long sticks, like gondoliers. Wearied and thirsty, we had before us a sleepless night in the desert of Porto Esperança.

Some sixty or seventy miles distant there was a largish cultivated area which we had chosen as our departure-base for the Caduveo. The *Fazenda francesa*, as it was called on the line, occupied a strip of some one hundred and twenty-five thousand acres alongside of which the train ran for about eighty miles. In all some seven thousand animals wandered here and there among this great expanse of brushwood and dry grasses (an animal needs, in the tropics, not less than fifteen or twenty-five acres to itself). Periodically, and thanks to the fact that the train stopped two or three times along the edge of the domain, these animals were exported to São Paulo. The halt which served the inhabited part of the area was called Guaycurus—a name that called to mind the great warrior-tribes that once ruled over the region; of these tribes the Caduveo are the last survivors.

Two Frenchmen managed the property, with the help of a few families of cowherds. I've forgotten the name of the younger Frenchman, but the other, who was rising forty, was called Félix R.—Don Félix, he was commonly named. He was later murdered by an Indian.

Our hosts had either grown up or served in the forces during the First World War. By temperament and by aptitude alike they were cut out to become settlers in Morocco, and I don't know what it was that led them to leave Nantes and head for a more precarious adventure in a derelict region of Brazil. The Fazenda francesa was, in any case, in a bad way. Ten years had passed since its foundation, all its capital had been absorbed by the initial purchase of the land, and the owners had nothing left with which to buy better beasts or newer equipment. Our hosts lived in a huge English-style bungalow. Half grocers, half cattle-raisers, they led an austere existence. The fazenda's sales-counter was, in effect, the only provision-store for sixty or seventy miles in any direction. The empregados, or employees—workers or peons—came and spent there with one hand what they had earned with the other; an entry in the books sufficed to turn them from creditors into debtors, and it was rare, in point of fact, for money actually to change hands. As most things were sold at two or three times their normal price—such was the accepted practice—it would have been quite a going concern if the shop had not occupied a merely subsidiary place in the whole venture. It was heart-rending to watch the workpeople on a Saturday. They would arrive with their little crop of sugar-cane, press it immediately in the fazenda's engenho (a machine made of trunks roughly squared off, in which the cane-stalks were crushed by the rotation of three wooden cylinders), evaporate the juice in a hot iron pan, and pour what remained into moulds, where it turned into tawny blocks, granular in consistency. Rapadura, these were called: and they would hand them in to the adjacent store. When evening came they would re-present themselves, this time as customers, and pay a high price for the right to offer their children their own product—refurbished, by then, as the *sertão's* only sweetmeat.

Our hosts took a philosophical view of their role as exploiters of the natives. They had no contact with their employees outside of working hours, and no neighbours of their own class (the Indian reserve stood between them and the nearest plantations on the Paraguayan border). The very severity of the life which they imposed on themselves was, no doubt, their best protection against discouragement. In dress and drink alone did they make some concession to their adopted continent. Living in a frontier-area where traditions were a mixture of Brazilian, Paraguayan, Bolivian, and Argentinian, they dressed pampastyle: a Bolivian hat of finely woven unbleached straw, with wide upturned brim and tall crown; and the *chiripa*, a grown-up's variant of swaddling clothes. Made of cotton and delicate in colour, with stripes of pink or blue or mauve, it left the legs and lower thighs bare. Cloth-topped white boots came well up the wearer's calves. When the weather turned cool, the *chiripa* gave place to the *bombacha*: billowing trousers such as zouaves wear, with rich embroidery down the sides.

Almost all their working hours were spent in the corral, where they 'worked over' their animals—looking them over, that is to say, and picking out those which were ready for sale. A storm of dust arose as the beasts, urged on by the *capataz'* guttural cries, filed past before their masters and were separated, some into one park, some into another. Long-horned zebus, fat cattle, and terrified calves went stumbling through the barriers. Sometimes a bull jibbed; and when this happened the *lassoeiro* would send his forty yards of finely plaited thong whirling through the air, and in a flash, as it seemed, the bull would be captured and horse and horseman pranced in triumph.

But twice a day—at eleven-thirty in the morning and seven in the evening—there was a general assembly underneath the pergola which ran round their house. The ritual in question was that of the *chimarrão*: maté drunk through a tube. The maté is a tree of the same family as our ilex; and its foliage, lightly roasted over the smoke of an underground fire, is pounded into a coarse powder, the colour of reseda, which keeps for a long time in kegs. I'm talking of the real maté, of course: the product sold in Europe under that name has usually undergone such sinister transformations as to bear no resemblance to the original.

There are several ways of drinking maté. When on an expedition we were too impatient for its immediate stimulus to do more than throw a large handful of the powder into cold water and bring it quickly to the boil. (It's vital, even then, to whip it off the fire at the very moment it boils: otherwise it loses all savour.) That is what is called *cha de maté*, an infusion in reverse, dark green in colour and almost oily, like a cup of strong coffee. When time was short, we made do with the *téréré*: this simply involved pouring cold water on a handful of the powder and sucking it up through a tube. Those who dislike a bitter taste often prefer the *maté doce*, favourite of the beauties of Paraguay: the powder, in this case, is mixed with sugar, turned to caramel over a quick fire, plunged into boiling water, and passed through a sieve. But I know of no amateur of maté who does not give pride of place to the *chimarrão*, which is at once a social rite and, as was the case at the *fazenda*, a secret vice.

All present sit in a circle around a little girl, the *china*, who has with her a kettle, a charcoal-stove, and a *cuia*, which may be either a calabash with a silver-mounted mouth, or, as at Guaycurus, a zebu horn sculpted by a peon. The *cuia* is two-thirds full of powder, and the little girl gradually saturates this with boiling water; as soon as the mixture has formed a paste she takes up a silver tube whose bulbous extremity is pierced with holes, and with this she carefully scoops out a hollow in the paste, so designed that the pipe rests at the very bottom of the *cuia*, in the little grotto where the liquid collects. The tube, meanwhile, must have just enough play not to spoil the equilibrium of the paste, but not too much: otherwise the water will not mix in properly. The *chimarrão* is then ready, and it only remains to let the liquid saturate fully before it is offered to the master of the house. He takes two or three draughts and gives the vessel back to the little girl; whereat the operation is repeated for everyone present—men first, and women later, if women are present at all. And so it continues until the kettle is empty.

The first draught or two will yield a delicious sensation—to the habitué, that is to say: the novice will often burn himself. This sensation is made up of the slightly greasy texture of the hot silver, the effervescent water, and the rich, foamy substance that is borne up with it: at once bitter and aromatic, as if a whole forest had been concentrated into half a dozen drops. Maté contains an alkaloid analogous to that found in coffee, tea, and chocolate, but on account of its dosage—and also perhaps because of the tartness of the liquid itself—it is as soothing as it is invigorating. After the vessel has been round a few times the maté begins to lose its quality, but if you explore carefully you can still plunge the pipe into anfractuosities as yet unexplored; these prolong the pleasure with fresh bursts of bitterness.

Maté is vastly superior, one must say, to the Amazonian *guarana*, of which I shall speak later; and, even more so, to the wretched *coca* of the Bolivian plateau: this is a most paltry compilation of dried leaves that soon degenerates into a fibrous ball, flavoured like a tisane, that acts as an anaesthetic on the mucous membrane and reduces one's tongue to the status of a foreign body. The only drink that can compare with maté is the richly orchestrated *chique* of betel-nut beaten up with spices; simply terrifying, to the unprepared palate, is the salvo of scents and savours which this can let off.

The Caduveo Indians lived in the low ground on the left bank of the Rio Paraguay, which was separated from the *Fazenda francesa* by the hills of the Serra Bodoquena. Our hosts regarded the Caduveo Indians as idlers and degenerates, thieves and drunkards, who were summarily turned out of the pasturelands when they attempted to penetrate them. Our expedition seemed to them doomed from the start; and although they gave us generous assistance, without which we should never have achieved our ends, they regarded the whole venture with disapproval. Great was their stupefaction when we returned some weeks later with oxen as heavily laden as those of a caravan: huge ceramic jars, painted and engraved, roebuck-hides decorated in arabesque, wooden sculptures representing a vanished Pantheon. . . . It was a revelation, and one which left them strangely changed: when Don Félix came to call on me in São Paulo, two or three years later, I understood from him that he and his companion, who had treated the local population so very much *de haut en bas*, had 'gone native', as the English say. The little bourgeois parlour of the *fazenda* was hung with painted skins, and native potteries were to be found in every corner. Our friends were playing at the bazaars of Morocco or the Sudan, like the exemplary colonial administrators whom they should really have been. And the Indians, now their official suppliers, were made warmly welcome at the *fazenda*; whole families were lodged there, in exchange for the objects they brought. Just how far did their intimacy go? It was difficult to imagine two bachelors able to resist the Indian girls when once they came to know them—so attractive were they, half naked on festival-days, with their bodies so patiently decorated with elegant blue and black scrolls and whorls that seemed to have been laid on the skin like a coating of elaborate lace. Be that as it may, Don Félix was murdered in 1944 or 1945: a victim not so much of the Indians, one might think, as of the disturbed state into which he had been thrown, a decade earlier, by the visit of us novice-anthropologists.

The *fazenda*'s store provided what we needed to eat: dried meat, rice, black beans, manioc flour, maté, coffee, and *rapadura*. We were also lent mounts: horses for the men, and oxen for our luggage, for we were taking with us a good deal of stuff to exchange for what we hoped to bring back: children's toys, glass necklaces, rings, scent; and also pieces of cloth, blankets, clothes, and tools. Some of the *fazenda* workers were to act as our guides—very unwillingly, as it happened, for we were taking them away from their families at Christmas-time.

The villagers were expecting us; no sooner had we arrived at the *fazenda* than Indian *vaqueiros* went off to announce that strangers bearing presents were on their way. This news was, if anything, disquieting to the Indians, who feared one thing above all: that we were coming *tomar conta*—to usurp their land.

16 *Nalike*

Nalike, capital of the Caduveo country, is about a hundred miles, or three days' ride, from Guaycurus. (The oxen were sent on ahead, because of their slower speed.) For our first day's march we planned to climb the slopes of the Serra Bodoquena and spend the night on the plateau in the last of the *fazenda*'s huts. We very soon got into narrow valleys where the grass stood so high that the horses could hardly make their way through it. Swampy ground underfoot made the going still more laborious: my horse would slip, struggle back to firm ground as and when it could, and find itself entirely surrounded by vegetation. We then had to take great care: for an innocent-looking leaf might secrete beneath it a wriggling egg-shaped mass of diminutive ticks, and these little orange-coloured brutes would get in under our clothes, spread all over our bodies like a table-cloth on the march, and bed down under our skin. The only remedy was for the victim to counter-attack immediately, jumping down off his horse, stripping off his clothes, and beating them out as hard as he could, while one of his companions searched his body. Less catastrophic were the bigger single parasites, grey in colour, which clung to the skin and inflicted no pain; hours or days later, when we happened to find them by touch, they had sunk into our flesh and had to be cut out with a knife.

Eventually the ground cleared and we got on to a stony track which led up to a dry forest, half trees and half cacti. A storm had been brewing since morning, and it broke just as we were rounding the top of some cactus-infested high ground We dismounted and looked for shelter in a hole in the rock: this turned out to be a grotto which, though damp in itself, would protect us from the storm. As soon as we got into it, there arose an immense whirring and stirring of bats: we had disturbed their slumbers.

The rain over, we rode on through the darkened and overgrown forest. It was full of cool smells and wild fruit: the heavy-fleshed, bitter-tasting *genipapo*, and in the clearings the *guavira* which was supposed to refresh every traveller with the perpetual coolness of its pulp, and the *caju* which proved that once the Indians had had a plantation there.

The plateau had the characteristic look of the Mato Grosso: high grass and scattered trees. We came up to our staging-point across a zone of marshland, where tiny waders cantered across the mud; by the corral, and then the hut, we recognized the Largon post, where the family was absorbed in the *mise à mort* of a *bezerro*, or young bull. They were getting to work on the body, while two or three naked children clambered over the bleeding carcass with cries of delight. Above the open fire which shone out in the twilight the *churrasco*, shiny with grease, was roasting, while the *urubus*—carrion vultures—came down by the hundred to the scene of the slaughter and fought with the dogs for the bloody remains.

From Largon onwards we followed the so-called 'Indians' route'. The serra ran steeply downhill—so much so that our horses took fright and we had to dismount and guide them. The track ran above a torrent and we could hear, even if we could not see, the water cascading down off the rocks; we ourselves slipped and slithered, meanwhile, on the damp stones or in the muddy pools left by the last fall of rain. Eventually, at the foot of the serra, we came to a circular clearing, the *campo dos indios*, where we and our mounts rested for a while before plunging again into the marshes.

Already at four in the afternoon we had to begin planning for our 'night's rest'. We sought out a group of trees from which to hang hammocks and mosquito-nets; our guides lit a fire and began preparing our meal of rice and dried meat. We were so thirsty that we drank deeply of the repellent mixture of earth, water, and permanganate which was all we had to drink. Night fell, and for a moment we watched the sky go scarlet behind the dirtier muslin of our mosquito-nets. Hardly had we gone to sleep before we had to be off again: at midnight, when the guides woke us, they had already saddled the horses. It was the hot season and we had to make the most of the cool of the night. We set off in the moonlight, still half asleep, shivering with cold, and generally fit for nothing. We watched for the dawn, hour after hour, as our horses stumbled forward. About four o'clock in the morning we got to Pitoko, where the Indians' Protection Service had once had an important outpost. All that remained of this was three ruined houses: just enough for us to swing our hammocks from. The

Rio Pitoko ran silently on towards the point, a mile or two farther on, where it vanished again into the pantanal. A marshland river, with neither source nor mouth, it harboured a mass of *piranhas*: dangerous to the unwary bather, these did not deter the wily and experienced Indians either from bathing or from drawing such water as they needed. A few families of Indians are still to be found here and there in the marshes.

Thenceforward we were in the pantanal proper: either shallow basins of floodland between wooden crests, or immense tree-less expanses of mud. A saddled ox would have served better than a horse; for, slow as he is, the massive ox, with the guiding rein passed through his nostril, is better able to stand the strain of plunging forward through mud that often comes up to his breast-bone.

We were in a plain that stretched as far, perhaps, as the Rio Paraguay, a plain so flat that the water could never drain off it, when there came down upon us the worst storm that I have ever had to face. There was no possibility of shelter—not a tree in sight in any direction—nothing to do but to go slowly forward, while to right and to left of us the thunder rolled and the lightning flashed like an artillery barrage, and the water ran down off horses and men alike. After a two hours' ordeal the rain stopped, and we could see the squall moving slowly across the horizon, as happens sometimes on the high seas. But already at the far edge of the horizon there was outlined a terrace of clay, perhaps a few dozen feet high, on which a group of huts stood out against the sky. We were approaching, not Nalike, but the nearby village of Engenho. We had decided to stay there in preference to Nalike, which in 1935 could muster only five huts in all.

To an inattentive eye these hamlets differed hardly at all from those of the nearest Brazilian peasants. Such, too, was the proportion of half-castes that the inhabitants were indistinguishable both in their way of dressing and in their physical type. But the language was a very different matter: the *guaicuru* manner of speech was delightful to the ear. They were headlong talkers, with a profusion of long words made up of the alternation of open vowels with dental and guttural sounds and an abundance of soft or liquid phonemes which sounded like a stream dancing over pebbles. The word 'caduveo' (pronounced 'cadiueu') is a corruption of the natives' own name for themselves: 'Cadiguegodi'. Our stay was too short for us to attempt to learn their language, especially as our new hosts' grasp of Portuguese was rudimentary in the extreme.

The 'houses' were supported by trunks, stripped of their bark, which stood firmly at the four corners; horizontal beams were lodged in the fork of the first branch, which the woodsman had been careful not to cut right through. A blanket of yellowed palm-leaves formed a roof that sloped down on both sides, but the huts differed from the Brazilian lodges in that they had no walls; they were, in fact, a compromise between the white men's huts (from which the roof had been copied) and the ancient native shelters, whose roofing had been flat and made of matting.

There was much to be learnt from the dimensions of these rudimentary homes. Rarely did they shelter a single family only; some were

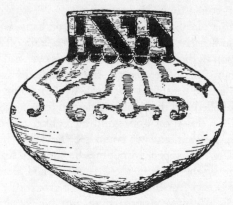

FIG. 5.   Water-jar, decorated in bright red
and varnished with black resin

like long narrow hangars, and housed as many as six families, each of whom had its clearly defined living-space. This was furnished with platform-beds made of planks, on which the tenants would spend their time: lying, sitting, or squatting, among the buckskins, lengths of cotton, calabashes, nets, and straw baskets which were laid, or heaped, or hung all over the place. In the corner could be seen the big decorated water-jars which stood on forked wooden supports: sometimes these supports were sculpted.

These constructions had once been 'long houses', not unlike those of the Iroquois, and some of them still looked to deserve the name. But it was now merely for reasons of convenience that several families would live in the same house, whereas formerly the residence had been matrilocal: the sons-in-law would congregate with their wives in the house of their parents-in-law.

'The past' was, in any case, far distant in this pitiable hamlet, where there remained not so much as a memory of the prosperity which the painter-explorer Guido Boggiani witnessed in 1892 and again in 1897. Boggiani's two journeys yielded both a delightful travel-diary and an important collection, now in Rome, of anthropological documents. The total population of the three centres was not above two hundred. They lived by hunting, collecting wild fruit, rearing a few cows and some farmyard animals, and cultivating a few strips of manioc on the far side of the little stream—their only one—which ran below the foot of the terrace. The water was opalescent and slightly sweet to the taste: we used it both for washing—mosquitoes notwithstanding—and for drinking.

Apart from straw-plaiting, the weaving of the cotton belts worn by the men, and the hammering-out of coins (nickel more often than silver) into discs or tubes that could be strung on necklaces, pottery was the main activity of the inhabitants. The women would mix the clay of the Rio Pitoko with pounded potsherds, roll the mixture into sausage-like pieces and press them together till the desired shape was formed; and when the clay was still damp they would embellish it with string impressions, painted over with a ferrous oxide found in the serra. Then it was baked in the open air, after which it only remained to go on with the decorations while the pot was still hot, with the help of two varnishes of juicy resin: the black of the *pau santo*, and the trans-lucent yellow of the *angico*. And when the pot had cooled they would go on to apply a white powder—chalk or ash—in order to touch up the impressions.

The women also made little figures for the children with whatever came nearest to hand: clay, or wax, or the dried pods of a large fruit which needed only minor additions or re-modellings.

The children also had little wooden statuettes, often clothed in rags, which they used as dolls. Some little statuettes, seemingly very like the others, would be preserved with love and care by some of the older women and put away at the bottom of their baskets. Were these toys? Or likenesses of the gods? Or ancestor-figures? It was impossible to say, so contradictory were the uses to which they were put: and all the more so as one and the same statue would sometimes serve now one purpose, now the other. In some cases—those now in the Musée de l'Homme, for instance—there can be no doubt that the meaning of the statue was religious: we can recognize the Mother of the Twins, for instance, or the Little Old Man—the god who had come down to earth and been ill-treated by mankind: now he was taking his revenge, and only that one family which had protected him was to be exempt from punishment. That the holy figures had been given over to the children as toys might, of course, be a symptom of the collapse of the faith in question; but this would be altogether too easy an interpretation. An identical instability, as it seems to us, was described by Boggiani in the 1890s, by Fritch a decade later, and by investigators who were there ten years later than myself. A situation which remains stationary for fifty years can only be called, in one sense, normal; and to interpret it we must realize not only that religious values are crumbling—as they undoubtedly are—but that the natives have a particular way, and a way that is more widespread than we sometimes suppose, of handling the relations between the sacred and the profane. The opposition of the two is neither so absolute, nor so constant, as some philosophers have liked to suppose.

In the hut next to mine there was a witch-doctor whose equipment included a round stool, a head-dress of straw, a gourd-rattle covered with a cotton net, and an ostrich-feather which he used to capture the *bichos*, or evil spirits, which were the cause of all illness. Such was the power of the witch-doctor's own *bicho* that the patient, once cured, would be relieved also of the evil spirit. The beneficent *bicho* was also a natural conservative: he forbade his protégé to let me have any of his equipment: 'I'm used to it,' was the message he sent.

While we were there, great celebrations were held to celebrate the puberty of a girl who lived in one of the other huts. They began by dressing her in the style of former days: in place of her cotton dress, a square piece of cloth swathed round her from her armpits downwards. Elaborate designs were painted on her shoulders, arms, and face, and all the necklaces that they could lay hands on were heaped round her neck. All this may, of course, have been not so much a matter of ancient tradition as an attempt to give us 'our money's worth'. Young anthropologists are always taught that primitive peoples are frightened of the camera and that it is best to allay their fears with a preliminary gift, either in cash or in kind. The Caduveo had brought this to perfection: not only did they insist on being paid before they would pose for pictures, but they actually forced me to photograph them in order that they should be paid for posing. Rare was the day on which a woman would not present herself in some freakish get-up or other and

FIG. 6. Three examples of
Caduveo pottery

FIG. 7. Two wooden statuettes: the Little Old
Man (*left*) and the
Mother of the Twins
(*right*)

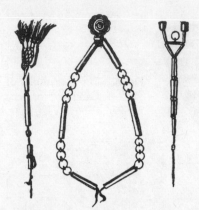

FIG. 8. Caduveo jewellery made
of hammered coins and
thimbles

insist that, whether I wanted to or not, I should photograph her and
make her a present of a few milreis. As I had no films to waste I would
often merely 'go through the motions' with the camera and hand over
the money.

Yet it would have been very bad anthropology to rebuff these
people, or even to regard them as a symptom of decadence or money-
mindedness. For their manœuvres were merely a transposed form of
certain characteristics of their tribal traditions: the independence and
authority of high-born women, ostentatiousness when faced with
strangers, and an insistence that the ordinary person should render
them due homage. My job was to re-transpose these traits into the
context of their former institutions.

Similarly with the festivities which followed the ceremonial
imposition of tribal dress upon our young lady-neighbour. From
afternoon onwards the *pinga* (cane-sugar alcohol) began to go round,
while the men, seated in a circle, laid loud claim to one rank or another
in the lower hierarchy of the army (the only one of which they knew
anything)—corporal, sergeant, lieutenant, captain. This was the
counterpart of the 'solemn drinking-parties' described by eighteenth-
century travellers, in which the chiefs, seated according to their rank,
would be served by equerries, and heralds would call out the titles of
each one, as he drank, and recite the list of his doughty deeds.

Drink affected the Caduveo in a curious way: after a period of high
excitement they fell into a doleful silence, which in its turn was succeeded by convulsive weeping. Two others, less far gone, would at
this stage take their despairing comrade by the arm and march him
up and down, murmuring words of consolation and affection until he

made up his mind to be sick. All three then returned to their places and fell to drinking again.

Meanwhile the women would repeat over and over again a brief three-note snatch of song. One or two of the older women would gather to one side and get under way with a drinking-bout of their own, gesticulating and speechifying with what appeared an almost complete incoherence. Laughter and mischievous comment broke out

FIG. 9. Statuettes of mythological personnages in stone (*left*)
and wood (*right*)

all around them. Yet, here also, it would have been wrong to regard all this merely as self-indulgence on the part of a set of drunken old women. The ancient authors bear witness that these festivities—and more especially those which marked some important stage in the growing-up of a child of noble birth—were marked by transvestite demonstrations on the part of the women of the tribe: military parades, dances, and tournaments. In the 1930s these ragged peasants were a pitiable sight in their forlorn and marshy habitat; but their wretchedness made it all the more striking that they should have clung so tenaciously to some vestige of their ancestral customs.

17 *A Native Society and its Style*

THE ensemble of a people's customs has always its particular style; they form into systems. I am convinced that the number of these systems is not unlimited and that human societies, like individual human beings (at play, in their dreams, or in moments of delirium), never create *absolutely*: all they can do is to choose certain combinations from a repertory of ideas which it should be possible to reconstitute. For this one must make an inventory of all the customs which have been observed by oneself or others, the customs pictured in mythology, and the customs evoked by both children and grown-ups in their games. The dreams of individuals, whether healthy or sick, and psycho-pathological behaviour should also be taken into account. With all this one could eventually establish a sort of periodical chart of chemical elements, analogous to that devised by Mendeleier. In this, all customs, whether real or merely possible, would be grouped by families, and all that would remain for us to do would be to recognize those which societies had, in point of fact, adopted.

These reflections are especially apt in the case of the Mbaya-Guaicuru: the Caduveo in Brazil are, with the Paraguayan Toba and Pilaga, the last representatives of this people. Their civilization immediately calls to mind something which our own society has pictured in one of its traditional distractions—something, too, whose essence was well captured by Lewis Carroll in *Alice in Wonderland*—for these Indian knights remind us of the court-cards in the pack. Their dress, to begin with: they wore tunics and leather surcoats which broadened their shoulders and hung stiffly down in folds, with painted patterns in red and black that reminded earlier travellers of Turkey carpets. To us, these patterns are notable for the motifs of the spade, the diamond, the club, and the heart: these recur over and over again. They had their kings and their queens; and like those in Lewis

Carroll, the Caduveo queens loved to play with the severed heads that their warriors brought back from battle. Nobles of both sexes delighted in tournaments and were absolved from all menial tasks by an enslaved people that had been installed there long before the Caduveo and differed from them both in language and in culture: the Guana. All that now remains of these is the Tereno, who live in a governmental reserve not far from the little town of Miranda. I went to see them there. In former times the Guana tilled the soil and paid the Mbaya lords a tribute of agricultural produce in exchange for their 'protection': as an insurance, that is to say, against pillage and sacking by bands of armed horsemen. A sixteenth-century German who ventured into the region described the relationship as similar to that then existing in central Europe between the feudal lords and their serfs.

The Mbaya were organized by castes; at the top of the social ladder the nobles were divided into two orders: the great hereditary nobles, on the one hand, and individuals who had been raised to the nobility —generally in order to sanction the coincidence that they had been born at the same time as a child of high rank. The great nobles were also divided into senior and junior branches. Next came the warriors: and the best of these were admitted, after initiation, into a brotherhood which entitled them to bear special names and use an artificial language made up (as in certain forms of slang) by the addition of a suffix to every word. The slaves, whether of Chamacoco or other extraction, and the Guana serfs constituted a plebs: the Guana serfs had, however, divided themselves for their own purposes into three castes similar to those of their masters.

The nobles bore, quite literally, the 'mark of their rank' in the form of pictorial designs—painted or tattooed—on their bodies. These were the equivalent of an escutcheon. They plucked out all their facial hair —eyebrows and lashes included—and recoiled in disgust from the bushy-browed European: 'the ostriches' brother' was their name for him. Men and women alike were accompanied in public by a suite of slaves and hangers-on: these vied with one another to spare them all effort. As late as 1935 their best draughtsmen, or draughtswomen, were hideous old monsters, heavily made up and weighed down with trinkets, who excused themselves for having had to give up their former accomplishments, now that they were deprived of the slaves who had once been at their service. There were always, at Nalike, a few former Chamacoco slaves: now part of the group, they were still treated with condescension.

Such was the cold arrogance of the great nobles that even the Spanish and Portuguese conquerors acknowledged it by according them the style of Don and Dona. A white woman who was captured in those days by the Mbaya was said to have nothing to fear: no Mbaya warrior would contaminate himself by union with her. Certain Mbaya ladies refused to meet the wife of the Viceroy: only the Queen of Portugal, they said, was worthy to associate with them. Another, while still a young girl, and known as Dona Catarina, returned a polite refusal when the Governor of the Mato Grosso invited her to Guiaba; as she was of marriageable age she assumed that the Governor would ask for her hand in marriage, and it was out of the question for her either to accept such an offer or to humiliate him by a refusal.

Our Indians were monogamous; but the girls sometimes chose, in adolescence, to follow the warriors in their adventures, serving them as equerries, pages, and mistresses. The noble ladies, for their part, had men to dance attendance upon them; often these were also their lovers, but no husband, in such a case, would deign to make any show of jealousy: by so doing he would have lost face. What we call 'natural' sentiments were held in great disfavour in their society: for instance, the idea of procreation filled them with disgust. Abortion and infanticide were so common as to be almost normal—to the extent, in fact, that it was by adoption, rather than by procreation, that the group ensured its continuance. One of the main objects of the warriors' expeditions was to bring back children. At the beginning of the nineteenth century it was estimated that not more than one in ten of Guaicuru group were Guaicuru by birth.

Such children as managed, in spite of this, to get born were not brought up by their parents, but fostered by another family. Their parents visited them only at rare intervals; and until they reached their fourteenth year they were daubed from head to foot with black paint and called by the name that the Indians applied also to negroes, when they came to know of them. They were then initiated, washed, and relieved of one of the two concentric crowns of hair which they had worn until then.

And yet the birth of a child of high rank was marked by festivities which were repeated at each stage in his growing-up: when he was weaned, when he learned to walk, when he first took part in games, and so on. Heralds would call out the family titles and predict a glorious future for him; another baby, born at the same moment, would be

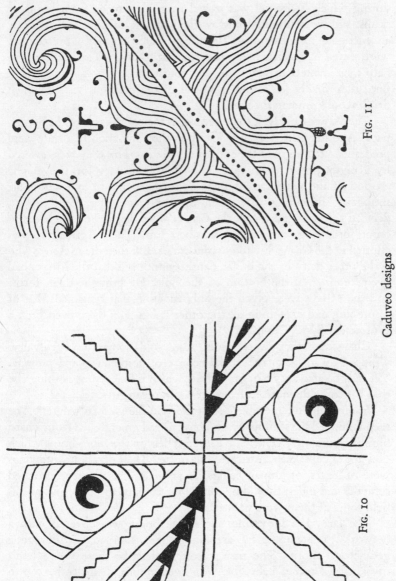

Fig. 11

Fig. 10

Caduveo designs

designated as his brother-in-arms; drinking-parties would be organized, during which hydromel was served in goblets made from horns or skulls; and women would borrow the warriors' armour and take one another on in mimic combat. The nobles, seated in order of precedence, were served by slaves who were forbidden to drink. Their task was to help their masters to vomit, in due course, and to watch over them until they finally fell asleep in search of the delicious visions which drink would procure for them.

They saw themselves, these people, as the court-cards of the human pack. And the pride was founded upon the conviction that they were predestined to rule over the entire human race. This they were assured by a myth, now known to us only in fragmentary form; even the erosion of the years cannot quite conceal its radiant and admirable simplicity. It tells us that when the supreme being, Gonoenhodi, decided to create humanity, the Guana were the first of the tribes to come forth from the earth; the others came later. Agriculture was allotted to the Guana, hunting to the others. But then the trickster, who is the other deity in the Indian pantheon, noticed that the Mbaya had been forgotten at the bottom of the hole. He brought them forth; and the Mbaya were given the only function that remained: that of oppressing and exploiting all the other tribes. Has there even been a profounder Social Contract?

Characters, they were, from some old romance of chivalry: wrapped up in their cruel make-believe of domination and prestige. Yet they created a style of graphic art which is like almost nothing else that has come down to us from pre-Colombian America.

In our tribe the men were sculptors and the women painters. The men fashioned the santons which I have already mentioned from a hard bluish lignum vitae. They also carved reliefs on the zebra-horns which they use as cups: men, ostriches, and horses. Their occasional drawings were of leaves, or human beings, or animals. The women decorated ceramics and hides; they also worked on the human body, and in this field some of them were past-masters.

The face, and sometimes the entire body, was covered with a network of asymmetrical arabesques that alternated with subtle geometrical motifs. The first person to describe these was a Jesuit missionary, Sanchez-Labrador, who lived among them from 1760 to 1770. But for an exact account we must wait another hundred years: for Boggiani's visits, in fact. In 1935 I myself made a collection of several hundred motifs. This is how I went about it: first I thought I

FIG. 13

FIG. 12

Motifs used in body-painting

would photograph them, but the ladies in question proved so demanding—financially speaking—that I had to abandon the idea. Next I tried
to draw human faces on sheets of paper and suggested to the native
women that they should ornament those faces, just as if they were
painting their own. This notion proved so successful that I was soon
able to give up my own clumsy sketches. The designers were not in the
least put off their stroke by the unfamiliarity of white paper, which
shows how little their art is concerned with the natural architecture of
the human face.

Only a few very old women seemed to have kept the virtuosity of
former times, and for a long time I believed that my collection had
been made at the last possible moment. It was, in fact, a surprise to me
when I received, some fifteen years later, an illustrated account of a
similar collection which had just been made by one of my Brazilian
colleagues. Not only did the specimens seem to have been carried out
with exactly the same assurance, but very often the motifs were
identical. Style, technique, and inspiration were unchanged, just as they
had been over the forty years between Boggiani's visit and my own.
This conservatism is the more remarkable in that it is not found at all
in Caduveo pottery, which would appear from such examples as have
lately been published to be in a state of complete degeneration. This
may point to the exceptional importance of body-painting, and above
all of face-painting, in Indian culture.

The motifs were, at one time, either tattooed or painted; but
tattooing has now quite dropped out. The painter, a woman, works on
the face or body of one of her fellow-women, or sometimes on those
of a small boy. (It's becoming rarer and rarer for a grown man to be
painted.) The artist uses a fine bamboo spatula dipped in the juice of
the *genipapo*—initially colourless, this later turns blue-black by
oxydization—and she improvises her design on the living model, with
neither sketch, nor prototype, nor 'focal point' to guide her. She
ornaments the upper lip with a bow-shaped motif finished off with a
spiral at either end. Then she divides the face with a vertical line; this
she occasionally cuts across horizontally. From this stage onwards the
decorations proceed freely in arabesque, irrespective of the position of
eyes, nose, cheeks, forehead, and chin—as if, in fact, the artist were
working on a single unbroken surface. Her compositions, perfectly
balanced for all their asymmetry, can begin from any corner of the face
and proceed without slip or hesitation to their final conclusion. The
basic shapes are relatively simple—spirals, S-forms, crosses, saw-edges,

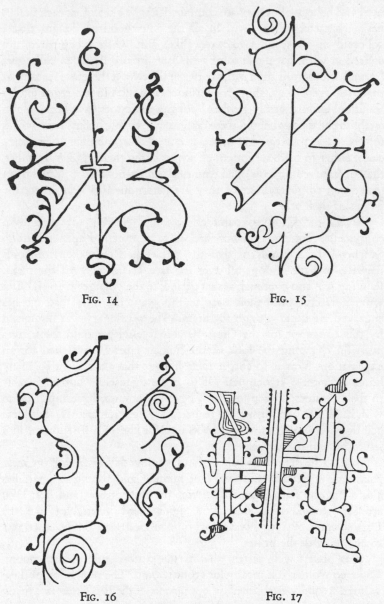

FIG. 14   FIG. 15

FIG. 16   FIG. 17

More motifs used in body-painting

nets, and helices—but they are combined in such a way that each design has a character of its own. In all the four hundred designs that I collected in 1935, no two were alike. But when I compared my collection with that made some years later by my Brazilian colleague, I found widespread similarities between the two. It therefore seems that the artists' repertory, though enormous, is none the less regulated by tradition. Unfortunately, neither I nor my successors have been able to establish the theory behind these designs; native informants have words for the basic patterns, but when it comes to combining them, they claim either to have forgotten, or not to know them. Either, in short, they operate on the basis of an empirical 'know-how' transmitted from generation to generation; or they are determined to keep intact the secrets of their art.

Today the Caduveo paint one another entirely for their own enjoyment; but the practice had once a much deeper meaning. Sanchez-Labrador tells us that the nobles had only their foreheads painted; to have it done all over the face was a mark of the plebs. Painting was also confined, at that period, to the younger women. 'Old women rarely waste their time in this way: the lines that age has engraved are quite enough for them.' The missionary was disquieted by this contempt for the Creator's activity: why should the natives insist on changing the look of the human face? He searched for an explanation. Was it to forget their hunger that they spent so many hours over these arabesques? Or to make themselves unrecognizable to their enemies? Deception does, beyond question, have much to do with it. Why? The missionary realizes, however reluctantly, that these paintings have a primordial importance for the Indians and are, in a sense, 'an end in themselves'.

And so he reproached them for spending day after day on these paintings, neglectful meanwhile of hunting and fishing and families alike. But the natives would answer the missionaries and say: 'You are the stupid ones, since you don't paint yourselves like the Eyiguayeguis.' Painting was a part of manhood: not to be painted was to be one with the brutes.

It is pretty well certain that if the custom still persists among Caduveo women it is mostly for erotic reasons. The reputation of these women is solidly established on both banks of the Rio Paraguay; many half-castes and Indians from other tribes have settled and married in Nalike. The painting of face and body may explain this attraction; certainly they reinforce and symbolize it. The delicate and subtle

FIG. 18. Drawings made by a young
Caduvean boy

contours are no less sensitive than those of the face itself; sometimes the one accentuates the other, sometimes it runs counter to it; in both cases the effect is deliciously provocative. As a result of this, as it were, pictorial surgery, art secures a sort of claw-hold upon the human body. When Sanchez-Labrador complains that the Indians prize 'an artificial ugliness above the graces of Nature' he very soon contradicts himself, saying a line or two later that even the most beautiful tapestries cannot compare with these paintings. Never, it seems, have the erotic effects of make-up been so consciously and so systematically exploited.

FIG. 19.   Another drawing by the same artist

The Mbaya manifested in their face-paintings that abhorrence of Nature which made them resort so freely to abortion and infanticide. Their art revealed, in fact, a sovereign contempt for the clay of which we are made; art, for them, comes dangerously close to sin. As a Jesuit and a missionary, Sanchez-Labrador showed an exceptional perspicacity when he divined the presence of the demon in these paintings. He himself underlined the Promethean aspect of this savage art when he described how the natives would cover the body with star-shaped motifs: 'Each Eyiguayegui sees himself,' he wrote, 'as an Atlas who bears, not only upon his hands and shoulders but upon his whole body, the weight of a clumsily charted universe.' And this may, indeed,

FIG. 20.   Two face-paintings, notable for the motif formed by two opposed spirals which represent—and are applied on—the upper lip

FIG. 21. Design painted on leather

explain the exceptional character of Caduveo art: that it makes it possible for Man to refuse to be made in God's image.

The recurrence in these paintings of lines, spirals, and curlicues must inevitably remind us of the iron- and stucco-work of Spanish baroque. Perhaps we are, in effect, faced with a style that has been borrowed from the Caduveo's conquerors? They did undoubtedly appropriate certain themes: we know of more than one example of this. In 1857, when a warship, the *Maracanha*, made its first appearance on the Paraguay a party of Indians paid her a visit; and on the following day they were seen to have drawn anchors all over their bodies. One Indian had gone so far as to cover all the upper half of his body with a complete representation of a white officer, complete with buttons, stripes, belt, and coat-tails. This only proves that the Mbaya were already habitual and accomplished painters. Their curvilinear style has few counterparts in pre-Colombian America, but it offers analogies with archaeological documents which have been discovered in more than one part of the continent: and some of these pre-date the discovery by several centuries. Hopewell, in the valley of Ohio, and the more recent caddo pottery in the Mississippi valley; Santarem and Marajo, at the mouth of the Amazon; Chavin, in Peru. This dispersion is in itself a sign of antiquity.

The real problem lies elsewhere. Any student of the Caduveo designs will soon realize that their originality does not lie in the elementary patterns, which are simple enough to have been invented rather than borrowed (probably they were both invented and borrowed); it lies in the combination of these initial patterns—in the result, that is to say—the finished work. But the compositional procedures are so systematic and so fastidious that they go far beyond any suggestions, in the same field, that the Indians might have picked up by way of European Renaissance art. Whatever the point of departure may have been, the development was so extraordinary that it can only be explained by features native to the Indians themselves.

In an earlier essay I tried to define some of these by comparing the art of the Caduveo with the analogous art of societies elsewhere: archaic China, the north-west coast of Canada and Alaska, New Zealand. My hypothesis here is a different one; but one that completes, rather than contradicts, my earlier suggestions.

As I noted then, Caduveo art is marked by a dualism: the men sculpt, the women paint; and whereas the sculpture is, for all its stylizations, representative and naturalistic, the paintings are non-representative. Painting alone concerns me here, but I should like to emphasize that this dualism may be found elsewhere and on more than one level.

Two styles are current among the women painters: abstraction and the decorative purpose are at the root of both. The one is angular and geometrical, the other free and curvilinear. Most compositions are based upon an orderly mingling of the two. One may be used, for example, for the border, or the frame, and the other for the central panel. Where pottery is concerned the combination is still more striking: the decoration of the neck being curvilinear, and that of the belly geometrical, or vice versa. The curvilinear style is more usually adopted for face-painting, geometry being reserved for the body; though at times each region may be adorned with a combination of the two.

In every case other principles may be seen to have been integrated; these always go in pairs. An initially linear contour may later, for instance, be 'blocked in' here and there. In most designs, two themes are to be found in alternation. And as a rule the subject and background are interchangeable, so that the design may be read in either of two ways: a positive and a negative. Often, too, principles of symmetry and asymmetry are put into practice simultaneously: the design being not so much cut up or divided off as gyronny or quartered, tranché or parted per bend sinister. (The heraldic terms are, in fact, very apt, since these principles have much in common with those of the escutcheon.)

Take an example: the simple-seeming body-painting which I reproduce opposite. It consists of undulating and accosted pales which mark out spindle-shaped fields whose centre is occupied (one to each field) by a small charge. This description is deceptive: let us look more closely. It may give some idea of the general appearance of the drawing, once it is completed. But the draughtswoman did not begin by tracing her wavy ribbons, and then go on to ornament each interstice with a charge. Her method was different, and more complicated. She worked like a paver, building up row after successive row with the help of identical elements. Each element is made up in the following way: a section of ribbon, made up of the concave part of one band and the convex part of the one next to it; a spindle-shaped field; a charge in the centre of that field. These elements overlap, disconnectedly, and it is only at the end that the whole design achieves a stability which at once confirms and denies the dynamic principle which has governed its execution.

The Caduveo style presents, us, therefore, with a whole series of complications. The dualism, to begin with, which recurs over and over again, on one level or another, like a hall of mirrors: men and women, painting and sculpture, abstraction and representation, angle and curve, geometry and arabesque, neck and belly, symmetry and asymmetry, border and centrepiece, figure and ground. But these antitheses are glimpsed *after* the creative process, and they have a static character. The dynamic of art—the way, i.e. in which the motifs are imagined and carried out—cuts across this fundamental duality at every level. The primary themes, initially disarticulated, are later blended into secondary themes which establish a sort of provisional unity among fragments borrowed from their predecessors, and these in their turn are juxtaposed in such a way that the original unity reappears, as if as the result of a conjuring-trick. And then the complicated decorations which have been arrived at by this means are themselves once again cut out and brought face to face with one another by means of escutcheon-like quarterings.

We may now understand why the Caduveo style strikes us as a subtler variant of that which we employ in our playing-cards. Each of

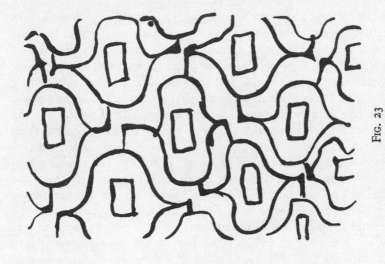

FIG. 23

FIG. 22

Body-painting: on the left as recorded by Boggiani in 1895 and on the right as recorded by the author in 1935

our card-designs corresponds to a twofold necessity and must assume a double function. It must be an independent object, and it must serve for the dialogue—or the duel—in which two partners meet face to face. It must also play the role which is assigned to each card, in its capacity as a member of the pack, in the game as a whole. Its vocation is a complicated one, therefore: and it must satisfy demands of more than one sort—symmetrical, where its functions are concerned, asymmetrical where its role is in question. The problem is solved by the use of a design which is symmetrical but yet lies across an oblique axis. (An entirely asymmetrical design would have sufficed for the role but not for the function; and vice versa in the case of a design that was wholly symmetrical.) Once again we have a complicated situation based upon two contradictory forms of duality, and resulting in a compromise brought about by a secondary opposition between the ideal axis of the object itself and the ideal axis of the figure which it represents. But in order to reach this conclusion we have had to go beyond the plane of stylistic analysis: we have had, in short, to ask: 'What is this object for?' And we have to ask the same question of Caduveo art.

We have replied in part to that question: or, rather, the Indians have replied for us. The face-paintings confer upon the individual his dignity as a human being: they help him to cross the frontier from Nature to culture, and from the 'mindless' animal to the civilized Man. Furthermore, they differ in style and composition according to social status, and thus have a social function.

Important as it is to grasp these facts, they will not in themselves account for the originality of Caduveo art; at most, they explain to us why it exists. Let us proceed with our analysis of Caduveo society: the Mbaya were divided into three castes, each dominated by preoccupations of social usage. For the nobles, and to a certain extent for the warriors also, prestige was the fundamental problem. Early travellers have described how they were paralysed by the necessity of not losing face, and above all of not marrying beneath them. Such a society would be in grave danger of segregation. Willingly or of necessity each caste tended to turn in upon itself, so that the cohesion of Society as a whole was threatened. In particular the endogamy of the castes and the multiplication of hierarchical nuances would make it very difficult to arrange unions of a kind which conformed to the concrete necessities of collective life. Only thus can we explain the paradox of a society which has a horror of procreation, and is so afraid of the risks of

Fig. 25

Fig. 24

Two face- and body-painting motifs

FIG. 26. A face-painting

internal misalliance that it practises a sort of racialism in reverse, and makes a regular practice of incorporating enemies and foreigners within its ranks.

In these conditions it is significant that, on the north-east and south-west extremes of the enormous territory controlled by the Mbaya, we come upon two almost identical forms of social organization, great as is the distance which separates them from one another. The Paraguayan Guana and the Bororo of the Mato Grosso had (and in the latter case still have) a hierarchical structure very similar to that of the Mbaya; they were, or are, divided into three classes which seem to have stood, in the past at any rate, for different social statuses. These classes were hereditary and endogamous. Yet the dangers which I have mentioned above were avoided in both cases by a vertical division which, in the case of the Bororo, also cut across the classes. Members of one class could not marry members of another, but in each class the members of one moiety were, on the contrary, compelled to marry members of the other moiety. It would therefore be fair to say that asymmetry of class was balanced, in a sense, by symmetry of 'moieties'.

Should we envisage this complicated structure as a systematized whole? Possibly: though it is also tempting to separate the classes from the moieties and regard one as more ancient than the other; arguments for this can be adduced from both sides.

But what interests us here is a question of quite a different kind. Brief as has been my description of the Guana and Bororo societies, it clearly suggests that on the sociological level these two societies have a structure comparable to that which we have detected, on the level of style, in Caduveo art. There is, in each case, a double antithesis. In the first instance a ternary and asymmetrical organization is opposed to one that is binary and symmetrical. In the second, social mechanisms based on reciprocity are opposed to social mechanisms based on hierarchy. In the effort to remain faithful to these contradictory principles the social group divides and subdivides itself into allied and opposed sub-groups. Just as an escutcheon is a symbolical assembly of prerogatives derived from many separate lines of descent, so is Society cut open, cut across, divided, and partitioned. As we shall see later, the organization of the ground-plan of a Bororo village is comparable to that of a Caduveo drawing.

It is as if the Caduveo and Bororo had been confronted with a contradiction in their social structure and managed to resolve or disguise it by strictly sociological methods. Perhaps they had had the moiety-system before they came under Mbaya influence: in that case the solution lay ready at hand. Or perhaps they invented or borrowed it later, when as a provincial people they lacked the standoffishness of the true aristocrat. Other hypotheses could be advanced. Anyway the Mbaya never adopted this solution: either because they did not know of it (though I find this hard to believe) or because it was incompatible with their fanaticism. So they were never lucky enough to resolve their contradictions, or to disguise them with the help of institutions artfully devised for that purpose. On the social level the remedy was lacking—unless they deliberately set their faces against it—but it never went completely out of their grasp. It was within them, never objectively formulated, but present as a source of confusion and disquiet. In fact, they dreamed of it: had they done so directly, it would have gone counter to their prejudices; but transposed, and present only in their art, it seemed harmless. The mysterious charm and (as it seems at first) the gratuitous complication of Caduveo art may well be a phantasm created by a society whose object was to give symbolical form to the institutions which it might have had in reality, had interest and superstition not stood in the way. Great indeed is the fascination of this culture, whose dream-life was pictured on the faces and bodies of its queens, as if, in making themselves up, they figured a Golden Age that they would never know in reality. And yet, as they stand naked before us, it is as much the mysteries of that Golden Age as their own bodies that are unveiled.

PART VI

The Bororo

18 *Gold and Diamonds*

Corumba, the gateway to Bolivia, lies facing Porto Esperança, on the right bank of the Rio Paraguay. Jules Verne might have imagined it: perched as it is on the top of a limestone cliff that overhangs the river. One or two little paddle-steamers (two storeys of cabins, a hull low in the water, a flimsy smoke-stack) were tied up, canoes all around them, to the quay whence mounted the path to Corumba. One or two buildings, at the outset, seemed disproportionately large: the Customs house, for instance, and the arsenal, which harked back to the time when the Rio Paraguay was the precarious frontier between States that had recently acquired their independence and were in a ferment of youthful ambition. And, also in those distant times, a mass of traffic had once passed up and down the river between Rio de la Plata and the interior.

When the path got to the top of the cliff it ran along its crest for a couple of hundred yards and then turned sharply to the right. Corumba was revealed: a long street of low, flat-roofed houses, roughly painted in white or beige. At the far end was a square where grass grew among *casalpiniae* that had acid green leaves and orange flowers; beyond, the stony countryside stretched as far as the hills that closed off the horizon.

There was only one hotel, and it was always full. A few rooms were to be had in private houses; but these were on the ground floor, damp with the dampness of the marshes, and haunted by bugs that turned the traveller into a modern variant of an early Christian martyr. The food, too, was execrable: the countryside being too poor, or too little cultivated, to meet the needs of the two or three thousand people—sedentary workers or travellers—who made up the population of Corumba. Prices were absurdly high, and the town had a look of frenzied animation which contrasted with the flat, deserted, spongy hinterland on the far side of the river. The atmosphere of Corumba was such as must have reigned, a century earlier, in the pioneer towns of California or the Far West. In the evenings the entire population would assemble on the cliff-road. The young men would sit, legs dangling, on the balustrade, while the girls filed past, whispering, in groups of three or four. It had an air of ritual, this solemn pre-nuptial parade, in the light of the flickering electric lamps, with three hundred miles of marshland all around and ostrich and boa to be found even at the gates of the town.

Corumba is, as the crow flies, a bare two hundred and fifty miles from Cuiaba. I witnessed the development of air travel between the two towns—from the little four-seaters that bumped their way across in a matter of two or three hours to the twelve-seater Junkers of 1938–9. But in 1935 the river was still the only means of travel, and the two hundred and fifty miles were doubled by the river's meanderings. During the rainy season it took eight days to reach the capital of the State; in the dry season it could be three weeks, so often did the steamers run aground, for all their shallow draught. Whole days were lost in the attempt to refloat the vessel, with the motor pulling its hardest on a cable tied to a stout tree on the bank. In the office of the shipping company a beguiling poster was to be found: on the opposite page is a rough transcription of its lay-out and style. The reality, needless to say, was very different.

And yet what a marvellous journey that was! Passengers were few: cattle-farmers and their families on their way back to their animals; a few Lebanese commercial travellers; some soldiers, garrison-bound; and a sprinkling of provincial officials. No sooner were these people on board than they changed, one and all, into the clothes which, for them, corresponded to a beach-suit: striped pyjamas (silk ones, where dandies were in question), through which much of their hairy persons could be glimpsed, and slippers. Twice a day we all sat down to a never-changing menu: a dish of rice, another of black beans, and a third of parched manioc flour; with these there went invariably a helping of beef, fresh or dried. This was called *feijoada*, after the *feijão*, or bean. To this daily pabulum my companions brought a critical sense as keen—and this was saying much—as their appetites. The *feijoada* would be pronounced *muito boa* (first-class) one day and *muito ruim* (disgusting) the next. When it came to the dessert (cream cheese and fruit jelly, eaten together from the sharp end of the knife) their vocabulary was even more restricted: it either was, or was not, *bem doce* (sweet enough).

IS YOUR EXCELLENCY PLANNING A TRIP?

If so, be sure to take the incomparable

S.S. CIDADE DE CORUMBA

of the **M . . . River Navigation Co.** A steamship equipped with first-quality furnishings, commodious bathrooms, electric light, running water in all cabins and all the conveniences of Gentlemen's Service Apartments.

The fastest and most comfortable ship on the Cuiaba–Corumba–Porto Esperança line.

By joining the **S.S. CIDADE DE CORUMBA** here in Corumba, or at Porto Esperança, Your Excellency will reach his destination **THREE DAYS OR MORE EARLIER** than with any other vessel. And as the **TIME** factor is of importance in activities such as yours, you will surely wish to patronize the ship which is fastest and has more comforts to offer.

STEAMSHIP GUAPORE

THE BETTER TO SERVE ITS HONOURED CLIENTS, the Company has just renovated the excellent steamship **GUAPORE,** moving the dining-room to the upper deck and so endowing the vessel with a magnificent **DINING SALOON** and a large area for the promenading of the distinguished passengers.

Choose, therefore, without hesitation the fast steamers **CIDADE DE CORUMBA** and **GUAPORE.**

Every twenty miles or so the ship stopped to take on wood; and if need be the halt was extended to two or three hours while the cook went off into the fields, lassoed a cow, cut its throat, and (with the help of the crew) skinned it. It was then hoisted on board and we set off again with several days' guaranteed provision of fresh meat.

For the rest of the time the ship steamed quietly along the narrow, winding river; it was said to be 'negotiating' the *estirões*—counting off, that is to say, the sections of the river which were bounded by corners sharp enough to cut off the view ahead. Sometimes the river wound round itself so completely that nightfall would find the ship only a few dozen yards from where it had started in the morning. Often, too, the boat would brush against the branches of the half-submerged forest that hung over the bank, while the sound of the engine made birds beyond number take wing: *araras* in a flash of blue, red, and gold; cormorants whose long necks were like winged snakes; parrots and parakeets whose loud cries were sufficiently like those of human beings for us to call them 'inhuman'. Prolonged study of a spectacle so monotonous and so near at hand induced in the traveller a sort of torpor, and only rarely was our interest quickened by something more unusual: a pair of deer or tapirs, swimming across the river; a *cascavel* (rattle-snake) or a *giboya* (python) as it came wriggling to the surface, light as a straw; or a group of *jacarés*—inoffensive crocodiles that we soon wearied of despatching with a carbine bullet straight in the eye. Fishing for *piranhas* was more eventful: somewhere along the river was a large *saladeiro* where meat hung drying from a sort of gibbet. Bones were strewn on the ground beneath wooden racks; on these lay the purplish remains above which vultures hovered. The river was stained red for several hundred yards below the slaughter-house. We had only to throw a line overboard and, before even the unbaited hook had reached the surface of the water, *piranha* after *piranha*, drunk with blood, would leap forward and hang its golden lozenge on the hook. But the fisherman had to be careful how he handled his catch; the *piranha* can sever a finger at a single snap.

After the junction of the São Lourenço—on the upper reaches of which we shall shortly travel to encounter the Bororo—the pantanal disappeared. The landscape to either side became one of grassy savannah. More houses began to appear, and herds could be seen grazing.

There was not much to draw Cuiaba to the traveller's attention: a paved ramp that ran down into the water, and above it the silhouette of the former arsenal. Thence a road bordered with countrified houses ran for more than a mile to the square where the cathedral stood, pink and white, between two rows of palm-trees. To the left, the Bishop's palace; to the right, the Governor's. At the corner of the main street was the inn—the only one, at that time—kept by a fat Lebanese.

I've described Goyaz; and if I were to go on about Cuiaba I could only repeat myself. The site is not so beautiful, but the town has the same sort of charm, with its austere houses, half cottage, half palace in style. As the site is sharply accidented the upper windows usually have an extended view: white houses roofed with orange titles, the fronds and foliage of the gardens, or *quintaes*. Around the central L-shaped square a network of alleyways reminds one of the colonial cities of the eighteenth century. Follow any one of them and you will come upon a patch of dead ground that serves for the caravan-trains, or an adumbrated avenue of mangoes and banana-trees with one or two mud huts among them; and then, in no time at all, the open country, with pasturing herds of oxen on their way to or from the *sertão*.

Cuiaba was founded in the middle of the eighteenth century. Towards 1720 Paulist explorers—*bandeirantes* was their name—penetrated the region for the first time and set up a little outpost, with a handful of colonists, only a few miles from where Cuiaba stands today. The territory was inhabited by *Cuxipo* Indians, some of whom agreed to help till the soil. One day a colonist, the aptly named Miguel Sutil, sent a small party of Indians to look for wild honey. They came back that same evening with their hands full of nuggets of gold that they had picked up off the ground. Sutil didn't waste a moment, but set off at once, with a companion named Barbudo—'the bearded one'—to the area in question. And within a month they got together five tons of gold-nuggets.

And so it's not surprising that parts of the country round Cuiaba look like a battlefield. Mound after mound, covered with brushwood and rough grass, bears witness to ancient frenzies. Even today a Cuiabano has been known to turn up a nugget of gold in his vegetable-patch. Gold is, in fact, always present in paillette form. The beggars of Cuiaba are 'gold-diggers' in the literal sense, and you can see them at work in the bed of the river that runs through the lower town. A day's exertions will bring them just enough to buy a meal, and in many shops in Cuiaba you can still find the little pair of scales which measures off a spoonful of powdered gold against a cut of meat or a pound of rice. Any heavy rainfall will send the water tumbling down the ravines, and at such times you will see the children rush out, ball of wax in hand, and plunge it into the current in the hope that tiny sparkling particles of gold will stick to it. The Cuiabanas claim that a rich seam of gold passes beneath their city at a depth of several yards; just below the modest premises of the Bank of Brazil there is more gold, they say, than is ever to be found in its old-fashioned safes.

Cuiaba has retained from its days of glory a style of life that is slow and ceremonious. The traveller's first day is taken up entirely with comings and goings across the square which separates the hotel from the palace of government. First, he leaves a card in token of his arrival; an hour later the compliment will be returned by the A.D.C., a moustached constable; after the siesta which paralyses the entire city from noon till four in the afternoon the traveller pays his respects to the Governor. The anthropologist receives a polite but unenthusiastic welcome. The Indians are, for the Governor, an irritating reminder that he himself has fallen out of favour, politically speaking, and been banished to a remote and backward area. The Bishop feels much the same; but I mustn't suppose, he tells me, that the Indians are as stupid and aggressive as one might think; why, one Bororo woman had actually been converted! And the Diamantino brothers had managed, after an unending struggle, to turn three Paressis into quite presentable carpenters! And as far as scholarship was concerned the missionaries had already taken note of all that was worth preserving. Did I realize that the unlettered officials of the Protection Service wrote 'Bororo' with an accent on the last vowel, whereas Father So-and-So had established a good twenty years earlier that it should fall on the middle one? And the fact that the Bororo knew of the Deluge was a sure sign that the Lord did not mean them to remain damned till the end of time. I was free to go among them, of course; but he did hope that I would do nothing to jeopardize the Fathers in their work. No trivial presents! No necklaces or hand-mirrors! Nothing but an axe or two, to remind those lazy creatures that work was sacred.

These formalities once discharged, one could get on to serious matters. Day after day would go by in the back-rooms of the Lebanese traders—*turcos*, they were called—who were half wholesalers and half usurers. Their stock of hardware, textiles, and medical goods was destined to dozen upon dozen of relations, clients, and protégés, who would buy on credit, take a canoe or a few oxen, and extort what they could from customers marooned deep in the bush or in some distant bend of the river. Life was as hard for the travelling trader as it was for his victim; but at least the trader could afford to retire after twenty or thirty years.

Or I would spend hour upon hour at the baker's, while he was preparing *bolachas* by the sackful. (*Bolachas* are loaves made with un-leavened flour that has been thickened with fat; they are hard as stone, but the oven gives them a marrowy quality, and when they have been shaken into small pieces on the road and impregnated with the sweat of the oxen they finish up as a form of food for which it is difficult to find a name: and as rancid, certainly, as the dried meat from the butcher.) Our butcher at Cuiaba was a natural dreamer, by the way, and all his thoughts were fixed upon an ambition unlikely ever to be realized: that a circus should visit Cuiaba in his lifetime. He would have loved to see an elephant: '*So* much meat! . . .'

And then there were two Frenchmen, the brothers B. Though Corsican by origin, they had lived in Cuiaba for a good many years: why, they didn't say. They spoke their mother-tongue with a distant, sing-song hesitation. They had been egret-hunters before turning to the garage trade; and they described their technique, which was to lay on the ground a series of cornets made of white paper. The egret, fascinated by a whiteness as dazzling as his own, would come down and thrust his beak into one of the cornets; thus blinded, he offered an easy prey, and during the mating season his beautiful feathers could be plucked out of the living flesh. Many a wardrobe in Cuiaba was full of such feathers, for which there was no longer any demand. The two brothers then turned to diamond-hunting. Eventually they set up a garage and specialized in fitting out heavy lorries with merchandise. These they launched as once men launched galleons across uncharted seas; both lorry and cargo might end up at the bottom of a ravine or a river, but there was also the possibility that they might get safely to their desti-nation, in which case a profit of four hundred per cent would make up for earlier losses.

I often travelled by lorry across the Cuiaba territory. On the day before departure we took on a special provision of petrol, bearing in mind that we needed enough for the entire journey from base back to base and that most of it would be covered in first or second gear. Next we packed our food, and our camping materials, in such a way that the passengers could take shelter in case of a rainstorm. On the inner walls of the lorry we hung all our jacks of tools, together with planks and rope to improvise a bridge where necessary. At dawn on the next day we climbed the cargo, as we might have climbed a camel, and took

our seats. The lorry began its quavering progress. By midday our
difficulties had begun: the road was flooded or swampy and had to be
paved with logs. I've spent three whole days in that way: laying and re-
laying a 'floor' of logs just twice the lorry's length until at last we were
out of the wet. Or else we ran into sand and had to stuff leaves and
branches under the wheels. Even where the bridges were intact we had
to unload everything, before the lorry could be coaxed across the
rickety structure, and then to reload on the far side. Where a bush-
fire had destroyed the bridge we set up our camp and built another.
But as we couldn't leave it there—the planks were too precious—we
had to dismantle the whole structure before going on our way. Finally,
we had to reckon with the major rivers: these could be crossed only on
rude ferry-boats made up of three canoes laid side by side. The lorry,
even unloaded, weighted these right down to the gunwale; and often
we got to the other side only to find that the bank was too steep, or
too muddy, for us to climb it. In such cases we had to improvise a
'road', sometimes for hundreds of yards, until we came to a better
landing-point, or a ford.

The men whose profession it was to drive these lorries were on the
road for weeks and even for months on end. They worked in pairs:
the driver and his assistant, the one at the wheel, the other on the
running-board, looking out for trouble. They had always a carbine to
hand, for often a tapir or a deer would pull up, intrigued rather than
frightened, in their path. They would shoot on sight and, if the shot
went well, they pulled up for the rest of the day. The prize had to be
skinned, gutted, and cut up into thin strips of meat, much as one peels
a potato in a spiral right through to the centre. These strips of meat
were then rubbed with a mixture, kept always ready for this purpose,
of pepper, salt, and crushed garlic. They were then laid in the sun for
several hours, and on the following day, and for several days after, the
process was repeated. The resulting *carne de sol* was not so delicious as
the *carne de vento*, which was dried on a tall stick in the wind, when sun
was lacking; also it did not keep so long.

These superb drivers led a strange existence: ready at any moment
to carry out the most delicate repairs, and ready too to improvise the
very road on which they were to drive, they sometimes had to stick
it out for weeks on end in the bush at the point where their lorry came
to grief. Eventually one of their rivals would pass that way and take
the news to Cuiaba; and at Cuiaba they would order the missing part
from Rio or São Paulo. Meanwhile the driver and his mate would

camp out, and hunt, and do their washing, and sleep it all off, and have patience. The best of my own drivers was a fugitive from justice; he never mentioned what he had done, but people in Cuiaba knew of it. No one ever gave him away, however; when it came to a dangerous run he was irreplaceable, and by the daily venturing of his own he life was thought to have paid, and paid liberally, for the life he had taken.

It was still dark when we left Cuiaba at four in the morning. The eye guessed at the churches, stucco-decorated over every inch of their height; the lorry bumped its way along the last streets, paved with pebbles and bordered with clipped mango-trees. The natural spacing of the trees gave the savannah an orchardy look, even when we were already well out in the bush, but before long the track became so rough as to leave us in no doubt that we had left 'civilization' behind. Up it climbed, above the river, winding along stony slopes with often a ravine or a muddy river-bed, overgrown with *capoeira*, to call for our attention. When we had climbed to a certain height we noticed a long thin pinkish shape on the horizon. It couldn't be the dawn, because it never varied in shape or texture, and yet for a long time we couldn't believe it was quite real. But after some four hours on the road we cleared a rocky hillside and were confronted with a vaster, more explicit perspective; from north to south a red wall ran six to nine hundred feet above the green hills. To the north it gradually subsided into the flatlands; but towards the south, where we were approaching, certain details were discernible. What had previously seemed unbroken was seen to have subsidiary features; narrow platforms, jutting prows of rock, balconies. Redoubts and defiles diversified the long barrier of stone. It would take the lorry several hours to climb the ramp—uncorrected, almost, by Man—which ends at the upper edge of the *chapada* of the Mato Grosso and allows us to penetrate the six or seven hundred miles of plateau, the *chapadão*, which runs very gently down towards the north and ends in the basin of the Amazon.

A new world was revealed to us. Rough grass, milky-green in colour, never quite concealed the underlying sand, itself white, pinkish, or ochre, which had resulted from the superficial decomposition of the underlying sandstone. The vegetation consisted merely of a few scattered shrubs, knotted and gnarled, which were protected from the dry season, which lasts for seven months of the year, by a thick bark, varnished leaves, and prickles. Yet a few days' rain could transform this desert of a savannah into a garden; the grass turned bright green and trees were soon covered with white and mauve flowers. But the

dominant impression remained one of immensity. So uniform is the
texture of the country and so gradual its inclination that the horizon
is pushed back for ten or twenty miles. You can motor for hours in
a landscape that never changes; today's prospect and yesterday's are
so alike, in fact, that memory and perception are blended in an
obsession with immobility. Such is the uniformity of the scene, such
the absence of landmarks, that one ends by mistaking the horizon-line
for cloud as it hangs high up in the sky. Yet the scene is too fantastic to
be called monotonous. From time to time the lorry traverses a watercourse which does not so much cross the plateau—since it has no banks
—as inundate it at certain seasons of the year. It is as if this area—
one of the most ancient in the world: a still-intact fragment of the
continent of Gondwana which once united Brazil to Africa—were still
too young for its rivers to have had time to hollow out their beds.

In European landscape it is the form which is exact and the light
which is diffused. Here the 'traditional' roles of earth and sky are
reversed; clouds build up into forms of extreme extravagance, whereas
the earth below remains milk-white and undefined. Shape and volume
are the sky's prerogatives; the earth is formless and insubstantial.

One evening we called a halt not far from a *garimpo*, or colony of
diamond-hunters. Before long shadowy figures appeared round our
fire: *garimpeiros* in rags who drew forth little tubes of bamboo and
emptied their contents into our hands: rough diamonds, these, which
they hoped to sell to us. But the B. brothers had told me a good deal
about the ways of the *garimpo* and I knew that there could be no
question, in all this, of a bargain. For the *garimpo* has its unwritten laws
and they are faithfully observed.

These men divide up into two categories: adventurers and men on
the run. The second group is the more numerous, and this is doubtless
why defections from the *garimpo* are few. Those who 'got there first'
have control of the river-beds in which the work is done. As they have
not resources enough to wait for the 'killing'—a rarity, in any event
—they organize themselves in bands. Each of these is led by a self-
styled 'Captain' or 'Engineer'; this leader has to have enough capital
to arm his men, equip them with the essentials of their trade—iron
sieve, wash-trough, diver's helmet, air-pump—and, above all, feed
them regularly. In exchange his men undertake not to sell his finds
except to authorized dealers (themselves working in association with
the big Dutch or British diamond-firms) and to share the proceeds with
their leader.

If they have to be armed, it is not only to ward off the menace of rival bands. Until quite lately, and sometimes even now, it was to keep the police at bay. The diamond-zone formed, in fact, a state within the State, and the one was often at war with the other. In 1935 we constantly heard of the war waged by the Engineer Morbeck and his bravoes, the *valentões*, against the State Police of the Mato Grosso. This had ended in a compromise. It must be said in defence of the rebels that the *garimpeiro* who was taken prisoner by the police rarely reached Cuiaba alive. One famous leader, Captain Arnaldo, was captured with his second-in-command. They were tied by the neck at the top of a tall tree, with their feet resting on a little board; and when they overbalanced from exhaustion they were left to hang.

So strictly are the 'laws' observed that at Lageado or Poxoreu, the centres of the *garimpo*, you can often see, in the inns, a table covered with diamonds that have been momentarily left behind by their owners. No sooner is a stone found than it is identified by its shape and colour and size. Such is the exactitude of these details, and such their emotional charge, that even years afterwards the lucky finder can distinguish each diamond from its fellows. 'When I looked at it,' one of my visitors said to me, 'it was as if the Holy Virgin had dropped a tear into my hand . . .' But the stones are not always so pure: often they are found in their attle and it's impossible to judge of their eventual value. The authorized buyer makes known his price (he is said to 'weigh' the diamond) and that price is final. Only when the grinder gets to work will the upshot of the speculation be known.

I asked if people didn't try to evade the regulations. 'Of course. But it never works.' A diamond offered to another buyer, or offered behind the leader's back, will be immediately 'burnt': *queimado*. That is to say that the buyer will offer a derisory price; and that price will get lower and lower with each subsequent attempt. So it is that the *garimpeiro* who tries to break the law can end by dying of hunger with a diamond in his hand.

Once the diamonds are sold it's a very different matter. Fozzi the Syrian is said to have grown rich by buying impure diamonds on the cheap, heating them on a Primus stove, and plunging them into a colour-bath; this gives the yellow diamond a more tempting surface and earns it the name of *pintado*, or painted diamond.

Another form of fraud is practised at a higher level. At Cuiaba and at Campo Grande I knew of men who made a living by evading the duty on diamonds destined for export. These professional smugglers were full of stories: of the imitation packets of cigarettes, for instance, that they would toss casually into the bushes if the police caught up with them, and the anxiety with which they would go back to look for them as soon as they were free to do so.

But that particular evening the talk around the camp-fire turned on the everyday hazards to which our visitors were exposed. I learnt, too, something of the picturesque language of the *sertão*. To render the English pronoun *one*, for instance, they have an immensely varied assortment of terms: *o homem*, the man; *o camarada*, the comrade; *o collega*, the colleague; *o negro*, the negro; *o tal*, so-and-so; *o fulano*, the fellow; and so on. As bad luck would have it, someone had just found gold in his wash-trough. This augurs ill for the diamond-hunter, whose only reaction is to throw it back into the river at once. (Weeks of ill fortune must otherwise follow.) Another hunter had been wounded by the tail of a poisonous skate. This was a hurt not easily cured, for he had to find a woman who would consent to undress and pass water on the wound. As the few women in the *garimpo* are nearly all peasant prostitutes this ingenuous remedy often brings in its train a particularly virulent form of syphilis.

It's the legendary 'stroke of luck' that draws these women to the area. The prospector may become rich overnight; and, if he does, his police record will force him to spend the money then and there. That's why the lorries lumber to and fro with their load of superfluous goods. The moment the cargo arrives at the *garimpo* it will be snapped up at no matter what price; not necessity, but the wish to show off, will be the motive. At first light, before we moved off, I called on a *camarada* in his little hut on the edge of the insect-infested river, only to find that he was already at work in his old-fashioned diver's helmet, scraping away at the bed of the stream. The inside of the hut was as wretched and as depressing as its site; but the man's mistress showed me with pride his twelve suits of clothes and her own silk dresses: the termites were feeding well upon them.

The night had been spent in singing and make-believe. Each of those present was invited to do a turn: something remembered, in most cases, from a distant evening at the music-halls. I found the same practice on the Indian frontier when minor officials met to dine together. In both cases monologues were welcome—or 'caricatures', as they were called in India—imitations, that is to say, of the noise made by a typewriter, or a motor-cycle misfiring, or, by strange contrast, a fairy-ballet and, in quick succession, a galloping horse. And, finally, a session of 'funny faces'.

I noted down, from this evening with the *garimpeiros*, some snatches of a traditional lament. It was the song of a private soldier who complained to his corporal of the food served to him; the corporal passes on the complaint to the sergeant, the sergeant to the subaltern, and so on from subaltern to captain, major, colonel, general, emperor. . . . The emperor passes it on to Jesus Christ; and Jesus, instead of passing it to God the Father, takes up his pen and consigns the whole lot of them to hell. Here is a little sample of this song of the *sertão*:

O Soldado . . .

O Offerece . . .

O Sargento que era um homem pertinente
Pego na penna, escreveu pro seu tenente

O Tenente que era homem muito bão
Pego na penna, escreveu pro Capitão

O Capitão que era homem dos melhor'
Pego na penna, escriveu pro Major

O Major que era homem como é
Pega na penna, escreveu pro Coroné'

O Coroné que era homem sem igual
Pego na penna, escreveu pro General

O General que era homem superior
Pego na penna, escreveu pro Imperador

O Imperador . . .
Pego na penna, escreveu pra Jesu' Christo

Jesu' Christo que e filho de Padre Eterno
Pego na penna et mando todos pros inferno

Yet they hadn't really much heart for the fun. The sands had been yielding fewer and fewer diamonds for quite some time, and the area

was infested with malaria, leshmaniosis, and ankylostomiasis. Yellow
fever had begun to appear a year or two before. And where once four
lorries had made the journey every week, there were now, at most,
two or three a month.

The 'road' we were about to embark on had been abandoned when
bush-fires had destroyed all the bridges. It was three years since a
lorry had ventured along it. No one knew at all in what state it
could be; but if we got to São Lourenço we'd be safe. There was a big
garimpo on the river-bank, and we'd find there everything we could
wish for: provisions, men, and canoes to take us as far as the Bororo
villages of the Rio Vermelho, which is a tributary of the São Lourenço.

I really don't know how we got through. The journey remains in
my mind like a confused nightmare; endless camping-out while we cut
our way through a few troublesome yards, loading and unloading, and
points at which we were so exhausted by having to lay the road, plank
by plank and length by length, that we fell asleep on the bare ground,
only to be woken in the middle of the night by a strange persistent
muttering beneath us: that of the termites as they set about the siege of
our clothes. Already they formed a compact, wriggling mass on the
outside of the rubberized capes which served us both as raincoats and
as improvised rugs. But at last the morning came when we trundled
downhill towards the São Lourenço, still thick with valley-mist.
Convinced that we'd accomplished a really extraordinary feat, we
announced our arrival with repeated blasts on our horn. But not so
much as a child came to meet us and all we could find on the river's
edge were four or five deserted huts. Not a soul to be seen: and a rapid
inspection satisfied us that the hamlet had been abandoned.

Our nerves were in shreds after the efforts of the previous few days;
we felt near to despair. Should we give the whole thing up? We decided
to make a last effort before turning back; each of us would start off in
a different direction and explore the outskirts of the village. Towards
evening we returned empty-handed—all save the driver, who had
found a family of fisherfolk and brought back the head of the family
with him. Bearded, and with the unhealthily white skin of someone
who had been too long in the water, he told us that the yellow fever
had come to the village some six months earlier. Those few who
survived it had scattered; but if we made upstream we should find one
or two people and an extra canoe. Would he come with us? Certainly:
for months he and his family had lived entirely on fish from the river.
The Indians would provide him with manioc and tobacco plants, and

we would give him a little money. On this understanding he would guarantee us a supplementary boatman; we could pick him up en route.

I shall have occasion to describe other boat-trips that I remember better than the one in question. I shall therefore say only that it took us eight days to work our way upstream, the river being swollen by the rains. Once when we were lunching on a little sandbank we heard the rustling movement of a boa, seven yards long, that we had awakened with our talk. It took a lot of lead to kill it; for the boa cares nothing for body-wounds: the head alone is vulnerable. When we came to skin it—it took us half a day—we found a dozen little boas, already alive and on the point of being born. The sun killed them off. And then one day, just after we'd shot an *irara*—a sort of badger—we saw two naked forms waving to us from the bank. These were our first Bororo. We tied up and tried to talk to them; all they knew, it seemed, was one word of Portuguese: *fumo*—tobacco—which they pronounced *sumo* (didn't the old missionaries say that the Indians were 'sans foi, sans loi, sans roi', because they could pronounce neither f, nor l, nor r?). They were farmers themselves, in a small way, but their product had none of the concentration of the tobacco, fermented and rolled rope-wise, with which we kept them liberally supplied. We explained to them by gesture that we were making for their village; they indicated that we should be there by nightfall, and that they would go on ahead to give warning of our arrival. They then disappeared in the forest.

Some hours later we pulled up at a bank of clay at the top of which we had seen a few huts. We were welcomed with fits of laughter by a group of naked men, painted red with urucu from their toe-nails to the roots of their hair. They helped us to disembark, grabbed hold of our luggage, and conducted us to a large hut in which several families were living. There the chief of the village made over to us his own corner; and for the duration of our visit he went to live on the opposite bank of the river.

19 *The Good Savage*

So PROFOUND, and yet also so confused, are one's first impressions of a native village whose civilization has remained relatively intact that it is difficult to know in what order to set them down. Among the Kaingang—and the same is true of the Caduveo—extremes of poverty inspire in the traveller an initial weariness and discouragement. But there are societies so vividly alive, so faithful to their traditions, that their impact is disconcertingly strong, and one cannot tell which of the myriad threads which make up the skein is the one to follow. It was among the Bororo that I first encountered a problem of this sort; and when I think back towards it I am reminded of my most recent experience of the kind. This was on the Burmese frontier; I had got to the top of a hill in a Kuki village—a climb that involved hour after hour of scrambling and hauling myself uphill, on slopes churned into slippery mud by the unceasing monsoon-rains. I was exhausted, hungry, thirsty, and disturbed in mind, as well; and yet despite the giddiness that overcame my whole being I had a heightened sense of both form and colour. I was vividly aware, for instance, of houses which, though flimsy, had a majesty of sheer scale about them. Their materials, and the uses to which they were put, were such as we encounter only in dwarfish state. For these houses were not so much built as knotted together, plaited, woven, embroidered, and given a patina by long use. Those who lived in them were not overwhelmed by great blocks of unyielding stone; these were houses that reacted immediately and with great flexibility to their presence, their every movement. The house was, in fact, subject to the householder, whereas with us the opposite is the case. The village served the villagers as a coat of light elastic armour; they wore it as a European woman wears her hats. It was an object of personal adornment on a mammoth scale, and those who built it had been clever enough to preserve something of the spontaneity of natural growth. Leafage and the springing branch were combined, in short, with the exactions of a carefully planned lay-out.

The inhabitants seemed protected in their nakedness by the fronded velvet of the partition-walls and the curtain-fall of the palms. And when they went forth from their houses it was as if they had just slipped out of an enormous dressing-gown of ostrich-feathers. Their houses were caskets lined with down, it might have seemed, and their bodies the jewels within them. They were delicately built, those bodies, and their basic tonalities were heightened with fards. These embellishments were as if designed to set off ornaments yet more splendid: feathers and flowers that served as a background for the broad shining teeth or tusks of jungle animals. It was as if an entire civilization were reaching out in a passion of tenderness towards the forms and the substances and the colours of life; as if it were striving to bedeck the human body with the richest essences of that life and had chosen, from among all its manifestations, those which, whether lasting or fugacious, had that particular quality in the highest degree and were, in one or the other respect, its privileged depositories.

As we proceeded to 'settle in' in the corner of the huge hutment I did not so much take in these things as allow myself to be impregnated by them. Certain details fell into place. The lay-out and the dimensions of the huts were as they had always been, but their architecture had already yielded to neo-Brazilian influences. They were no longer oval, but rectangular in shape; and although roof and walls were still made of palm-leaves laid on a substructure of branches, the two elements were not distinct from one another and the roof, instead of being rounded, was in the shape of an inverted V and came down almost to the ground. Yet the village of Kejara, where we had just arrived (together with the two others which comprised the Rio Vermelho group: Pobori and Jarudori), was one of the few in which the influence of the Salesian Fathers was not yet preponderant. These were the missionaries who, in collaboration with the Protection Service, had managed to put a stop to the conflicts between settlers and Indians. They had also carried out some admirable pieces of ethnographical field-work. (On the Bororo their work is, indeed, the best source available to us, after the earlier studies of Karl von der Steinen.) Unfortunately this went hand in hand with a systematic attempt to exterminate the Indians' culture.

Two things showed to what an extent Kejara was one of the last bastions of independence. It was, to begin with, the residence of the chief of all the Rio Vermelho villages. This haughty and enigmatic figure knew, or pretended to know, no Portuguese. Though attentive to our wants and curious as to the motives of our visit he never communicated with me directly. Considerations of prestige, as much as of language, enjoined him to negotiate through the members of the Council in whose company all his decisions were made.

Secondly, there was at Kejara a native destined to act as my inter-preter, and also as my principal informant. He was about thirty-five years old and spoke tolerable Portuguese. He claimed, in fact, that as a result of the missionaries' exertions he had once been able both to write and to read in Portuguese. The Fathers took such a pride in this that they had sent him to Rome, where he had been received by the Holy Father in person. Apparently they had wanted him, on his return, to get married according to the Christian rites and in disregard of the traditional practices of his tribe. This had led to a spiritual crisis from which he emerged reconverted to the ancient Bororo ideal; and he went to Kejara and had lived there, for the last ten or fifteen years, the life of a savage in every particular. Stark naked, painted scarlet, with his nose and lower lip transpierced by nasal and lip-plugs, the Holy Father's befeathered Indian turned out to be a most remarkable exponent of Bororo sociology.

For the moment we were surrounded by scores of Indians; laughter and horseplay broke out all around us as they discussed the news of our arrival. The Bororo are the tallest and the most finely built of all the Brazilian Indians. They are roundheads, with elongated faces, regular, vigorous features, and the bearing of athletes; they reminded me of certain Patagonian types and it may be that they have affinities with them from the racial point of view. The women as a rule are small and sickly, with irregular features; it is rare to find among them that bodily harmony which distinguishes their men. The high spirits of the men contrasted from the very beginning with the more rebarbative attitude of the other sex. The population seemed, on the whole, to be strikingly healthy in spite of the epidemics which had ravaged the region. There was, however, one leper in the village.

The men were entirely naked, save for a little straw sheath that covered the extremity of the penis. This was kept in position by the foreskin, which was stretched through an opening on the top of the sheath and bulged out over it. Most of them had painted themselves red from head to foot with urucu seeds mashed up with fat. This was

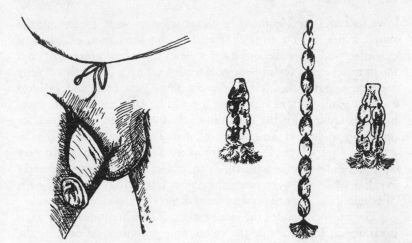

FIG. 27. Penis-sheath   FIG. 28. Lip-plug and ear-rings
                                        of mother-of-pearl and
                                        feather

applied even to their hair, which they wore either at shoulder-length
or cut round at the level of their ears. All looked, therefore, as if they
were wearing helmets. Other paintings were added to this scarlet
ground: a horseshoe pattern in shining black resin often covered the
forehead and came down on either cheek to the level of the mouth.
Sometimes strips of white down were stuck on to shoulders or arms;
or micaceous powder together with pounded mother-of-pearl was
rubbed into shoulders and chest. The women wore a belt of stiff bark
round their waists, and this held in place a white strip of softer bark
which passed between their legs. On top of these was a loincloth of
cotton steeped in urucu, and across the chest and over their shoulders
they wore a double skein of finely plaited cotton. Their costume was
completed by little bands of cotton, drawn tight around ankles, wrists,
and biceps.

Gradually they all went away and we were left to share the hut,
which measured forty feet by fifteen, with a sorcerer and his wife
(silent and hostile, these two), and an old widow who lived on the
charity of relations in huts nearby. Often they neglected her, and she
would sing of her five husbands who had died, one after the other, and
of the happy days when she lacked neither manioc, nor maize, nor fish,
nor game.

Outside men were beginning to sing. Their songs, heavily accented, low, sonorous, and guttural in character, were sung in unison; the simple tunes, their continual repetition, the alternation of solo and ensemble, and the virile and tragic style of the whole proceedings put me in mind of the warrior-songs of some Germanic *Männerbund*. Why were they singing these songs? Because of the *irara*, I was told. We had brought game with us and before it could be eaten an elaborate ritual had to be gone through. The spirit of the *irara* had to be placated, for one thing, and the chase itself consecrated. Too exhausted to behave as a good anthropologist should, I dropped off at nightfall into an uneasy sleep and did not wake again till dawn. Much the same happened every evening while we were there; the nights were given over to the life of religion and the natives slept from dawn till noonday.

The ritual demanded the intervention, at certain moments, of wind instruments; but as a rule the voices were accompanied only by the rattling of calabashes filled with pebbles. It was marvellous to hear what could be done with them: sometimes they would abruptly arrest, or as abruptly unleash, the singers in their singing; sometimes they would fill in a silence with a long-held crescendo or decrescendo; and sometimes, again, they gave the lead to their dancers by alternations of sound and silence so varied in their duration, quality, and intensity that not even our 'star conductors' could have asked for a more flexible or a more responsive instrument. It's not surprising that in former times the natives of other tribes and even the missionaries were convinced that the devil himself was speaking to the Indians through this music. The traditional beliefs in the sound-language of the drum have turned out to be unfounded, but it seems probable that among certain peoples at any rate there did really exist a codified sound-language of an extremely simplified and symbolical sort.

I got up at daybreak to make a tour of the village; and as I went out of the door I stumbled over a pathetic huddle of disfeathered birds. These were the domesticated *araras* which the Indians make pets, the better to pluck out the feathers from the living bird, thus equipping themselves with the raw material of their coiffures. The naked and grounded birds were like chickens ready for the spit, with beaks all the more enormous for the loss of half the body behind them. On the roofs other *araras* were solemnly perching; but these had new-grown feathers and looked like heraldic emblems enamelled with gules and azure.

I was in the middle of a clearing bordered on one side by the river and tapering off, on the others, into the forest; gardens lay hidden on

the very edge of the forest and in the distance, between the trees, I
could glimpse a backcloth of hills patched with red sandstone. The
circumference of the clearing was marked out by huts—twenty-six in
all—identical with my own. They were arranged in a circle, and in the
centre was a hut at least sixty feet long and twenty-five feet wide:
much larger, that is to say, than the others. This was the *baitemannageo*
or men's house. The unmarried men all slept there and in the daytime,
when they were not out hunting or fishing, or engaged in some public
ceremony on the dancing-ground, all the men of the tribe could be
found there. (The dancing-ground was a large oval space immediately
to the west of the bachelors' house.) Women were strictly forbidden to
enter the *baitemannageo*; the perimeter huts were their domain and the
men would go back and forth several times a day along the path
through the brushwood which led from their club to their conjugal
hearth. Seen from the top of a tree, or from a roof, the Bororo village
looked like a cart-wheel, with the bachelors' house as the hub, the
established paths as the spokes, and the family huts to make up the rim.

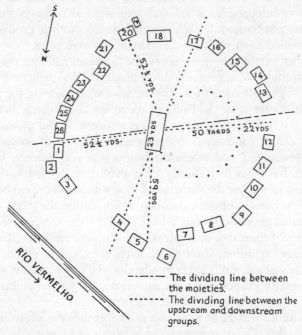

- - - - - - The dividing line between
the moieties.
· · · · · · · The dividing line between the
upstream and downstream
groups.

Fig. 29. Plan of Kejara village

All the villages were laid out in this way at one time, except that their populations were much higher than they usually are today. (At Kejara there were a mere one hundred and fifty, for instance.) Consequently the family houses were laid not in one but in several concentric circles. These circular villages can be found, with certain local variations, among all the tribes of the Gé linguistic group, which occupy the plateau of central Brazil between the Araguaya and the São Francisco rivers. The Bororo are probably the southernmost representatives of this group. But we know that their nearest neighbours to the north, the Cayapo, who live on the right bank of the Rio dos Mortes, build their villages in the same way, as do also the Apinayé, the Sherenté, and the Canella.

So vital to the social and religious life of the tribe is this circular lay-out that the Salesian missionaries soon realized that the surest way of converting the Bororo was to make them abandon their village and move to one in which the huts were laid out in parallel rows. They would then be, in every sense, dis-oriented. All feeling for their traditions would desert them, as if their social and religious systems (these were inseparable, as we shall see) were so complex that they could not exist without the schema made visible in their ground-plans and reaffirmed to them in the daily rhythm of their lives.

To this extent we can absolve the Salesian Fathers: they took infinite trouble to understand this difficult cultural structure and to preserve the recollection of it. Anyone who works among the Bororo must first master what the Fathers have to say about them. But at the same time it was urgently necessary that someone should measure their findings against conclusions drawn in regions where missionaries had not yet penetrated, and where the system was still in force. Guided, therefore, by what had already been published, I tried to get my informants to analyse the structure of their village. We spent our days going from house to house, counting heads, noting the status of each inhabitant, and marking out on the sand of the clearing the ideal boundaries of the elaborate networks, which corresponded respectively to privilege, tradition, hierarchical status, rights, and duties. I shall simplify my account of all this by adapting the compass, as it were, to my immediate purposes: for the natives do not set the points of the compass as precisely as do our geographers.

The circular village of Kejara lies at a tangent to the left bank of the Rio Vermelho. The river flows roughly from east to west. The population is divided into two groups by a line that cuts straight across the village and in theory runs parallel to the river. Those to the north are the Cera; those to the south, the Tugaré. It seems, though it's not absolutely certain, that the first name means 'weak' and the second one 'strong'. Be that as it may, the division is fundamental for two reasons: one, that each individual belongs indissolubly to the same group as his mother; and the other, that he is compelled to marry a member of the other group. If my mother is Cera, I too am Cera, and my wife must be Tugaré.

The women live in, and inherit, the house in which they are born. When he marries, therefore, a male Bororo crosses the clearing, steps over the ideal frontier which separates one moiety from the other, and goes to live on the other side. The men's house lies partly in one moiety, partly in the other, and to this extent 'breaks the fall', as it were. But the 'rules of residence' lay down that the door which gives on to Cera territory shall be called 'the Tugaré door', and vice versa. Men only may use them, of course, and all those who live in the one sector were born in the other.

The married man never feels 'at home' in his wife's house. 'His' house, the one where he was born, and the one he remembers from childhood, lies on the other side of the village. His mother and his sisters, and now his brothers-in-law, live there. But he can go back there whenever he likes and be assured of a warm welcome. And when the atmosphere of his wife's house becomes oppressive—when his brothers-in-law come visiting, for instance—he can always go and sleep in the men's house. There he will find much to remind him of his adolescence. The atmosphere is one of masculine camaraderie, and the religious environment not so strong as to prevent an occasional flirtation with unmarried girls.

The function of the moieties goes far beyond marriage. Rights and duties relate directly to the other moiety, since some must be enjoyed with its help, and others carried out to its benefit. The funeral rites of a Cera, for instance, are performed by a Tugaré, and vice versa. The two moieties are partners, in short, and all social or religious undertakings involve the participation of an 'opposite number', whose role is complementary to one's own. The element of rivalry is not excluded, however: each moiety takes a pride in itself and on occasion is jealous of the other. It's rather as if two football teams, instead of trying to defeat one another, were to vie with each other in demonstrations of generosity.

A second diameter ran from north to south, at right angles to the

first. All those born east of this line were 'upstreamers'; all those born
west of it, 'downstreamers'. We therefore have four sections, as well as
two moieties, and both Cera and Tugaré are subdivided. Unfortunately
no observer has as yet fathomed the role of this second diameter.

The population is also divided into clans. These are groups of
families which consider themselves to be related through the female line
by descent from a common ancestor. This ancestor is mythological in
character and sometimes nobody knows who he is. Let us therefore say
that the members of the clan recognize one another by the fact that
they bear the same name. It is probable that at one time there were
eight clans in all—four for the Cera and four for the Tugaré. But since
then some clans have died out and others have subdivided. The
empirical situation is therefore considerably confused. It remains true,
in any case, that the members of a clan, with the exception of its
married men, all live either in the same hut or in huts adjacent to one
another. Each clan has therefore its own place in the circle of huts and
will be either Cera or Tugaré, upstream or downstream, or yet further
subdivided, should the second diameter happen to pass through the
hutments of the clan in question.

Yet another complication: each clan includes hereditary sub-groups
which also descend through the female line. Each clan has, in fact, its
'red' families and its 'black' families. Formerly, too, each clan was
divided into three classes: higher, middle, and lower. This may be a
reflection, or a transposition, of the hierarchized castes of the Mbaya-
Caduveo; I shall come back to that point. What makes this hypothesis
plausible is the fact that these classes seem to have been endogamous:
a 'higher' person could only marry another 'higher' person (from the
other moiety), and so on. We can only surmise in these matters: such
is the total collapse, demographically speaking, of the Bororo villages.
Now that they have only a hundred or at most two hundred
inhabitants, as against a thousand or more in former times, many
categories are perforce unrepresented. Only the rule of the moieties
is strictly respected, and even there certain upper-class clans may be
exempted; for the rest, the Indians improvise as best they can when
faced with unforeseen situations.

The clan system constitutes, beyond a doubt, the most important of the divisions in which Bororo society seems to take pleasure.
In the general system of marriages between one moiety and the other
the clans were formerly united by special affinities: one of the Cera
clans allying itself, by preference, with a particular Tugaré clan, and

FIG. 30. Wooden club
used in fishing

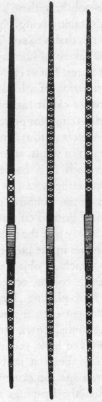

FIG. 31. Bows decorated with
rings of bark in the
fashion characteristic
of the owner's clan

vice versa. The clans also varied in their social standing. The chief of
the village was always chosen from a particular Cera clan, and the title
went in the female line from the maternal uncle to his sister's son. There
were 'rich' clans and 'poor' clans. In what, though, did these differences
of 'wealth' consist?

Our conception of wealth is primarily economic; modest as is the
Bororo's standard of life, there are some who live better than their
fellows. Some are better at hunting or fishing: others, more lucky or
harder working. One or two people at Kejara had the beginnings of
professional status. One man, for instance, was an expert at the making

of stone-polishers; these he exchanged for food, and he seemed to make a comfortable living. Yet these differences remained individual: ephemeral, that is to say. The only exception to this was the chief, who received tokens of homage from all the clans, in the form of food and manufactures. But as each gift entailed a subsequent obligation, he was in the situation of a banker: wealth passed through his hands, but he could never call it his own. My collections of religious objects were built up in return for presents which the chief would at once redistribute among the clans, thus conserving his 'balance of payments' intact.

Wealth of status, as between one clan and another, is quite another matter. Each clan has a capital of myths, traditions, dances, and functions, either social or religious. The myths are, in their turn, at the bottom of the technical privileges which are one of the most curious features of Bororo culture. Almost all Bororo objects are emblazoned in such a way that the owner's clan and sub-clan may be identified. The privilege lies in the use of certain feathers, or colours of feathers; in the way in which an object is carved or cut; in the disposition of feathers differing in colour, or species; in the execution of certain decorative work: fibre-plaiting, for instance, or feather-mosaics; in the use of particular patterns, and so on.

Ceremonial bows, for instance, are embellished with feathers, or with rings of bark, according to the canons prescribed for each clan. The arrow bears at its base, between the feathering, which keeps it straight, a specific ornamentation. The pieces of mother-of-pearl out of which the lip-plugs are made are worked in designs: oval, rectangular, or pisciform, according to the clan. Fringes vary in colour. And the feathered diadems worn during the dance bear a mark of the same sort: generally a strip of wood covered with a feather-mosaic. On festive occasions even the penis-sheath goes into regalia and is equipped with a ribbon of stiff straw decorated or cut out with the colour and the emblem of the clan.

These privileges (they may be bought and sold, by the way) are the object of watchful, not to say quick-tempered supervision. It's inconceivable, people say, that one clan should usurp the prerogatives of another; civil war would result. But from this point of view the differences between the clans are enormous; some live in luxury, some in squalor; a glance at the interior of the huts will prove this. The distinction is not so much between 'rich' and 'poor' as between bumpkins and sophisticates.

The material equipment of the Bororo is marked by simplicity on

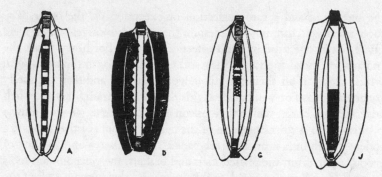

FIG. 32. Arrow shafts bearing clan ornamentation between the feathering

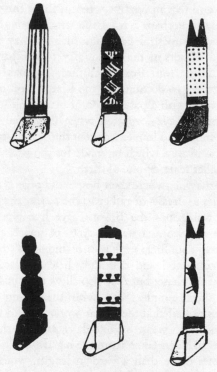

FIG. 33. Emblazoned penis-sheaths

the one hand and a rare perfection of execution on the other. The tools remain archaic in style, despite the axes and knives which were given out at one time by the Protection Service. For heavy work the Indians use metal tools; but they still carve and polish the clubs with which they kill off their fish, their wooden bows, and their delicately barbed arrows. For work such as this they have a traditional tool, half adze and half burin, which they use on all occasions, as we would use a pocket-knife. It consists of one of the curved incisors of the *capivara*, a rodent which lives near the river-banks, tied sideways-on to a stick of wood. Apart from the plaited mats and baskets, the weapons and tools —made from bone or wood—of the men, and the digging-stick of the women who work in the fields, there's not much to be seen in the huts. A few calabashes; some black pots,. bowls and shallow basins, with sometimes a long handle, ladle-wise. These objects have a great purity of form, and this purity is underlined by the austerity of their component materials. One strange thing: it seems that Bororo pottery used to be decorated, and that in relatively recent times this was forbidden on religious grounds. Perhaps it is for the same reason that the Indians no longer carry out rupestral paintings such as may still be found in rock-protected shelters of the chapada: yet these paintings contain many elements taken from Bororo culture. To make quite sure of this I once asked them to decorate for me a large sheet of white paper. A native set to work with a paste made of urucu and some resin; and although the Bororo have forgotten when they used to paint those rocky walls, and indeed no longer frequent the escarpments where they are to be seen, the picture which he made for me was an almost exact version, on a smaller scale, of one of them.

Austere they may be, where their household objects are concerned; but when it comes to dress—or rather to the accessories of dress which are their entire wardrobe—the Bororo give free rein to fancy. To luxury, too: for the women own caskets of jewels and pass them on from mother to daughter: necklaces of monkeys' teeth or jaguars' fangs mounted on wood and delicately held in place with strings. These are relics of the chase; but they also allow their husbands to pluck the hair from their temples, and with these hairs the husbands weave long ropes of hair that they wear wound round their heads like a turban. The men also wear, on fête-days, crescent-shaped pendants made up of a pair of claws taken from the big armadillo—that monster burrower, at times more than a yard in length, which has changed hardly at all since the tertiary era—and embellished with incrustations

FIG. 34.   Black pottery bowl

FIG. 36.   Crescent-shaped pendant
decorated with jaguar
teeth

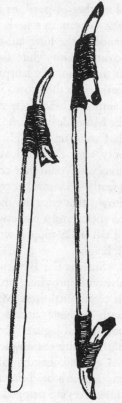

FIG. 35.   Two examples,
one single and
one double, of a
Bororo 'pocket-
knife'

FIG. 37.   Improvised ornaments:
painted crowns of
dried straw

of mother-of-pearl, or a fringe of feathers or cotton. Or there may be seen a toucan's beak fastened to a feathered stalk; egrets by the handful; the long tail-feathers of the *arara*, stuck into bamboo-stalks covered with white down: all these ornament the chignon, natural or made-up, like hairpins devised to balance, at the rear, a diadem of feathers on the brow. Sometimes these two features are combined in a composite head-dress which takes hours to set in place. I got one for the Musée de l'Homme in Paris in exchange for a rifle, after negotiations that went on for eight days. It was indispensable to their rituals, and only after they had assembled a duplicate collection of the feathers involved would they consent to sell. It consists of a fan-shaped diadem; a feathered visor that covers the upper part of the face; a tall cylindrical crown that encircles the head, and is made up of harpy-eagle feathers on sticks; and a basketwork plaque into which is stuck a whole bushful of tall stalks topped with feathers and down. The ensemble is six feet in height.

Such is the Bororo's love of display ornament that the men are always improvising ornaments for themselves even when they are not in ceremonial dress. Many wear crowns: bandeaux of fur embellished with feathers; circlets of basketwork, again with feathers inserted; coronets of jaguars' claws mounted on a circle of wood. But they are pleased with the simplest things: a ribbon of dried straw, picked up off the ground, hastily painted and pulled into shape, will give delight enough, as a head-dress, until some other fantasy takes its place. Sometimes trees are stripped of their flowers to this end. A piece of bark and a feather or two will be quite enough to give these tireless man-milliners the elements of a pair of sensational ear-rings. Enter the men's house and you will see how hard these virile giants work to make themselves beautiful: in every corner someone is at work with knife or chisel or burin; shells from the river are taken to pieces and polished on millstones to make necklaces; fantastic constructions of feathers and bamboo are in process of creation. These are men built like stevedores; but no dressmaker could better the application with which they stick down on to one another's skins and finish up looking like day-old chicks.

But the men's house is not only a workshop. Adolescents sleep in it; and when there is no work to be done the married men go there for siestas, or to talk things over and smoke the big cigarettes that they roll in a dried leaf of maize. They also take some of their meals there; for a minutely organized system of obligations compels all the clans in turn to serve in the *baitemannageo*. Every two hours or so one of the men goes over to his family hut and fetches a bowl of the dish, made from boiled maize, which is called *mingau*. Great shouts of joy greet his arrival: 'Au, au!' resounds through the silence of the day. Ceremony requires him to invite a group of six or eight of his fellows to partake of the dish; this they proceed to do, with ladles made of pottery or shells. Women are forbidden, as I said earlier, to enter the men's house. Married women, that is to say: for unmarried girls take good care not to go too near it; they know too well that if they stray too near, either from inadvertence or from the wish to provoke, the men may dart out and rape them. And, once in each woman's life, she must enter the men's house of her own free will: in order to 'propose' to her future husband.

20 *The Living and the Dead*

THE *baitemannageo* is many things in one: workshop, club, dormitory, *maison de passe*, and, finally, temple. There it is that the religious dancers make themselves ready and that certain ceremonies are held, out of sight of the women of the village: the construction and whirling of the bull-roarers, likewise. These bull-roarers are musical instruments, made of wood and richly painted. They have the outline of a long flat fish and their length varies between one and five feet. When they are made to wheel round on the end of a length of rope they make a sort of low roaring noise—hence their name; this noise is attributed to the visiting spirits of whom the women are supposed to be terrified. Any woman who sees a bull-roarer is ill-fated; even today, as like as not, she will be clubbed to death. When I first watched them in process of construction I was assured that they were cooking utensils. The natives' extreme reluctance to let me have a few of them to keep was explained not so much by the work that would have to be done over again as by fear that I might betray their secret. I had to take one of my kit-cases to the men's house under cover of darkness; the bull-roarers, already wrapped and parcelled, were laid inside and the case shut and locked; I had to promise not to open it till I got to Cuiaba.

There is something almost scandalous, to a European observer, in the ease with which the (as it seems to us) almost incompatible activities of the men's house are harmonized. Few peoples are as deeply religious as the Bororo; few have so elaborate a system of metaphysics. But their spiritual beliefs and their habits of every day are so intimately mingled that they seem not to have any sensation of passing from one to the other. I met with the same artless religiosity in the Buddhist temples of the Burman frontier, where the bonzes live and sleep in the room in which their services are held, with their pots of pomade and the contents of their medicine-chest laid out at the foot of the altar; nor did they disdain to caress their pupils in the interval between two lessons in the alphabet.

This nonchalance with regard to the supernatural was the more surprising to me in that my only contact with religion goes back to a stage in my childhood at which I was already an unbeliever. During the First World War I lived with my grandfather, who was the rabbi of Versailles. His house stood next to the synagogue and was linked to it by a long inner corridor. Even to set foot in that corridor was an awesome experience; it formed an impassable frontier between the profane world and that other world from which was lacking precisely that human warmth which was the indispensable condition to my recognizing it as sacred. Except at the hours of service the synagogue was empty; desolation seemed natural to it, and its brief spells of occupation were neither sustained enough nor fervent enough to overcome this. They seemed merely an incongruous disturbance. Our private religious observances suffered from the same offhand quality. Only my grandfather's silent prayer before each meal reminded us children that our lives were governed by a higher order of things. (That, and a printed message which hung on a long strip of paper in the dining-room: 'Chew Your Food Properly: Your Digestion Depends On it.')

It was not that religion had more prestige among the Bororo: on the contrary, it was taken for granted. In the men's house people went through the motions of religious observance in a consummately casual

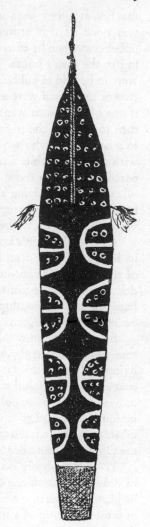

Fig. 38.   A bull-roarer

manner, as if they were actions performed for a specific purpose; there was none of that attitude of respect which comes over even the unbeliever when he enters a sanctuary. That afternoon they were singing in the men's house, in preparation for the evening's rites, which were to be held in public. In one corner boys were snoring or chatting; two or three men were intoning to the accompaniment of rattles. But if one of those men wanted to light a native cigarette, or if it was his turn to dig into the maize gruel, he would either pass his instrument to a neighbour, who would take over where he had left off, or go on with one hand, while scratching himself with the other. If one dancer paraded round to show off his latest creation, everyone would stop whatever he was doing and give his opinion. The 'service' seemed to have been forgotten—until suddenly in another corner the incantation would begin again where it had been left off.

And yet the men's house has a significance over and above that of its being, as I have described, the centre of the social and religious life of the village. The lay-out of the village does not only allow full and delicate play to the institutional system; it summarizes and provides a basis for the relationship between Man and the Universe, between Society and the Supernatural, and between the living and the dead.

Before going into this new aspect of Bororo culture, I must say something in parenthesis about relations between the dead and the living. Without this, it would be difficult to grasp the particular character of the solution which Bororo thought has applied to this universal problem—a solution remarkably similar to that which may be found at the other extreme of the western hemisphere, among the inhabitants of the forests and prairies of north-eastern North America: the Ojibwa, for instance, and the Menomini, and the Winnebago.

There is probably no such thing as a society which does not treat its dead with consideration. At a time when mankind as we know it had hardly come into being, Neanderthal Man already buried his dead in tombs made up of a few rough stones. No doubt funerary practices vary from one group to another. Can we say that these variations are negligible, in relation to the unvarying sentiment which underlies them? Even when we simplify, as far as we possibly can, the respective attitudes maintained in this matter by one society or another, we still have to acknowledge one great distinction: two poles, that is to say, linked by a whole series of intermediary positions.

Certain societies leave their dead in peace. In return for periodical acts of homage the dead, in such cases, give the living no trouble. If they come back to take a look at them, it is at foreseeable intervals and on the foreseeable occasions. And their visits bring only good: the punctual movement of the seasons, fertility in gardens and in women—all are guaranteed by the dead. It is as if the dead and the living had made a pact together: in return for certain sober marks of attachment the dead will remain where they are, and in such momentary encounters as may take place the interest of the living will always be put first. One of the universal themes of folklore puts this formula very well: the so-called motif of the 'grateful dead'. A rich hero buys back a dead body from creditors who had refused to allow it to be buried, and gives it formal burial. The dead man then appears to his benefactor in a dream and promises him success, on condition that the benefits resulting from this are shared equally between the two of them. And, sure enough, the hero soon wins the love of a princess, whom he manages, with the help of his supernatural protector, to rescue from one danger after another. Is he to share her favours with the dead man? The princess lies under a spell and is half woman, half serpent. The dead man claims his share, the hero keeps to their bargain, and the dead man, well pleased with this loyal observance, takes for himself the bewitched half of the princess, leaving the hero with a wife entirely human.

As antithesis to that notion, we have another theme from folklore: 'the enterprising knight', as I like to call it. This time the hero is not rich, but poor. His only possession is a grain of corn which he manages, such is his cleverness, to exchange for a cock, in the first place, and later for a pig, an ox, and finally a dead body, which he barters for a live princess. Here the dead body is rather object than subject: no longer a partner to be negotiated with, it is an instrument to be played upon in a speculation in which untruths and swindling are involved. Certain societies maintain an attitude of this sort towards their dead. They do not allow them to rest, but rather conscript them: literally at times, when cannibalism and necrophagy are based upon the wish to annex for oneself the merits and capacities of the dead; and also symbolically, in societies where competitive prestige plays a great part and the peoples concerned must continually, as it were, summon the dead to their rescue. Evocation of their ancestors and artful genealogies are two of the means by which they try to justify their prerogatives. Such societies feel themselves particularly harassed by the dead whom they exploit. They think that the dead pay them back in kind for their persecution: ever more exacting and irascible, the dead get their own back on those of the living who aim to profit by them. But, whether it is a matter of 'fair shares', as in my first example, or of unbridled speculation, as in the second, the relation is never, and cannot be, one-sided.

Between the two extremes are a number of intermediary positions. The Indians on the west coast of Canada and the Melanesians summon all their ancestors to appear in ceremonies in which they bear witness in favour of their descendants; in certain ancestor-cults, in China or Africa, the dead keep their personal identity—but for a few generations only; among the Pueblos, in the south-west of the U.S.A., they immediately lose their identities but share out among themselves a certain number of specialized functions. Even in Europe, where the dead have become anonymous and lost all character, folklore still preserves certain vestiges of a quite different eventuality in the belief that there are two different kinds of dead person: those borne off by 'natural causes', who form a corps of protective ancestors, and those who died by their own hand, or were murdered or magicked away; the latter turn into jealous and maleficent spirits.

If we confine ourselves to the evolution of western civilization, there is no doubt that we tended less and less to speculate on the dead, and more and more to enter into contractual agreement with them. Eventually this gave place to an indifference foreshadowed, perhaps, in the New Testament phrase: 'Let the dead bury their dead.' But there is no reason to suppose that this evolution corresponds to any universal pattern. It would seem, rather, that all societies have a certain obscure awareness of both possible formulas. No matter towards which of the two they incline, they will always take superstitious precautions against the possible validity of the other—as do we ourselves, whatever the faith, or lack of faith, which we profess. The originality of the Bororo, and of the other peoples whom I have cited as examples, lies in their having clearly formulated both possibilities and built up a system of ritual and belief applicable both to the one and to the other: machinery, that is to say, with the aid of which they can pass to and fro in the hope of a twofold conciliation.

I should express myself imperfectly if I were to say that there is no such thing, for the Bororo, as natural death. A man is not, for them, an individual, but a person. He is part of a sociological universe: the village which exists for all eternity, side by side with the physical universe, itself composed of other animate beings; celestial bodies and meteorological phenomena. Nor is this affected by the fact that the village itself rarely remains more than thirty years in any one place, so rapidly is the soil brought to the point of exhaustion. The village does not, in fact, consist either of the land on which it stands, or of the huts which comprise it at any one time; it consists in the lay-out which I have described above. And this lay-out never varies. That is why, in putting a stop to it, the missionaries destroyed an entire culture.

As for the animals, some belong to the world of men—birds and fish, above all—and some, as in the case of certain terrestrial animals, to the physical universe. The Bororo consider, therefore, that their human shape is transitory: midway between that of the fish (whose name they have adopted for themselves) and the *arara* (in whose guise they will complete the cycle of their transmigrations).

If the Bororos' thought—like that of the anthropologist—is dominated by the fundamental opposition between Nature and culture, it follows that they go beyond even Durkheim and Comte and consider that human life should itself be regarded as a department of culture. To say, therefore, that death is either natural or unnatural is meaningless. In fact and law alike, death is both *natural* and *anti-cultural*. That is to say that, whenever a native dies, an injury is done not only to those near to him, but to Society as a whole; and Nature, in consequence, is held to be in debt to Society. It is, in fact, as a debt that we may best interpret the notion, essential to the Bororo, of the *mori*. When a native dies, the village organizes a collective hunt, incumbent on the moiety of which the dead man was not a member. The object of this expedition is to make Nature pay her debt; the natives hope, by killing some sizable creature—a jaguar, for preference—to bring home a skin, and a set of teeth and nails, which will constitute the dead man's *mori*.

A man had just died when I arrived in Kejara but, unluckily, he had died some way away, in another village. I could not, therefore, witness the double burial ceremony: first, the body is put in a ditch, covered with branches, in the middle of the village, and then, when putrefaction has been completed, the bones are washed in the river. Next, they are painted and ornamented with feather-mosaics stuck on with glue and, finally, they are sent down in a basket to the bottom of a lake or a running stream. All the other ceremonies at which I was present were in strict traditional style, inclusive of the ritual scarification of the relatives at the place where the provisional tomb had had to be dug. I was also unlucky in that the collective hunt had taken place either the day before, or on the afternoon of, my arrival, so that I could not witness it. Nothing had been killed, in any case, and an old jaguar-skin was brought into service for the funeral dances. I even suspect that our *irara* was commandeered to take the place of the missing prey. They would never tell me if this was the case—and more's the pity: for, had it really been so, I could have claimed for myself the role of the *uiaddo*, or chief huntsman and representative of the dead man. His family would have presented me with an armband of human hair and a *poari*, or mystic clarinet: this was made up of a little befeathered calabash which served as amplifier to the bamboo reed-pipe on which the huntsman would play when the kill had been completed; and, later, it would be attached to the skin. I should have shared out, as I was bound to do, the meat, the hide, the teeth, and the nails among the dead man's relatives; and they would have given me in exchange a ceremonial bow and arrows, another clarinet in commemoration of my services in the field, and a necklace of flat discs made from shells. I should also, no doubt, have had to paint myself black in order to escape the notice of the evil spirit which had been responsible for the man's death. By the rules of the *mori*, this spirit would be incarnate in the animal I should set out to kill; and, although it had to offer itself by way of compensation for the harm it had done, it would be filled with a vindictive hatred for its executioner. For, in a sense, the Bororo's murderous Nature is human and operates through the intermediary of a special category of souls, answerable directly to her and not to Society.

As I said above, I was sharing a sorcerer's hut. The *bari* formed a special category of human beings and did not belong completely either to the physical universe or to the world of Society; their role was rather to mediate between these two estates. It is possible, though not certain, that they were all born in the Tugaré moiety; mine certainly was, since our hut was Cera and he lived, as was the rule, with his wife. A man becomes a *bari* by vocation. Often this follows upon a revelation whose central motif is a pact concluded with certain members of a very complex collectivity of evil, or perhaps merely formidable, spirits. These are in part celestial (and in control, therefore, of the phenomena of astronomy and meteorology), in part animal, and in part subterranean. Their numbers are continually increasing, as the souls of dead sorcerers arrive to swell the ranks: and they have in their charge the operation of the solar system, the wind and the rain, sickness and death. Their appearance varies, but is in every case terrifying: matted with hair, some say, and with holes in their heads from which tobacco-fumes emerge when they smoke; monsters of the air with immensely

long nails and rain pouring from
their eyes, nostrils, and hair; one-
legged creatures with huge bellies
and the soft and downy body of
a bat.

The *bari* is asocial. By reason
of his personal links with one or
more spirits, he is a privileged being:
when he goes out hunting by himself, for instance, supernatural help
is forthcoming; he can turn himself
into an animal at will; he has the
gift of prophecy and knows the
secrets of disease. Neither an animal
killed in the chase, nor the first
fruits of a garden, can be eaten till
he has had his share. This last is the
mori owed by the living to the spirits
of the dead. Its role in the system is,
therefore, symmetrical with, and the
obverse of, that of the funerary hunt
which I have described.

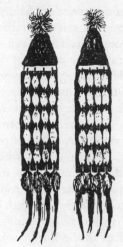

FIG. 39. Ceremonial ear-
rings made of
pieces of mother-
of-pearl fastened
to strips of bark,
and trimmed
with feathers
and hair

But the *bari* is also under the
dominion of one or more guardian
spirits. They make use of him for their own incarnation; at such times
the *bari*, with the spirit, as it were, in the saddle above him, is subject
to trances and convulsions. In return for his guardianship the spirit
watches the *bari*'s every movement; he is the true proprietor, not merely
of the sorcerer's possessions, but of his very body. For every broken
arrow, every broken pot, every fingernail, or lock of hair not accounted
for, the sorcerer is answerable to the spirit. As none of these things may
be destroyed or thrown away, the *bari* drags along behind him the
debris of all his past existence. The old adage about the quick and the
dead here takes on an unexpected and terrible significance; for, between
the spirit and the sorcerer, the bond is of so jealous a nature that one
can never be quite sure which of the two partners is, in the end, the
master, and which the servant.

Clearly, therefore, for the Bororo the physical universe consists in
a complex hierarchy of individualized powers. Their personal nature
is directly manifested; but this is not the case with their other attributes,

for these powers are at once beings and things, living and dead. In Society, the sorcerer is the intermediary between mankind and the equivocal universe of evil spirits who are at one and the same time persons and objects.

The sociological universe has characteristics quite different from those of the physical universe. The spirits of ordinary men (those, I mean, who are not sorcerers) do not identify themselves with the forces of Nature, but form a society, as it were, of their own; but, conversely, they lose their personal identity and merge in that collective being, the *aroe*, a term which, like the ancient Bretons' *anaon*, should doubtless be translated as 'the souls' society'. This society is, in point of fact, twofold, since the souls are divided after the funeral ceremonies into two villages, of which one is in the east and the other in the west. Over these villages stand guard, respectively, the two great hero-divinities of the Bororo Pantheon: in the west, the older of the two, Bakororo, and in the east the younger, Ituboré. This east-west axis corresponds, by the way, to the course of the Rio Vermelho. It is therefore probable that there is a relation, as yet unillumined, between the duality of the villages of the dead and the secondary division of the village itself into an upstream and a downstream moiety.

The *bari* serves, therefore, as intermediary between human society and the evil spirits, individual or cosmological. (The spirits of the dead *bari* are both at once, as we have seen.) There is also another mediator— one who presides over relations between the society of the living and the society of the dead (this last being beneficent, collective, and anthropomorphic). This is the *aroettowaraare*, or 'Master of the spirits' road'. His distinguishing marks are the opposite of the *bari*'s. He and the *bari* hate and fear one another, what is more. The Road Master is not entitled to receive offerings, but he must keep strictly to certain rules: there are things that he must not eat, and he must be very quietly dressed. All ornament, all brightly coloured clothing, is forbidden him. Nor is there any pact between him and the spirits, and these are always present to him and, in a sense, immanent. Instead of taking possession of him when he is in a trance, they appear to him in dreams; if he calls upon them from time to time, it is always to someone else's advantage.

If the *bari* has the gift of foreseeing illness and death, the Master is both nurse and healer. It is said, by the way, that the *bari*, as the embodiment of physical necessity, is always ready to confirm his prognostications by killing off any invalid who is too slow to realize his grim predictions. But it must be noted here that the Bororo do not share our conception of the relation between life and death. Someone said to me one day, of a woman who was lying in a high fever in the corner of her hut: 'She's dead'—meaning that they had given up her case as hopeless. And, after all, this is not so different from our army's way of lumping together dead and wounded under the single heading of 'casualties'. As far as immediate effectiveness goes, they are indeed one and the same, even if, from the wounded man's point of view, there is an undeniable advantage in not being among the dead.

The Master can, like the *bari*, turn himself into an animal at will. But he never turns himself into a man-eating jaguar, symbol (until he is killed in his turn) of the power of the dead to exact their *mori* from the

FIG. 40. Bororo paintings of cult objects

living. The Master chooses, rather, one of the provider-creatures: the fruit-picking *arara*, the fish-catching harpy-eagle, or the tapir, on whose flesh the whole tribe can feast. The *bari* is possessed by its spirits; the *aroettowaraare* sacrifices himself for the salvation of mankind. Even the revelation which makes him aware of his mission has its painful side; he recognizes it, initially, by the dreadful stench which follows him everywhere. This stench recalls, no doubt, the smell which hangs over the village at the time when a dead body is given provisional 'burial' at ground-level, in the middle of the dance-area; but at the moment of revelation it is associated with a mystical being, the *aije*. The *aije* is a mythical monster of the aquatic deep, repellent, evil-smelling, and affectionate: it appears before the budding *aroettowaraare* and forces him to endure its caresses. The scene is mimed, during the funeral ceremony, by young men daubed with mud who throw their arms

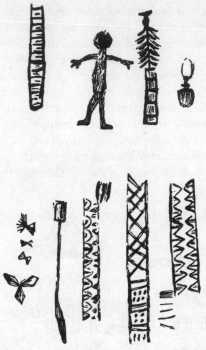

FIG. 41. Bororo painting of an officiant,
trumpets, a rattle, and various
ornaments

round the fancy-dressed impersonator of the young spirit. The natives
have so clear an idea of the *aije* that they can even paint his portrait;
and they give it the same name as is given to the bull-roarer, whose
humming announces the emergence of the animal and imitates its cries.

And so it is not surprising that the funeral ceremonies go on for
several weeks. Their functions, many and various, are situated on the
two planes which we have just distinguished. Seen from an individual
point of view, every day is the pretext for negotiations between
Society and the physical universe. The hostile forces which compose
the physical universe have done harm to Society, and that harm must
somehow be put right: that is the role of the funerary hunt. Once the
dead man has been at once avenged and redeemed by the hunters, as a
group, he must be admitted to the society of spirits. That is the function
of the *roiakuriluo*, the great funeral dirge which I was about to have the
good fortune to hear.

In a Bororo village, one moment in the day has a particular importance: the evening roll-call. As soon as night falls a great fire is lit on the dancing-place, and the chiefs of the clans assemble there. A herald calls out in a loud voice to each group: *Badedjeba*, the chiefs; *O Cera*, those of the ibis; *Ki*, those of the tapir; *Bokodori*, those of the big tattoo; *Bakoro* (from the name of the hero Bakororo); *Boro*, those of the lip-plugs; *Ewaguddu*, those of the buriti-palm; *Arore*, those of the caterpillar; *Paiwe*, those of the hedgehog; *Apibore* (a word whose meaning is uncertain). . . . As and when each group arrives, the orders for the morrow are made known to them, still in a tone of voice that can be heard even in the most distant huts in the village—or would be, if those huts were not by now more or less empty. As the mosquitoes vanish with the last of the light, the men all move away from the family houses, whither they had returned towards six in the evening. Each has under his arm the mat that he will spread out on the beaten earth of the dance-plaza that lies to the west of the men's house. There they stretch themselves out, wrapped in a cotton blanket died orange by long contact with bodies stained with urucu; the Service de Protection would hardly recognize in these blankets one of its benefactions to the region. There are also larger mats, on which five or six men can lie together, occasionally exchanging a word or two. Some are quite on their own, and amble about among the prostrate bodies of their fellows. As the roll-call proceeds, the head of one family after another will rise to his feet in answer to his name, receive his orders, and once again lie down, face upwards towards the stars. The women, too, have left their huts, and stand in groups on the threshold. Conversation dies down and gradually, led at first by two or three officiants and growing even greater in volume as more and more people arrive, we begin to hear, first from the depths of the men's house and eventually on the plaza itself, the songs, recitatives, and choruses which will continue all night.

The dead man was a member of the Cera moiety; the Tugaré officiated, therefore, at his funeral. In the centre of the square, branches had been strewn to 'stand in' for the tomb itself. These are flanked to right and to left by raised bundles of arrows, before which bowls of food had been set out. Priests and singers numbered about a dozen, and most of them had on a large diadem of brilliantly coloured feathers (others wore this on their buttocks), with, on their shoulders, a rectangular wickerwork fan, kept in place by a thin cord round their necks. Some were entirely naked and painted either in red (all over or striped) or in black, or else covered with long thin strips of white down; others wore a long straw skirt. The main character, whose role it was to personify the young spirit, had a change of costume to suit the various stages of the action. Sometimes he appeared clad in fresh green leaves, wearing on his head the enormous diadem I described above, and carrying, like a ceremonial train, a jaguar-skin; this last was held up behind him by a page. On other occasions he was naked and painted black, with no ornament but what looked like a huge pair of glassless straw spectacles round his eyes. This detail is especially interesting in that it is analogous to the motif by which Tlaloc, the rain-god of ancient Mexico, may be recognized. Perhaps the Pueblo Indians of Arizona and New Mexico hold the key to the mystery, for the spirits of their dead turn into the gods of rain; and they also have certain beliefs relating to magical objects which protect the eyes and allow their possessor to become invisible at will. I have often noticed that spectacles exert a great fascination among South American Indians—so much so that on my last expedition I took along a great quantity of glassless spectacle-frames. These had a great success among the Nambikwara—as if their traditional belief made them particularly welcome. We had had no record of straw spectacle-frames among the Bororo, but as black paint is said to render the wearer invisible, it may well be that spectacles do the same—as they do, for that matter, in Pueblo mythology. And, finally, the *butarico* (the spirits responsible for rain among the Bororo) are described as having the same redoubtable aspect—hooked hands and great fangs—as the Maya goddess of water.

During the first few nights we witnessed, one after another, the dances of the Tugaré clans; *Ewoddo*, those of the palm-tree, and *Paiwe*, those of the hedgehogs. In both cases the dancers were covered with leaves from head to foot and, as their heads were invisible, we took them to be higher than they really were—on the level, in fact, of the feathered diadem which stood up in so imposing a fashion that we involuntarily took the dancers to be enormously tall. In their hands they held palm-stems or sticks ornamented with leaves. There were two sorts of dances. In the one, the performers came on alone divided into two quadrilles which faced one another at the two extremities of the square, ran towards one another with cries of 'Ho, ho!' and whirled round and round each other until they were facing the opposite way from which they had come. Later, women would weave in among the men dancers, and the dance became an interminable farandole which formed up, moving forward or simply marking time, led by

naked coryphées who walked backwards, waving their rattles, while
other men squatted on the ground and sang.

Three days later the ceremonies were interrupted, so that Act II,
the *mariddo* dance, could be got ready. Teams of men went off into the
forest, returning with armfuls of green palms: these were stripped of
their leaves and the stems were cut into sticks, each about a foot in
length. With crude ropes of plaited foliage these were roughly tied
together, in bundles of two or three, to form the steps of a flexible
ladder several yards in length. Two such ladders were made, of different lengths; and they were then rolled up to form two wheel-like
shapes. Each stood on its narrow breadth, and they rose to a height of

Fig. 42. Diadem of yellow and blue *arara*
feathers carrying clan marking

roughly five feet in the one case and four in the other. The sides were
then decorated with a network of foliage, held together with thin
ropes of plaited hair. The two objects, when complete, were solemnly
taken to the middle of the square and put down side by side. These
were the *mariddos*, male and female, whose construction was the
responsibility of the Ewaguddu clan.

Towards evening two groups, each of five or six men, made off
respectively to east and to west. I followed the first group to the point,
some fifty yards distant, at which I could watch them at their preparations. Hidden from the public by a screen of trees, they were
covering themselves with leaves, like dancers, and fitting their diadems
in place. But on this occasion secrecy was essential to their role: like

the other group, they represented the spirits of the dead who had come from their villages in, respectively, the west and the east to welcome the new addition to their number. When all was ready they headed, whistling, towards the square, where the eastern group was already in position (the westerners had come 'upstream', in symbolical terms, so that it was natural for them to take longer than those who had come 'downstream' from the east).

Their hesitant and fearful bearing was admirably descriptive of the plight of the shades; I thought of how, in Homer, Ulysses strives to keep hold of the phantoms conjured up by blood. But all at once the ceremony became more lively: men seized one of other of the *mariddos* (all the heavier, these, for being made up of fresh-cut branches), hoisted them at arm's length, and danced beneath them until they dropped from exhaustion, leaving the *mariddo* for some rival to continue the dance. The scene lost its initial, mystical character and became a fairground on which the young men of the village showed off their muscles in an environment of sweat, horseplay, and crude joking. The sport is one that recurs among certain related peoples in a purely profane sense—in, for instance, the log-races of the Gé on the Brazilian plateau; but among the Bororo it still retains its full religious significance; the hilarious and disorderly scene is one in which the native really feels that he is playing with the dead and wresting from them the right to go on being alive.

This opposition—the living *against* the dead—is expressed, in the first place, by the division of the villagers, throughout the ceremonies, into participants and spectators. But the real participants are the men, protected as they are by the secrecies of the communal house. The lay-out of the village must, therefore, have a significance even deeper than that which we ascribed to it on the sociological level. When a villager dies, each half takes it in turn to play the living, or the dead, in relation to the other. But this game of poise and counterpoise mirrors another, in which the roles have been distributed once and for all; for the men who have grown up in the *baitemannageo* symbolize the society of spirits, whereas from the huts all around, which belong to the women (who have no part in the most sacred of the rites and are, therefore, predestined spectators), is drawn the audience of the living.

We have observed already that the supernatural world is itself twofold, since it includes both the domain of the priest and the domain of the magician. The magician is the master of the celestial and terrestrial powers, from the tenth heaven (the Bororo believe in a plurality of heavens, each superimposed upon the other) down to the depths of the earth. The forces he controls—and on which he depends —are, therefore, disposed along a vertical axis; whereas the priest, Master of the spirits' road, presides over the horizontal axis which unites east and west, where the two villages of the dead are situated. But much goes to show that the *bari* is invariably Tugaré in origin, and the *aroettowaraare* Cera; this suggests that the division into halves is also expressive of this duality. It is a striking fact that all the Bororo myths present the Tugaré heroes as creators and demiurges and the Cera heroes as men of peace and organization. The Tugaré heroes are answerable for the existence of things: water, rivers, fish, vegetation, manufactured objects. The Cera heroes have put creation in order, delivering the human race from monsters and assigning to each animal its specific nourishment. One myth even tells how the supreme power once belonged to the Tugaré, who voluntarily made it over to the Cera —as if the antithesis of the moieties was intended to symbolize, in native thought, the passage from an unbridled Nature to an ordered Society.

This explains the apparent paradox by which the Tugaré are known as 'the strong', while the Cera, though the repository of political and religious power, are known as 'the weak'. The Tugaré stand closer to the physical universe, and Cera to the human universe: and the latter is not the more powerful of the two. Social order cannot cheat the hierarchy of the cosmos and get away with it. Even among the Bororo, Nature can be vanquished only if we recognize her authority and allow her fatalities their true role. A sociological system such as theirs allows them, in any case, no choice: a man can never belong to the same moiety as either his father or his son, since it is to his mother's side that he owes allegiance: only with his grandfather and grandson is he again at one in the matter of moieties. If the Cera should wish to justify their power by claiming an exclusive affinity with the founder-heroes, they set themselves, in so doing, at a further distance of one whole generation—becoming, in effect, the heroes' 'grandsons', whereas the Tugaré would become their 'sons'.

But to what extent are the natives bemused by the logic of their system? I cannot, after all, dismiss the feeling that the dazzling metaphysical cotillon which I witnessed can be reduced, in the end, to a rather gruesome farce. The men's brotherhood claimed to be impersonating the dead in order that the living should have the illusion of a visit from the spirits; the women were excluded from the rites and deceived as to their true nature—doubtless to sanction the division of rights by which they take priority, where housing and birth rights are in question, leaving the mysteries of religion to their men. But their credulity, whether presumed or authentic, has also a psychological function: that of giving, for the benefit of both sexes, an affective and intellectual content to fantasy-figures which might otherwise be altogether less meaningfully manipulated. If we bring up our children to believe in Father Christmas, it is not simply because we want to mislead them: it is also because their enthusiasm gives ourselves fresh warmth. Through them, we contrive to deceive ourselves also, and to believe, as they believe, that a world of unqualified generosity is not absolutely incompatible with reality. And yet men die, and die never to return; and all forms of social order draw us nearer to death, in so much as they take something away from us and give back nothing in exchange.

For, the moralist, Bororo society has one particular lesson. Let him listen to his native informers: they will describe to him, as they described to me, the ballet in which the two halves of the village set themselves to live and breathe in and for one another; exchanging women, goods, and service in a kind of shared passion for reciprocity; inter-marrying their children; burying one another's dead; offering each other guarantees that life is eternal, that human beings help one another, and that Society is based on justice. To bear witness to these truths, and back them up in their convictions, the wise men of the tribe have evolved a grandiose cosmology which is writ large in the lay-out of their villages and distribution of their homes. When they met with contradictions, those contradictions were cut across again and again. Every opposition was rebutted in favour of another. Groups were divided and redivided, both vertically and horizontally, until their lives, both spiritual and temporal, became an escutcheon in which symmetry and asymmetry were in equilibrium—just as they are in the drawings with which a Caduveo beauty, equally though less explicitly a prey to the same preoccupations, will ornament her face. But what remains of all that, what is left of the moieties and the counter-moieties, the clans and the sub-clans, when we draw the conclusions which seem to proceed inevitably from certain recent observations? In a society whose complexities seem to spring from a delight in complication for its own sake, each clan is subdivided into three groups: upper, middle, and lower. One regulation takes prece-dence over all others: that an 'upper' should marry another 'upper', a 'middle' another 'middle', and a 'lower' another 'lower'. Despite, that is to say, all the appearances of institutionalized brotherhood, the Bororo village is made up in the last analysis of three groups, each of which always marries within its own numbers. Three societies which, all unknowingly, remain for ever distinct and isolated, each imprisoned within its own vainglory, dissimulated even from its own self by

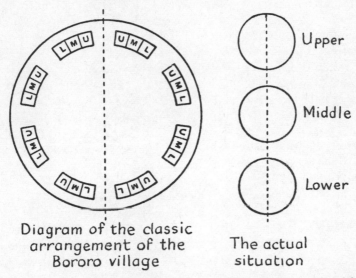

Diagram of the classic
arrangement of the
Bororo village

The actual
situation

FIG. 43.   Diagram showing the real and apparent social structure of the
Bororo village

misleading institutions; with the result that each of the three is the unwitting victim of artificialities whose purpose it can no longer discover. Try as the Bororo may to bring their system to full flowering with the aid of a deceptive prosopopoeia, they will be unable, as other societies have also been unable, to smother this truth: that the imagery with which a society pictures to itself the relations between the dead and the living can always be broken down in terms of an attempt to hide, embellish or justify, on the religious level, the relations prevailing, in that society among the living.

PART VII

The Nambikwara

21   *The Lost World*

Aｎ ａｎｔｈｒｏｐｏｌｏｇｉｃａｌ expedition to central Brazil was being got into shape at the intersection of the Rue Réaumur and the Boulevard de Sébastopol. There it is that the wholesalers of the dress-and-clothing trade congregate; and there, if anywhere, that we could find goods acceptable to the fastidious Indians.

A year had passed since my visit to the Bororo; and, during that year, all the conditions required to make an anthropologist of me had been fulfilled. Lévy-Bruhl, Mauss, and Rivet had given me their blessing—even if only after the event; my collections had been shown in an art gallery in the Rue du Faubourg St Honoré; I had lectured and written articles. Thanks to Henri Laugier, who presided over the youthful destinies of the department of scientific research, I had been accorded funds for a more ambitious venture. It remained for me to assemble my equipment; my three months' intimacy with the natives had taught me to know their needs, and those needs were much the same—amazingly so, in fact—from one end of the South American continent to the other.

And so, beset by Czech importers, in a part of Paris as unfamiliar to me as the Amazon itself, I began my strange negotiations. Knowing nothing of their affairs, I was not even able to explain what I wanted. All I could do was to apply the Indians' own criteria. I picked out, for instance, the smallest of the embroidery pearls ('pebbles' was their name in the trade) which, strung together in heavy ropes, filled rack upon rack. I tried to break them between my teeth, to test their strength; I sucked them to see if they were coloured all the way through and would not turn transparent after their first dip in the river; I bought in quantities which varied according to the Indian colour-canon: equal amounts of black and white, to begin with; red, next; yellow, in much smaller amounts; and merely token quantities of the colours—blue and green—which the Indians would, as like as not, disdain altogether.

These preferences are perfectly comprehensible. When the Indians make their own pearls, and do it by hand, they set the highest value upon those which involve the most, and the most skilled, work: the smallest, that is to say. As raw material they use the black rind of the palm-nut and milky, mother-of-pearly shells from the river-bed; they enjoy playing off the one against the other. Like everyone else, they like best what they already know: I should be most successful, therefore, with my blacks and my whites. Red and yellow often fall, for the Indians, into one and the same category: such is the result of using urucu dyes which vary, according to the quality of the seeds and the degree of their development, between vermilion and a yellowy-orange, red predominates, none the less, by reason of an intensity which certain seeds and certain feathers have long made familiar to the Indians. As for blue and green, these are comparatively cold colours, illustrated in Nature by short-lived vegetable substances; hence the Indians' indifference towards them and, what is more, the indifference of their language to nuances of blue, which is seen rather as a department of black, in some regions, and of green, in others.

My needles had to be large enough to admit a good stout thread, yet not so large as to prevent the threading of tiny pearls. The thread itself had to be strong in colour, preferably red (the Indians dye theirs with urucu), and made up with a good firm twist to give it a look of hand-made craftsmanship. Generally speaking I was wary of junk jewellery and gewgaws; the Bororo had taught me a profound respect for native techniques. Life in the bush soon shows up any shortcomings of quality; and if I was not to lose face, paradoxical as this may seem, I had to offer the natives the finest-quality steels, glass coloured through and through, and thread worthy of the Queen of England's saddle-maker.

Sometimes I fell upon wholesalers who delighted in the special problems of my mission and were ready to adapt their special knowledges to its exoticism. I remember a fish-hook maker near the Canal Saint-Martin who let me have all his remnants at a bargain price: for a whole year I tramped the bush with bundle after bundle of these hooks, but nobody would take them on—they were too small and too fine for any fish worthy of the Amazonian angler. In the end I got rid of them on the Bolivian frontier. All my purchases had to serve a double function: on the one hand, I needed to barter with, or, on occasion, to give them away to, the Indians; and on the other I used them to buy myself goods or services in distant regions where white traders rarely or never penetrated. At the end of the expedition, when I had spent all my money, I kept going for several weeks by opening a shop in a hamlet of rubber-gatherers. The local prostitutes would exchange—and not without bargaining—one of my necklaces for two eggs.

I planned to spend a whole year in the bush, and had hesitated for a long time as to where, and for what reason, I was to go. In the end, with no notion that the result would be quite contrary to my intentions, and being anxious rather to understand the American continent as a whole than to deepen my knowledge of human nature by studying one particular case, I decided to examine the whole breadth of Brazil, both ethnographically and geographically, by traversing the western part of the plateau, from Cuiaba to Rio Madeira. Till quite recently, this was the least-explored part of the country. The Paulist explorers of the eighteenth century got hardly any farther than Cuiaba, so discouraging were the desolation of the landscape and the hostility of the Indians. Even at the start of the twentieth century the thousand miles between Cuiaba and the Amazon were still forbidden ground—so much so that, in order to go from Cuiaba to Manaus or Belem, on the Amazon, the simplest method was to go by way of Rio de Janeiro and continue northwards by sea, or up the estuary of the Amazon. Only in 1907 did General (then Colonel) Candido Mariano da Silva Rondon begin to penetrate the area; and it took him eight years, first to explore the region, and second to establish the strategically important telegraph wire that for the time established a link between Cuiaba, the federal capital, and the frontier posts to the north-west.

From the reports of the Rondon Commission (not yet published in full, by the way); from some of the General's lectures; from the recollections of Theodore Roosevelt, who accompanied the General on one of his expeditions; and from a delightful book, *Rondonia*, published in 1912 by the late Roquette-Pinto, who at the time was Director of the National Museum, I had gleaned certain summary indications about the very primitive peoples who had been discovered in the region. But since then, and for a long time, the ancient curse seemed to have fallen once again upon the plateau. Not one professional anthropologist had penetrated it. I was much tempted to follow the telegraph line, or what remained of it, and in so doing to try to find out exactly who were the Nambikwara—and who, too, were those enigmatic peoples, farther to the north, whom no one had seen since Rondon had left a bare mention of their existence.

Interest had centred hitherto on the tribes along the coast, and those who lived in the great river-valleys which were the traditional high-roads into the Brazilian interior. By 1939, however, the Indians of the plateau were already a subject for speculation. My own experience of the Bororo had persuaded me that, on both the religious and the sociological levels, tribes sometimes dismissed as 'primitive' were often, on the contrary, possessed of an exceptional degree of refinement. People had become aware of the researches then being made by a German anthropologist, now dead, called Kurt Unkel: Unkel had taken the native name of Nimuendaju and, after spending some years in the Gé villages of central Brazil, had confirmed that the Bororo were not an isolated phenomenon, but rather a variation upon a theme fundamental to, and shared with, a number of other peoples. The savannahs of central Brazil were occupied, therefore, to a depth of nearly fourteen hundred miles by the survivors of a remarkably homogeneous culture. The marks of this culture were a language diversified by a number of interrelated dialects and a relatively low standard of living: in contrast to this latter, social organization and religious thought had attained a high level of development. Surely these were the original inhabitants of Brazil—peoples either forgotten in the depths of the bush or driven back into inhospitable country, not long before the discovery of Brazil, by more warlike tribes who had come from no one knows where to appropriate for themselves the coast-line and the river-valleys?

In the sixteenth century travellers encountered, along more or less the whole length of the coast, representatives of the great Tupi-guarani culture. These were in occupation of almost all Paraguay, and of the Amazon from source to sea. Their territories comprised, that is to say, a broken ring, two thousand miles in diameter, which the area between Paraguay and Bolivia interrupted hardly at all. These Tupi, who had certain obscure affinities with the Aztecs—the very group who had belatedly taken possession of the Mexico valley—these Tupi were themselves newcomers: in the valleys of the Brazilian interior they did not, for instance, complete their occupation until the nineteenth century. Possibly they had begun their dispersal, several centuries before the discovery of Brazil, in the belief that somewhere on earth there was a country where death and evil did not exist. Such was still their conviction at the end of their migrations when, in the last years of the nineteenth century, little groups of them appeared on the São Paulo littoral, guided by their sorcerers, dancing, singing the praises of the land where death was unknown, and fasting for long periods to make themselves worthy of it. In the sixteenth century, in any case, they were engaged in bitter struggles for the possession of the coast; we know little of their opponents, the former occupants of the area, but they may have been those we know as the Gé.

To the north-west of Brazil the Tupi co-existed with other peoples: the Caraïbes or Caribs, who ended by conquering the Antilles. Though different from them in their language, they were very similar in their culture. There were also the Arawaks, a rather mysterious people. Older, and of greater refinement than the other two, they formed the majority of the population of the Antilles and had spread as far as Florida. Though unlike the Gé in that they enjoyed a high degree of material culture—notable in pottery and wood-sculpture—they were not unequal to them in the complexity of their social organization. Caribs and Arawaks seemed to have penetrated the continent much earlier than the Tupi: already in the sixteenth century they were massed in the Guianas, in the estuary of the Amazon, and in the Antilles. But small colonies may still be found in the interior, on certain tributaries of the right bank of the Amazon: the Xingu and the Guaporé. The Arawaks even have descendants in upper Bolivia. It was probably they who brought the art of ceramics to the Mbaya-Caduveo, since the Guana (who, as the reader will remember, were reduced to slavery by the Mbaya-Caduveo) spoke an Arawak dialect.

By traversing the least-known part of the plateau, I hoped to find in the savannah the most westerly representatives of the Gé group; and, once in the Madeira basin, I hoped to be able to study the unpublished vestiges of the three other linguistic families on the borders of their great highroad into the interior: the Amazon.

If these hopes were only partly realized, it was because of our over-simplified view of pre-Colombian history in America. Today, in the light of recent discoveries, and thanks, as far as I myself am concerned, to years spent in the study of North American ethnography, I realize that the western hemisphere must be considered as a whole. The social organization and religious beliefs of the Gé correspond curiously to those found in the forests and prairies of North America, just as the analogies between the tribes of the Chaco, such as the Guaicuru, and those of the plains of Canada and the U.S.A. have long been evident, even if no conclusion was drawn from them. The civilizations of Mexico and Peru were certainly in touch with one another, at many moments in their history, through the intermediary of rafts plying along the Pacific coasts. All this had not been much examined, because American studies were dominated for a very long time by the conviction that only 'recently' (i.e. five thousand or six thousand years before Christ) had America first been penetrated. That penetration was attributed entirely, what is more, to Asiatic peoples who had made their way in by way of the Bering Strait.

The fact had therefore to be explained away that somehow, in the course of a very few thousand years, these nomads had established themselves from one end to the other of the western hemisphere: adapting themselves perfectly to its wide varieties of climate and discovering, developing, and distributing over immense areas of land the wild plants which turned, in their hands, into tobacco, beans, manioc, sweet potatoes, potatoes, ground-nuts, cotton, and, above all, maize. Successive civilizations had to be accounted for: in Mexico, central America, and the Andes there were born and brought to maturity the civilizations of which Aztecs, Mayas, and Incas were but the distant descendants. All this called for a kind of historical marquetry in which every new development had to fall neatly into place, a mere century or two after its predecessor. Pre-Colombian history in America became a succession of kaleidoscopic images in which the whims of the theoretician would summon forth, instant by instant, an entirely new picture. It was as if those who specialized in the subject were bent on imposing on 'primitive' America that shallowness which characterizes the history of the New World in modern times.

All this was knocked sideways, or rather backwards, by discoveries which proved that Man had, in point of fact, penetrated the American continent very much earlier than had been supposed. We know that Man knew of, and hunted, animals now extinct in America—sloth, mammoth, camel, an archaic form of bison, and the antelope—whose bones have been found side by side with his stone weapons and instruments. That some of these animals should have been found in, for instance, the Mexico valley is proof that the climate there was once very different from what it is now. Such a change can only take place over a period of many thousands of years. Similar results have been given when radio-activity has been used to determine the antiquity of archaeological remains. We have therefore to admit that men lived in America at least twenty thousand years ago; in certain regions maize was cultivated more than three thousand years ago. Over more or less the whole of North America remains dating from fifteen to twenty thousand years ago have been found. And, by measuring the residual radio-activity of the carbon in the earliest known archaeological remains of the American continent, we have been able to back-date those remains between five and fifteen hundred years. Like those Japanese flowers, made out of flat paper, which open out when put in water, pre-Colombian history acquired overnight that volume in time which it had hitherto lacked.

And yet . . . we are faced with a difficulty just the opposite of that with which our predecessors had to wrestle. How are we to furnish these enormous areas of time? We realize that the migrations which I mention above exist on the surface of the truth, and that something must have preceded the great civilizations of Mexico and the Andes.

FIGS. 44–45. People of ancient Mexico, on the left from the south-east (American Museum of Natural History), on the right from the Gulf coast (Exposition d'Art Mexicain, 1952)

Already in Peru, and in many parts of North America, vestiges of the first inhabitants have come to light: tribes that knew nothing of agriculture gave place to tribes that settled in villages, had gardens of their own, and yet had neither maize nor pottery; next, as we also know, came groups that sculptured in stone and knew how to work in precious metals in a style freer and more inspired than any which was to follow. We had inclined to believe that the whole of American history came to full bloom and achieved, as it were, a perfect synthesis in the Incas of Peru and the Aztecs of Mexico. But now we know that these civilizations were as distant from their sources as is our *style Empire* from the Egypt and the Rome to which it owes so much. All

242 The Nambikwara

three were totalitarian arts, harking avidly back to that colossal scale
of activity for which ignorance and clumsiness had been originally
responsible—a scale appropriate to a State anxious above all to give
expression to its power, and concentrating not so much upon refinement of manner as upon efficiency in administration or the making of
war. Even the Mayas' monuments now seem to us to mark, however
flamboyantly, the decadence of an art which reached its zenith a
thousand years earlier.

Where did these founder-fathers come from? Our forbears thought
they knew for certain, but we have to admit that we simply do not
know at all. Population movements in the Bering Strait region have
been of great complexity. Quite recently, the Eskimoes took part in
them. They were preceded over a period of about a thousand years by
the paleo-Eskimoes whose culture is evocative of archaic China and the
Scythians; and for a very long time indeed, from about 8000 B.C. up
till the eve of the Christian era, other and different populations have
been traced there. Sculptures going back to the first millennium B.C.
suggest that the ancient inhabitants of Mexico may have been of a
physical type very different from that of today's Indians: well-fleshed
Orientals whose clean-shaven features were flabbily modelled, and, with
them, bearded and aquiline profiles which put us in mind of the
Renaissance. Evidence of another kind is provided by the geneticists,
who tell us that at least forty vegetable species which grew wild,
or were cultivated, in pre-Colombian America, have either the same
chromosomic composition as corresponding species in Asia, or a
composition derived from the same source. Should we infer that
maize, which is on the list, was brought in from south-east Asia? And
how could this be, if the Americans were growing maize four thousand
years ago, at a time when the art of navigation was in its infancy?

Without going so far as to follow Heyerdahl in his audacious
theory that Polynesia was colonized by primitive Americans, we must
admit that the voyage of the *Kon-Tiki* proves that trans-Pacific
contacts could have taken place, and taken place often. But at the time,
towards the beginning of the first millennium B.C., when great civilizations were already in existence in America, the Pacific islands were
empty: nothing has been found, at any rate, which dates so far back.
We should therefore look beyond Polynesia, towards Melanesia, which
may already have been inhabited, and towards the whole length of the
Asiatic coast. We now know that communications between Alaska and
the Aleutians, on the one hand, and between Alaska and Siberia on the

FIGS. 46 7.   On the left Chavin culture, northern Peru (after Tello); on the
right Monte Alban, southern Mexico (from bas-reliefs known
as 'the dancers')

FIG. 48.   Hopewell culture, eastern United
States (after Charles C. Will-
oughby. *The Turner Group of
Earthworks*, Papers of the Pea-
body Museum, Harvard Uni-
versity, Vol. VIII, No. 3, 1922)

other, went on without interruption. Towards the beginning of the Christian era, iron tools were in use in Alaska, though the natives there knew nothing of metallurgy; similar types of pottery may be found from the region of the Great Lakes in North America to central Siberia, as can also the same legends, the same rites, the same myths. At a time when the West lived shut in upon itself, it would appear that all the northern peoples, from Scandinavia right across to Labrador, by way of Siberia and Canada, were in close and constant contact with one another. If the Celts took certain of their legends from that sub-Arctic civilization, of which we know almost nothing, we can understand why it is that the Grail cycle is closer to the Indian myths which flourished in the forests of North America than to any other mythological system. Nor is it, in all probability, by chance that the Lapps are still building conical tents identical with those of the North American Indians.

In southern Asia, American civilizations give rise to echoes of another sort. On the frontiers of southern China are peoples ('Barbarians', the Chinese call them) with an extraordinary affinity with those of America; and this is still more the case with the primitive tribes of Indonesia. In the interior of Borneo, anthropologists have recorded myths, elsewhere missing, which are among those most widely known in North America. And, then again, specialists have long pointed out the similarities between archaeological documents found in south-east Asia and those which belong to the proto-history of Scandinavia. Probably, therefore, these three regions—Indonesia, the American north-east, and Scandinavia—formed the trigonometrical points of the pre-Colombian history of the New World.

One of the major events in human history is the emergence of neolithic civilization, with its widespread use of pottery and weaving, the beginnings of agriculture and livestock-farming, and the first experiments in the field of metallurgy. Originally this was confined to the region, in the Old World, between the Danube and the Indus. But may it not have provoked an uprush of excitement among the most 'backward' peoples of Asia and America? It is difficult to understand the origins of American civilization without admitting the hypothesis of an intense activity on both the Asiatic and the American coasts of the Pacific. For thousands of years this activity may well have been a carrier of ideas along the whole length of these coasts. Formerly we refused to allow pre-Colombian America the space, as it were, to breathe in history, on the grounds that that space had also been denied to post-Colombian America. We may still be falling into a second

Fig. 49.   Chavin, northern Peru (after Tello)

error—that of thinking that for twenty thousand years America was cut off from the rest of the world, simply because, during that time, she was cut off from western Europe. Everything points, on the contrary, to the hypothesis that, while the Atlantic remained in total silence, a humming as of innumerable bees could be heard all around the periphery of the Pacific.

Be that as it may, at the beginning of the first millennium B.C., an American hybrid seems to have already engendered three sub-species, solidly grafted on to problematic variants traceable to an earlier stage of evolution. Among rustic cultures, the Hopewell culture, which occupied or contaminated all that part of the U.S.A. which lies east of the plains, corresponds to the Chavin culture in the north of Peru (this in its turn is echoed in the south by Paracas). Chavin, for its part, resembles the earliest manifestations of the so-called Olmec civilization and foreshadows the development of Maya civilization. In all three cases, we are faced with an art that is cursive, free, supple, and marked by an intellectual delight in double-meanings (in Hopewell, as in Chavin, certain motifs bear one meaning when read normally, and quite another when read upside-down). There is as yet almost no sign of the angular stiffness, the immobilism, which we associate with pre-Colombian art. Sometimes I try to persuade myself that the drawings of the Caduveo are, in their way, a continuation of this distant tradition. Was it at that time that the civilizations of America began to draw away from one another, with Mexico and Peru taking the initiative and marching ahead with 'giant's strides', while the others kept to an intermediary position or fell behind, gradually sinking into a state of near-savagery? We shall never know exactly what happened in tropical America, because climatic conditions there do not favour the preservation of archaeological remains; but it is a disturbing fact that the social organization of the Gé—and even the lay-out of the Bororo villages—is similar to what we have been able to reconstruct of such vanished civilizations of pre-Inca times as those of Tiahuanaco in upper Bolivia.

These considerations have carried me a long way from the preparations for my expedition into the western Mato Grosso. But they were indispensable if I was to give the reader an idea of the intense excitement which attaches to all American studies, whether on the archaeological or the anthropological level. Such is the scale of the problems, so narrow and so precarious are the paths hitherto trodden, so final the annihilation of tract after immense tract of the past, and so

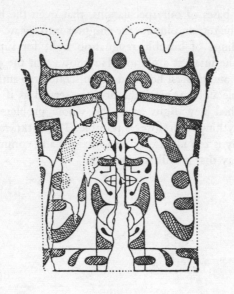

Fig. 50. Hopewell, eastern United States (after W. K. Moorehead, the Hopewell mound. . . . Field Museum, Chicago Anthropol. Series, Vol. VI, No. 5, 1922)

uncertain the bases of our speculations, that even the briefest reconnaissance on the terrain plunges the enquirer into a state of indecision, in which feelings of humble resignation fight for supremacy with moments of the insanest ambition. He knows that the essentials have gone for ever and that all he can do is to scratch the surface. Yet may he not stumble upon some indication, preserved as if by a miracle, which will shed new light upon the whole problem? Nothing is possible: everything, therefore, is possible. The darkness in which we grope our way is too intense for us to hazard any comment on it: we cannot even say that it will last for ever.

22 *In the Sertão*

Back in Cuiaba, after a two years' absence, I tried to find out exactly what the position was in respect of the telegraph line three or four hundred miles to the north.

That line was detested in Cuiaba, and for more than one reason. Since the foundation of the town in the eighteenth century, such rare contacts as it had had with the north had always been made by water, along the middle reaches of the Amazon. For supplies of their favourite stimulant, the *guarana*, the inhabitants of Cuiaba relied on expeditions by dug-out canoe on the Tapajoz: these might last as long as six months at a time. This *guarana* is a hard paste, chestnut in colour: the *Maué* Indians are almost the only people who make it, and they use as its base the fruit of a liana, the *Paullinia sorbilis*. They take a short sausage of this paste and grate it on the bony tongue of a fish, the *pirarucu*: these tongues are kept in a buckskin purse. These are important details, for the use of a metallic grater, or of a purse made from any other skin, would cause the precious substance to lose all its powers. (The Cuiabanos also believe that their ropes of tobacco must be torn open and shredded by hand; cut with a knife, they might lose their flavour.) The *guarana* powder is then poured into sugared water, where it does not dissolve but floats around in a compact mass. The taste is faintly chocolatey. I myself never found that it had the slightest effect, but for the peoples of the central and northern Mato Grosso the *guarana* is as important as is the maté for the peoples more to the south.

People thought it worth while, in any case, to go to great trouble to get supplies of *guarana*. Before venturing among the rapids, a group of men were left behind on the bank, where they cut away a corner of the forest and planted manioc and maize, so that the expedition should find fresh provisions waiting for it on its way home. But, since the development of the steam-ship, *guarana* could be had quicker and in greater quantity from Rio de Janeiro, whither the coastal-steamers would bring it from Manaus and Belem. The expeditions along the Tapajoz were relegated, therefore, to a heroic and already forgotten past.

And yet, when Rondon announced that he was about to open the north-western part of the area to civilizations, memories revived. A little was known of the edges of the plateau, where two hamlets, Rosarion and Diamantino, respectively sixty-five and a hundred miles north of Cuiaba, were drowsing their existences away now that their veins and gravels were exhausted. Beyond, the journey would have to be made over land, fording one after another the little rivers which made up the tributaries of the Amazon, instead of canoeing down them: an enterprise, this, as dangerous as it would be lengthy. Towards 1900 the northern region was still mythical territory, and people even believed in the existence there of a mountain-range, the Serra do Norte, which was even marked on their maps.

This state of ignorance, when allied to the still-recent opening-up of the American Far West and the consequent Gold Rush, led to the craziest aspirations among the peoples of the Mato Grosso, and even, too, among those along the coast. Once Rondon's men had laid their telegraph line, a great flood of emigrants would invade the territory, exploit its undreamed-of resources, and build there a Brazilian Chicago. A great disappointment was in store: like that north-easterly region in which is the ill-omened territory described by Euclides da Cunha in *Os Sertões*, the Serra do Norte proved to be a semi-desert, a savannah as inhospitable as any in America. And, what is more, the telegraph line lost all importance after the beginnings, in 1922, or thereabouts, of radio-telegraphy: these coincided with the completion of the line, which became overnight an object of merely archaeological interest, veteran of a period in the development of science which came to an end just as the line was ready to come into service. It did, however, enjoy its hour of glory when, in 1924, the federal government was cut off from all contact with the interior by the insurrection of São Paulo. Only by telegraph could Rio remain in contact with Cuiaba, by way of Belem and Manaus. Then began the days of decline, and those few enthusiasts who had thought to seek employment in the telegraph service dropped away or lingered on, forgotten. When I reached them, it was several years since they had been sent any provisions. Nobody quite dared to shut the line down; but nobody thought of using it, either. The poles were left to tumble down, the wire to go rusty; as for the last survivors of the staff, they had neither the courage nor the means to leave; and so, slowly, one after another, eaten away by sickness, hunger, and solitude, they were dying off.

All this weighed the more heavily upon the consciences of the Cuiabanos because their hopes, though dashed, had none the less produced one small tangible result: the exploitation of those employed in the telegraph service. Before leaving to take up their posts, every employee had to nominate a *procurador*, or representative, who would collect their salaries for them and use them 'according to instructions'. These instructions were limited, as a rule, to requests for the purchase of cartridges, paraffin, salt, sewing needles, and cloth. All these were accounted for at high prices, thanks to an understanding between *procuradores*, Lebanese merchants, and caravan-managers. After a few years the wretched employee was so heavily in debt as to be even less able than before to envisage escaping from the bush. The line was best forgotten, beyond a doubt; and my project of using it as a base was generally discouraged. And when I tried to seek out the retired N.C.O.s who had served under Rondon I could get nothing out of them but a sombre, ever-repeated '*um pais ruim, muito ruim, mais ruim que qualquer outro . . .*' 'a ghastly country, simply ghastly, more ghastly than anything anywhere . . .' A country, they said, to keep out of at all costs.

And then there was the problem of the Indians. In 1931 unidentified Indians had come down from the valley of the Rio de Sangue, which had been believed to be uninhabited, and attacked and destroyed the telegraph station at Parecis, in a relatively frequented region two hundred miles north of Cuiaba and a mere fifty miles from Diamantino. These wild people had been nicknamed the 'wooden muzzles', on account of the wooden discs which they had mounted in their lower lips and in the lobes of their ears. They had continued their sorties, at irregular intervals, and as a result the line had had to be moved some fifty miles to the south. As for the Nambikwara nomads who had been in intermittent contact with the outposts since 1909, their relations with the whites had been marked by ups and downs of fortune. Cordial enough at first, they had got progressively worse until, in 1925, they invited seven white workpeople to visit their villages: nothing more was heard of these guests, and from that moment onwards the Nambikwara and the staffs of the telegraph service kept well clear of one another. In 1933 a Protestant mission established itself not far from the station at Juruena; relations would seem to have been embittered almost from the start, the natives being displeased with the gifts, insufficient in their eyes, with which the missionaries rewarded them for their help in building a house and laying out its garden. A few months later, an Indian with high fever came to the mission-post and was given two aspirins, which he swallowed in front of his friends. He then went off for a bathe in the river, caught pneumonia, and died. As the Nambikwara are expert poisoners, they could only imagine that their friend had been murdered; reprisals were taken, in the course of which six inhabitants of the mission—among them a baby aged two —were massacred. A rescue party from Cuiaba arrived to find only one woman still alive. Her story, as it was repeated to me, tallied exactly with that given to me by the originators of the attack, who served me faithfully for several weeks as companions and informers.

Since this incident, and one or two others which followed upon it, the atmosphere had remained tense along the whole length of the line. When I at last managed, at the main post office of Cuiaba, to get into contact with the main stations—a task which took several days to accomplish, in every case—the news was uniformly depressing. One post had just been been threatened with an Indian attack; another had not seen any Indians for three months, which in a way was just as bad; a third, which had once had Indians working nearby, reported that they had reverted to their wild state, become *bravos*, and so on. Only one indication was—or so I was assured—encouraging: three Jesuit Fathers had been trying for the last few months to settle in near Juruena, on the edge of Nambikwara territory, four hundred miles north of Cuiaba. I could always go and see them, get the news from them, and make my final plans afterwards.

And so I spent a month at Cuiaba, getting my expedition ready. Having once got leave to go, I was determined to see the thing through; a six months' journey in the dry season across a plateau described to me as more or less a desert, with no grazing animals, and no game. I had therefore to take with me all the food I should need, not only for my men, but for the mules which would serve us as mounts until we got to the basin of the Madeira and could continue by canoe. A mule that has no maize to eat is in no state to travel. To carry all this food, I needed oxen, which are more hardy and can get by on leaves and dry grass. Even so, some of my oxen might well die of hunger and exhaustion; it would not do to take too few. And as I should have to have herdsmen to drive the oxen, and to unload and load them at each halting-place, our numbers would be correspondingly increased.

More food, therefore; and more mules; and more oxen to carry the food for those men and those mules. . . . It was a vicious circle. In the end, after consultation with experts in the matter, I settled for fifteen men, fifteen mules, and thirty oxen. Where mules were concerned, I had no choice: within a radius of thirty miles around Cuiaba there were not more than fifteen for sale. I bought the lot, at prices ranging, at the 1938 rate of exchange, from one hundred and fifty to one thousand francs a head, according to their looks. As leader of the expedition, I kept the best for myself: a majestic white animal, bought from the nostalgic, elephant-loving butcher of whom I spoke earlier.

The real problem began with the recruitment of my men. The scientific personnel, including myself, were four in number at the time we set out, and we knew very well that our success, our safety, and even our lives, would depend on the loyalty and competence of the team I was about to engage. For days on end I picked over the bad-hats and adventurers who formed the lowest depths of Cuiaban society: then an elderly 'colonel' of sorts recommended to me a former herdsman of his, now living in an isolated hamlet, whom he described as poor, reliable, and high-principled. I went to call on him, and he won me over at once by that instinctive nobility which is often found among the peasants of the Brazilian interior. Instead of begging me, as did the others, for the rare privilege of a year's paid employment, he made certain conditions: that he alone should decide on the choice of both men and oxen, and that I should allow him to bring along one or two horses, which could be sold at a good price, he thought, in the north. I had already bought a herd of ten oxen from a caravan-manager in Cuiaba; what had tempted me was their great stature and, even more, their saddles and harnesses, which were made from tapir-hide in a style already historic. Moreover the Bishop of Cuiaba had persuaded me to take on a protégé of his as my cook. After a few days' march he turned out to be a *veado branco*, or white roebuck—a homosexual, that is to say—and so badly afflicted with piles that he could no longer sit on a horse. He was only too glad to drop out. My magnificent oxen (who had just walked three hundred miles—a fact unknown to me) had not an ounce of fat on their bodies. One after another they began to suffer great pain from the fact that saddles bit into their skins and, despite all the skill of our *arreieros*, their hide was soon worn through. Great openings appeared, streaming with blood, infested with worms, and offering a clear view of the spinal column. These skeletal, festering beasts were our first casualties.

Luckily Fulgencio—pronounced 'Frugencio'—my head-man, was able to make up for this by buying a number of oxen which, though nothing much to look at, managed for the most part to complete the journey. As for his own team, he recruited it in his village, or thereabouts, relying on very young men who had known him from their childhood onwards and had a great respect for his skills. Most of them came from old Portuguese families that had settled in the Mato Grosso a hundred or two hundred years earlier and still kept to their austere and ancient traditions.

Poor as they were, each one of these recruits possessed a hand-towel, embroidered and lace-bordered, which had been made for them by their mother, sister, or fiancée: and never, at any point on the journey, would they have dried their faces on anything else. But when I offered them a ration of sugar to go with their coffee, I met with a proud refusal. They were not *viciados* (perverted), they said. I had one or two difficulties with them, because they, like myself, had made up their minds once and for all about the problems involved in our journey. For instance, I only just escaped having a mutiny on my hands where our victualling arrangements were concerned. They were convinced that they would die of hunger if I did not devote all the available space to rice and beans. They would just tolerate the idea of dried meat, although they were convinced that we should never go short of game. But sugar! Dried fruit! Preserves! Such notions appalled them. They would have died for us, but never could we expect to be called 'Sir'. Nor would they do any washing, except on their own behalf: such duties were fit only for women. The bases of our contract were as follows: for the duration of the expedition each of them would be lent a mount and a rifle; and over and above his food he would get five francs a day, at the 1938 rate of exchange. This, they insisted, should be kept back until they were home again—by which time they would have put by one thousand five hundred or two thousand francs: a nest-egg large enough for a man to get married, in some cases, or start a cattle-farm, in others. . . . It was also agreed that Fulgencio would pick up a few young Indians, half-civilized Paressi, at the moment when we crossed the former domain of that tribe, which today provides the great majority of those responsible for the upkeep of the telegraph line on the edge of the Nambikwara territories.

And so, slowly, by groups of two or three men and a few animals, our expedition got organized in one hamlet or another all round Cuiaba. We were due to assemble one day in June 1938 at the gates of

Cuiaba, whence oxen and riders were to set off to rendezvous with Fulgencio, taking some of our baggage with them. Our oxen could carry from one hundred and twenty to two hundred and fifty pounds avoirdupois apiece, according to their strength, the weight being distributed in two bundles, one exactly as heavy as the other, on either side of a wooden pack-saddle; this saddle was padded round with straw, and the whole apparatus covered with dried skins. Our day's march averaged about eighteen miles, but at the end of a week our animals needed to rest for several days. So we decided to let them go on ahead, with as light a load as possible, while I myself would come up behind with a heavy lorry as far as the track allowed—to Utiarity, that is to say, some three hundred and thirty-five miles north of Cuiaba. Utiarity was a telegraph station, over the borders of Nambikwara territory, on the bank of the Rio Papagaio: here the raft used as a ferry was too fragile to bear the weight of my lorry. Beyond that point, adventure began.

Eight days after the departure of our troop—*tropa* is the word for a caravan of oxen—our lorry and its cargo were on the move. Barely thirty-five miles along the road we came upon our men and their beasts, peacefully encamped in the savannah, at a time when I had supposed them to be almost at Utiarity. It was the first, and not the last, time that I got angry. After one or two more disappointments of this sort I began to realize, however, that the idea of time had no currency in the universe I had just entered. It was not I who was the leader of the expedition; nor was it Fulgencio; it was our oxen. These ponderous creatures turned into so many duchesses, whose every whim, moment of fatigue, or sudden shift of temper had to be carefully watched. An ox that is too heavily laden or suddenly feels tired will give no warning of these facts; he will go steadily on, till quite suddenly he collapses, dead—or, if not dead, so exhausted that it will take six months' rest to get back his strength. In either case, he must be abandoned. The herdsmen are, therefore, the servants of their oxen, every one of whom has a name that corresponds to his colour, his way of walking, or his temperament. Mine, for instance, were called: Piano (the musical instrument); Maça-Barro (mud-squasher); Salino (Fond of salt); Chicolate (my men had never tasted chocolate, but this was their name for a mixture of hot sweetened milk and egg-yolk); Taruma (palm-tree); Galão (big cock); Lavrado (red ochre); Ramalhete (bouquet); Rochedo (reddish); Lambari (a fish); Açanhaço (a blue bird); Carbonate (an impure diamond); Galala (?); Mourinho (half-caste); Mansinho (gentle); Correto (correct); Duque (duke); Motor (motor, because, his driver told me, he 'had such a good engine inside him'); Paulista; Navigante (navigator); Moreno (brown); Figurino (model); Brioso (lively); Barroso (muddy-looking); Pai de Mel (bee); Araça (a wild fruit); Bonito (pretty); Brinquedo (toy); Pretinho (swarthy).

The whole troop came to a halt whenever the herdsmen thought it necessary. One by one, the oxen were unloaded and camp set up. If it was safe, the oxen were allowed to roam freely; if not, they had to graze under supervision. (*Pastorear* was the word, in the latter case.) In the morning, men would scour the country for miles around until each animal had been located. That was called *campiar*. The *vaqueiros* speak of their animals as deeply mischievous by nature: likely, in fact, to run away from sheer devilry, hide themselves, and evade capture for days on end. Was I not once immobilized for a week because one of our mules, they said, had gone off into the *campo*, walking now sideways, now backwards, in such a way that his *rastos*, or traces, were indecipherable?

When the animals had been got together their sores had to be inspected and covered with ointment, and the load had to be readjusted so that the pack-saddles did not bear directly on a sore place. And they had still to be harnessed and laden. Next began a further drama: four or five days' rest had left the oxen quite out of practice. No sooner did they feel the pole on their backs than some of them would kick up their heels and send the carefully balanced load flying in all directions: all had to be begun again from the beginning. We counted ourselves lucky if none of the recalcitrants had headed at top speed for open country. For, if that occurred, camp had to be set up afresh: unloading, *pastorear*, *campiar*, and so on—all had to be gone through before the troop could be reassembled and the loading gone through for the fifth or sixth time until, for no apparent reason, all went smoothly.

Myself less patient, even, than my oxen, I took weeks to resign myself to this whimsical manner of progress. Leaving the troop behind us, we arrived at Rosario Oéste, a little town of a thousand inhabitants, black for the most part, dwarfish, and be-goitred, lodged in *casebres*, mud huts a flaring red in colour beneath fronds of bright green palm-leaves, aligned in long straight avenues with tall grasses running wild in the roadway.

I remember my host's little garden: it might have been a living-room, so minutely was it organized. The earth was swept and beaten, and the plants set out as carefully as the furniture in a drawing-room:

two orange-trees, a lemon-tree, a pimento-plant, ten stems of manioc, two or three *chiabos* (an edible hibiscus), the same number of stems of vegetalbe silk, two rose-trees, a small group of banana-trees, and another of sugar-canes. Lastly, a parrot in a cage and three chickens, each tied by one foot to a tree.

At Rosario Oéste, dishes for 'state occasions' are divided down the middle: half of each chicken is served roasted and hot, the other half cold, with a sauce piquante. Half of each fish is fried, and the other half boiled. The meal is rounded off with a *cachaça*, an alcoholic drink made from sugar-cane; with this there goes a ritual salutation: *cemiterio, cadeia, cachaça não e feito para uma so pessoa*. This means: 'The three Cs—cemetery, prison, brandy-wine—never visit the same person together.' Rosario is already in the middle of the bush, and its inhabitants—sometime prospectors for rubber, gold, and diamonds—might have useful advice to give me as to the route to be followed. I listened, with this object in mind, to my visitors' life-histories, in which legend and personal experience were inextricably mingled.

I could not bring myself to believe, for instance, that *gatos valentes*, super-cats produced by the cross-breeding of the jaguar and the domestic cat, were to be found in the north. But another story may be worth telling, even if nothing remains of it in the end but the style, the turn of mind, of the *sertão*.

At Barra dos Bugres, a little town in the western Mato-Grosso, in upper Paraguay, there lived a *curandeiro*, a bone-setter who also cured snake-bites. First he made an incision in the victim's forearm with the teeth of the *sucuri*, or boa. Next he drew on the ground, in gunpowder, a cross and set it on fire while the victim held his arm in the smoke. Finally he took a piece of cotton, singed it with an *artificio* (a tinder-box whose tinder is made of lint screwed up into a cornet-shaped receptacle), dipped it in *cachaça*, and made the victim drink the mixture. That was all.

One day the leader of a *turma de poaieros* (a troop of ipecacuanha-pickers) witnessed one of these 'cures' and asked the bone-setter to wait till the following Sunday, when his men would arrive and, beyond a doubt, would want to have themselves vaccinated (at five milreis a time, or, in 1938, five francs). The bone-setter agreed. On the Saturday morning a dog was heard howling outside the *barracão*, or collective cabane. The troop-leader sent a camarada to see what was the matter: *a cascavel*, or rattle-snake, was running wild. The troop-leader told the bone-setter to capture the snake, and when he refused the troop-leader said: 'No snake, no vaccinations.' And so the bone-setter reached for the snake, got bitten, and died.

The man who told me this added that he had himself been vaccinated by the bone-setter and that, shortly afterwards, he had deliberately let himself be bitten by a snake, to see how far the vaccination was effective. It worked perfectly. 'By the way,' he added, 'it wasn't a poisonous snake.'

I tell this story because it illustrates very well the combination of malice and naivety in regard to incidents, in themselves tragic, which the peoples of the Brazilian interior treat as the small change of everyday life. This combination is typical of their way of thinking, and the conclusions drawn from it are only superficially absurd. I heard much the same kind of reasoning from the leader of the neo-Moslem Ahmadi sect, who had invited me to dinner in Lahore. The Ahmadis strayed from orthodoxy in that they believed, for instance, that all those who, in the course of history, had claimed to be Messiahs (and Socrates and Buddha were among those whom they included) had in fact deserved the title; God would otherwise have chastised them for their impudence. My friend in Rosario no doubt thought, in the same way, that if the bone-setter's magic had not been authentic the supernatural powers would have exposed him by making a poisonous snake out of one that was normally harmless. As the cure was considered to be magical, he had verified it on a level which was also, in its way, that of magic.

We had been assured that the 'road' to Utiarity had no surprises in reserve for us: none comparable, at any rate, to those I had encountered two years earlier on the route to the Rio São Lourenço. And yet, when we reached the summit of the Serra do Tombador, at the point known as Caixa-Furada, one of the pinions of our driving-shaft broke. We were some twenty miles from Diamantino, whither our drivers set off on foot to telegraph to Cuiaba. Rio could fly the necessary spare part to Cuiaba, and it could be sent up to us by lorry: with luck the whole operation would take eight days, by which time our oxen would have overtaken us.

So we set our camp on the heights of the Tombador, a rocky spur about a thousand feet high, at the end of the *chapada* over the basin of the river Paraguay. On the other side, stream after little stream was already swelling the tributaries of the Amazon. What were we to do in this spiky savannah, once we had found the few trees on which were hung hammocks and mosquito-nets? Sleep, daydream, hunt? The dry season had begun a month before; we were in June; apart from one or two half-hearted showers in August—the *chuvas de caju,* and even they never came in 1938—not a drop of rain would fall before September. The savannah had already taken on its winter-time look: plants were faded and dried-up, burnt in places by bush-fires, with the sand showing through in big patches beneath the scorched brushwood. It was the season at which such game as was wandering across the plateau was concentrated in those impenetrable round thickets, the *capões,* whose domed outlines marked the point at which a spring bubbled up: there, a yard or two of still-green pasture could be found.

During the rainy season, from October to March, when rain fell almost every day, the temperature rose to forty-two or forty-four degrees Centigrade during the day. The nights were cooler, with on occasion a sudden chill at dawn. During the dry season, on the contrary, changes of temperature were very great—sometimes from a maximum of forty degrees in the day to a minimum of eight or ten degrees at night.

As we sat round our camp-fire drinking maté we listened to the tales of adventure in the *sertão* which were being told by our drivers, and by the two brothers who were our particular servants. They described how it is that the big ant-eater, the *tamandua,* is quite harmless in the *campo,* where he loses his balance if he attempts to stand upright. In the forest he leans up against a tree, steadying himself with his tail, and smothers, with his forepaws, whatever comes within reach. The ant-eater has no fear of night attack, what is more, for 'he sleeps with his head folded back along his body, and not even the jaguar can make out where he has put it'. In the rainy season, one ear must be kept on the alert for the wild pigs (*caetetu*) which go about in bands of fifty or more; the grinding of their teeth can be heard for miles around (whence their second name of *queixada,* from *queixo,* the chin). The hunter should take to his heels when he hears this sound, for if any one of the pigs is killed or wounded the others will make a mass attack on their adversary, whose only course is to climb a tree, or a *cupim* (anthill).

One man told of how once, when travelling with his brother, he heard someone crying for help but, for fear of the Indians, did not do anything about it till the morning. The cries went on, meanwhile, till dawn—when they found a hunter perched up in a tree, with his rifle fallen to the ground and an angry circle of pigs all around him.

His fate was less tragic than that of another hunter, who, hearing the wild pigs in the distance, took refuge on an anthill, where the pigs surrounded him. He fired into them until his last cartridge was spent, and he could only defend himself with the woodcutter's knife or *facão*. The next day a rescue-party came out to look for him, and before long they knew, from the *urubus*, or carrion-birds, that were circling overhead, just where he must be. Nothing remained on the spot but his skull and the gutted carcasses of the pigs he had killed.

The talk took a more humorous turn: how the *seringueiro*, or rubber-prospector, once met a hungry jaguar. Each followed the other round and round a big clump of trees till suddenly the man dodged in the wrong direction and came face to face with the jaguar. Neither dared to move. The man didn't even dare to cry out: 'and it was only after half an hour that he got cramp, made an involuntary movement, and noticed he was carrying a gun'.

Unluckily our camp was infested with the usual insects: *maribondo* wasps, mosquitoes, *piums*, and *borrachudos* (tiny blood-sucking flies that came up by the swarm), and with these the *pais-de-mel*, honey-fathers— bees, in a word. South American bees have no sting, but they plague the visitor in quite another way. Delighting in human sweat, they battle for their favourite positions at the corners of the eye, the lip, and the nostril. Once established, they seem to become completely intoxicated by their victim's secretions, preferring rather to die *in situ* than to take refuge in flight. Further connoisseurs then fly up, attracted by the sight of such corpses as linger on one's skin. Thence their nick- name of *lambe-olhos*: eye-lickers. The bees are the real plague of the tropical bushlands, worse even than the mosquitoes and the blood- suckers, to whose infections one's system adapts itself at the end of a few weeks.

But where there are bees, there is honey: and honey that can be collected with impunity, gutting the bees' above-ground shelters, or finding in a hollow tree shelf upon shelf of spherical cells, each as big as an egg. Each species of bee produces a honey with its own special flavour—I counted at least thirteen—and all of them so pungent that we soon learned to do as the Nambikwara do and dilute them with water. The scents are deep-lying and slow to reveal themselves in their entirety—in this respect they are like the wines of Burgundy—and they have a disconcerting strangeness. I found something of the same sort in a condiment, produced in south-east Asia from cockroach glands and worth its weight in gold. The merest touch of it is enough to scent a whole dish. Also very near to it is the smell given off by a French coleoptera, dark in colour, which is called *procuste chagriné* (shagreen procuste).

At long last the rescue-lorry arrived with the new part and a mechanic to fix it in place. Off we went again, through half-ruined Diamantino in the valley that looked over towards the Rio Paraguay, and up on to the plateau—uneventfully, this time. Skirting the Rio Arinos which sends its waters to the Tapajoz, and thence to the Amazon, we turned off to the west, towards the accidented valleys of the Sacre and the Papagaio—contributors, both, to the Tapajoz—who mark their arrival by falls two hundred feet high. At Paressi, we stopped to inspect the weapons left behind them by the Beiços de Pau who were said, once again, to be not far away. A little farther on, we spent a sleepless night in the marshlands, disturbed by the native camp-fires whose smoke was rising, a mile or two away, into the cloudless skies of the dry season. One more day, to see the river-falls and get together a little information in a village of Paressi Indians. And there we were, at the Rio Papagaio, a hundred or more yards wide, with its waters, flowing by at ground-level, so clear that we could see deep, deep down to the rocky river-bed. On the far side, a handful of straw huts and mud-walled sheds: the Utiarity telegraph station. We unloaded the lorry, sent over our luggage and our stores of food by the raft which served as a ferry, and took leave of our drivers. Already on the farther shore we could glimpse the naked bodies of the Nambikwara.

23 *On the Line*

Living on the 'Rondon Line' was much like living on the moon. Imagine a territory the size of France, three-quarters of it unexplored; inhabited only by little bands of nomads, who are among the most genuinely 'primitive' of the world's peoples; and traversed from one end to the other by a telegraph line. The *picada*, or summary track which runs alongside it, is for nearly five hundred miles the region's only landmark. The Rondon Commission undertook a reconnaissance or two to the north and the south, but except for these the traveller may be said to step into the unknown the moment he leaves the *picada*—and even the *picada* itself is sometimes not easily distinguished. There remains, you may say, the wire itself: but the wire, obsolete from the day of its completion, hung down from poles never replaced when they go to rot and tumble to the ground. (Sometimes the termites attack them, and sometimes the Indians, who mistake the humming of the telegraph wires for the noise of bees on their way to the hive.) In places the wire trails on the ground, or has been carelessly draped across the nearest little tree. Paradoxically, in short, the line rather aggravates than takes away from the prevailing atmosphere of desolation.

An entirely virgin landscape is so monotonous as to deprive its wildness of all meaning. It does not so much defy us as return a blank stare: almost it abolishes itself as we look at it. And, in this bush that seems to go on for ever, the narrow slit of the *picada*, the contorted outlines of the remaining poles, the reversed arcading of the pendent wires—all put us in mind of those incongruous objects which float in a vast loneliness in the paintings of Yves Tanguy. Bearing witness, as they do, to the passage of western Man and the vanity of his efforts, they mark out, more clearly than if they had not been there, the extreme limit that he has attempted to cross. The erratic nature of the enterprise

and the total reverse in which it culminated give a final authenticity
to the surrounding wastelands.

About a hundred people in all lived 'on the line'. Some of them
were Paressi Indians, recruited on the spot, in days gone by, by the
Telegraph Commission. The army had taught them to keep the
wires in good condition and operate the machinery—not that this
stopped them from hunting with bow and arrows, in traditional style.
The rest were Brazilians who had been attracted to the job by the hope
of finding either an Eldorado or a second Far West. These hopes had
long been dashed: the farther they advanced into the plateau, the rarer
became the 'deposits' of diamonds.

Deposit, or 'form', was the name given to the little stones, notice-
able either by their colour or by their strangeness of form, which are
to the diamond what footprints are to an animal. 'Anywhere where you
see those stones, there've been diamonds.' There are, for instance, the
emburradas, 'stuffed pebbles'; the *pretinhas*, 'little negresses'; the
amarellinhas, 'golden sovereigns'; the *figados-de-gallinha*, 'chicken-
livers'; the *sangues-de-boi*, 'Bull's blood'; the *feijões-reluzentes*, 'shining
beans'; the *dentes-de-cão*, 'dog's teeth'; the *ferragems*, 'tools'; and also the
carbonates, lacres, friscas de ouro, facieras, chiconas, and so on.

Diamonds in short supply, therefore: game almost non-existent;
and among these sandy wastes, where rain fell in torrents for one half
of the year and not a drop could be expected during the remaining six
months, nothing grew but a few spiky, mis-shapen shrubs. As has often
happened in the history of Brazil, a handful of adventurers, madmen,
and starvelings had been swept into the interior on an impulse of high
enthusiasm, only to be abandoned, forgotten, and cut off from all
contact with civilization. Each little 'station' consisted of a group of
straw huts, fifty or seventy-five miles from its nearest neighbour—a
distance which could, in any case, be covered only on foot—their
isolation was complete, and each individual wretch had to adapt
himself to it by devising his own particular brand of insanity.

Every morning the telegraph system came momentarily to life.
News was exchanged: one station had seen the camp-fires of a band of
Indians, bent on their extermination: another reported the disappearance of two Paressis, victims no doubt of those same Nambikwara
bands whose reputation was firmly established along the whole length
of the line. They had been sent, beyond all question, *na invernada do ceu*
—'to hibernate in heaven'. The tale is retold, with grim humour, of
the missionaries who were massacred in 1933, or the telegraphist who

was found buried up to his waist, with his chest riddled with arrows and his automatic sender perched on his head. For the Indians have a morbid fascination for the servants of the line. On the one hand, they represent a continuous danger, the more intense for the play of fancy; and on the other the visits of their little nomadic bands constitute the sole distraction of the telegraphist's life—and, more than that, his only opportunity of human contact. So that when they turn up, once or twice a year, many pleasantries fly to and fro between the reputed killers and their potential victims—each jest being couched, of course, in the weird jargon of the line, which is made up of, in all, some forty words, half Portuguese, half Nambikwara.

Apart from these episodes, each of which has its moment of vicarious excitement for those who are listening in, every 'head of station' develops a personal style all his own. Take, for example, the fanatic who never bathes in the river without loosing off half a dozen rounds with his Winchester rifle. He hopes in this way to intimidate the Indian bands who would otherwise, he feels sure, spring upon him from both banks of the river and cut his throat: but the only result is that he squanders his irreplaceable store of ammunition. This activity is known as *quebrar bala*, or breaking a cartridge. Then there is the man of the world who had been a student of chemistry in Rio and still imagines himself to be passing the time of day on the Largo-do-Ouvidor. But as he has now nothing whatever to say his conversation consists merely of empty mimicry, stray clackings of fingers and tongue, and 'meaningful' glances: in the days of the silent cinema he would have passed as a *boulevardier*. Nor should the man of prudence be forgotten: for he it is who has contrived to maintain his family in a state of equilibrium, biologically speaking, with a band of deer which drinks regularly from a nearby spring. Every week he kills just one of these animals, never less, never more; and so both game and station manage to keep going. But for the last eight years—since the annual revictualling of the stations, by a caravan of oxen, was discontinued—he and his family have eaten nothing but deer.

An equally picturesque note of quite another kind was struck by the Jesuit Fathers who had had a few weeks' start of us and had just settled down near the station of Juruena, some thirty-five miles from Utiarity. There were three of them: a Dutchman who thought only of his devotions, a Brazilian who planned to civilize the Indians, and a Hungarian, a one-time squire and inveterate lover of the chase, whose role it was to provide the mission with fresh meat. Not long after their

arrival they were visited by their Provincial, an elderly Frenchman
with a prodigious roll to his r's who seemed to have stepped straight
out of the reign of Louis XIV; from the gravity with which he spoke
of the 'savages'—he never spoke of the Indians in any other way—you
would have thought that he had disembarked in a new Canada, with
Cartier or Champlain at his side.

Hardly had he arrived when the Hungarian was seized with one
of the attacks which are known among French colonials as the *coup de
bambou*. (He was said to have been prompted to enter his Order by the
repentance consequent upon a first youth spent in debauch.) Insult
after insult rang through the compound as he set upon his superior, and
the Provincial, more than ever perfectly in character, exorcized him in
a flurry of signs of the cross and cries of '*Vade retro, Satanas!*' The
Hungarian, delivered at last of his demon, was put on fifteen days'
bread and water: a punishment which remained symbolical, since
bread was not to be had at Juruena.

Both Caduveo and Bororo could, without any play upon words,
be called in their different ways 'learned societies'. The Nambikwara,
by contrast, brought the observer back to what he might readily,
though mistakenly, suppose to be the childhood of our race. We had
set up our camp on the edge of the little village, beneath a half-
dismantled straw roof which had been used as a store-room at the time
when the line was being laid. The Indians' camp was only a few yards
away, and consisted of a score or so of people, making up six families
in all. The little band had arrived there a few days before us, during
one of its nomadic sorties.

For the Nambikwara year is divided into two distinct parts. During
the rainy season, from October to March, each group takes up its
lodging on a little hill overlooking a river-bed and builds for itself
rough and ready huts with branches and palm-leaves. In a burnt-out
clearing in the forest gallery which fills the damp lower part of each
valley they plant and till their gardens. These include above all manioc
(both bitter and sweet), several kinds of maize, tobacco, sometimes
some haricot beans, cotton, ground-nuts, and calabashes. The women
grate the manioc on flat spiky strips of palm-wood; when one of the
poisonous species is in question, they get rid of the juice by pressing
the fresh pulp into a taut-drawn piece of bark. From these gardens they
get enough food to keep them going during part of their sedentary
period. To keep 'something in the larder', cakes of manioc-pulp are carefully buried in the earth and dug up, half-rotten, weeks or months later.

At the beginning of the dry season they abandon their village and split up into small roving bands. For seven months these nomadic groups wander across the savannah in search of game: tiny animals above all—grubs, spiders, grasshoppers, rodents, snakes, lizards—and, with these, fruit, seeds, roots, wild honey—everything, in short, which might prevent them from dying of starvation. When they set up camp, it is for a day or two, or sometimes for a few weeks, and each family makes for itself a rude shelter of branches and palm-leaves stuck into the sand in a semi-circle and tied together at the top. As the day progresses the shelter is moved round, in such a way that its protective screen stands always between its inmates and the sun—or, as the case may be, the wind or the rain. The search for food is uppermost, however, in everyone's mind. The women arm themselves with pointed sticks, to dig up roots or, on occasion, to kill off any little animal that presents itself. The men go off hunting with big bows made of palm-wood: their arrows are of several sorts. For birds they use a blunted point, so that the arrow shall not get caught in a high branch. For fish a longer arrow is used. It has no feathering, but is divided at one end into either three or five tapering points. There are also poisoned arrows, whose tips are dipped in curare and protected by a bamboo sheath: these are for game of medium size. For 'big game'—jaguar or tapir—an arrow with a spear-shaped head of bamboo is used: this brings on a haemorrhage, since the dose of poison carried by any one arrow would not be effective.

After the splendour of the Bororo palaces, the material poverty of the Nambikwara seems almost beyond belief. Neither sex wears any clothing at all and their physical type, as much as the poverty of their circumstances, marks them out at once from their neighbours. They are small in stature: just over five feet, in the case of a man, and about three inches less among the women. As is the case with so many other South American tribes, the women have no very clearly modelled waist; but their limbs are unusually graceful, and their hands and feet more elegantly made than is generally the case. Their skin is darker too: many are afflicted with skin diseases that cover their entire bodies with patches of violet, but, among those not so affected, the skin is powdered with the sand in which they love to roll themselves; this gives it, after a time, a look and feel of velvety beige which can, above all in the case of the younger women, be enormously attractive. The head is elongated, the features often delicate and well shaped, the eye lively, the body hair better developed than among most peoples of

Mongolian origin, and the hair of the head wavy and not, as a rule, quite black. Earlier visitors to the region were so impressed by the Nambikwara's physical type that they put forward the hypothesis of cross-breeding with negroes who had escaped from their plantations in order to take refuge in the *quilombos*, or colonies of rebel slaves. But, if the Nambikwara had been so crossed in recent times, the admixture of negro blood would make it out of the question for them all to belong to blood group O, as our researches confirmed that they do: for this group implies, if not a purely Indian origin, at any rate a demographic isolation of several centuries' duration. Today the Nambikwara's physical type seems to us less problematical, since it harks back to that of an ancient race whose bones have been found in Brazil in the caves of Lagoa Santa, one of the sites in the State of Minas Geraes. I myself was amazed to find myself reminded of the almost-Caucasian faces, found in certain statues and bas-reliefs in the region of Vera Cruz, which are now attributed to the oldest of Mexican civilizations.

This similarity was all the more disturbing because the indigence of the Nambikwara's material culture disposed one not to associate them with the loftiest cultures of central and southern America, but rather to treat them as survivors of the stone age. The women wore, at most, a single strand of shell-beads round their waists and another strand or two as necklaces or as shoulder-belts; their ear-rings were of feathers or mother-of-pearl, their bracelets were carved from armadillo-shell or, at times, made up from straw or cotton (woven by their men) and tied round their ankles or biceps. The men's wardrobe was even more summary, except that some of them wore a tuft of straw that hung from their belts just above their genitals.

In addition to bow and arrows, their armament consisted of a sort of flattened spike. But this seemed to relate as much to magic as to the hunt, for I never saw it used except to deflect a hurricane or to kill off, with a well-directed throw, the *atasu*, or evil spirits of the bush. The name of *atasu* is given also to the stars, and to our oxen, of whom they lived in terror. (And yet they will readily kill and eat mules, though they made their acquaintance at the same time as that of the oxen.) My wrist-watch was also called an *atasu*.

The Nambikwara's entire possessions can be assembled, therefore, in the baskets which the women carry, slung over their shoulders, during the nomadic season. These baskets are of plaited bamboo, worked in an openwork pattern with six strands of split bamboo (two pairs running perpendicularly and one cross-wise) made up into an open network of large hexagonal shapes: at the top they spread slightly outwards, and at the bottom they form a shape like a finger-stall. They can be as much as five feet high—as tall, that is to say, as the women who bear them: at the bottom, a few cakes of raw manioc are covered over with leaves. Next comes their furniture and their stock of tools: calabashes used as receptacles; knives made from a sharp splinter of bamboo, roughly flaked stones, scraps of iron (obtained, these, by barter) stuck with wax, or tied with string, between two pieces of wood that serve as a handle; drills made up of a sharp flake of stone or iron point, mounted on the end of a wooden stem that can be rotated between the palms of the hands. They also have the axes and hatchets which the Rondon Commission gave them, so that their stone axes are now used mainly as anvils when fashioning objects from bone or shell: grinders and polishers are still made from stone, however. Among the western groups, with whom I began my enquiries, pottery was unknown: and elsewhere it is exceedingly crude. The Nambikwara have no canoes, and when they come to water they swim across it, helping themselves at times with buoys made of faggots.

All this equipment was so primitive as hardly to merit the name of 'manufactures'. The Nambikwara basket contains above all the raw materials from which tools can be put together as and when they are needed: woods of various kinds, and notably those which can be used as fire-drills; lumps of wax or resin; bunches of vegetable fibres; the bones, teeth, and claws of animals; odd bits of fur; feathers; hedgehogs' quills; nutshells, and shells taken from the river; stones; cotton; and seeds. All this has such a haphazard appearance that the collector may well be discouraged and see in the whole assemblage the result not so much of human activity as of that of some race of giant ants. And there is, in effect, a resemblance between a column of ants and a Nambikwara band as it marches in single file through the tall grasses, each of the women encumbered with her plaited basket, much as an ant which forms part of a colony on the move is encumbered with the egg it has to carry.

The Indians of tropical America invented the hammock. Not to know of the hammock, and not to have any convenience of that kind for rest or sleep, is for them the very symbol of poverty. The Nambikwara sleep naked on the bare earth. As the nights of the dry season are cold they keep warm by sleeping close to one another, or by drawing nearer and nearer to the remains of the camp-fire—so much so, in fact, that they often wake up at dawn sprawled in the still-warm ashes of the fire. For this reason the Paressi have a nickname for them —*uaikoakoré*, 'those who sleep on the ground'.

As I said before, the band who were our neighbours at Utiarity, and later at Juruena, was made up of six families: the leader's, with his three wives and his adolescent daughter; and five others, each made up of a married couple and one or two children. All were interrelated, for the Nambikwara prefer to marry a niece (their sister's daughter), or a kinswoman of the kind which anthropologists call 'cross-cousin': the daughter of their father's sister, or of their mother's brother. Cousins of this sort are called, from birth, by a name which means husband or wife, while the other cousins (the children respectively of two brothers or two sisters and called, therefore, by anthropologists 'parallel' cousins) call themselves, and treat one another as, brothers and sisters and may not intermarry. All the Indians seemed to be on very good terms with one another: yet even so small a group—twenty-three persons in all, counting the children—sometimes ran into trouble. A young widower had just married a rather good-for-nothing girl who refused to take any interest in the children of his first marriage—two little girls, one six years old and the other two or three. Despite the kindness of the elder child, who acted as 'mother' to her little sister, the baby was very neglected. The grown-ups would have been delighted for me to adopt her, for she was being passed from one family to the next, and not all were glad to care for her. The children, however, had a solution which they preferred, and which seemed to them a tremendous joke: they brought me the little girl, who could as yet barely walk, and suggested, with gestures which could have only one meaning, that I should take her for my wife.

Another family was composed of father and mother, no longer young, and their pregnant daughter, who had come back to them now that her husband had abandoned her. And then there was a young couple, with a child still at the breast. These were still suffering from the prohibitions which are enforced upon parents whose child is still unweaned. They were filthy, because they were not allowed to bathe in the river; thin, because most kinds of food were forbidden them; and idle, because they were excluded, for the time being, from the collective life of the band. Sometimes the man went off on his own to hunt or collect food; the woman was fed by her husband or her relations.

The Nambikwara make no difficulties and are quite indifferent to the presence of the anthropologist with his notebooks and camera. But certain problems of language complicated matters. They are not allowed, for instance, to use proper names. To tell one from another we had to do as the men of the line do and agree with the Nambikwara on a set of nicknames which would serve for identification. Either Portuguese names, like Julio, José-Maria, Luisa; or sobriquets such as *Lebre*, hare, or *Assucar*, sugar. I even knew one whom Rondon or one of his companions had nicknamed Cavaignac on account of his little pointed beard—a rarity among Indians, most of whom have no hair on their faces.

One day, when I was playing with a group of children, a little girl was struck by one of her comrades. She ran to me for protection and began to whisper something, a 'great secret', in my ear. As I did not understand I had to ask her to repeat it over and over again. Eventually her adversary found out what was going on, came up to me in a rage, and tried in her turn to tell me what seemed to be another secret. After a little while I was able to get to the bottom of the incident. The first little girl was trying to tell me her enemy's name, and when the enemy found out what was going on she decided to tell me the other girl's name, by way of reprisal. Thenceforward it was easy enough, though not very scrupulous, to egg the children on, one against the other, till in time I knew all of their names. When this was completed and we were all, in a sense, one another's accomplices, I soon got them to give me the adults' names too. When this was discovered the children were reprimanded and my sources of information dried up.

The second linguistic difficulty arose from the fact that the Nambikwara speak a number of different dialects, all of which are unknown. The termination of the nouns, and certain verbal forms, distinguish one dialect from another. On the 'line' a kind of pidgin language is spoken, and this is useful only at the very beginning. The good nature and lively intelligence of the Indians were such that I soon picked up the rudiments of their speech. Luckily, their language includes a number of key words—*kititu* in the eastern dialect, *dige*, *dage*, or *tchore* elsewhere—which when added to a noun turn it into a verb with, if need be, a negative particle. In this way one can say more or less whatever one wants to, even if this 'basic Nambikwara' does not allow of any very subtle processes of thought. The natives are well aware of the uses of this short cut, and when they try to speak Portuguese they employ much the same methods. Thus 'ear' and 'eye' become respectively 'to hear' (or 'to understand') and 'to see', and they render the contrary notion by saying, for instance, *orelha acabo* or *olho acabo*: 'Ear [or eye] I finish. . . .'

The Nambikwara language has a rather clouded or fogged sound to it, as if it were being whispered and spoken 'on the breath'. The women like to emphasize this by slurring certain words (thus *kititu* becomes *kediutsu* when they pronounce it): they articulate with the tip of the tongue, affecting a babyish, mumbled utterance. They are perfectly aware of the mannered, not to say precious, character of their diction; and when I did not understand them and had to ask them to say something again they exaggerated all the more, out of mischief. If I gave up in discouragement they would burst into laughter and make fun of me: they had got the better of it.

I soon realized that apart from the verbal suffix the Nambikwara language included a dozen others, which marked off objects and living things into categories. Hair, body hair, feathers; pointed objects and orifices; bodies, whether supple or stiff; fruits, seeds, rounded objects; things which hung down or trembled; bodies that swelled out or were full of liquid; barks of trees, hides, and other forms of covering, etc. This suggested a parallel with a linguistic family in central America and the north-west of South America: *Chibcha*, once spoken by a great civilization in what is now Colombia, an intermediary between the civilizations of Mexico and Peru. Could the Nambikwara language be a southerly offshoot of this? This was yet another reason not to be taken in by appearances. For all their physical poverty, natives who hark back in physical type to the most ancient of the Mexicans and in language-structure to the *Chibcha* empire are not at all likely to be 'primitives' in the true sense of the word. Rather should they be compared to a stock of prodigal sons for whom history has never killed the fatted calf. Why this should be so we do not know: but the answer may be found, one day, in their past, of which we as yet know nothing, and in the inhospitable character of the terrain in which they are now living.

24 *Family Life*

The Nambikwara wake up at dawn, relight their fires, warm themselves up as best they can after the chill of the night, and make a light meal of whatever has been left over from the previous day. Shortly after this the men go off hunting, individually or in groups. The women stay behind in the encampment and busy themselves in the kitchen. They take their first bathe when the sun begins to get up. Women and children often bathe together, for the fun of it; and sometimes they light a fire so that when they come out of the water they can squat in front of it and warm themselves—making the most, again in fun, of such momentary shivers as may overtake them after their bathe. Other bathes follow during the course of the day. There is not much variety in their occupations. The most exacting, in terms of time and trouble, is the preparation of their food: the manioc has to be grated and pressed, and its pulp dried and cooked; or else it's a matter of shelling and boiling the *cumaru* nuts which add a scent of bitter almonds to so many of their dishes. When supplies run short the women and children go off on an expedition to collect and gather. When there's enough to eat the women turn to spinning, squatting or kneeling the while, with their buttocks resting on their heels. Or else they trim, polish, and string together their 'pearls'—nut-kernels or river-shells—and with these they make ear-rings and other ornaments. And if they don't feel like work they pick off one another's lice, or idle about, or go to sleep.

In the heat of the day the camp falls silent. Its inhabitants, speechless if not actually asleep, make for the precarious shade of their huts. At other times everybody talks all the time, no matter what he is doing. Laughter and high spirits are general and there's a constant flow of joking and teasing, obscene or scatological references being greeted with particular approval. An enquiry or the arrival of a visitor brings

272

all work to a halt; and if two dogs or birds should chance to copulate everyone downs tools and watches closely and with fascination. Work does not begin again until this important event has been discussed at appropriate length.

The children laze about for most of the day, and although the girls may give their elders some momentary assistance the boys enjoy a more leisurely life, with some occasional fishing. Men who have not gone hunting devote themselves to wickerwork, or make arrows or musical instruments, or do a little to 'help in the house'. Most households are perfectly harmonious. Towards three or four in the afternoon the hunters return home. The camp then becomes more lively, conversation takes a brisker turn, and the groups that form and re-form have no longer a family basis. Dinner consists of flat cakes of manioc and whatever has been found during the day. At nightfall the women take it in turns to go out into the bush and cut down or otherwise collect enough wood for the night. Back they come, stumbling in the half-light under the load that pulls tight the porter's bandeau across their foreheads. Eventually they squat down and lean a little backwards, so that the big basket of plaited bamboo rests on the ground and the bandeau loosens.

The wood is heaped in one corner of the camp and everyone takes what he needs. Family groups re-form as the fires begin to blaze and the evening is spent either in talk or in singing and dancing. Sometimes this is kept up well into the night; but usually, after some preliminary caresses and a bout or two of affectionate tussling, each couple draw more closely together, the mother takes her sleeping child in her arms, all fall silent, and nothing is heard in the night but the crackling of a log, the light step of someone looking after the fire, the barking of a dog, or a child crying.

The Nambikwara have few children; childless couples are not uncommon, though one or two children constitute the norm, and it is quite exceptional for there to be more than three in one family. Sexual relations between parents are forbidden while their child remains unweaned: often, that is to say, until it is three years old. The mother carries her child astraddle on her thigh, and keeps it in place with a broad shoulder-strap of cotton or bark; as she also has to carry a large basket on her back, one child is clearly her maximum load. Living, as they do, a nomadic life in a very poor environment, the natives have to be very careful; and the women do not hesitate to resort to abortion of one kind or another—medicinal plants, or some mechanical device—in case of need.

They both feel and show, none the less, the liveliest affection for their children; and this affection is returned. Sometimes, however, this is masked by extreme nervousness; instability takes its toll. A little boy, for instance, is suffering from indigestion; between headache and vomiting he spends half his time groaning aloud and the other half in sleep. Nobody pays the slightest attention to him and he is left completely alone all day. But when evening comes his mother comes across to him, tenderly picks off all his lice as he falls asleep, signs to the others not to come near, and makes for him a kind of cradle with her arms.

Or, it may be, a young mother is playing with her baby. Playfully she gives him slap after little slap on the back; he loves it, and to make him laugh the louder she slaps harder and harder till he bursts into tears; then she stops and consoles him.

Once I saw the little orphan of whom I spoke earlier literally trampled underfoot during a dance; in the general excitement she had fallen down and nobody had noticed.

When they are crossed, children often hit out at their mother, and their mother does nothing to stop it. The children are not punished, and I never saw one of them beaten—not even in pantomime—except by way of a tease. Sometimes a child cries because he's hurt himself, because he's hungry, because he's had a quarrel, or because he doesn't want to have his fleas picked off—but this last is rare: delousing seems to be as much fun for the patient as for the operator, and it is prized as a mark of interest and affection. A child—or husband—who feels in need of it will lay his head on the woman's knees, offering first one side and then the other. She will then part his hair, ridge by ridge, and peer through. A louse, once caught, is instantly eaten. Any child who cries during the proceedings is consoled by an older child or a member of his family.

And so there's a delightful gaiety in the spectacle of a mother with her child. Sometimes she dangles an object in front of him through the straw walls of their hut and whips it away just as he reaches out for it: 'There—you missed it! Grab it at the front—or the back!' Or else she takes up the child and with great shouts of laughter threatens to throw him down to the ground. '*Amdam nom tebu!* I'll drop you!' And the child pipes up: '*Nihui!* No, please don't!'

There's something correspondingly uneasy and exacting about the loving kindness with which the children surround their mother. They want to be quite sure that she gets her fair share of the spoils of the hunt. The child has lived very close to its mother. When they move camp she carries the child until it can walk; later, it hurries along at her side. It stays with her in their camp, or their village, while its father goes hunting. Eventually, however, certain distinctions of sex may be remarked. A father is more interested in his son than in his daughter, because his son has to be taught the techniques of manhood; and the same is true of mother and daughter. But the relations between father and children are marked by the tenderness and solicitude which I have described above; a father will take his child for a walk on his shoulder and carve for him weapons appropriate to his tiny arm.

It's also the father's duty to tell his children the traditional legends of the tribe—transposing them down, of course, in terms acceptable to the infant mind: 'Everyone was dead! No one left! Not one man! Nothing!' Thus begins the South American children's version of the Flood in which all humanity was once engulfed.

In cases of polygamy a special relationship exists between the children of the first union and their youthful stepmothers: a free-and-easy comradeship which is extended to all the other girls in the group. Small in numbers as this group may be, there may none the less be distinguished within it a society of adolescent girls and young women who band together to go bathing in the river, troop off into the brushwood to satisfy the needs of Nature, organize smoking-parties, enjoy private jokes, and delight in games which we might consider in dubious taste—taking it in turns, for instance, to squirt their saliva in each other's faces. The relationship between members of the band is a close one, and all prize it, but there is no great courtesy about it; in this it resembles our own schoolboy groups. Rarely will one of the girls render another a service or show her any particular attention; but one interesting result of it all should be remarked—that the girls come to independence much more quickly than the boys. They follow the young women and take part in their activities, whereas the boys, left entirely to themselves, make timid and largely ineffective attempts to band together in the same way, remaining meanwhile mother-bound until their first childhood is over.

The Nambikwara children know nothing of games. Sometimes they make toys of a kind out of rolled or plaited straw, but in general their only pastime is wrestling—or some other form of shared physical exertion—and their existence is one long imitation of the grown-ups. Little girls are taught to spin, or left to play around, laugh among themselves, or fall asleep. Little boys of eight or ten begin to play with miniature bows and arrows and learn the rudiments of masculine activity. But girls and boys alike soon learn that the basic, and sometimes the tragic, preoccupation of Nambikwara life is how to get enough to eat; and they learn that they are expected to take an active part in it. Collecting and gathering are tasks to which they lend themselves with great enthusiasm. When food runs short they can often be seen scavenging on the outskirts of the camp, digging away at roots or tiptoeing in the grass, stick in hand, in search of grasshoppers. The little girls know the role of their sex in the economic life of the tribe and are impatient to make themselves worthy of it.

Once I met a little girl who was carrying a puppy in the shoulder-carrier that her mother used for her little sister. Seeing her, I said: 'Stroking your puppy-baby?' And she replied, in all seriousness: 'When I'm big I shall kill all the wild pigs and all the monkeys. I'll kill them every one when the dog barks!'

Actually she made a grammatical mistake which her father was delighted to point out. Instead of saying '*tilondage*' for 'when I'm big' she used the masculine form: '*ihondage*'; thus revealing a woman's feminine ambition to raise the economic activities which are peculiar to her sex to the level of those that are the privilege of manhood. As the precise sense of the phrase which she used was 'kill by a heavy blow with a club or stick' (a digging-stick, in this case) it would seem that she was unconsciously trying to identify the women's scrounging for food (their capture of, at most, very small animals) with the men's true hunting with bow and arrow.

Another special relationship exists between those children whose degree of cousinage is such that they are allowed to call one another 'Husband' and 'Wife'. Sometimes they behave like a real married couple and, at nightfall, they leave the family circle, take a few warm logs into a corner of the camp, and light a fire. After which they 'set up house' and demonstrate their affections, in so far as they can, just as their elders do; the grown-ups glance their way in amusement.

I must also say a word about the household pets; these live in intimacy with the children and are indeed themselves treated as children. They share in the family meals and receive the same marks of interest or tenderness as do the human beings: their lice are picked for them, they take part in games, and people talk to them and caress them. The Nambikwara have a wide range of pets: dogs, first of all, and cocks and hens—descendants of those introduced into the region by the Rondon Commission—monkeys, parakeets, birds of many kinds, and even wild pigs, wild cats, and coatis. The dog alone serves a specific purpose: it helps the women when they go hunting with sticks. (Men never use dogs when they go out with bow and arrow.) The other animals are reared purely as pets. They are never eaten; nor, for that matter, are the eggs which the hens lay in the undergrowth. But if a young bird dies during the process of taming it is eaten without hesitation.

When the Nambikwara move on, all the pets, save those able to walk, are included in their baggage. The monkeys get a firm hold in the women's hair, rising above it helmet-wise, with their tails wound round the bearer's neck for double security. Hens and parakeets perch on top of the baskets; other animals are carried bodily. None is very well fed; but all—even when food is short—get something. In return they act as fools and jesters to the company.

To turn to the grown-ups: the Nambikwara attitude to matters of love can be summed up in their formula '*Tamindige mondage*', of which an exact if inelegant translation would be: 'It's good to make love.' Daily life is impregnated, as I have said, with eroticism. Love-matters arouse their interest and curiosity in the highest possible degree; they never tire of discussing them, and conversation in the camp is full of undertone and allusion. Most sexual activity takes place at night—near the camp-fires, at times, but more often the partners go off a hundred yards or so into the neighbouring brushwood. Their departure, immediately noticed, is the subject of widespread jubilation; jokes are made, speculations exchanged; even the children are carried away by an excitement whose origins they know perfectly well. Sometimes a little group of men, young women, and children will dart off, whispering and laughing the while, in pursuit of such glimpses of the proceedings as they can secure through the branches. The protagonists don't at all care for this, but they have to put up with it, just as they have to put up with the teasing that will greet them as they return to the camp. Sometimes a second couple will follow their example and make off into the isolation of the bush.

Yet these occasions are rare. Nor is their rarity due altogether to formal prohibition. The real obstacle would seem to lie rather in the Nambikwara temperament. Never in all the amorous exercises to which they devote themselves publicly and with such relish have I seen even the beginnings of an erection; and yet often they go quite far. The pleasure they seek would seem to be playful or sentimental, rather than directly physical. This is perhaps why the Nambikwara, in contrast to almost all the other populations of central Brazil, wear the penis uncovered. It is in fact probable that the penis-sheath, when used, is intended not so much to prevent an erection as to make plain the peaceful condition of him who wears it. Peoples who live entirely naked are not ignorant of what we call 'modesty': they simply have another frontier-line. Among the Brazilian Indians, as among certain Melanesian peoples, modesty has nothing to do with how much or how little of the body is exposed; tranquillity lies on one side of the frontier, agitation on the other.

These nuances sometimes gave rise to misunderstandings between ourselves and the Indians for which neither side was responsible. It was difficult to remain indifferent to the pretty girls who would tease us as they sprawled in the sand at our feet, naked (and supple) as worms. When I went to bathe in the river I was often embarrassed by the onslaught of a group of five or six people, young or old, whose one object was to rob me of my soap, of which they were so particularly fond. These liberties extended to every aspect of daily life. Often I had to make the best of a hammock stained red by a native who had used it at siesta-time after painting her body with urucu. And when I was at work, sitting on the ground in the middle of a circle of informants, I sometimes felt a hand tugging at my shirt-tails; some woman was finding it easier to wipe her nose on my shirt than to go in search of the little branch, folded in two like a pair of pincers, that usually did duty in this respect.

To understand the attitude of the sexes towards one another we must first bear in mind the fundamental character of the couple among the Nambikwara. The couple is, both economically and psychologically, *par excellence, the* unit in Nambikwara life. Among these bands of nomads, where each band forms and re-forms unceasingly, the couple represents—in theory at any rate—stable reality. The couple forms, moreover, the only subsistence-unit known to the Nambikwara. They live, after all, in a double economy: fishing and gardening on the one hand, collecting and scavenging on the other. The man takes care of one, the woman of the other. While the men troop off for a day's hunting with bow and arrow, or, during the wet season, work in the garden, the women wander off, stick in hand, into the savannah with their children and fall upon everything that may come in useful for food: seeds, fruit, berries, roots, tubers, eggs, small animals of every sort. At the end of the day the couple reunites around the fire. When the manioc is ripe, and there is still some left, the man brings home a great load of roots and the woman shreds and presses them to make cakes. If the hunt has gone well the game is cut in pieces and cooked quickly beneath the hot ashes of the family fire. But for seven months of the year manioc is hardly ever seen; hunting is a matter of luck in this sandy desert where the game, such as it is, rarely stirs from the shaded pastures of the springs; between each spring and the next is a considerable expanse of largely inhospitable undergrowth. And so it's the women, with their gathering, who keep the family alive.

I have often shared the grisly dolls' dinners which, during half the year, are the Nambikwara's only means of not dying of hunger. When the man returns tired and silent from a fruitless day's hunting, the woman turns to her basket and brings out a touching collection of oddities: the orange-coloured fruit of the *buriti* palm, two large and poisonous spiders, a lizard or two and some of their tiny eggs, a bat, some little nuts from the *bacaiuva* or *uaguassu* palms, and a handful of locusts. The fleshed fruits are crushed by hand in a calabash filled with water, the nuts are broken open with a stone, and the animals and larvae bundled higgledy-piggledy in among the ashes; and all sit down gaily enough to a meal which, while it would barely take the edge off a white man's hunger, must here suffice for a whole family.

The Nambikwara use the same word for 'young' and for 'pretty', and the same one also for 'old' and 'ugly'. Their aesthetic judgments are based therefore on human, and above all on sexual, values. But the interest of one sex for the other is a complicated matter. Men regard women, comprehensively speaking, as not quite of the same stuff as themselves; their behaviour towards them is coloured by—as the case may be—desire, admiration, or tenderness. The terminological confusion on which I remarked above is in itself a form of homage. The sexual division of labour does of course give the woman a role of capital importance (since it is her collecting which, in large measure, keeps the family alive); but this collecting is none the less regarded as an inferior type of activity. The ideal life is seen in terms of hunting or farming: the possession of great quantities of manioc and game of superior size and quality is a dream continually cherished, though not often realized. Provender got together as luck wills it is regarded, quite rightly, as a miserable minimum. In Nambikwara folklore 'to eat locusts' has in a much stronger degree the pejorative sense of our 'to take pot-luck'. And it's the women and children who provide the locusts.

In the same way a woman is regarded as a secondary possession: prized and loved, perhaps, but secondary. It's the custom among men to speak of women with pitying goodwill, and to address them with a slightly teasing indulgence. Men constantly say: 'Children don't know, and women don't know, but I *do* know'; and women in general, *doçu*, with their jokes and their endless talk, are the subject of much tender mockery. But this is merely a social attitude. When the man and his woman are alone beside their fire he will listen to her complaints, take note of her wishes, and in his turn ask her help in a hundred-and-one little things; masculine braggadocio gives place to the collaboration of two partners who know very well that the one cannot get along without the other.

This ambiguity in the men's attitude towards their women has its exact counterpart in the women's attitude towards their men. The women think of themselves as a distinct group. We've already noticed that they do not speak as the men speak: this is true above all of young women, particularly when they have not yet had children, and of concubines. Among mothers and older women the differences are much less marked. Young women enjoy the society of children and adolescents and amuse themselves a great deal in their company; and it's the women, too, who look after the animals with that humanity which characterizes certain South American Indians. All this creates around the women, within the interior of the group, a quite special atmosphere: at once childish, high-spirited, mannered, and provocative; and the men fall in with this when they come back from hunting or gardening.

But when the women turn to those activities which are their special preserve, their attitude becomes quite different. If it's a matter of working with their hands they manifest an exemplary skill and patience as they sit in a circle, back to back, in the hushed encampment. While travelling they loyally hump the heavy baskets which contain food for the journey, the family's combined belongings, and the arsenal of arrows. Their menfolk meanwhile march at the head of the column, bow at the ready, with one or two arrows merely and a wooden spear or digging-stick: their job is to spot the occasional fruit-tree or the animal that breaks cover; while the women, with their carriers' headbands braced across their foreheads, and the long narrow basket (shaped like an overturned elongated bell) laid along their backs, march on for mile after mile with their characteristic gait: thighs held stiffly together, knees joined, ankles wide apart, and feet well forward, with the weight on the outer edge of the foot and their haunches swaying. They are brave women, and energetic, and gay.

This contrast between the women's psychological attitude and their economic function is to be found also on the religious and philosophical plane. Relations between men and women among the Nambikwara oscillate between the two extremes around which their existence is organized: on the one hand the settled existence of the gardening period, based on the two masculine activities of hut-building and cultivation, and on the other the nomadic period, during which women are almost entirely responsible for the supply of food. One stands for security and a copious menu, the other for hazard and near-starvation. To these two forms of existence, winter and summer, the Nambikwara react in very different ways. They speak of winter with that melancholy that comes from the conscious and resigned acceptance of our human condition: a dismal doing-over-and-over of an unchanging routine. Summer on the other hand is a matter for excited discussion, with the element of discovery always present.

Where metaphysics are concerned, these relationships are seen in reverse. The souls of Nambikwara men are incarnated, after death, in jaguars; but the souls of women and children vanish into the air and no more is heard or seen of them. This distinction explains why women are excluded from the more sacred ceremonies: these are held at the beginning of the cultivation period and consist in the manufacture of bamboo flutes fed with offerings; the men play on these instruments, after first withdrawing out of sight of the women.

Although the flutes were, as it were, 'out of season', I was very anxious to hear them played and to acquire a few of them. A group of men, yielding to my insistence, set off on an expedition to the distant forest in which the big bamboos were to be found. Three or four days later the returning travellers woke me up in the middle of the night; they had waited for the women to go safely to sleep. We all trooped off to a point about a hundred yards distant, where bushes hid us from the rest of the camp, and the men set to work to construct their flutes. When they were ready, four players struck up in unison; but as the flutes were not quite in tune the effect was one of some harmonic illusion. The tune was different from the Nambikwara songs with which I had become familiar. (The melodic structure of these songs reminded me of the *rondes* of the French countryside.) They differed also from the strident calls which could sometimes be heard on the three-holed nose-ocarina which was made up of two fragments of a calabash stuck together with wax. The range of the flageolets was restricted to a few notes, but the tunes were marked by a chromaticism and rhythmic resource which seemed to me strikingly similar to certain passages in Stravinsky's *Sacre du Printemps*—notably to the woodwind modulations in the passage entitled 'Action rituelle des ançêtres'. Any woman who ventured upon the scene would have been struck down at once. As with the Bororo, the women are the subject of a veritable metaphysical curse; but the women of the Nambikwara differ from those of the Bororo in that they do not enjoy special status in law— although it seems that among the Nambikwara descent also follows the maternal line. In a society as little organized as theirs, these tendencies remain a matter of implication, and the synthesis operates on a basis of informal practice and non-crystallized attitudes.

When the men describe the kind of life which is summed up in the temporary shelter and the everlasting basket-load, they speak as tenderly as if they were caressing their wives. Each day they extract, collect, or capture the most incongruous means of subsistence. They live exposed to rain, wind, and cold. And this existence leaves behind it no more trace than the spirits, dispersed by wind and storm, of the women on whose activity it fundamentally resides. They conceive of their sedentary life quite differently, though its specific and ancient character is attested by the original species which they cultivate. The unchanging sequence of agricultural activity confers on the sedentary life a perpetuity identical with that of the reincarnated spirits of the men, the long-lasting winter-house, and the gardens which will go on living and producing 'when the death of the farmer's predecessor will have been forgotten'.

Perhaps this explains the extraordinary instability of the Nambik-wara, and the speed with which they pass from cordiality to hostility? The few observers who have got near to them have all been struck by this. The Utiarity band was the one that, five years earlier, had mur-dered a group of missionaries. My male informants took pleasure in describing this incident, and disputed with one another for the honour of having struck the decisive blows. I must admit that I couldn't blame them for it. I've known many missionaries. Some, certainly, had great merits both as men of science and as human beings. But the American Protestant missions which tried to penetrate the central Mato Grosso around the year 1930 were of a kind all their own. They came from peasant families in Nebraska or Dakota and, as adolescents, had been brought up to believe literally in hell-fire and cauldrons of boiling oil. Some of them became missionaries in the way that other people take out an insurance policy. Once assured of their salvation they felt no need to do anything else to deserve it; and in the exercise of their profession they were often revoltingly hard and inhuman.

How did the massacre come about? That I discovered as the result of a piece of awkwardness which nearly got me into serious trouble. The Nambikwara are accomplished toxicologists. They manufacture curare for their arrow-heads, for instance, beginning with an infusion made from the red skin which covers the roots of certain *strychnos*; this they heat over a fire until the mixture attains the consistency of a paste. They also employ other vegetable poisons, and carry them about with them in feather or bamboo tubes, wrapped round with cotton thread or bark. These poisons are used to avenge hurts, whether amorous or commercial; I shall have more to say of them.

These are poisons of a scientific sort, whose manufacture is carried out quite openly, with none of the precautions and magical complexities which surround the making of curare in more northerly regions. The Nambikwara have also others, more mysterious in their nature. In tubes identical with those used for authentic poisons, they collect particles of the resin exuded by a tree of the genus *bombax*, whose trunk swells out half-way up. They believe that if they project one of these particles on to an adversary, he will take on the physical condition of the tree: swell up, that is to say, and die. Authentic poisons and magical substances are alike designated by the name of *nandé*, which goes far beyond the narrow meaning of our 'poison'. It connotes, in fact, every kind of threatening action—as well as all the products or instruments which may be useful when such action is taken.

I had in my luggage a few of those large and many-coloured silk-paper balloons that are used by the thousand in Brazil on the feast-day of St John. (You fill them with hot air by fixing a little torch underneath them.) One evening I had the unhappy idea of showing the natives how they worked. The first balloon caught fire on the ground—an incident which was received with general laughter, it being clear that they had no idea of what ought to have happened. The second balloon went off all too well, mounting rapidly into the upper air and eventually mingling its tiny flame with those of the stars; after vagabonding above us for some time it disappeared. The spectators meanwhile had ceased to be amused. Quite other sentiments overcame them; the men watched fixedly and in great annoyance, while the women cowered together in terror, hiding their heads in their arms. I heard the word *nandé* used over and over again. The next morning a deputation of the men came to see me, demanding to inspect my stock of balloons and make sure that no *nandé* was hidden among them. The inspection was extremely thorough; thanks, however, to the Nambikwara's remarkably positive turn of mind (despite all that I have just said) my demonstration, with the aid of a fire and a few shreds of paper, of the power of hot air to make objects rise, was, if not understood, at any rate accepted. As usually happened when something had to be excused, the whole thing was blamed on the women who 'understood nothing', had 'got the wind up', and were in terror of calamities of every kind.

I wasn't deceived: things might well have turned out very badly indeed. Yet neither this incident nor others which I shall describe later could detract from the feelings of friendship which the Nambikwara inspire in those, and those only, who live in intimacy with them for a considerable period. I was therefore amazed to read the description given by a foreign colleague of his encounter with the same band of natives that I had known, ten years previously, at Utiarity. When he went there in 1949 two missions were working there: the Jesuits of whom I have spoken, and some American Protestants. The native band had dwindled to eighteen: this is what our author has to say about them:

'Of all the Indians which I have visited in the Mato Grosso, the members of this band of the Nambikwara were the most miserable. Of the eight men, one had syphilis, another had some kind of infection in his side, another had an injured foot, another was covered with some kind of scaly disease from head to foot, and another was deaf and dumb. The women and children, however, appeared to be healthy. Owing to the fact that they use no hammocks but sleep on the ground, they are always covered with dirt. On cold nights they remove the fires and sleep in the warm ashes. . . . They wear clothes only when they are given by the missionaries, who ask that they be worn. Their distaste for bathing permits not only a covering of dust and ashes to accumulate on their skins and hair but also particles of decayed meat and fish which, combined with stale sweat, makes proximity to them rather distasteful. They also appear to be heavily infected with internal parasites, for their stomachs are distended and they are continually passing wind. On several occasions when a number of them had crowded into the small room we used for working we had to cease work in order to air the room.

The Nambikwara are surly and impolite even to rudeness. On many occasions when I went to visit Julio at his camp he was lying down near a fire and, as he saw me approach, he turned his back to me, saying he did not want to talk. The missionaries informed me that a Nambikwara will ask for some object several times, and if it is not given he will try to take it. In order to keep the Indians out they would sometimes close the screen door, but if a Nambikwara really wanted to enter he would tear a hole in the screen and walk in. . . .

One does not have to remain long among the Nambikwara in order to feel this underlying hatred, mistrust and despair, which create in the observer a feeling of depression not unmixed with sympathy.'[1]

When I myself had known them, the diseases introduced by white men had already decimated them; but there had not been, since Rondon's always humane endeavours, any attempt to enforce their submission. I should prefer to forget Mr Oberg's harrowing description and remember the Nambikwara as they appear in a page from my notebooks. I wrote it one night by the light of my pocket-lamp:

'The camp-fires shine out in the darkened savannah. Around the hearth which is their only protection from the cold, behind the flimsy screen of foliage and palm-leaves which has been stuck into the ground where it will best break the force of wind and rain, beside the baskets filled with the pitiable objects which comprise all their earthly belongings, the Nambikwara lie on the bare earth. Always they are haunted by the thought of other groups, as fearful and hostile as they are themselves, and when they lie entwined together, couple by couple, each looks to his mate for support and comfort and finds in the other a bulwark, the only one he knows, against the difficulties of every day and the meditative melancholia which from time to time overwhelms the Nambikwara. The visitor who camps among the Indians for the first time cannot but feel anguish and pity at the sight of a people so totally dis-provided for; beaten down into the hostile earth, it would seem, by an implacable cataclysm; naked and shivering beside their guttering fires. He gropes his way among the bushes, avoiding where he can the hand, or the arm, or the torso that lies gleaming in the firelight. Laughing whispers can still make light of the Nambikwara's poverty. Their embraces are those of couples possessed by a longing for a lost one-ness; their caresses are in no wise disturbed by the footfall of a stranger. In one and all there may be glimpsed a great sweetness of nature, a profound nonchalance, an animal satisfaction as ingenuous as it is charming, and, beneath all this, something that can be recognized as one of the most moving and authentic manifestations of human tenderness.'

[1] K. Oberg, *Indian Tribes of the Northern Mato Grosso, Brazil.* Smithsonian Institution, Institute of Social Anthropology. Publ. no. 15, Washington 1953, pp. 84–85.

25 *A Writing Lesson*

I WANTED somehow to arrive at a figure, however approximate, for the total of the Nambikwara population. In 1915 Rondon had put it at twenty thousand, which was probably too high. But at that time the nomadic bands were of several hundred people apiece, and all the indications I had collected along the line pointed to a rapid decline. Thirty years ago, for instance, the known fraction of the Sabané group comprised more than a thousand individuals; when that same group visited the telegraph station of Campos Novos in 1928 it consisted of one hundred and twenty-seven men, plus their women and children. In November 1929, moreover, an influenza epidemic broke out when the group was camping at the point known as Espirro. The disease turned into a form of pulmonary oedema, and three hundred Indians died of it within forty-eight hours. The whole group disintegrated, leaving the sick and dying to fend for themselves. Of the thousand Sabané who had once been known of, only nineteen men and their families were still alive in 1938. This decline is due not only to the epidemic, but also to the fact that some years ago the Sabané were in a state of war with some of their easterly neighbours. But a large group installed not far from Tres Buritis was wiped out by influenza in 1927: of the six or seven survivors, only three were still alive in 1938. The Tarundé group, once one of the largest, numbered twelve men, with their families, in 1936: three years later these twelve were reduced to four.

What was the position at the time of my arrival? Probably a bare two thousand Indians were scattered about the territory. I could not hope to make a systematic count, because certain groups were always hostile, and because, during the nomadic season, all the bands were continually on the move. But I tried to persuade my friends at Utiarity to take me to their village at a time when a rendezvous had been arranged with other allied or related bands. Thus I hoped to estimate the present

286

size of a gathering of this sort and to compare it with the reunions that had been scrutinized in earlier years. I promised to bring them presents, and effect some exchanges, but the leader of the band remained hesitant: he was not sure of his guests, and if my companions and I were to disappear in the region where no white men had penetrated since the incident of the seven telegraph-workers in 1925, then the precarious peace which existed there would be compromised for a long time to come.

In the end he agreed, on condition that we cut down the size of our party, and took only four oxen to carry our presents. Even so, he said, we should have to forswear the usual tracks, because our beasts would never get through the dense vegetation which abounded in the lower reaches of each valley. We should have to go by the plateau, improvising our route as we went along.

This was a very dangerous expedition, but it now seems to me largely grotesque. We had hardly left Juruena when my Brazilian colleague remarked to me on the absence of the Nambikwara women and children: only the men were with us, each armed with bow and arrows. All the literature of travel indicated this as a sign that an attack was imminent. Our feelings were mixed, therefore, as we went forward, verifying from time to time the position of our Smith and Wesson revolvers ('*Cemite Vechetone*' was our men's name for them) and our rifles. These fears proved misplaced: towards the half-way point of the day's march we caught up with the remainder of the band, whom their provident chief had sent on ahead of us, the day before, knowing that our mules would make much better time than the women, laden as these were with their baskets and encumbered with little children.

Soon after this, however, the Indians got lost. The new itinerary was not as straightforward as they had supposed. Towards evening we had to come to a halt in the bush. We had been promised that there would be game thereabouts and the Indians, counting on our rifles, had brought no food with them. We, for our part, had brought only emergency rations which could not be shared out all round. A troop of deer which had been nibbling away at the edge of a spring fled at our approach. The next morning everybody was in a thoroughly bad humour: ostensibly, this took for its object the leader of the band, whom they considered to be responsible for the venture which he and I had devised between us. Instead of going off to hunt or collect wild food on their own account, they decided to spend the day lying in the shade, leaving it to their leader to find the solution to their problem.

He went off, accompanied by one of his wives: towards evening we saw them coming back with their baskets heavy-laden with grasshoppers that they had spent the entire day in collecting. Grasshopper pie is not one of their favourite dishes, but the entire party fell on it, none the less, with relish. Good humour broke out on all sides, and on the next morning we got under way again.

And, at last, we got to the rendezvous. This was a sandy terrace above a watercourse, bordered with trees between which the Indians had laid out some little gardens. Incoming groups arrived at intervals during the day and by the evening there were seventy-five people in all: seventeen families, grouped under thirteen crude shelters hardly more solid than those which served in camp. I was told that when the rains began the whole company would take refuge in five round huts built for several months' wear. Many of the natives seemed never to have seen a white man, and their more than dubious welcome combined with their leader's extreme nervousness seemed to suggest that he had forced their hand, somewhat, in the whole matter. Neither we nor the Indians felt at all at our ease and, as there were no trees, we had to lie, like the Nambikwaras, on the bare ground. No one slept: we kept, all night long, a polite watch upon one another.

It would have been rash to prolong the adventure, and I suggested to the leader that we should get down to our exchanges without further delay. It was then that there occurred an extraordinary incident which forces me to go back a little in time. That the Nambikwara could not write goes without saying. But they were also unable to draw, except for a few dots and zigzags on their calabashes. I distributed pencils and paper among them, none the less, as I had done with the Caduveo. At first they made no use of them. Then, one day, I saw that they were all busy drawing wavy horizontal lines on the paper. What were they trying to do? I could only conclude that they were writing—or, more exactly, that they were trying to do as I did with my pencils. As I had never tried to amuse them with drawings, they could not conceive of any other use for this implement. With most of them, that was as far as they got: but their leader saw further into the problem. Doubtless he was the only one among them to have understood what writing was for. So he asked me for one of my notepads; and when we were working together he did not give me his answers in words, but traced a wavy line or two on the paper and gave it to me, as if I could read what he had to say. He himself was all but deceived by his own play-acting. Each time he drew a line he would examine it with great care, as if its mean-

ing must suddenly leap to the eye; and every time a look of disappointment came over his face. But he would never give up trying, and there
was an unspoken agreement between us that his scribblings had a
meaning that I did my best to decipher; his own verbal commentary
was so prompt in coming that I had no need to ask him to explain what
he had written.

And now, no sooner was everyone assembled than he drew forth
from a basket a piece of paper covered with scribbled lines and pretended
to read from it. With a show of hesitation he looked up and down his
'list' for the objects to be given in exchange for his people's presents.
So-and-so was to receive a machete in return for his bow and arrows,
and another a string of beads in return for his necklaces—and so on for
two solid hours. What was he hoping for? To deceive himself, perhaps:
but, even more, to amaze his companions and persuade them that *his*
intermediacy was responsible for the exchanges. He had allied himself
with the white man, as equal with equal, and could now share in his
secrets. We were in a hurry to get away, since there would obviously
be a moment of real danger at which all the marvels I had brought
would have been handed over. . . . So I did not go further into the
matter and we set off on the return journey, still guided by the
Indians.

There had been something intensely irritating about our abortive
meeting, and about the mystifications of which I had just been the unknowing instrument. Added to that, my mule was suffering from
aphtha, and its mouth was causing it pain, so that by turns it hurried
inpatiently forward and stopped dead in its tracks. We got into a
quarrel with one another and, quite suddenly, without realizing how it
happened, I found myself alone, and lost, in the middle of the bush.

What was I to do? What people do in books: fire a shot in the air
to let my companions know what had happened. I dismounted and did
so. No reply. I fired again, and as there seemed to be an answer I fired a
third shot. This scared my mule, who went off at a trot and pulled up
some distance away.

I put weapons and photographic equipment neatly at the foot of a
tree, memorized its position, and ran off to recapture my mule, who
seemed quite peaceably disposed. He let me get right up to him and
then, just as I reached for the reins, he made off at full speed. This
happened more than once until in despair I jumped at him and threw
both my arms round his tail. This unusual proceeding took him by surprise, and he decided to give in. Back in the saddle, I made as if to

collect my belongings, only to find that we had twisted and turned so often that I had no idea where they were.

Demoralized by this episode, I decided to rejoin our troop. Neither my mule nor I knew where they had gone. Sometimes I would head him in a direction that he refused to take; sometimes I would let him lead, only to find that he was simply turning in a circle. The sun was going down, I was no longer armed, and I expected at every moment to be the target of a volley of arrows. I was not, admittedly, the first white man to penetrate that hostile zone. But none of my predecessors had come back alive and, quite apart from myself, my mule was a tempting prey for people who rarely have anything very much to get their teeth into. These dark thoughts passed, one by one, through my mind as I waited for the sun to go down, thinking that since I at least had some matches with me I could start a bush-fire. Just as I was about to strike the first match I heard voices: two of the Nambikwara had turned back, the moment my absence was noticed, and had been following me all afternoon. For them to recover my equipment was child's play and, at nightfall, they led me to the camp where our whole troop was waiting for me.

Still tormented by this absurd incident, I slept badly. To while away the hours I went back, in my mind, to the scene of the previous morning. So the Nambikwara had learnt what it meant to write! But not at all, as one might have supposed, as the result of a laborious apprenticeship. The symbol had been borrowed, but the reality remained quite foreign to them. Even the borrowing had had a sociological, rather than an intellectual object: for it was not a question of knowing specific things, or understanding them, or keeping them in mind, but merely of enhancing the prestige and authority of one individual—or one function—at the expense of the rest of the party. A native, still in the period of the stone age, had realized that even if he could not himself understand the great instrument of understanding he could at least make it serve other ends. For thousands of years, after all, and still today in a great part of the world, writing has existed as an institution in societies in which the vast majority of people are quite unable to write. The villages where I stayed in the Chittagong hills in Pakistan are populated by illiterates; yet each village has a scribe who fulfils his function for the benefit both of individual citizens and of the village as a whole. They all know what writing is and, if need be, *can* write: but they do it from outside as if it were a mediator, foreign to themselves, with whom they communicate by an oral process. But the scribe is rarely a functionary or an employee of the group as a whole; his knowledge is a source of power—so much so, in fact, that the functions of scribe and usurer are often united in the same human being. This is not merely because the usurer needs to be able to read and write to carry on his trade, but because he has thus a twofold empire over his fellows.

Writing is a strange thing. It would seem as if its appearance could not have failed to wreak profound changes in the living conditions of our race, and that these transformations must have been above all intellectual in character. Once men know how to write, they are enormously more able to keep in being a large body of knowledge. Writing might, that is to say, be regarded as a form of artificial memory, whose development should be accompanied by a deeper knowledge of the past and, therefore, by a greater ability to organize the present and the future. Of all the criteria by which people habitually distinguish civilization from barbarism, this should be the one most worth retaining: that certain peoples write and others do not. The first group can accumulate a body of knowledge that helps it to move ever faster towards the goal that it has assigned to itself; the second is confined within limits that the memory of individuals can never hope to extend, and it must remain the prisoner of a history worked out from day to day, with neither a clear knowledge of its own origins nor a consecutive idea of what its future should be.

Yet nothing of what we know of writing, or of its role in evolution, can be said to justify this conception. One of the most creative phases in human history took place with the onset of the neolithic era: agriculture and the domestication of animals are only two of the developments which may be traced to this period. It must have had behind it thousands of years during which small societies of human beings were noting, experimenting, and passing on to one another the fruits of their knowledge. The very success of this immense enterprise bears witness to the rigour and the continuity of its preparation, at a time when writing was quite unknown. If writing first made its appearance between the fourth and third millennium before our era, we must see it not, in any degree, as a conditioning factor in the neolithic revolution, but rather as an already-distant and doubtless indirect result of that revolution. With what great innovation can it be linked? Where technique is concerned, architecture alone can be called into question. Yet the architecture of the Egyptians or the Sumerians was no better than the work of certain American Indians who, at the time America was discovered, were ignorant of writing. Conversely, between the invention of writing and the birth of modern science, the western world has lived through some five thousand years, during which time the sum of its knowledge has rather gone up and down than known a steady increase. It has often been remarked that there was no great difference between the life of a Greek or Roman citizen and that of a member of the well-to-do European classes in the eighteenth century. In the neolithic age, humanity made immense strides forward without any help from writing; and writing did not save the civilizations of the western world from long periods of stagnation. Doubtless the scientific expansion of the nineteenth and twentieth centuries could hardly have occurred, had writing not existed. But this condition, however necessary, cannot in itself explain that expansion.

If we want to correlate the appearance of writing with certain other characteristics of civilization, we must look elsewhere. The one phenomenon which has invariably accompanied it is the formation of cities and empires: the integration into a political system, that is to say, of a considerable number of individuals, and the distribution of those individuals into a hierarchy of castes and classes. Such is, at any rate, the type of development which we find, from Egypt right across to China, at the moment when writing makes its débuts; it seems to favour rather the exploitation than the enlightenment of mankind. This exploitation made it possible to assemble workpeople by the thousand and set them tasks that taxed them to the limits of their strength: to this, surely, we must attribute the beginnings of architecture as we know it. If my hypothesis is correct, the primary function of writing, as a means of communication, is to facilitate the enslavement of other human beings. The use of writing for disinterested ends, and with a view to satisfactions of the mind in the fields either of science or the arts, is a secondary result of its invention—and may even be no more than a way of reinforcing, justifying, or dissimulating its primary function.

There are, however, exceptions to this rule. Ancient Africa included empires in which several hundred thousand subjects acknowledged a single rule; in pre-Colombian America, the Inca empire numbered several million subjects. But, alike in Africa and in America, these ventures were notably unstable: we know, for instance, that the Inca empire was established in the twelfth century or thereabouts. Pizarro's soldiers would never have conquered it so easily if it had not already, three centuries later, been largely decomposed. And, from the little we know of the ancient history of Africa, we can divine an analogous situation: massive political groups seem to have appeared and disappeared within the space of not many decades. It may be, therefore, that these instances confirm, instead of refuting, our hypothesis. Writing may not have sufficed to consolidate human knowledge, but it may well have been indispensable to the establishment of an enduring dominion. To bring the matter nearer to our own time: the European-wide movement towards compulsory education in the nineteenth century went hand in hand with the extension of military service and the systematization of the proletariat. The struggle against illiteracy is indistinguishable, at times, from the increased powers exerted over the individual citizen by the central authority. For it is only when everyone can read that Authority can decree that 'ignorance of the law is no defence'.

All this moved rapidly from the national to the international level, thanks to the mutual complicity which sprang up between new-born states—confronted as these were with the problems that had been our own, a century or two ago—and an international society of peoples long privileged. These latter recognize that their stability may well be endangered by nations whose knowledge of the written word has not, as yet, empowered them to think in formulae which can be modified at will. Such nations are not yet ready to be 'edified'; and when they are first given the freedom of the library shelves they are perilously vulnerable to the ever more deliberately misleading effects of the printed word. Doubtless the die is already cast, in that respect. But in my Nambikwara village people were not so easily taken in. Shortly after my visit the leader lost the confidence of most of his people. Those who moved away from him, after he had tried to play the civilized man, must have had a confused understanding of the fact that writing, on this its first appearance in their midst, had allied itself with falsehood; and so they had taken refuge, deeper in the bush, to win themselves a respite. And yet I could not but admire the genius of their leader, for he had divined in a flash that writing could redouble his hold upon the others and, in so doing, he had got, as it were, to the bottom of an institution which he did not as yet know how to work. The episode also drew my attention to a further aspect of Nambikwara life: the political relations between individuals and groups. This I was shortly to be able to scrutinize more directly.

We were still at Utiarity when an epidemic of purulent ophthalmia broke out among the natives. This infection, gonococchic in origin, soon spread to every one of them. Apart from being terribly painful, it led to what threatened to be permanent blindness. For several days the entire band was paralysed. They treated their eyes with water, in which a certain kind of bark had been soaked: this they introduced into the eye with the help of leaves rolled into the shape of a funnel. The disease spread to my own group. My wife was the first to catch it. She had taken part in all our previous expeditions and had taken her full share in the study of material culture: but now she was so seriously ill that I had to send her back home. Most of our bearers went sick, and so did my Brazilian associate. Before long it was out of the question to go any farther. I ordered the main body of our party to rest, left our doctor behind to do what he could for them, and myself pushed on with two men and a few animals to the station of Campos Novos, near which a number of Indian bands had been reported. There I spent a fortnight in semi-idleness, picking the barely ripe fruit of an orchard which had 'gone back to Nature': guavas whose bitter taste and stony texture belied the promise of their scent; *caju*, vivid in colour as any parakeet, with a flesh that concealed within its spongy cells an astringent, delicately flavoured juice. And when the larder was empty we had only to get up at dawn and make our way to a thicket, a few hundred yards from the camp, where wood-pigeons would turn up, sharp on time every day, and offer themselves as our prey. At Campos Novos, too, I met two bands which had arrived from the north, drawn by the rumour of the presents I had brought with me.

These two bands were as ill disposed towards one another as they were towards me. From the outset, my gifts were not so much solicited as exacted. During the first few days only one of the bands was in evidence, together with a native from the Utiarity group who had gone on ahead of me. Did he show too much interest in a young woman who belonged to our hosts' group? I believe he did. Relations were bad, almost from the start, between the strangers and their visitor, and he dropped into the habit of coming over to my camp in search of a more cordial welcome. He also shared my meals. This fact was taken note of: and one day when he was out hunting I was visited by a delegation of four Indians. There was a distinct menace in the tone of voice in which they urged me to put poison into his food. They would bring me all that I needed: four little tubes bound together with cotton and filled with grey powder. I was very much put out: yet, as an outright refusal would turn the whole band against me, I felt it best to go carefully, in view of their maleficent intentions. So I decided to know less of their language than I really did. Faced with my look of total incomprehension, the Indians repeated to me over and over again that my guest was *kakoré*, very wicked, and that I should get rid of him as soon as possible. Eventually they made off, with every sign of discontentment. I warned my guest of what had occurred, and he at once took to his heels; not till months later, when I revisited the region, did I see him again.

Luckily the second band arrived on the following day, giving the Indians a new target for their hostility. The meeting took place at my camp, which was both neutral ground and the terminal-point of their respective journeyings. I had, therefore, a front seat in the stalls. The men of each party came up on their own; a lengthy conversation followed between their respective leaders, consisting mainly of monologues, in alternation, on a plaintive, nasal note that I did not remember having encountered before. 'We are very angry!' one group kept on whining. 'You are our enemies!' To which the others replied: 'We are not at all angry! We are your brothers! Friends! We can understand each other!' and so on. Once this exchange of protests and provocations was over, a common camp was set up, close to my own. After some dancing and singing, during which each group played down its own contribution and glorified that of its adversaries—'The Tamaindé sang so well! And we sing so badly!'—quarrelling began again, and before long tempers began to run high. The night had hardly begun when the noise of argument-cum-singing set up a tremendous row, the significance of which was lost upon me. Threatening gestures could be seen, and once or twice men actually came to blows and had to be separated. The menaces consisted, in every case, of gestures relating in some way to the sexual organs. A Nambikwara shows hostility by taking his penis in both hands and pointing it towards his adversary. This is the prelude to an attack on the adversary in question, with a view to wrenching off the tuft of *buriti* straw that hangs down from the front of his belt, just above his private parts. These parts are 'hidden by the straw' and the point of fighting is to get the other man's straw away from him. This is an entirely symbolic action, for the masculine *cachesexe* is so fragile, and in any case so insubstantial, that it serves neither to protect nor, in any true sense, to dissimulate the parts in question. Another mark of victory is to wrest your opponent's bow and arrows from him and put them down some distance away. At all such times the Indians take on attitudes of extreme intensity, as if in a state of violent contained rage. Eventually these individual quarrels end up in a general pitched battle. But on this occasion they

died down at dawn. Still in the same state of evident exasperation, and
with the roughest of gestures, the adversaries began to scrutinize one
another closely, fingering an ear-ring here and a cotton bracelet or
feathered ornament there, and muttering rapidly throughout: 'Give . . .
give . . . give . . . look at that . . . how pretty!' to which the owner
would reply: 'No, no . . . it's ugly, old, worn-out. . . .'

This reconciliatory inspection marks the end of the conflict. It introduces, as between the two groups, another kind of relationship: that of
the commercial exchange. The material culture of the Nambikwara
may be of the rudest, but each band's manufactures are, none the less,
highly prized in the outer world. Those in the east are short of pottery
and seed-beads. Those in the north consider that their southerly neighbours make particularly beautiful necklaces. The meeting of two
groups, once established upon a pacific level, will therefore engender a
whole series of reciprocal gifts: the battlefield turns into a market-place.

But the exchanges go forward almost imperceptibly: the morning
after the quarrelling everyone went about his normal occupations, and
objects or products changed hands without either donor or recipient
making any outward allusion to what was going forward. Balls of
thread and raw cotton; lumps of wax or resin; urucu paste; shells, ear-
rings, bracelets, and necklaces; tobacco and seed-beads; feathers and
strips of bamboo that could be made into arrowheads; bunches of palm-
fibres and porcupine-quills; complete pots and potsherds; calabashes.
This mysterious traffic went on until the day was half over, when the
two groups separated and went off, each on his own way.

The Nambikwara leave everything, on such occasions, to the generosity of their 'opposite number'. Totally foreign to them is the notion
that anyone could set a price on any object, discuss that price, haggle
over it, insist on getting it, or 'chalk it up' as a debt. I once offered an
Indian a forest-knife in return for his having carried a message to a
nearby group. When he came back I did not immediately give him the
knife, because I assumed that he would come and ask for it. But nothing
of the kind: and the next day I couldn't find him anywhere. His friends
told me that he had gone away in a rage, and I never saw him again. I
had to entrust the present to another Indian. This being so, it is not surprising that when the exchanges are over one side or the other is often
discontented with the result; and that, as weeks and then months go by,
and he counts up, over and over again, the presents he received, and
compares them with those he has given, he becomes more and more
bitter. Often this bitterness turns to aggression. Many a war has broken

out for no other reason. There are other causes, of course: a murder, or a rape to be either brought off or avenged. It does not seem as if a band feels itself bound to take collective reprisals for an injury done to any one of its members. But such is the animosity which reigns between groups that often every advantage is taken of pretexts of this kind, especially if the group in question feels itself in a strong position. The case is then presented by a warrior, who sets out his grievances in the same tone and in much the style of the encounter-ritual: 'Hallo there! Come here! Now look here—I'm very angry! Really very angry indeed! Arrows! Big arrows!'

Specially dressed for the occasion—tufts of *buriti* straw striped with red, jaguar-skin helmets—the men assemble behind their leader and dance. A divinatory rite must be observed: the chief, or the sorcerer, if one exists, hides an arrow in a corner of the bush. The next day the men search for the arrow and, if it is stained with blood, war is declared: if not, they call it all off. Many expeditions that begin in this way come to an end after a few miles' march. The war-party loses all its enthusiasm and excitement and turns back towards home. But sometimes the venture is pressed to its conclusion, and blood is shed. The Nambikwara attack at dawn, after having first scattered to create the conditions of an ambush. The signal to attack passes from man to man by means of the whistle that each carries round his neck. This whistle, made up of two tubes of bamboo tied together with cotton, makes a noise like that of the cricket and, doubtless for that reason, bears the same name. The war-arrows are those used in peace-time for hunting the bigger game, but their points are cut to a saw-edge. Arrows poisoned with curare, though common in hunting, are never used in battle, because anyone wounded by one of them would get it out before the poison had had time to get into his veins.

26 *Men, Women, and Chiefs*

Beyond Campos Novos, at the highest point of the plateau, was the post of Vilhena. In 1938 it consisted of a few huts in the middle of a lengthy clearing several hundred yards wide. This clearing marked the point at which the builders of the line had hoped that the Chicago of the Mato Grosso would one day be built. I believe it is now a military airfield, but in my time its only inhabitants were two families who had not had any supplies of food for the previous eight years. They it was who, as I described earlier, had managed to keep in biological equilibrium with the herd of deer which provided them with a modest living.

There I met two new nomadic bands. One of them numbered in all eighteen persons, and their dialect was not far distant from the one which I was beginning to speak; the other, thirty-four strong, talked an unknown language—and one that I never succeeded in identifying. Each was led by a chief. In the case of the smaller of the two bands, his attributes seemed to me entirely secular. But the chief of the larger band was soon revealed to me as a sorcerer of some kind. His group were called the Sabané, and the others the Tarundé.

Except for the language, there was no telling them apart: looks and culture were identical. This was already the case at Campos Novos; but at Vilhena the two bands, so far from being on bad terms, lived in perfect harmony. Their camp-fires were some way apart, but they travelled together, camped side by side, and seemed to be indissolubly allied, for all that they spoke different languages, and that their chiefs could communicate with one another only through the intermediary of one or two men, in either group, who could act as interpreters.

Their union must have been a recent one. Between 1907 and 1930, as I explained earlier, epidemics traceable to the arrival of white men had decimated the Indians. Consequently there were bands so reduced in numbers that they could not pursue an independent existence. At

Campos Novos I had examined the internal antagonisms of Nambikwara society and watched the forces of disintegration at work. At
Vilhena, by contrast, I was faced with an attempt at reconstruction.
For there was no doubt that this was the two bands' conscious aim. The
grown men of the one band addressed the women of the other band
as 'sisters' and were called by them 'brothers' in return. As for the men,
they addressed the men of the other band by the words which, in one
language or the other, mean 'cousin' of the type which anthropologists
call 'crossed': this corresponds to the relationship which we define as
that of 'brothers-in-law'. Given the marriage-laws of the Nambikwara,
this means that all the children of the one band are potentially the
husbands or wives of children of the other band, and vice versa. By
the time that the next generation has grown up, therefore, the two
bands will have merged completely.

But there were still obstacles to this grand design. A third band,
enemies of the Tarundé, was in the neighbourhood. Sometimes their
camp-fires were within sight of our own camp, and the Tarundé made
themselves ready for any emergency. As I could understand the
Tarundé up to a point, and the Sabané not at all, I found myself more
in sympathy with the Tarundé. Also the Sabané, with whom I had no
means of communication, were much less trusting in their relations
with me. So it is not for me to expound their point of view. In any case,
the Tarundé were not sure that the Sabané's motives in uniting with
them were altogether disinterested. They were frightened of the third
group, and what frightened them still more was the possibility that the
Sabané might suddenly decide to go over to the other side

A strange incident soon showed that there was foundation for their
fears. One day, when the men had gone out hunting, the Sabané chief
did not come back at his usual time. Night fell, and by nine or ten
o'clock in the evening consternation reigned in the camp—above all in
the home of the vanished chief, where his two wives and one child
were huddled together in tears at the presumed death of their husband
and father. At that moment I decided to go for a tour of the area, taking
a few Indians with me. Hardly had we gone two hundred yards when
we came upon our man, squatting on the ground and shivering in the
dark. He was entirely naked—stripped, that is to say, of his necklaces,
bracelets, ear-rings, and belt. By the light of my torch we could see
that he was haggard and distraught. He offered no resistance as we
helped him back to our camp, where he sat, speechless, in an attitude of
dejection which was really quite startling.

Eventually his disquieted audience got the story out of him. He had been swept away by the thunder, he said. (*Amon* is their word for a storm, harbinger of the rainy season, and a storm had, in fact, just taken place.) This thunder had carried him up in the air and set him down at a point eighteen miles from our camp. It had stripped him of all his ornaments and brought him back to the place where we had found him. Everyone dropped slowly off to sleep as they hashed over the story, and by next morning the Sabané chief was back in his best humour and, what is more, had recovered all his ornaments. No one seemed surprised by this: nor did he attempt to explain it. But before long a very different account of the episode was being put about by the Tarundé. They declared that under cover of his high adventure the Sabané chief had been negotiating with the other band of Indians who were camping nearby. These insinuations were never brought up in public, and the official account of the incident was still given official credence. But in private the Tarundé chief made no secret of his anxieties. As the two groups moved off shortly afterwards I never heard the end of the story.

This incident, allied to my previous observations, caused me to reflect on the nature of the Nambikwara bands and on the political influence exerted within them by their chiefs. There is no social structure more fragile, or shorter-lived, than the Nambikwara band. If the chief is too exacting, if he allots to himself too large a share of the women, or if he cannot find enough food for his subjects during the dry season, discontentment follows immediately. Individuals, or whole families, will break away from the group and go off to join a band with a better reputation. This other band may be better fed, thanks to the discovery of better places for hunting and scavenging; or it may have a larger store of ornaments, thanks to favourable exchanges with neighbour-bands; or it may even have become more powerful as a result of a victorious campaign. One day the leader will find himself at the head of a group too small either to cope with the difficulties of everyday life or to protect its women from the designs of outsiders. When that happens he will just have to give up his position and ally himself and his few supporters with some more fortunate group. From all this it will be clear that the Nambikwara social structure is essentially fluid. Bands are constantly forming and being dissolved, doubling their numbers or disappearing altogether. A few months may suffice for their composition, numbers, and general character to change beyond recognition. Domestic political intrigues and conflicts between neighbour-bands impose their separate rhythms upon these variations, and both individuals and groups pass from zenith to nadir, and vice versa, in a way that is often disconcerting.

Why, therefore, do the Nambikwara divide themselves into bands at all? Economically speaking, they could hardly do otherwise than break up into small groups, given their extreme poverty in natural resources and the large area of ground which is needed, in the dry season, to keep even one Indian alive. The problem is not why, but how, they should so divide themselves. Initially there is a small group of acknowledged leaders who constitute the nucleus around which each band forms itself. On the ability of the leader to consolidate his position and keep his followers in their place will depend the importance of his band and the quasi-permanence of its character throughout the dry season. Political power does not seem to result from the community's needs; rather does the little community derive its characteristics—form, size, origins even—from the potential leader who existed before the group came into being.

I knew two of these chiefs very well: the one at Utiarity, whose band was called Wakletoçu, and the Tarundé chief. The first was remarkably intelligent, active, resourceful, and well aware of his responsibilities. He forsaw the consequences of any new situation; drew up an itinerary expressly adapted to my needs; and elucidated it, where necessary, by drawing a map in the sand. When we reached his village we found that stakes to which we could tether our animals had already been planted by a party which he had sent on ahead for the purpose.

As an informant he was invaluable to me, in that he understood my problems, solved my difficulties, and took a real interest in my work. But his functions preoccupied him, and for days together he would go off hunting, or on reconnaissance, or to see if the fruit- or seed-bearing trees were doing well. There were also his wives, whose continual invitations to amorous amusements of one sort or another found in him the readiest of partners.

In general his activites revealed a logic, and a capacity for sustained effort, which are rare among the Nambikwara. (Instability and caprice are more the rule.) His conditions of life were precarious, and his means derisory: yet he had great powers of organization and took upon himself entire responsibility for his group. He was a thoroughly competent leader, though somewhat given to speculation.

The Tarundé chief was, like his colleague, about thirty years old. He was equally intelligent in his quite different way. The Wakletoçu chief struck me as an informed and resourceful leader, who was always turning over in his mind some possible political manœuvre. His colleague was a man, not of action, but of contemplation: he had an attractive and poetical turn of mind and was unusually sensitive. He realized that his people were decadent, and for this reason his conversation had often a note of melancholy. 'I used to do that once,' he would say, 'but now it's finished . . .' as he spoke of the days when his group, so far from being too small to carry on the traditions of the Nambikwara, ran to several hundreds, every one of them a fervent upholder of those ancient customs. He was as interested in our own ways, and in those of other tribes that I had examined, as I was in his own. With him, the anthropologist's work was never one-sided: he saw it as an exchange of information, and always had a cordial welcome for all that I could tell him. Often, indeed, he would ask me for, and carefully keep, drawings of the feather-ornaments, the head-dresses, and the weapons that I had noted down among peoples near or far. Did he hope that these would help him to perfect the material and intellectual equipment of his own band? Conceivably—although his day-dreamer's temperament did not lend itself well to practical activity. And yet when, one day, I asked him about the Pan-pipe, with a view to verifying the position of the air-holes on that instrument, and he, never having heard of it, asked me to draw him a picture of one, he later contrived to make himself such a flute, roughly but serviceably constructed, on the basis of my drawing.

The exceptional qualities manifested by both these chiefs derived from the manner of their designation—for political power is not hereditary among the Nambikwara. When a chief grows old, falls ill, or feels that he can no longer shoulder his heavy burdens, he himself chooses his successor: 'That one shall be chief . . .' But this autocracy is more apparent than real. We shall see later on how slender is the chief's authority; and in this matter, as in others, the final decision would seem to be preceded by an appeal to public opinion, so that the heir finally appointed is the man most acceptable to the majority. But the choice of the new chief is not dictated entirely by the wishes or preferences of the group; the leader-designate must be willing to take on the job and, not uncommonly, he answers with a violent: 'No, I don't want to be chief!' A second choice must then be made. There does not, in fact, seem to be any great competition for power, and the chiefs whom I knew were more likely to complain of their heavy burdens and manifold responsibilities than to talk with pride of the chief's lofty position. What, in fact, are the chief's privileges, and what are his obligations?

Around the year 1560 Montaigne met, in Rouen, three Brazilian

Indians who had been brought back by some early navigator. What, he asked one of them, were the privileges of a chief ('king' was what he said) in their country? The Indian, himself a chief, said: 'He's the first man to march off to war.' Montaigne tells this story in his *Essays* and marvels at the proud definition. It was a matter, for me, of intense astonishment and admiration that I received the same reply, nearly four centuries later. The civilized countries do not show anything like the same constancy in their political philosophy! Striking as it is, the formula is not so fraught with meaning as the choice of the word for 'chief' in Nambikwara language. *Uilikandé* seems to mean 'the one who unites' or 'the one who binds together', and it suggests that the Indian mentality is aware of the phenomenon which I have already underlined: that the chief is rather the cause of the group's wish to constitute itself as a group, than the effect of the need, felt by an already-existing group, for a central authority.

Personal prestige and the ability to inspire confidence are the foundations of power in Nambikwara society. Both are indispensable to the man who will be their guide in the adventurous, nomadic life of the dry season. For six or seven months the chief will be entirely responsible for the leadership of his band. He it is who organizes their departure, chooses their itinerary, and decrees where and for how long they will stop. He decides on the expeditions—hunting, fishing, collecting, scavenging—and he deals with relations with neighbour-bands. When the chief of a band is also the chief of a village (by this I mean a semi-permanent installation for use during the rainy season) his obligations go further. He determines the time and the place for the sedentary life. He supervises the gardens and says what crops are to be planted. More generally, he adapts his band's activities to the needs and possibilities of the season.

Where these manifold functions are concerned it should be said at once that the chief cannot seek support either in clearly defined powers or in a publicly recognized authority. Consent lies at the origins of power, and consent also confers upon power its legitimacy. Bad conduct (from the Indians' point of view, needless to say) or marks of ill will on the part of one or two malcontents may throw the chief's whole programme out of joint and threaten the well-being of his little community. Should this happen, the chief has no powers of coercion. He can disembarrass himself of undesirable elements only in so far as all the others are of the same mind as himself. And so he needs to be clever: and his cleverness is not so much that of an all-powerful sovereign as that of a politician struggling to maintain an uncertain majority. Nor does it suffice for him merely to keep his group together. They may live in virtual isolation during the nomadic season, but they never forget that neighbour-groups are not far away. The chief must not merely do well: he must try, and his group will expect him to try, to do better than the others.

How does the chief fulfil his obligations? The first and the main instrument of his power is his generosity. Generosity is among most primitive peoples, and above all in America, an essential attribute of power. It has a role to play even in those elementary cultures where the notion of property consists merely in a handful of rudely fashioned objects. Although the chief does not seem to be in a privileged position, from the material point of view, he must have under his control surplus quantities of food, tools, weapons, and ornaments which, however trifling in themselves, are none the less considerable in relation to the prevailing poverty. When an individual, a family, or the band as a whole, wishes or needs something, it is to the chief that an appeal must be made. Generosity is, therefore, the first attribute to be expected of a new chief. It is a note which will be struck almost continuously; and from the nature, discordant or otherwise, of the sound which results the chief can judge of his standing with the band. His 'subjects' make the most of all this: of that there can be no doubt. The chiefs were my best informers; and as I knew the difficulties of their position I liked to reward them liberally. Rarely, however, did any of my presents remain in their hands for more than a day or two. And when I moved on, after sharing for several weeks the life of any particular band, its members rejoiced in the acquisition of axes, knives, pearls, and so forth from my stores. The chief, by contrast, was generally as poor, in material terms, as he had been when I arrived. His share, which was very much larger than the average allowance, had all been extorted from him. This often reduced the chief to a kind of despair. A chief who can say 'No' in such situations is like a Prime Minister, in countries subject to parliamentary democracy, who can snap his fingers at a vote of confidence. A chief who can say: 'I'll give no more! I've been generous long enough! Let someone else take a turn!' must really be sure of his authority if he is not to provoke a moment of grave crisis.

Ingenuity is generosity transposed to the level of the intellect. A good chief gives proofs of his initiative and skill. He it is who prepares the poison for the arrows. He, likewise, who constructs the ball of wild rubber which is used on Nambikwara sports days. He must also be able to sing and dance, with a repertory large enough to amuse the band at any time and distract them from the monotony of their everyday life. These functions might easily make of him something of a shaman, and some chiefs do, in fact, combine the roles of warrior and witch-doctor. But mysticism in all its forms remains well in the background of Nambikwara life, and the gift of magic, when present, is merely one of the secondary attributes of command. It is more common for one person to assume the temporal and another the spiritual power. In this the Nambikwara differ from their neighbours, the Tupi-Kawahib, whose chiefs are also shamans much given to premonitory dreams, visions, trances, and the dissociation of personality.

But the skill and ingenuity of the Nambikwara chief are none the less astonishing for being directed towards a more positive outlet. He must have a minute knowledge of the territories frequented by his band and by its neighbours: the hunting-grounds must have no secrets from him, and he must know just when each clump of wild fruit-trees will be ripe for plucking. Thus instructed, he can work out a rough itinerary for each of his neighbour-bands, whether friendly or hostile; and, as he needs to be constantly on the move, reconnoitring or exploring, he may well seem to be not so much leading his band as circling rapidly round it.

Apart from one or two men who have no real authority, but are prepared to collaborate if paid to do so, the passivity of the band is in striking contrast to the dynamism of its leader. It is as if, having handed over to him certain advantages, they expect him to take entire charge of their interests and their security. This attitude was well displayed in the episode which I have already described of the journey on which, when we lost our way and had not enough food, the Indians lay down on the ground instead of going off to look for some, leaving it to the chief and his wives to remedy the situation as best they could.

I have often spoken of the chief's 'wives'. He is, practically speaking, the only polygamist in the band: and this is both a consolation, moral and sentimental, for the heavy burdens of office, and one of the means of shouldering those burdens. With rare exceptions the chief and the witch-doctor (when these functions are shared between two men) are the only people to have more than one wife. But this polygamy is of a special type: it is not plural marriage in the strict sense, but rather a normal monogamous marriage to which are added relationships of a a different sort. The first wife fulfils the normal role of the wife in monogamous marriages, in that she does the work usually attributed to her sex, looks after the children, does the cooking, and goes out to collect such food as she can. Later unions, though recognized as marriages, are of a different kind. The wives come, to begin with, from a younger generation, and the first wife addresses them as 'daughter' or 'niece'. Nor do they obey the rules of the division of labour between the sexes, but do the work of either men or women, as they please. In camp, they regard 'house-work' as beneath them and live in idleness, either playing with children nearer their own age, or making love with their husband, while the first wife busies herself with the routine work of the home. But when the chief goes hunting or exploring, or on some other masculine errand, his secondary wives go with him and give him both physical and moral support. Boyish in appearance, and chosen from the prettiest and healthiest girls of the group, they are, indeed, more mistresses than wives, and he lives with them in an atmosphere of amorous camaraderie which is in striking contrast to the conjugal atmosphere of his first union.

Men and women do not as a rule bathe together, but the chief can sometimes be seen in the river with his secondary wives, and these occasions are marked by a great deal of splashing about, horse-play, and jokes of every kind. In the evening he plays with them. Sometimes the games are clearly erotic, and they roll about, two, three, or even four together, closely entwined on the sand. Sometimes they are more childish in tone: for instance the Wakletoçu chief and his two wives would lie on the ground in the shape of a three-leafed clover, with their feet together in the middle, and then, raising their legs in the air, would bring them together, clapping the soles of their feet together in unison.

This form of polygamy represents, therefore, a normal mono-gamous marriage, to which is added a pluralist variant of amorous camaraderie. It is also an attribute of power, and has a functional value in both the moral and the economic spheres. The wives generally live together in harmony, and, although the lot of the first wife may seem thankless, she seems to feel, or at any rate to show, no bitterness as she toils away while her husband and his little playmates amuse themselves and, at times, go to the limits of erotic enjoyment, within sight and sound of her. This distinction between the original wife and her succes-sors is not, in any case, immutable. It happens, though less often, that the first wife may join in the fun: nor is she in any way excluded from the lighter sides of family life. And the fact that she takes less part in their dalliances is balanced by the greater respect, and to some extent the obedience, which is owed to her by her youthful successors.

This system has serious consequences for the life of the group. By withdrawing, as he does, a number of young girls from the normal matrimonial cycle, the chief creates a disequilibrium between the number of young men and the number of available girls. The young men suffer most from this, for they are condemned either to remain single for years, or to ally themselves with widows or older women whose husbands have had enough of them.

The Nambikwara have, however, another way of resolving the problem, and that is by homosexual relations or, as they call them, *tamindige kihandige*: 'the loving lie'. These relations, common among the younger men, are carried on with a publicity uncommon in the case of more normal relations. The partners do not go off into the bush, as they would with a partner of the opposite sex, but get down to it beside the camp-fire, much to the amusement of their neighbours. The incident provokes a joke or two, on the quiet, the relations in question being regarded as childishness and of no serious account. It remains doubtful whether these exercises are carried to the point of complete satisfaction or whether, like much that goes on between husbands and wives among the Nambikwara, they are limited to sentimental out-pourings and a certain amount of erotic fore-play.

Homosexual relations are only allowed between adolescent boys who stand to one another in the relations of crossed cousins—cases, that is to say, in which one partner would normally marry the other's sister and is taking her brother as a provisional substitute. Whenever I asked an Indian about a relationship of this sort, the answer was always the same: 'They are two cousins (or brothers-in-law) who make love together.' Even when fully grown, the brothers-in-law are still very free in their ways, and it is not unusual to see two or three men, all married and the fathers of children, walking round in the evening with their arms round one another's waists.

The privilege of polygamy, which gives rise to these makeshift arrangements, is clearly an important concession to the chief on the part of the entire group. How does he see it? The fact of being able to pick and choose among the prettiest young girls gives him great satisfaction —a satisfaction not so much physical, for reasons I have already given, as sentimental. But, above all, polygamy and its specific attributes are the means put by the group at the disposition of their chief in order to help him to carry out his duties. Were he alone, he could only with difficulty do more than the others. His secondary wives, freed, in virtue of their special status, from the normal bondage of their sex, can help and comfort him. They are both the reward and the instrument of power. Can we say, however, that from the Indian's point of view the reward is adequate? To get an answer to that, we must examine the question more generally and see what the Nambikwara band, if considered as an elementary social structure, has to teach us about the origins and function of power.

The evidence of the Nambikwara runs, to begin with, clean counter to the ancient sociological theory, now temporarily resurrected by the psycho-analysts, according to which the primitive chief derives from a symbolical Father. This view goes on to assert that the forms of the State have developed, from this starting-point, on the analogy of family life. At the foundations of power in one of its most primitive forms, on the other hand, we have discerned a decisive phase which introduces, in relation to the phenomena of biology, quite a new element: this phase consists in the *giving of consent*. Consent is at the origins, and at the same time at the furthest limit, of power. What are in appearance one-sided relations (those existing, for instance, in a gerontocracy, an autocracy, or any other form of government) may arise among groups whose structure is already complex; but in forms of social organization as simple as the one I am now trying to describe they are inconceivable. In such cases, political relations may be reduced to a kind of arbitration between, on the one hand, the talents and authority of the chief and, on the other, the size, coherence, and good will of the group. All these factors exert a reciprocal influence upon one another.

I should like to be able to show how markedly, in this regard, contemporary anthropology supports the theses of the eighteenth-century *philosophes*. Doubtless Rousseau's schema differs from the quasi-contractual relations which obtain between the chief and his companions. Rousseau had in mind quite a different phenomenon—the renunciation by the individual of his own autonomy in the interests of the collective will. It is none the less true, however, that Rousseau and his contemporaries displayed profound sociological intuition when they realized that attitudes and elements of culture such as are summed up in the words 'contract' and 'consent' are not secondary formations, as their adversaries (and Hume in particular) maintained: they are the primary materials of social life, and it is impossible to imagine a form of political organization in which they are not present.

As a consequence of all this, it is clear that power is founded, psychologically speaking, in consent. But in daily life it finds outlet in the game of oath and counter-oath which is played out by the chief and his companions. Another of the attributes of power is, in effect, the notion of reciprocity. The chief has power, but he must be generous. He has duties, but he can also have several wives. Between himself and the group there is a constantly adjusted equilibrium of oaths and privileges, services and responsibilities.

But in the case of marriage the whole thing goes one stage further. By conceding to its chief the privilege of polygamy, the group exchanges the individual elements of security guaranteed by the rule of monogamy and receives in return the collective security which it expects from Authority. Each man receives his wife from another man, but the chief receives his several wives from the group as a group. In return, he offers to guarantee the group in times of danger or need; and this guarantee is offered not to the individuals whose daughters or sisters he marries, nor even to those who, as a result of this, will have to remain single. It is offered to the group as a group, for it is the group as a group which has suspended the common law to his personal advantage. These reflections may be of interest to any theoretical study of polygamy: but above all they remind us that the conception of the State as a system of guarantees, renewed after discussion of a national insurance system such as that put forward by Beveridge and others, is not a purely modern development. It is a return to the fundamental nature of social and political organization.

Such is the group's point of view, where power is concerned. What, now, is the chief's own attitude to his function as chief? From what motives does he accept an office which is not always a very pleasant one? The Nambikwara chief knows that his is a difficult role, and that it will take all he has to sustain it adequately. If, what is more, he does not succeed in continually enhancing his personal standing he may easily lose what he has taken months or years to acquire. That is why many men decline the position of power. But why is it that others accept it, and indeed go out of their way to get it? It is never easy to judge of psychological motives, and it becomes almost impossible to do so when the culture in question is so very different from our own. One can say, however, that the privilege of polygamy, however attractive from the sexual, social, and sentimental points of view, would not in itself be enough. Polygamous marriage is one of the technical conditions of power: as far as private satisfactions are concerned, it can offer only an auxiliary significance. Nor is that all: for when I call to mind the moral and psychological characteristics of the Nambikwara chiefs, and try to capture the fugitive nuances of their personality (these nuances cannot be analysed scientifically, but where the experiment of friendship is concerned, or the intuitive feeling of human communication, they may be of great value), I am carried irresistibly forward to the following conclusion: that if there are chiefs, it is because there are, in every group of human beings, men who, unlike their companions, love importance for its own sake, take a delight in its responsibilities, and find rewards enough in those very burdens of public life from which their fellows shrink. Certainly these individual differences are developed and find outlet in a manner, and to a degree, which will itself differ from one culture to another. But the fact that they exist in a society so largely un-competitive as that of the Nambikwara would suggest that their origin is not entirely social. Rather are they a part of that raw material of psychology in which every society somewhere finds it foundations. Men are not all alike, and even in primitive tribes, which sociologists have portrayed as crushed by all-powerful tradition, the differences between one man and another are noted as exactly, and exploited with as much pertinacity, as in what we call our 'individualist' society.

This is, in another form, precisely the 'miracle' of which Leibnitz speaks, in connection with the American savages whose ways, as des-cribed by early travellers, taught him 'never to mistake the hypotheses of political philosophy for demonstrations'. For my own part, I went to the ends of the earth in search of what Rousseau called 'the barely perceptible advances of the earliest times'. Beneath and beyond the veil of the all-too-learned laws of the Bororo and the Caduveo I had gone in search of a state which, to quote once again from Rousseau, 'no longer exists, perhaps may never have existed, and probably will never exist'. 'And yet,' he goes on, 'without an accurate idea of that state we cannot judge properly of our present situation.' Myself luckier than he, I thought that I had come upon that state in a society then nearing its end. It would have been pointless for me to wonder whether or not it was a vestigial version of what Rousseau had in mind; whether tradi-tional or degenerate, it brought me into contact with one of the most indigent of all conceivable forms of social and political organization. I had no need to go into its past history to discover what had maintained it at its rudimentary level—or what, as was more likely, had brought it thus far down. I had merely to focus my attention on the experiment in sociology which was being carried out under my nose.

But that 'experiment' eluded me. I had been looking for a society reduced to its simplest expression. The society of the Nambikwara had been reduced to the point at which I found nothing but human beings.

PART VIII

The Tupi-Kawahib

27 By Canoe

I HAD left Cuiaba in June, and it was now September. For three months I had wandered across the plateau, camping with the Indians while my animals had a rest, or pushing on interminably from one point to the next, asking myself the while what it would all add up to in the end. Meanwhile the jerky motion of the mule gave me sore places so atrociously painful, and yet so familiar, that I ended up by feeling that they were a permanent part of my anatomy and that I should even miss them if they were not there the next morning. Boredom got the upper hand of adventure. For weeks on end the same austere savannah would unroll before me—a land so dry that living plants could scarcely be distinguished from the dead stumps that marked the place where someone had lately struck camp. And as for the blackened remains of bush-fires, they seemed merely the natural culmination of a territory where it was the destiny of everything, sooner or later, to be burnt to a cinder.

From Utiarity we went to Juruena, and thence to Juina, Campos Novos, and Vilhena. September saw us moving towards the last stations on the plateau: Tres-Buritis first, and then Barão de Melgaço, which was already at the foot of the plateau. At more or less every station we had lost one or two of our oxen, either from thirst, or from hunger, or from *hervado*—eating poisonous grasses, that is to say. When we crossed a river by a bridge that was crumbling into ruins, several oxen fell into the water, together with our baggage, and it was with great difficulty that we saved the most precious fruits of our expedition. But such incidents were rare: every day was spent in exactly the same way: setting up camp, slinging our hammocks, with their mosquito-nets, putting our baggage and pack-saddles out of reach of the termites, seeing to our animals, and making ready for the same procedures, in reverse, the next morning. Should an Indian band come in sight, we put another routine into action, making a census, taking note of the names given to the various parts of the body and to certain family relationships, drawing up genealogies, and making an inventory of the natives' possessions. If this was 'escape', I was one of escape's bureaucrats.

We had had no rain for five months, and there was no game to be seen. It was a great day for us if we could shoot an emaciated parrot, or capture a big *tupinambis* lizard that could be boiled with our rice, or roast in their shells a tortoise or an oily, black-fleshed armadillo. We had to content ourselves, most often, with *xarque*: that eternal dried meat, prepared months previously by a butcher in Cuiaba. The thick slices would be swarming with worms when we unrolled them each morning in the sun: we cleaned them as best we could, only to find them in the same state next day. Just once, however, someone killed a wild pig. Its bleeding flesh seemed to us more heady than any wine, and as we tore into it, eating at least a pound a head, I could well understand the supposed 'gluttony' which so many travellers had instanced as proof of the savage's barbaric state. Once one had lived as they live, and eaten as they eat, one well knew what hunger could be, and how the satisfaction of that hunger brought not merely repletion, but happiness itself.

Gradually the landscape changed its character. The former crystalline and sedimentary soils, which make up the central plateau, gave way to a base of clay. The savannah was replaced by zones of dry chestnut-forest (not our own chestnuts, but the Brazilian *Bertholletia excelsa*), and forests too of the balsam-secreting copaiba-tree. The once limpid streams became clouded with yellow, foul-smelling waters. Landslides could be seen on every hand: eroded hills with, at their feet, marshes full of *sapézals* (tall grasses) and *buritizals* (palm-trees). On the verges of these, our mules would pick their way through fields of wild pine-apples—little fruit with orange-yellow skins whose flesh was full of big black seeds, with a taste midway between that of the cultivated pineapple and the richest of raspberries. From the soil there arose a smell we had not smelt for months past: that of a hot chocolate-flavoured tisane, which is in reality nothing more than the smell of tropical vegetation and organic decomposition. Suddenly one realized, when confronted with this smell, how this soil could produce cocoa, just as sometimes in Haute-Provence the scent of a field full of half-faded lavender will explain how that same earth can secrete the truffle. A last ledge in the terrain brought us to the edge of a meadowland immediately above the telegraph station of Barão de Melgaço. And from there, as far as the eye could see, the Machado valley stretched out into the Amazonian forest that went on for another thousand miles, right up to the Venezuelan frontier.

At Barão de Melgaço there were meadows of green grass surrounded by humid forest lands loud with the trumpet-note of the *jacu*, or barking-bird After two hours in these surroundings one could be confident of coming back to camp with one's arms full of game. A kind of gastronomic frenzy took hold of us, and for three days we did nothing but cook and eat. Thenceforward we should never go short: our so carefully husbanded stocks of sugar and alcohol melted away as we got our first taste of Amazonian dishes: above all the *tocari* or Brazil-nuts, whose meat, when grated, enriched our sauces with a smooth white cream. Here are some details of our culinary adventures that I have retrieved from one of my notebooks:

Humming-bird (called in Portuguese *beija-flor*, or flower-kisser) roasted on a needle and *flambé* in whisky.
The grilled tail of a caiman.
A parakeet roasted and *flambé* in whisky.
A salmis of *jacu* in a fruit-salad made from the fruits of the *assaï* palm-tree.
A ragout of *mutum* (a sort of wild turkey) and palm-buds, with pepper and a *tocari* sauce.
Roast *jacu* with caramel.

After these debauches and certain no less necessary ablutions—for we had spent many days without a chance of taking off the overalls which, together with cap and boots, made up our entire wardrobe—I began to draw up my plans for the rest of the journey. From that point onwards we would do better to keep to the rivers, rather than hazard ourselves in the overgrown forest. I had, in any case, only seventeen of my original oxen still with me, and their state was such that they could not have gone on, even on easy ground. We would split up into three groups. My troop-leader and some of his men would go overland towards the nearest of the rubber-seekers' posts, and there try to sell our horses and some of our mules. Other men would stay with our oxen at Barão de Melgaço, to allow them time to recover their strength in pastures of *capim-gordura*, or fat grasses. Tiburcio, their old cook, was the more ready to take command of them in that they all loved him. He had a good deal of African blood in him, and they said of him that he was 'black in colour and white in quality'—which shows, by the way, that the Brazilian peasant is not exempt from racial prejudices. In Amazonia a white girl who has a black suitor will often say: 'Have I such a white carcass that an *urubu* comes and perches on my belly?' In this she harks back to the familiar spectacle of the dead crocodiles who float downstream with a black-feathered vulture picking away at the belly of each for days together.

Once the oxen were better, the troop would turn in its tracks and go back to Utiarity. There we foresaw no trouble, since the oxen would have nothing to carry and the now-imminent rains would have turned the desert into a prairie. Finally, the scientific personnel and the remainder of our men would take our baggage and convey it in canoes to the inhabited areas in which we should go our separate ways. I myself intended to cross into Bolivia by the Madeira, fly across the country, go back to Brazil by way of Corumba, and thence to Cuiaba, and on to Utiarity, in the month of December or thereabouts, to rejoin my *comitiva*—my men and animals—and bring the expedition to a close.

The chief of the Melgaço station lent us two *galiotes*—light coracles made of planks—and some men to paddle them. And so it was good-bye to our mules! For now we had only to go down with the stream of the Rio Machado. Month after month of dryness had made us careless, and on our first evening we did not bother to hang our hammocks in a sheltered place, but simply slung them between the trees on the bank. The storm broke out in the middle of the night with a noise like a horse at full gallop and, before we had even woken up, our hammocks were awash with water. We unfolded an awning as best we could to shelter us from the rain: actually to erect it was quite impossible in such a deluge. Nor was there any question of going to sleep: squatting in the water, with the sheet draped over our heads, we had to keep a constant watch on the folds of the canvas which kept filling up with water and had to be shaken out before the water had time to get through. To pass the time, the men told one another stories: I remember one that Emydio told us.

'A widower had an only son, who was already almost grown up. One day he sent for him and told him that it was high time he got married. "What must I do to get married?" the boy asked. "It's very simple," his father said. "All you have to do is to go and see our neighbours and try to get their daughter to like you." "But I don't know how to make a girl like me!" "Well then—play the guitar, and

laugh, and sing her a song or two!" The son did as he was told. But as
he arrived just as the girl's father was dying his behaviour was thought
to be most unsuitable and they drove him away and threw stones after
him. He went home and complained to his father, who told him how he
ought to behave in such cases. The boy went off to his neighbours again
and arrived just as they were killing a pig. Remembering the latest of
his lessons he burst into tears: "How sad! How good he was! How we
loved him! We shall never find a better!" Once again the neighbours
drove him away in exasperation. He described all this to his father,
and once again he was told exactly how to behave in such circumstances.
When he paid his third visit, his neighbours were busy clearing the
caterpillars from their garden. Always one lesson behind, he burst out
with: "What an abundance of good things! May you have more and
more such animals on your property! May they never be lacking!" And
he was chased away again.

'After this third rebuff the father told his son to build himself a hut.
He went into the forest to cut down the necessary trees. A werewolf
passed by in the night, thought the site a good one for himself to settle
in, and went to work. Next morning the boy came back to the clearing
and found the work well advanced. "God is giving me a hand!" he
thought to himself delightedly. And so they worked in double shifts, the
boy by day and the werewolf by night. Before long the house was ready.

'By way of house-warming the boy decided to feast off a roebuck.
The werewolf preferred a human body. The one brought the buck by
day, the other a corpse during the night. And when the boy's father
came along to join in the feast he saw a dead man on the table as *pièce de
résistance* and said to his son: "Ah, my boy, I'm afraid you'll never be
up to anything much. . . ." '

The next day it was still raining and as we sailed down to the
Pimenta Bueno station we had to bail the whole time. The station stood
at the point where the river from which it took its name joined the Rio
Machado. About twenty people lived in it: a few whites from the
interior, and some Indians of varied extraction who were working to
maintain the line—Cabishianas from the Guaporé valley, and Tupi-
Kawahibs from the Rio Machado. All were to provide me with important information. Some of it had to do with the Tupi-Kawahibs who
were still completely primitive: older reports had made out that these
had disappeared. Of this I shall say more later. Other stories related to
an unknown tribe which seemed to live some days distant, by canoe,

along the Rio Pimenta Bueno. Immediately I wondered how I could get to meet them and, as luck would have it, a black man named Bahia was passing through the station. He was a commercial traveller, and something of an adventurer, who made, every year, a most remarkable journey. First he would go down as far as the Madeira and stock up with the merchandise to be found in the riverside warehouses. Then he would canoe upstream along the Machado and, for two days, up the Pimenta Bueno. There he knew of a track which allowed him to drag his canoes and their load through the forest for three solid days until he came to a little tributary of the Guaporé. At this point he could dispose of his stock at prices all the more exorbitant for the fact that the region served by this little river had no other source of supplies. Bahia said that he was quite ready to go up the Pimenta Bueno beyond the normal limit of his itinerary, on condition that I paid him not in money but in merchandise. This was a sound speculation on his part, in that the Amazonian wholesale prices were higher than those I had paid at São Paulo. So I handed over to him some lengths of red flannel: these had lost their charm for me ever since, at Vilhena, I had offered one to the Nambikwara, only to see, on the following day, that not only they themselves, but their dogs, monkeys, and tame boars were dressed from head to toe in red flannel. (An hour later, the joke being exhausted, the flannel was strewn about the bush in ribbons and no one paid any more attention to it.)

Our team was soon made up: with two canoes borrowed from the station, four paddlers, and two of my own men, we were ready to set off on our improvised adventure.

Nothing is more exciting for an anthropologist than the prospect of being the first white man to penetrate a native community. Already in 1938 this greatest of compensations could be procured only in a very few parts of the world—few enough, in fact, to be counted on the fingers of one hand. Today the possibilities are still more restricted. In my journey I was to re-live the experience of the travellers of old; and at the same time I should be faced with that moment, so crucial to modern thought, at which a community which had thought itself complete, perfected, and self-sufficient, is made to realize that it is nothing of the kind. The counter-revelation, in short: the fact that it is not alone in the world, that it is but part of a vast human ensemble, and that to know itself it must first look at the unrecognizable image of itself in that mirror of which one long-forgotten splinter was about to give out, for myself alone, its first and last reflection.

Perhaps my enthusiasm was out of place in the twentieth century? The Indians of the Pimenta Bueno were 'unknown', certainly: but I could hardly expect to get from them a shock of the kind felt, four hundred years earlier, by the great pioneers, Léry, Staden, and Thevet, who were the first to set foot on Brazilian territory. What they then saw, our eyes could not hope to see again. The civilizations which they were the first to consider had developed on lines different from our own, but they had none the less reached the maximum point of plenitude and perfection which was compatible with their nature. The societies which we could study today, in conditions which it would be a great illusion to compare to those of four centuries ago, were enfeebled in body and mutilated in form. Distant as they were from the western world, and weird as had been the intermediaries between themselves and it (just how weird these had been was a source of amazement to me, when I managed to reconstruct the chain of events involved), they had been pulverized by the development of western civilization. For them, as for so large and so innocent a fraction of the human race, this development had come as a monstrous and unintelligible cataclysm. We in the West should remember that that development has put upon the matter a second face, as truthful and as indelible as its predecessor.

The men might have changed, but the conditions of the journey remained the same. After the back-breaking ride across the plateau I gave myself up to the delights of navigation. Our maps did not indicate the course of that delectable river, but its every detail put me in mind of narratives long cherished.

I had to relearn the habits of river life that I had picked up, three years before, on the São Lourenço: to recognize, for instance, the different types and respective merits of the canoes, some cut out of a tree-trunk, others assembled from planks, which are called, according to shape and size, *montaria, canoea, uba,* or *igarité*. I had to get used, once again, to squatting for hours together in the water that seeped in through cracks in the wood and had to be bailed out continually with a little calabash. Stiff as I was, I had to stretch myself slowly and with the utmost care if I were not to capsize my boat. (As the Indians said, '*agua não tem cabellos*': 'Water has no hair.' If ever I fell out, there would be nothing to hold on to.) And I needed great patience: for, whenever an obstacle presented itself, we had to unload the provisions and the equipment that I had stowed away with such an extremity of care, and carry both them and the canoes along the rocky bank to a point, several hundred yards distant, at which the whole operation could be begun all over again.

These obstacles were of several kinds: *seccos*, where the river-bed was dry; *cachoeiras*, rapids; *saltos*, falls. Each type was soon given a vivid nickname by our oarsmen: a detail of the landscape, such as *castanhal*, *palmas*; an incident of the chase, *veado*, *queixada*, *araras*; or a name suggestive of some more directly personal relationship with the traveller: *criminosa*, the criminal; *encrenca*, an untranslatable noun which describes the feeling of being caught in a trap; *apertada hora*, the 'confined hour', or the hour of anguish; *vamos ver*, 'we shall see . . .'

And so I got away to an experience which, in its beginnings, was familiar enough. We let the rowers space out the rhythms in traditional style: first a series of short strokes, plouf, plouf, plouf . . . after which the boat really gets under way, with two sharp taps on the gunwale between each stroke, tra-plouf, tra-plouf, tra . . . and finally the long-distance rhythm. In this last, the oar only goes *into* the water on every other stroke, alternating with a mere caress of the surface which is preceded and followed by a tap on the gunwale. The rhythm is, therefore, tra-plouf, tra, sh, tra . . . and so on. In this we saw first the blue and then the orange side of each oar, hardly more heavy, as it skimmed above the water, than the reflection (and at times the oars themselves seemed no more than their own reflection) of the large groups of *araras* which flew across the river with either their golden-yellow bellies or their sky-blue backs sparkling all together in the sunlight. The air no longer had the transparency that it had had in the dry season. At dawn everything was wrapped in a kind of thick rosy-pink froth as the mists of morning rose slowly from the river. It was already very warm, but little by little this indirect warmth declared itself more exactly. What had been merely a diffused heat became the strong downbeat of the sun upon one part or another of one's face and hands. One began to know just why one was sweating. The pink of the mist grew lighter here, darker there. Islets of blue made their appearance. The mist seemed, in fact, to be getting richer in colour, whereas it was really only dissolving.

Going upstream was hard work, and our rowers needed an occasional rest. The morning was then spent in catching, with the help of a coarse line baited with wild berries, enough fish for the *peixada* or Amazonian bouillabaisse: *pacus* yellow with fat and eaten in slices held by the backbone as one holds a cutlet by its 'handle'; silvery, red-fleshed *piracanjubas*; the vermilion chrysophrys; *cascudos*, with black armour-plate as heavy as a lobster's; speckled *piaparas*; *mandi*; *piava*;

curimbata; jatuarama; matrinchão. . . . But we had to look out for the poisonous rays and the *puraké*, or electric fish; this latter can be caught without bait, but its electric charge is strong enough to kill a mule. To pass water in the river was still more dangerous for, according to our men, there were tiny fish that could climb up the jet of urine and get into one's bladder. . . .

Alternatively we would watch the vast thickets of green mould that formed in the forest at the water's edge for the sudden irruption of a band of many-named monkeys: the shrieking *guariba*, the *coata* with its spidery limbs, the capuchin or 'nail-monkey', and the *zog-zog*, which wakes the whole forest with its cries in the hour before dawn. With his big almond-eyes, his lofty carriage, and his silken billowy coat, the *zog-zog* could pass for a Mongol prince. With these came the whole tribe of smaller monkeys: the *saguin*, which we call the ouistiti; the *macaco da noite*, or night-monkey, with its dark gelatinous eyes; the *macaco de cheiro*, or scent-monkey; the *gogo de sol*, or sunny-throat, and so on. . . . A shot fired at random into their troop would almost certainly bring one down. Roasted, it would look like a mummified child with clenched hands; in a ragout, it would taste like duck.

Towards three in the afternoon there came a clap of thunder, the sky darkened, and rain masked one half of the sky with a great vertical bar. Would it reach us? The black bar became streaky, tore itself open, and revealed on the far side of it a glimmer of light which, at first golden in colour, turned later to a faded blue. Only the centre of the horizon was now dark with rain. But the clouds melted away, and the rain-patch thinned down to left and to right and finally disappeared. All that remained was a composite sky, with blue-black masses super-imposed upon a background of blue and white. This was the moment, before the next storm, to tie up at a point where the forest seemed not quite so thick. We would quickly cut away a little clearing with our sabres, and look closely at the trees thus brought into the open. One of them might boast the *pau de novato*, or novice-tree, so called because the greenhorn who slings his hammock to it will be invaded by an army of red ants; or the garlic-scented *pau d'alho*; or the *cannela merda*, whose name speaks for itself. Perhaps too, if we were lucky, there would be the *soveira*, whose trunk, when cut into in a circle, will in the space of a few minutes pour out more milk than any cow. Its milk is creamy and foaming but, if drunk neat, will cover the inside of one's mouth with an insidious thin rubbery skin. Or the *araça*, whose purplish fruit, about as big as a cherry, has the smell of turpentine and, with it an acidity so light that the water in which one squeezes it will seem to fizz; the pod-bearing *inga*, whose pods are full of sweet-tasting down; the *bacuri*, a pear such as one might steal from the orchards of Paradise; and finally the *assaï*, greatest of forest delicacies, whose liquid, when drawn off, is like a thick raspberry syrup. Leave it overnight, and it will turn into a fruity and slightly sour cheese.

Some of our men would look to the food, while others slung the hammocks beneath shelters of branches covered with a light roof of palms. This was the moment for stories round the camp-fire—stories full of ghosts and apparitions: the *lobis-homem*, or werewolf, or the headless horse, or the old woman with a skeleton's head. Always in any troop there is an old *garimpeiro* who looks back with nostalgia to that wretched way of life and its daily increment of hope. 'I was writing one day'—'writing' means sifting the gravel—'when I saw a tiny grain of rice glittering in the wash-trough. Shining out like a lighthouse it was! *Que cousa bounita!* I doubt if there is anywhere in the world *cousa mais bounita*, a more beautiful sight. . . . When you looked at it, it almost gave you an electric shock!' And a discussion began: 'Between Rosario and Laranjal there is a stone on a hill that sparkles. You can see it from miles away, especially at night.' 'Perhaps it's crystal?' 'No, crystal doesn't light up at night. But diamonds do.' 'And no one goes to get it?' 'With diamonds like that, it's been settled—oh, ages and ages ago—who's going to find them, and when!'

Those who are not sleepy go and stand, sometimes till dawn, at the water's edge, where they have seen the tracks of a boar, a capivara, or a tapir; they try, in vain, the *batuque* hunt—beating the ground at regular intervals with a thick stick: poum . . . poum . . . poum. . . . The animals mistake this for the noise of fruit falling from the bough, and it seems that they always come up in the same order—the boar first, and then the jaguar.

Some there are, too, who simply keep the fire going. And so, after the incidents of the day have been talked over and the maté has been passed round, nothing remains but for each of us to slip into his hammock. Around him is his mosquito-net, half cocoon in construction and half kite, kept together and in place by an elaborate apparatus of string and thin sticks. Once inside, he takes care to raise its skirts so that none of them is trailing on the ground: and he bunches them together, forming a kind of pocket which he wedges shut with the heavy revolver that he keeps always within reach. Before long the rain begins to fall.

28 Crusoe Country

For four days we had been working our way upstream. So numerous were the rapids that we had to unload our boats, hump the cargo overland, and reload as many as five times a day. The water ran down between rock formations that divided the river into several arms; in the middle, trees that had floated downstream, complete with branches, roots, earth, and attendant vegetation, were lying, caught on the reefs. On these improvised islands vegetable life had been quick to reassert itself, indifferent even to the chaotic state in which the last flood-waters had left it. Trees grew in every direction, with flowers in full bloom across waterfalls. It was difficult to tell whether the river's main purpose was to irrigate this astonishing garden, or whether it would be quite simply overwhelmed by the multiplicity of plants and liana which had arrogated to themselves not merely the vertical dimension, but all space's dimensions, now that the ordinary distinctions between earth and water had been abolished. One could no longer say 'Here is the river' or 'Here is the bank'; rather was there a labyrinth of bouquets kept ever fresh by running water, with earth burgeoning on the crest of the waves. This friendship between the elements extended to living creatures also: the native tribes needed an immense amount of ground to keep themselves alive, but in these reaches the superabundance of animal life made it clear that for many years past Man had been powerless to disturb the natural order of things. The trees seemed to bear almost as many monkeys as leaves: it was as if living fruits were dancing on their branches. Near the rocks which stood just at water-level you had only to stretch out your hand to stroke the jet-black plumage of the big coral- or amber-beaked *mutum*, or the *jacamin*, with its watered silky-blue, like that of labradorite. These birds did not fly off at our approach, and when, like so many precious stones in motion, they picked their way between the water-rounded liana and the many-leaved torrents, they put me in mind of those paintings from the studio of Breughel in which Paradise is portrayed as a place in which plants, animals, and human beings live together in tender intimacy: a place in which there has, as yet, been no cleavage in the animal universe.

On the afternoon of the fifth day a slender canoe, tied up to the bank, told us that we had reached our destination. A thinly spread clump of trees would serve as our camping-ground. The Indian village was just over half a mile inland: its garden, about a hundred yards wide at its broadest point, stood in an egg-shaped clearing in which were three collective huts, hemispherical in shape, with their central pole sticking out of the top like a mast. The two main huts faced one another in the broader section of the egg, on the edge of a dance-floor of beaten earth. The third stood at the pointed end of the clearing and was linked to the 'main square' by a footpath that led through the garden.

There were twenty-five people in the village, in all, plus a small boy of about ten who was, so far as I could make out, a prisoner of war. He was treated, in any case, just like the other children. Clothes, for men and women alike, were as scanty as with the Nambikwara, except that all the men wore a conical penis-cover like that used by the Bororo and almost everyone wore the straw pom-pom, above their private parts, which was known, though less common, among the Nambikwara. Men and women alike wore lip-pieces of hardened resin that looked almost like amber, and necklaces of either discs or plaques of shining mother-of-pearl or, on occasion, shells, polished and entire. Wrists, biceps, calves, and ankles were adorned with tight-drawn strips of cotton. And the women had pierced their nasal septum to make way for an ornament made up of black and white discs, in alternation, strung together and drawn tight along a length of stiff fibre.

The physical appearance of the Tupi-Kawahib was very different from that of the Nambikwara. They had very light skins, squat sturdy bodies, and short legs. Their pale skin combined with a faintly Mongolian cast of feature to give some of the natives a Caucasian look. The Indians pluck out all their facial hair with the most minute care: the lashes by hand, and the eyebrows with wax which they allow to harden *in situ* for a number of days before getting down to work. In front, the hair of the head was cut—or, more exactly, burnt—off in a rounded fringe which left the forehead bare. The temples were bared by a procedure which I have never encountered elsewhere, the hair being pulled back in the knot of a thick rope twisted back upon itself. The operator takes one end between his teeth: with one hand he keeps the loop of the rope open, while with the other he pulls so hard on the free end of the rope that it draws itself tighter and tighter, pulling out the hair by the roots as it does so.

These Indians referred to themselves by the name of Mundé, and there had been no previous mention of them in anthropological literature. They spoke a high-spirited language, in which the words ended with a sharply accented syllable, *zip, zep, pep, zet, tap, kat*: these underlined what they had to say with a noise like the clashing of cymbals. Their language had affinities with the now-vanished dialects of the Bas-Xingu, and with others recently recorded on the tributaries of the right bank of the Guaporé: and the Mundé live very near, be it remembered, to those sources. No one, to my knowledge, has visited the Mundé since I was there, save for a woman missionary who met some of them, a little before 1950, on the Haut Guaporé, where three families had taken refuge. I spent a very agreeable week with them: rarely can hosts have been more unaffected, more patient, or more cordial. They invited me to admire the gardens in which they were growing maize, manioc, sweet potatoes, ground-nuts, tobacco, gourds, and several sorts of broad and haricot beans. When they clear a patch of ground they take care not to damage the palm-stumps, so rich in the fat white larvae which they eat with immense relish: there results from all this a curious farmyard, in which agriculture and stock-breeding are carried on side by side.

The round huts allowed a diffused light, flecked with sunshine, to filter through from outside. They were very carefully built, with a dome-like interior made of long poles, planted in a circle, and curved towards the top to fit into a number of forks, which stood at an oblique angle to them and acted as buttresses. Between these ten or a dozen hammocks of stitched cotton were slung. At a point twelve or thirteen feet from the ground all the poles met and were tied to the central pole, or mast, that pushed on up through the roof. Horizontal circles of branches completed the main structure, and on top of that was a cupola of palm-leaves which had been folded in the same direction, one on top of another, to form a tile-like roof. The biggest hut was nearly forty feet in diameter. Four families lived in it, and each had to itself the area between two buttresses There were in all six such areas, but the two immediately facing the front and back doors were left empty, to allow people to come and go. I spent my days sitting on one of the little wooden benches which the natives used. These were made up of the scooped-out half of a palm-log, laid with the flat part downwards. We ate maize-seed grilled on a flat pottery plate and drank *chicha* of maize—a drink half-way between beer and soup—out of calabashes blackened on the inside with some sort of carbonaceous glazing. On the outside these were decorated with lines, zigzags, circles, and polygons, incised or poker-worked.

Even without knowing the language, and although I had no interpreter, I could try to penetrate certain aspects of the natives' thought, and of their society: the composition of the group, relationships and the names given to them, the names of the parts of the body, and the vocabulary of colour, according to a scale which I kept always with me. The words for relationships, for the parts of the body, colours, and forms (those drawn on the calabashes, for instance) have often common properties which put them half-way between vocabulary and grammar: each group forms a system, and the manner in which different languages choose to separate or commingle the relationships therein expressed gives rise to a certain number of viable hypotheses, even where it does not define the distinctive characteristics, where these things are concerned, of this or that society. . . .

And yet, although this adventure was begun with such high enthusiasm, it left me with a feeling of emptiness.

I had wanted to pursue 'the primitive' to its furthest point. Surely my wish had been gratified by these delightful people whom no white man had seen before me, and none would ever see again? My journey had been enthralling and, at the end of it, I had come upon 'my' savages. But alas—they were all *too* savage. Having encountered them only at the last moment, I could not put aside the time that was indispensable if I were to hope to know them properly. My resources needed careful husbanding, my companions and I myself were physically near to exhaustion—a state shortly to be aggravated by the fevers which would follow the rains. Consequently, where I should have spent a month in serious consecutive study, I could snatch at most a few days for the purpose. There they were, all ready to teach me their customs and beliefs, and I knew nothing of their language. They were as close to me as an image seen in a looking-glass: I could touch, but not understand them. I had at one and the same time my reward and my punishment, for did not my mistake, and that of my profession, lie in the belief that men are not always men? That some are more deserving of our interest and our attention because there is something astonishing to us in their manners, or in the colour of their skins? No sooner are such people known, or guessed at, than their strangeness drops away, and one might as well have stayed in one's own village. Or if, as in the present case, their strangeness remained intact, then it was no good to me, for I could not even begin to analyse it. Between these two extremes, what are the equivocal cases which afford us the excuses by which we live? Who is, in the end, the one most defrauded by the disquiet which we arouse in the reader? Our remarks must be pushed a certain distance, if we are to make them intelligible, and yet they must be cut off half-way, since the people whom they astonish are very like those for whom the customs in question are a matter of course. Is it the reader who is deceived by his belief in us? Or ourselves, who have not the right to be satisfied before we have completely dissolved that residuum which gave our vanity its pretext?

Let the earth speak, therefore, since the men are beyond our grasp. Over and above the delights which it had given me by the river's edge, let it at last answer up and yield the secret of its unspoiledness. What lay behind those confused appearances which are everything and nothing at one and the same time? If I take any particular scene and try to isolate it, that tree, that flower could be any other tree, any other flower. Could that also be a lie, that whole which gave me such delight, that whole whose parts vanished as soon as I tried to examine them individually? If I had to admit that it was real, I wanted at last to master it, all of it, down to its smallest detail. I turned a prosecutor's eye upon the enormous landscape, narrowing it down to a strip of clayey river-marge and a handful of grasses: nothing, there, to prove that when I next raised my eyes to the world about me I should not find the Bois de Boulogne stretched out all round that insignificant patch of ground. Yet that same ground was trodden daily by the most authentic of savages, though Man Friday's print had yet to be found there.

The journey downstream went remarkably quickly. Our oarsmen, still carried away by the charm of the Mundé, disdained to get out and carry our baggage. When faced with a stretch of rapids they pointed the prow of their canoe towards the foaming waters and, for a second or two, the landscape whizzed by at a tremendous pace and we ourselves had the sensation of being brought to a halt and violently shaken. Then suddenly all was calm again and we were safely through the rapids and into dead water: only then did we feel dizzy.

In two days we got to Pimenta Bueno, where I made a new plan —one not to be understood without one or two moments of explanation. Towards the end of his explorations, in 1915, Rondon came upon

several Tupi-speaking native groups and managed to get into contact
with three of them: the remainder proved irreducibly hostile. The
largest of the groups was installed on the upper reaches of the Rio
Machado, two days' march from the left bank and on a secondary
tributary, the Igarapé do Leitão (or 'sucking-pig stream'). This was the
band, or clan, or of the Takwatip or 'bamboo'. The term 'clan' may
not be quite apt, for the Tupi-Kawahib bands usually formed a single
village, owned hunting-grounds whose frontiers were jealously guar-
ded, and practised exogamy rather from a wish to form alliances
with neighbouring bands than from the application of any strict rule.
The Takwatip were led by the chief Abaitara. On the same side of the
river there were, to the north, a band known only by the name of its
chief, Pitsara. To the south, on the Rio Tamuripa, the Ipotiwat (the
name of a liana), whose chief was called Kamandjara: and then,
between Rio Tamuripa and the Igarapé du Cacoal, the Jabotifet, or
'tortoise-people', whose chief was called Maira. On the left bank of
the Machado, in the valley of the Rio Muqui, lived the Paranawat,
'river-people', who are indeed still there, but respond to any attempt
to make contact with them with a shower of arrows; and, a little farther
to the south, on the Igarapé de Itapici, another unknown band. Such, at
any rate, was the information which I was able to secure in 1938 from
the rubber-collectors who had been in the area since the time of
Rondon's expedition. Rondon himself had given only fragmentary
information about the Tupi-Kawahib.

Talking to the civilized Tupi-Kawahib at the station of Pimenta
Bueno, I managed to get together some twenty names of clans. The
researches of Curt Nimuendaju, who was a man of learning as much as
a field-anthropologist, have likewise thrown some light on the past
history of the tribe. The term 'Kawahib' harks back to the name of an
ancient Tupi tribe, the Cabahiba, which is often quoted in documents
of the eighteenth and nineteenth centuries and was then located on the
upper and middle reaches of the Rio Tapajoz. It would seem to have
been progressively driven out of that area by another Tupi tribe, the
Mundurucu: and, on its way towards the west, to have broken up into
several groups, of which the only ones now known are the Parintintin
of the lower reaches of the Machado and the Tupi-Kawahib, farther to
the south. There is therefore every possibility that these Indians may
be the last descendants of the great Tupi populations of the middle and
lower reaches of the Amazon. These were related to the populations
along the coast who were known, at the time of their apogee, to the

European travellers of the sixteenth and seventeenth centuries whose narratives laid the fuse for the anthropological studies of our own time; for it was under their unknowing influence that the political and moral philosophy of the Renaissance set out on the road which was to lead it to the French Revolution. To be, as seemed very possible, the first man to penetrate a still-intact Tupi-Kawahib village was to go back more than four hundred years and join hands with Léry, with Staden, with Soares de Souza, with Thevet, and even with Montaigne, who ruminates in one of his essays (the one on cannibals) on a conversation with Tupi Indians whom he had met in Rouen. What a temptation!

At the moment when Rondon made contact with the Tupi-Kawahib, the Takwatip, under the leadership of an ambitious and energetic chief, were in the process of extending their hegemony over a number of other bands. After spending months in the more or less desert-like solitudes of the plateau, Rondon's companions were dazzled by the 'mile upon mile' (the language of the *sertão* lends itself readily to exaggeration) of plantations which the people of Abaitara had opened up in the humid forest or on the *igapos*, banks safe from inundation. Thanks to these plantations the Abaitara were able to revictual without any difficulty the explorers who had been until then directly under the shadow of famine.

Two years after their first meeting, Rondon persuaded the Tupi-Kawahib to transfer their village to the right bank of the Machado, at the point still marked as *aldeia dos indios*, opposite the mouth of the Rio São Pedro (11.5°S. and 62.3°W.) on the *International Map of the World* on a scale of 1/1,000,000. This facilitated the work of victualling and surveillance, and it also made it easier to get Indian canoeists: on waters studded with rapids, falls, and narrow straits, the natives knew just how to manoeuvre their light bark shells.

That 'new' village had disappeared, but I could still get a description of it. As Rondon had noted at the time of his visit to the forest village, the huts were rectangular, had no walls, and consisted of a two-piece palm-roof supported by trunks planted firmly in the earth. About twenty huts, measuring about four yards by six, were set out in a circle some twenty yards in diameter, in the middle of which were two more spacious habitations (eighteen yards by fourteen). One of these latter was occupied by Abaitara himself, with his wives and young children, and the other by his youngest married son. The two elder unmarried sons lived like the rest of the population in the peripheral huts. Like the other bachelors, they were fed in the chief's hut. Many chicken-runs were laid out in the area between the central huts and those of the outer circle.

All that was far removed from the vast Tupi dwellings described by the travellers of the sixteenth century, but from the five to six hundred inhabitants of Abaitara's time to the villages of today the distance is greater still. In 1925 Abaitara was murdered. The death of this emperor of the upper Machado initiated a period of violent happenings in a village already reduced by the influenza epidemic of 1918–20 to twenty-five men, twenty-two women, and twelve children. In that same year, 1925, four people, among them the murderer of Abaitara, were killed in acts of vengeance, most of them sexual in origin. Shortly after this the survivors decided to abandon the village and go back to the station of Pimenta Bueno, two days' journey upstream by canoe. In 1938 their strength was down to five men, one woman, and one little girl. They spoke a kind of rusticated Portuguese and appeared to have thrown in their lot with the neo-Brazilian population of the post. It might have seemed as if the history of the Tupi-Kawahib had come to an end—at any rate as regards the right bank of the Machado, and with the exception of an irreducible group of Paranawat on the left bank, in the village of the Rio Muqui.

And yet when I arrived at Pimenta Bueno in October 1938 I learned that in 1935 an unknown group of Tupi-Kawahib had appeared on the river; they had been seen again two years later and the last surviving son of Abaitara (who bore his father's name and will be so designated in this story) had gone to see them in their village, which was an isolated point in the forest, two days' march from the Rio Machado and with no path to point the way. He had persuaded the chief of the little group to promise that he would come, with his people, and pay him, Abaia Abaitara, a visit during the following year—at about the time, that is to say, at which we ourselves arrived at Pimenta Bueno. This promise had a great importance for the native inhabitants of the post. Themselves suffering from a shortage of womenfolk (one grown woman to five men), they had been particularly attentive to young Abaitara's description of how, in the unknown village, there were a number of superfluous women. Himself a widower for some years past, he expected that the establishment of friendly relations with his savage kindred would allow him to procure himself a wife. These were the circumstances in which, not without difficulty (for he feared that the adventure might have bad consequences), I persuaded him to bring about a meeting before the appointed time, and to act as my guide.

The point at which we had to plunge into the forest to get to the Tupi-Kawahib was at the mouth of the Igarapé do Porquinho, three days downstream by canoe from the post of Pimenta Bueno. The Igarapé was a slender little stream that debouched into the Machado. Not far from there, we happened on a little natural clearing, which was safe from floods since the banks at that point were several yards high. There we disembarked our equipment: a few boxes of presents for the natives and provisions of dried meat, beans, and rice. We set up a camp rather more solid than usual, since it had to last until we got back to it. A whole day was spent in this, and in the organization of our journey— a rather complex matter, this last. I had separated from part of my troop, as I have already explained, and as bad luck would have it Jehan Vellard, the expedition's doctor, had an attack of malaria and had had to go on ahead to rest in a little rubber-collectors' post, three days upstream by boat—and these distances have to be doubled or tripled when it is a question of going upstream in such difficult waters. We were thus reduced to Luis de Castro Faria, my Brazilian companion, Abaitara, myself, and five men, two of whom would guard the camp while the other three followed us into the forest. With such restricted numbers, and as each of us was already loaded up with hammock, blanket, mosquito-net, gun, and ammunition, it was out of the question to take with us food other than a little coffee, some dried meat, and some *farinha d'agua*. This form of *farinha* is made from manioc soaked in the river (whence its name) and then fermented. It comes in the form of small lumps, hard as stone, which, when suitably moistened, taste deliciously of butter. For the rest we counted on the *tocari*—Brazil-nuts —which abound in the area. One single *ouriço*, or 'hedgehog', of these (a hard round clump of nuts which can kill a man if it falls on him from a height of seventy or a hundred feet) can provide several people with a meal of thirty to forty big triangular nuts apiece, each with a milky and bluish meat to it, if the 'hedgehog' is held firm between one's feet and suitably attacked with a *terçado*.

We left before dawn, traversing to begin with the *lageiros*, areas almost bare of vegetation, in which the rock of the plateau, shortly to disappear beneath the alluvial soil, can still be seen in large disgarnished patches. Next came fields of *sapézals*, tall spear-shaped grasses: and, two hours later, we were in the forest.

29　*In the Forest*

Eᴠᴇʀ since my childhood, the sea has aroused mixed feelings in me. The shore itself, and that marginal area ceded from time to time by the reflux which prolongs it—these I find attractive by reason of the challenge which they offer to our undertakings, the unexpected universe which lies hidden within them, and the possibilities which they offer of observations and discoveries most flattering to the imagination. Like Benvenuto Cellini, whom I find more sympathetic than the masters of the Quattrocento, I enjoy walking on shores left bare by the receding tide, following, round some steep slope, the itinerary which that tide has imposed upon me; picking up stones with holes through the middle of them, shells whose geometry has been reshaped by the motion of the waves, or spectral fragments of sea-wrack, and making a private museum of these things: a museum which, for a moment, seems quite the equal of those other museums to which only masterpieces are admitted. Perhaps, after all, those masterpieces derive from methods of work which, though rooted in the mind rather than in the palpable world, may not be fundamentally different from those with which Nature amuses herself.

But as I am neither sailor nor fisherman, I feel myself diminished by this mass of water which robs me of half my universe—more than half, indeed, since it makes its presence known some way inland, giving the landscape, as often as not, a touch of austerity. It seems to me that the sea destroys the normal variety of the earth. Enormous spaces and supplementary colours it may offer to the eye—but at the price of a deadening monotony, a flat sameness, where never a hidden valley keeps in reserve the surprises on which my imagination feeds.

And, what is more, the pleasures which the sea has to offer are now no longer available to us. Like an animal whose carapace thickens with age, forming an impenetrable crust through which the epidermis can no longer breathe, thus hastening the onset of old age, most European countries have allowed their coasts to become cluttered with villas, hotels, and casinos. Whereas the littoral once gave a foretaste of the ocean's great solitudes, it has become a kind of front line, where mankind from time to time mobilizes all its forces for a full-scale attack on liberty: but the value of that liberty is marked down by the very conditions in which we allow ourselves to grasp hold of it. A beach was once a place where the sea yielded up the results of commotions many thousands of years in the making, admitting us, in this way, to an astonishing museum in which Nature always ranked herself with the avant-garde; today that same beach is trodden by great crowds and serves merely as a depository for their rubbish.

So I prefer the mountains to the sea; and for some years past this preference has taken the form of a jealous passion. I hated all those who shared my predilection, for they were a menace to the solitude I value so highly; and I despised those others for whom mountains meant merely physical exhaustion and a constricted horizon and who were, for that reason, unable to share in my emotions. The only thing that would have satisfied me would have been for the entire world to admit to the superiority of mountains and grant me the monopoly of their enjoyment. I must add that my feelings did not extend to *high* mountains: these had already disappointed me, because of the ambiguous character of the delights—and I do not deny them—that they have to offer; these delights are physical in the extreme—organic, one might say, in view of the efforts involved. But they have a formal, almost an abstract quality in so much as one's attention, absorbed by problems of a technical character, is often drawn away from the splendours of Nature and entirely engrossed by preoccupations relating rather to mechanics or geometry. What I liked best were pasture-mountains and, above all, the zone between four thousand five hundred and six thousand seven hundred and fifty feet: the heights are not great enough, as yet, to impoverish the landscape, as is the case higher up, and while they make it difficult to cultivate the land they seem, in other respects, to urge Nature on to an activity more vivid, more sharply contrasted than that found in the valley below. On these lofty balconies, and with that undomesticated landscape before one, it is easy, though doubtless erroneous, to imagine that Man in his beginnings was confronted with just such a sight as meets one's eyes.

If the sea presents, in my opinion, a landscape many degrees below proof, mountains offer, by contrast, a world in a state of intense concentration. Concentrated it is, in fact, in the strict sense of the word, in that the earth is pleated and folded in such a way as to offer the maximum amount of surface for a given area. A denser universe, it keeps its promises longer: the instability of the climate and the differences due to the height, the nature of the soil, and the fact of its exposure to the air—all favour a sharp and direct contrast between one season and another, and likewise between level ground and steep slopes. Unlike so many people, I was not at all depressed by a sojourn in a narrow valley where the slopes, so close to one another as to take on the look of high walls, allowed one to glimpse only a small section of the sky and to enjoy at most a few hours of sunlight. On the contrary, I found an immense vitality in the upended landscape. Instead of submitting passively to my gaze, like a picture that can be studied without one's giving anything of oneself, the mountain scene invited me to a conversation, as it were, in which we both had to give of our best. I made over to the mountains the physical effort that it cost me to explore them, and in return their true nature was revealed to me. At once rebellious and provocative, never revealing more than half of itself at any one time, keeping the other half fresh and intact for those complementary perspectives which would open up as I clambered up or down its slopes, the mountain scene joined with me in a kind of dance—and a dance in which, I felt, I could move the more freely for having so firm a grasp of the great truths which had inspired it.

And yet I have to admit that, although I do not feel that I myself have changed, my love for the mountains is draining away from me like a wave running backwards down the sand. My thoughts are unchanged, but the mountains have taken leave of me. Their unchanging joys mean less and less to me, so long and so intently have I sought them out. Surprise itself has become familiar to me as I follow my oft-trodden routes. When I climb, it is not among bracken and rock-face, but among the phantoms of my memories. Those memories have lost their charm for me, on two separate counts: first, because long usage has robbed them of all novelty; and second, because a pleasure which grows a little less vivid with each repetition can only be had at the price of an effort which grows greater and greater with the years. I am getting older, but the only evidence of it is that the cutting edge of my projects is growing steadily blunter. I can still carry them through, but their fulfilment no longer brings me the satisfaction on which I could so often and so undisappointedly count.

What attracts me now is the forest. It has the same magic as the mountains, but in a more peaceable, more welcoming form. Having to cross and recross the desert-like savannahs of central Brazil has taught me to appreciate anew the luxuriant Nature beloved of the ancients: young grass, flowers, and the dewy freshness of brakes. No longer could I look to the stony Cevennes with the intransigent passion of old; and I realized that my generation's enthusiasm for Provence was a ruse of which we were first the authors and later the victims. In the interests of discovery—that greatest of joys, and one of which civilization was soon to deprive us—we sacrificed to novelty the objective which should justify it. We had neglected that department of Nature, while there were others for us to batten on. Now that the finest was no longer available to us, we had to scale down our ambitions to those which were still within our reach, and set ourselves to glorify what was dry and hard, since nothing else remained to us.

But in that forced march we had forgotten the forest. As dense as our cities, it was inhabited by other beings—beings organized in a society which, better than either the high peaks or the sun-baked flatlands, had known how to keep us at a distance: a collectivity of trees and plants that covered our tracks as soon as we had passed. Often difficult to penetrate, the forest demands of those who enter it concessions every bit as weighty, if less spectacular, than those exacted by the mountains from the walker. Its horizon, less extensive than that of the great mountain ranges, closes in on the traveller, isolating him as completely as any of the desert's empty perspectives. A world of grasses, flowers, mushrooms, and insects leads there an independent life of its own, to which patience and humility are our only passports. A hundred yards from the edge of the forest, and the world outside is abolished. One universe gives place to another—less agreeable to look at, but rich in rewards for senses nearer to the spirit: hearing, I mean, and smell. Good things one had thought never to experience again are restored to one: silence, coolness, peace. In our intimacy with the vegetable world, we enjoy those things which the sea can no longer give us and for which the mountains exact too high a price.

For me to have been convinced of this, it may well have been indispensable that the forest should first appear to me in its most virulent form, so that its universal traits were immediately evident. For between the forest as we know it in Europe, and the forest into which I plunged en route to the Tupi-Kawahibs, the distance is so great that I do not know how best to express it.

Seen from outside, the Amazonian forest looks like a great heap of stationary bubbles, a vertical accumulation of green blisters. It is as if the river-marge had been visited, everywhere and at the same time, by some pathological affliction. But once the film is broken, and the traveller penetrates into the interior, all is changed: seen from within, the confused mass becomes a monumental universe The forest is no longer a scene of terrestrial disorder and could rather be taken for a new planetary world, which is as rich as our own and has taken its place.

Once the eye has adjusted itself to the nearness of one plane to another, and the mind has overcome its first sensation of being overwhelmed, a complicated system presents itself. Storeys superimposed one on the other may be discerned, and for all the abrupt changes of level and intermittent mulching which interfere with their alignment, these are all constructed in the same way. First comes the head-high crest of plants and grasses. Next, the pale trunks of trees and liana, free for a brief space to grow untrammelled by vegetation. Shortly, however, these trunks vanish, masked by the foliage of bushes or the scarlet flowers of the wild banana or *pacova*. The trunks re-emerge fleetingly, only to disappear again among the palm-leaves, and make a third appearance at the point where their first branches stand out horizontally. They are leafless; but, just as a ship has its rigging, so have these branches an outcrop of epiphytal plants—orchids or bromeliaceae. And finally, almost out of sight, the forest-universe ends in huge cupolas, some green, some shorn of their leaves; these latter are covered with flowers—white, yellow, orange, purple, or mauve—in which a European spectator is amazed to recognize the freshness of the European spring, but on a scale so disproportionate that he can only compare it with, if anything, the majestic and luxurious blaze of colour which we associate with autumn.

To these aerial storeys others closely corresponding may be found beneath the traveller's feet. For it would be an illusion to suppose that he is walking 'on the ground'. That ground is buried deep beneath tangle upon tangle of roots, suckers, mosses, and tufts of grass. Let him tread too heavily on unsteady ground, and he may find himself falling —disconcertingly far, at times. In my case, Lucinda's presence added a further complication.

Lucinda was a little female monkey with a prehensile tail. Her skin was mauve and her fur miniver. She was of the species *Lagothryx*, commonly called *barrigudo*, because of its characteristic big belly. I got her, when she was a few weeks old, from a Nambikwara woman who had taken pity on her and carried her, night and day, clamped to the head-dress which represented for the little creature the furred backbone of her mother. (Mother monkeys carry their young on their backs.) I fed her on spoonfuls of condensed milk, and at night a drop or two of whisky would send her into the soundest of sleeps, leaving me free. But during the daytime I could get her to make, at most, a compromise: that she would leave go of my hair and settle for my left boot instead. And there she would cling, with all four paws, just above my toes, from morning till night. On horse-back this was all very well, and it was manageable when we were in our boats. But on foot it was quite a different matter, for at every bramble, every hollow in the ground, every low branch, she would give a loud cry. All my attempts to make her move to my arm, my shoulder, and even to my hair, were in vain. Only the left boot would do: it was her only protection, her sole point of security in the forest. She was a native of that forest, and yet a month or two in the company of human beings had made her as great a stranger to it as if she had grown up among the refinements of civilization. And so it was that, as I limped along with my left leg, doing my best not to lose sight of Abaitara's back, my eardrums were pierced by Lucinda's cries of alarm. Abaitara forged ahead with a short and rapid step in the green half-light, working his way round trees so thick that I would think for a moment that he had disappeared, cutting a path through bushes and liana, and darting off to left or to right on an itinerary which, though unintelligible to the rest of us, took us ever deeper into the forest.

To forget my tiredness, I let my mind go free. Short poems formed in my head to the rhythm of our march and I would run over them, hour by hour, till they were like a mouthful of food so often chewed as to have no longer any flavour, and yet so acceptable, for its modest companionship, that one hesitates either to swallow it or to spit it out. The aquarium-like environment of the forest prompted this quatrain:

> Dans la forêt céphalopode
> gros coquillage chevelu
> de vase, sur des rochers roses qu'érode
> le ventre des poissons-lune d'Honolulu

Or else, no doubt for the sake of contrast, I summoned up the dismal memory of a Parisian suburb:

On a nettoyé l'herbe paillasson
les pavés luisent savonnés
sur l'avenue les arbres sont
de grands balais abandonnés

And then this last one, which never seemed to me quite finished, though it is complete in form. Even today it torments me when I go for a long walk:

Amazone, chère Amazone
vous qui n'avez pas de sein droit
vous nous en racontez de bonnes
mais vos chemins sont trop étroits

Towards the end of the morning we were working our way round a big bush when we suddenly found ourselves face to face with two natives who were travelling in the opposite direction. The older of the two was about forty. Dressed in a tattered pair of pyjamas, he wore his hair down to his shoulders. The other had his hair cut short and was entirely naked, save for the little cornet of straw which covered his penis. On his back, in a basket of green palm-leaves tied tightly round the creature's body, was a large harpy-eagle. Trussed like a chicken, it presented a lamentable appearance, despite its grey-and-white-striped plumage and its head, with powerful yellow beak, and crown of feathers standing on end. Each of the two natives carried a bow and arrows.

From the conversation which followed between them and Abaitara it emerged that they were, respectively, the chief of the village we were hoping to get to, and his right-hand man. They had gone on ahead of the other villagers, who were wandering somewhere in the forest. The whole party was bound for the Machado with the object of paying their visit, promised a year previously, to Pimenta Bueno. The eagle was intended as a present for their hosts. All this did not really suit us, for we wanted not only to meet them, but to meet them in their own village. It was only after they had been promised a great many gifts when they got to the Porquinho camp that they agreed, with the greatest reluctance, to turn in their tracks, march back with us, and make us welcome in their village. This done, we would set off, all together, by river. Once we had agreed on all this, the trussed eagle was jettisoned without ceremony by the side of a stream, where it seemed inevitable that it would very soon either die of hunger or be eaten alive by ants. Nothing more was said about it during the next fifteen days, except that a summary 'death certificate' was pronounced: 'He's dead, that eagle.' The two Kawahib vanished into the forest to tell their families of our arrival, and we continued on our way.

The incident of the eagle set me thinking. Several ancient authors relate that the Tupi breed eagles, feed them on monkeys' flesh, and periodically strip them of their feathers. Rondon had noted this among the Tupi-Kawahib, and other observers reported it among certain tribes of the Xingu and the Araguaya. It was not surprising, therefore, that a Tupi-Kawahib group should have preserved the custom, nor that the eagle, which they considered as their most precious property, should be taken with them as a gift, if these natives had really made up their minds (as I was beginning to suspect, and as I later verified) to leave their village for good and throw in their lot with civilization. But that only made more incomprehensible their decision to abandon the eagle to its pitiable fate. Yet the history of colonization, whether in South America or elsewhere, is marked by these radical renunciations of traditional values and repudiations of a style of life, in which the loss of certain elements at once causes all other elements to be marked down: perhaps I had just witnessed a characteristic instance of this phenomenon.

We made a scratch meal of a few strips of grilled and still-salted *xarque*, enlivened with what we could get from the forest: some *tocari* nuts; the fruit—white-fleshed, acid in taste, foamy in texture—of the wild cocoa-plant; berries from the *pama* tree; fruit and seeds from the *caju* of the woods. It rained all night on the palm-leaf awnings that protected our hammocks. At dawn the forest, silent during the day, was torn from end to end for several minutes by the cries of monkey and parrot. And on we went, trying never to lose sight of the back of the man immediately ahead of us, convinced that even a few yards 'off course' would put us out of earshot, with no hope of retrieving the path. For one of the most striking characteristics of the forest is its way of seeming to merge into an element heavier than air: such light as gets through is greenish and enfeebled, and the human voice does not carry. The extraordinary silence which reigns—as a consequence, perhaps, of this condition—would communicate its example to the traveller if he were not already disinclined to speak, so intent is he upon not losing his way. His moral situation combines with his physical state to create an almost intolerable feeling of oppression.

From time to time our guide would lean over the edge of his invisible track, deftly lift the corner of a leaf, and show us the sharp point of a stick of bamboo that had been planted obliquely in the ground to pierce the foot of any enemy who happened to come by. These spikes are called *min* by the Tupi-Kawahib, who use them to protect the outskirts of their villages: the Tupi of former times used larger ones.

During the afternoon we reached a *castanhal*, or group of chestnut-trees around which the natives (who exploit the forest systematically) had opened up a little clearing, the better to collect such fruit as fell from

FIG. 51.   Bamboo sticks guarding the approach-way
to the village

the trees. The whole strength of the village had camped out there, the men naked save for the penis-cap which we had already encountered on the chief's lieutenant, and the women also naked, but for the slip of woven cotton round their loins: originally this was dyed red with urucu-dye, but with use it had faded to a russet colour.

There were in all six women and seven men, one of the men being an adolescent, and three little girls who seemed to be aged one, two, and three respectively. One could hardly conceive of a smaller group holding out for at least thirteen years (since the disappearance of Abaitara's village, that is to say), cut off from any contact with the outer world. Among the company were two people paralysed from the waist down: a young girl who supported herself on two sticks and a man, also young, who dragged himself along the ground like a legless cripple. His knees stood out above his fleshless legs, which were swollen on their inner side and looked as if they were afflicted with serosity. The toes of the left foot were paralysed, but those of the right foot could still be moved. Yet these two cripples managed to cover long distances in the forest with no apparent difficulty. Was it poliomyelitis, or some other virus, which had gone on ahead of any real contact with civilization? When I was confronted with these unhappy people, who had been left to their own devices in the midst of a Nature as hostile as any that men have to face, it was heart-rending to think back to the page on which Thevet speaks with such admiration of the Tupi whom he visited in the sixteenth century: 'A people,' he says, 'made of the same stuff as ourselves, who have never as yet been afflicted with leprosy, or paralysis, or lethargy, or chancres, or other bodily ailments which are apparent to the eye.' He had no idea that he and his companions were the advance guard of these evils.

30 *The Crickets' Village*

Towards the end of the afternoon we got to the village, which stood in an artificial clearing immediately above the narrow valley of a torrent, which I was able later to identify as the Igarapé do Leitão, a tributary of the right bank of the Machado, into which it flows a mile or two downstream from the confluence of the Machado and the Muqui.

The village consisted of four more or less square houses that stood in line parallel to the course of the torrent. Two of the houses—the largest—were lived in: so much was evident from the hammocks, made from cotton strings knotted together and strung up between stakes. The two others, one of which stood between the two inhabited houses, had not been occupied for a long time and looked rather like shelters or store-houses. At first glance these houses looked to be identical with the Brazilian dwelling-houses of the same region. But in reality they were differently conceived, in that the lay-out of the stakes which supported the high gabled roof of palm-leaves was similar to that of the wooden substructure of the roof itself, except that it was smaller, so that the building had the profile of a square mushroom. And yet this structure was not clear to the eye, because of the false walls which encircled the house up to the level of the roof but were not joined on to it. These palisades—for that is what they were—consisted of palm-trunks split down the middle, planted side by side, and tied one to the other, with their convex side looking outwards. In the case of the principal house—that which stood between the two store-houses—these trunks were cut out to allow of the making of five-sided loopholes, and their outer surface was covered with paintings roughly executed in red and black with urucu and resin. These pictures represented, according to one of the natives, successively a human being, some women, a harpy-eagle, some children, an object in the shape of a loophole, a

342

toad, a dog, a large unidentified quadruped, two strips of zig-zag shapes, two fish, a jaguar, and finally a symmetrical motif composed of squares, crescents, and arches.

These houses were not at all like the native habitations of the neighbouring tribes. It is probable, however, that their form is traditional. When Rondon discovered the Tupi-Kawahib, their houses were already square or rectangular, with a gabled roof. Nor does the mushroom-like structure correspond to any Brazilian technique. The existence of these high-roofed houses is, moreover, confirmed by

FIG. 52. Detail of the paintings on the outside of a hut

archaeological documents dating back to more than one pre-Colombian civilization.

Another point of originality among the Tupi-Kawahib: like their Parintintin cousins, they neither cultivate nor use tobacco. When he saw us unpacking our stores of tobacco-rope, the chief of the village said sarcastically: '*Ianeapit*—human droppings!' The reports of the Rondon Commission relate, moreover, that when they first made contact with the Tupi-Kawahib, the Indians were so exasperated by the presence of any smoker that they would snatch his cigar or cigarette out of his mouth. And yet, unlike the Parintintin, the Tupi-Kawahib have a word for tobacco: *tabak*, the same word as we have in French, which derives from the ancient lingo of the natives of the Antilles and may well be of Carib origin. There may be a link with the dialects of the Guaporé, which have the same term, either because they have borrowed it from the Spanish (the Portuguese say *fumo*) or because the Guaporé cultures represent the farthest point reached to the south-west by an ancient Caribbean civilization (and there is much to support this hypothesis) which may in this way have left its traces in the lower valley of the Xingu. I must add that the Nambikwara are inveterate smokers, whereas the other neighbours of the Tupi-Kawahib, the Mundé and the Kepkiriwat, take their tobacco in powder form with the aid of tubular inhalers. So that there is something enigmatic about the presence in the middle of Brazil of a group of tobaccoless tribes—and all the more so if we consider the Tupi of ancient times were great tobacco-users.

For lack of tobacco we were going to be received in the village by what the French travellers of the sixteenth century called a *cahouin—kaui* is the Tupi-Kawahib word—or, in other words, a drinking-party at which would be served a *chicha* made from maize: several varieties of maize were grown in patches of ground burnt clear for the purpose on the outskirts of the village. Our ancient authors have described the great pots, each as tall as a man, in which the liquid was prepared, and the role assigned therein to the virgins of the tribe (each had to spit copiously into the brew to make sure that it fermented). Perhaps the Tupi-Kawahib pots were too small: perhaps the village was short of virgins. The three little girls were summoned, at any rate, and made to spit into the decoction of pounded seed. As the delicious drink, as refreshing as it was reborative, was drunk that same evening its fermentation can hardly be said to have been accelerated.

While visiting the gardens I noted, first, the big wooden cage in which the eagle had been kept; it was still strewn with bones. There were little plantations of ground-nuts, beans, peppers of various kinds, little yams, sweet potatoes, manioc, and maize. The natives supplemented these resources by the collection of whatever grew wild near at hand. For this purpose they exploited the tall grasses of the forest, tying the tops of several stalks together in such a way that the fallen seeds collected in little heaps on the ground. These they heated on a flat piece of pottery till they burst open like popcorn—whose taste is not dissimilar, by the way.

While the *cahouin*, enriched by various blendings and ebullitions, was going from hand to hand, distributed by the women with ladles made from the halves of a calabash, I took advantage of the last hours of daylight to scrutinize the Indians.

Apart from their cotton loincloths, the women wore tight little wrist- and ankle-bands, and necklaces made of tapirs' teeth, or carved pieces of deer-bone. Their faces were tattooed with the blue-black juice of the *genipa*: on their cheeks, a thick oblique line ran from the lobe of the ear to the corner of the lips, which was marked with four little vertical lines. On the chin were four horizontal lines, one above the other, each ornamented on its underside with a fringe of vertical

FIG. 53. Another example of hut-paintings

stripes. The hair, usually short, was often combed with a large-toothed comb, or with some more delicate instrument, made of thin sticks of wood held in place with cotton.

The men wore nothing but the conical penis-cover which I have already described. One native was making himself a new one at that very moment. He took a fresh *pacova* leaf, peeled off the two sides from the central stalk, and relieved them of their tough outer edge. Then he folded them in two, lengthwise. By making the two pieces overlap, one over the other (they were about a foot long and three inches broad), so that the two folds joined at right angles, he got a sort of square, with two thicknesses of leaf on the sides and four at the top, where the two bands crossed over one another. This 'square' was then folded back upon itself diagonally, and its two arms were cut off and thrown away, leaving the craftsman with a little isosceles triangle made up of eight thicknesses of leaf. This triangle he rounded on his thumb, working from front to back, the points of the two sharper angles being cut open and the sides sewn up with a wooden needle and some vegetable thread. The little object was ready: all that remained was to put it in position, pulling back the foreskin across the opening so that it would not fall off, and so that the tension of the skin would keep the member vertical. All the men wore an accessory of this sort and if any of them were to lose his cap he would at once draw the pulled-back extremity of his prepuce under the cord which he wore round his loins.

The houses were almost empty. I noticed hammocks made of cotton thread: a few earthenware pots and a basin in which maize or manioc pulp could be dried over the fire; some calabashes: a few wooden pestles and mortars; some manioc-scrapers made of thorn-inlaid wood; some wickerwork sieves; burins made of rodents' teeth; a few spindles; and some bows, about five feet in length. The arrows were of several kinds; either with points and bamboo—sharpened for hunting, saw-edged for war—or with multiple points; these last were used for fishing. Lastly I noted some musical instruments; Pan-pipes with thirteen tubes, and four-holed flageolets.

When night fell, the chief ceremoniously brought us the *cahouin* and a ragoût of giant beans and peppers. Hot as these were to the palate, they were a delight after six months among the Nambikwara, who know nothing of either salt or pepper and whose palates are so delicate that all food has to be drenched in water, and thus effectively cooled, before they can begin to eat. The native salt came in a little calabash; it was a brownish liquid so bitter that the chief, who contented himself with watching us eat, insisted on tasting it in our presence to reassure us that it was not a poison. This condiment is prepared with the ashes of the *toari branco* wood. Modest as the meal was, it was served with a dignity which reminded me that the Tupi chiefs of old were in honour bound, as one traveller put it, to 'keep open house'.

A still more curious detail is that, after a night in one of the store-houses, I found that my leather belt had been half-eaten by crickets. Never, in all the tribes whose existence I had shared, had I suffered such an assault; neither among the Kaingang, nor the Caduveo, nor the Bororo, nor the Paressi, nor the Nambikwara, nor the Mundé. It was among the Tupi that I was destined to re-live the misadventures familiar four centuries earlier to Yves d'Evreux and Jean de Léry: 'I must tell of these little creatures, no bigger than our crickets, who make for the camp-fire at night in great troops and bands, and eat into anything that they can find. But above all things they make for the leather of shoes or neckbands, eating away the whole of the outer cover, so that when those who own such things wake up in the morning they find them white and flaky.' Unlike the termite, and many another destructive insect, the cricket merely eats into the outer surface of the leather, so that my belt was, in effect, 'white and flaky' when I reached for it, witnessing to a strange and exclusive association, many centuries old, between a species of insect and a group of human beings.

As soon as the sun was up one of our men went into the forest to shoot at the pigeons which were fluttering about in the clearing. After a little while we heard a shot. No one paid any attention until a native came running up, livid and in high excitement: he tried to explain what had happened. Abaitara was not at hand to interpret, but we could hear from the direction of the forest loud cries growing steadily nearer, and soon a man came running across the plantations, holding his right fore-arm in his left hand. From that fore-arm there was dangling a hand reduced to bleeding ribbons. He had leaned on the barrel of his gun, and the gun had gone off. Luis and I discussed what should be done. Three fingers were blown practically off and the palm seemed to be more or less in pieces. It looked as if the hand would have to be amputated. Yet we ourselves did not quite dare to do this: to make a cripple, that is to say, of Emydio, whom we had recruited, together with his brother, in a little village on the outskirts of Cuiaba. His youth made us feel particularly responsible for him, and he had shown peasant qualities of loyalty and fine feeling which had made us very fond of him. His job in life was to look after beasts of burden: and the proper loading of mules and oxen calls for great manual skill. For him to lose a hand would be a catastrophe. Not without apprehension, we decided to put the fingers back in place, as best we could, dress and bandage the wound with the means at our disposal, and start back at once. Once back at our camp, Luis would take the wounded man to Urupa, where our doctor was, and if the natives were to agree to this scheme I would stay and camp out with them on the river-bank, until the galiot came back to fetch me fifteen days later (it would take three days to go downriver and about a week for the return trip).

The Indians were terrified by the accident and seemed afraid that it might make us less well disposed towards them. They accepted, therefore, every suggestion that was made to them; and while they once again made ready to leave we plunged into the forest.

It was a nightmarish journey, and I remember very little about it. The wounded man was delirious all the way, and walked so fast that we couldn't keep up with him. He took the lead, marching ahead even of the guide, never showing the slightest hesitation about our route, though no trace of it seemed to remain. At night we contrived to put him to sleep with drugs, and as he luckily had no experience of medicines our draughts took their full effect. When we got to our camp on the afternoon of the following day we found that his hand was full of worms, which were causing him intolerable pain. But when we got him to the doctor three days later the wound was clear of gangrene, the worms having eaten the bad flesh as and when it putrefied. There was no longer any need to amputate, and after a month-long series of small surgical operations (Vellard's skills as vivisector and entomologist were very useful there) we got Emydio's hand back into shape. Arriving at Madeira in December, I sent him back to Cuiaba by air, to gather strength; he was then still convalescent. But when I went to call on his parents in January, at a time when I was revisiting all our troop, one by one, I found them full of reproaches: not for their son's sufferings, which they regarded as an everyday incident in *sertão* life, but for my barbaric action in exposing him to the dangers of the skies—a diabolical situation, in their view, and one to which they found it inconceivable that a Christian should be submitted.

31 *The Japim Bird Takes the Stage*

MY NEW family was made up as follows: first of all Taperahi, the chief of the village, and his four wives—Maruabai, the eldest; Kunhatsin, her daughter by a previous union; Takwame; and Ianopamoko, the young paralytic. This polygamous household was bringing up five children: Kamini and Pwereza, two boys who looked to be about seventeen and fifteen respectively, and three little girls: Paerai, Topekea, and Kupekahi.

Potien, the chief's lieutenant, aged about twenty, was the son of an earlier marriage of Maruabai's. There was also an old woman, Wirakaru; her two adolescent sons, Takwari, and Karamua, of whom the first was unmarried and the second was married to his barely nubile niece; and, finally, their cousin, a young paralytic, Walera.

Unlike the Nambikwara, the Tupi-Kawahib do not make a mystery of their names. And, as the sixteenth-century travellers noted, each name has a meaning. 'As we do with dogs and other animals,' Léry wrote, 'so do they deal out names from stock—Sarigoy, for instance, for a four-legged animal; Arignan, a hen; Arabouten, the Brazil-tree; Pindo, a tall grass; and so on.'

This was true of every case in which the natives gave me an explanation of their names. Taperahi was a little bird with black and white feathers, and Kunhatsin a white or light-skinned woman; Takwame and Takwari were names derived from *takwara*, a species of bamboo; Potien was a freshwater shrimp; Wirakaru, a parasite that attached itself to human beings (in Portuguese, a *bicho de pe*); Karamua, a plant; and Walera, another species of bamboo.

Staden, another sixteenth-century traveller, said that the women 'usually take the names of birds, fish, or fruit', and he added that whenever the husband killed a prisoner he and his wife took a new name. My companions did the same. Karamua, for instance, was also called Janaku because, said my informant, 'he has already killed a man'.

349

The natives also acquired new names as they passed from childhood to adolescence and from adolescence to manhood. Each had, therefore, two, three, or four names, all of which he would readily communicate to me. These names have a considerable interest, because the members of each lineage prefer to take names that stem from kindred roots. These names belong to the clan. Most of the inhabitants of 'my' village belonged to the *Mialat,* or Wild-boar clan, but this clan had been formed by intermarriage with other clans, notably the *Paranawat,* or River clan, and the *Takwatip,* or Bamboo clan. But all the members of this last-named clan had names deriving from its eponym: Takwame, Takwarumé, Takwari, Walera (a big bamboo), Topehi (a fruit of the same family), and Karamua (also a plant, but an unidentified one).

The most striking characteristic of our Indians' social organization was the quasi-monopoly enjoyed by the chief in respect of the women of the group. Of the six women who had got beyond puberty, four were his wives. Of the two others, one, Penhana, was his sister, and therefore forbidden; the other, Wirakaru, was an old woman who no longer interested anybody. It is clear, therefore, that Taperahi had attached to himself the maximum possible number of women. In his household it was Kunhatsin who took first place. She was also the youngest, with the exception of Ianopamoko the paralytic, and native opinion coincided with that of the anthropologist in finding her a great beauty. From the hierarchical point of view Maruabai was a secondary wife and her daughter took precedence over her.

The principal wife seemed to help her husband more directly than the others, who were concerned with household chores, kitchen duties, and the care of the children, who were all brought up together, passing indifferently from one breast to another—so much so, in fact, that I could never quite decide which children belonged to which mother. By contrast the principal wife accompanied her husband from place to place, helped him to receive visitors, took care of presents received, and kept the entire family under supervision. The situation is the opposite of that which I had observed among the Nambikwara, where it is the principal wife who stays at home and looks after the house, while the young concubines take a full share in the men's activities.

The chief's hold upon the women of the group seemed to derive primarily from the notion that his was no ordinary nature. His temperament was acknowledged to be quite exceptional. He was subject to trances, during which he had sometimes to be held in check, lest he should commit homicide (I shall later describe an instance of this). He had the gift, among other things, of prophecy, and his sexual appetites were held to be so powerful that he needed to have many wives in order to satisfy them. During the two weeks in which I shared the life of their camp, I was often struck by the abnormal behaviour—abnormal in relation to that of his companions—of Taperahi, the chief. He seemed to be afflicted with ambulatory mania: three times a day at least he would move his hammock and its protective awning of palm-leaves to another part of the camp, accompanied in each instance by his wives, Potien his lieutenant, and his babies. Every morning he disappeared into the forest with his wives and children—'to make love', said the natives. Half an hour or an hour later they would troop back and move house again.

The chief's privileged position, where polygamy is concerned, is to some extent counterbalanced by the loan of his wives to his companions, and also to strangers. Potien is not merely his assistant: he also takes part in the chief's family life, eats at his 'table', nurses the babies from time to time, and enjoys other favours. As for the stranger from the world outside, every sixteenth-century author has much to say about the liberality with which he was received by the Tupinamba chiefs. This hospitable duty operated in favour of Abaitara, as soon as I arrived in the village, and he was lent Ianopamoko. She was pregnant at the time, but until the day I left she shared Abaitara's hammock and was fed by him.

From what Abaitara told me privately, this generosity was not disinterested. Taperahi was proposing to Abaitara that he should make over the girl to him once and for all in exchange for his little daughter, Topehi, who was then aged about eight: '*karijiraen taleko ehi nipoka*'— 'the chief wants to marry my daughter'. Abaitara was not very enthusiastic, for Ianopamoko, a cripple, could not be much of a companion to him. 'She can't even go and fetch water from the river,' he said. It really was not a fair exchange: a grown-up, physically handicapped, against a healthy and very promising little girl. Abaitara had other ideas, in any case: he would have liked to exchange Topehi for the two-year-old Kupekahi—the point being, he said, that she was the daughter of Takwame who, like himself, was a member of the Takwatip clan. He could therefore exert over her the privilege of a uterine uncle. Takwame herself was to be made over, according to his plan, to another native from the post of Pimenta Bueno. Matrimonial equilibrium would be partly re-established thereby, in that Takwari was, for his part, 'engaged' to the little Kupekahi. Once all these transactions were completed, Taperahi would have lost two of his four wives, and gained a third one, in the person of Topehi.

I do not know what was the outcome of these discussions. But during the fifteen days of life in common, they led to great tension among those immediately concerned; at times the situation was really disquieting. Abaitara was absolutely set on having his two-year-old fiancée, for, although he was himself thirty to thirty-five already, he saw in her a wife after his own heart. He made her little presents, and when she played on the river's edge he never tired of admiring, and urging me to admire, her robust little body. How beautiful she would be in ten or twelve years' time! Although he had already been for some years a widower, the long wait had no terrors for him. (Admittedly he had Ianopamoko to be going on with, meanwhile.) The tender feelings which he cherished for the baby girl were mingled with innocent erotic daydreams of what was to happen in years to come, with a fatherly feeling of responsibility towards the little creature, and with the affectionate camaraderie of an elder brother who had belatedly acquired a baby sister.

Another factor which helped to balance the unequal distribution of wives was the levirate, or inheritance of the wife by the brother. This was how Abaitara had come to marry the widow of his dead brother. He had not wanted to do it, but his father had insisted—as had, indeed, the widow herself who, he said, 'couldn't keep her hands off me'. The Tupi-Kawahib also practise fraternal polyandry, of which an example was provided by the little Penhana, a skinny creature, barely at the stage of puberty, who shared herself out between her husband Karamua and her brothers-in-law Takwari and Walera. Walera was a brother of the other two in terms of classification only: 'He lends [his wife] to his brother', for 'the brother is not jealous of the brother'. Normally brothers- and sisters-in-law, without avoiding one another, take up an attitude of mutual reserve. When the wife has been lent, the fact may be inferred from the familiarity with which she then treats her brother-in-law. They talk and laugh together and her brother-in-law gives her her food. One day when Takwari had 'borrowed' Penhana he was lunching next to me. As he began his meal he asked his brother to 'get Penhana to come and eat'. Penhana was not hungry, because she had already lunched with her husband. But she came, accepted a mouthful, and went away at once. In the same way, Abaitara left my own hearth and took his meal over to Ianopamoko so that he could eat with her.

The Tupi-Kawahib combine, therefore, polygyny with polyandry in order to resolve the problems set by the chief's prerogatives. A bare week or two after taking leave of the Nambikwara, it was striking to note to what a degree groups geographically very near to one another can find different solutions for identical problems. For among the Nambikwara also, as we have seen, the chief has a polygamous privilege, whence there results, once again, a disequilibrium between the number of young men and the number of available unattached wives. But instead of having recourse to polyandry, as the Tupi-Kawahib do, the Nambikwara allow their adolescents to practise homosexuality. The Tupi-Kawahib have strong words for such habits and are outwardly much against them. But, as Léry remarked maliciously of their ancestors: 'From the fact that sometimes, in a quarrel, one will call the other *Tyvire* (the Tupi-Kawahib have almost the same word: *teukuruwara*), or bugger, it could be conjectured, though I do not myself affirm anything of the kind, that this abominable crime is committed among them.'

Among the Tupi-Kawahib, the hierarchy of power was the object of a complex organization, to which our village remained attached in a symbolical way, much as in our own former monarchies some faithful subject is usually ready to act out the role of Lord High Chamberlain and so save the dignity of the former sovereign. This, it seemed, was Potien's role in relation to Taperahi. Such was his assiduity in serving his master, such the respect that he showed him, and such the deference which he was shown, in return, by the other members of the group, that one might sometimes have thought that Taperahi held sway, as Abaitara had done in his time, over thousands of subjects or thanes. At that time there were at least four grades of rank at the court: chief, bodyguard, minor officers of state, and companions. The chief had the right of life or death over his people. As in the sixteenth century, execution was usually by drowning—a duty accorded to the minor officers of state. But the chief also took care of his people, and had charge of negotiations with the outer world: these he conducted with considerable presence of mind, as I was to see for myself.

I possessed a large aluminium basin, which we used for cooking rice. One morning Taperahi, accompanied by Abaitara as his interpreter, came and asked me for this basin, promising in exchange that for as long as we were with him he would keep it constantly topped up with *cahouin*, for us to drink from as we pleased. I tried to explain that the basin was indispensable to our culinary arrangements; and I

was amazed to see that while Abaitara was translating my remarks
Taperahi went on smiling all over his face, as if what I had to say was
exactly what he had most wanted to hear. And, sure enough, when
Abaitara completed his exposé of the situation, Taperahi, still in the
best of spirits, seized hold of the basin and put it without more ado
among his own equipment. There was nothing for me to do but give
in. Taperahi kept his promise, moreover, and for a week on end I was
served with a *cahouin de luxe*, made up of a mixture of maize and *tocari*.
This I disposed of in enormous quantities—quantities limited only,
indeed, by the necessity of not overtaxing the salivary glands of the
three babies. The incident reminded me of a passage in Yves d'Evreux:
'If any one among them wants something belonging to one of the
others, he tells him so, quite openly: and, unless the thing asked for is
very dear indeed to its owner, it will be handed over at once, with the
condition, however, that if the one who asks has among his own possessions something that the giver would like to have, he will give, in
his turn, all that he is asked for.'

The Tupi-Kawahib's conception of the role of the chief differs
radically from that current among the Nambikwara. When pressed for
an elucidation, they will say: 'The chief is always happy.' And the best
commentary on that statement was the extraordinary dynamism which
Taperahi did, in effect, display at all times. Individual aptitudes could
not explain it altogether, since the chiefs of the Tupi-Kawahib, unlike
those of the Nambikwara, inherit in the masculine line. Pwereza would
succeed his father, but he looked younger than his brother Kamini,
and I noticed other indications that the younger of the two might turn
out to be the more important. In the past, one of the chief's duties
was to organize feasts, of which he was said to be the 'master' or the
'owner'. Men and women painted their bodies all over (notably with
the violet juice of an unidentified leaf which was also used in the
painting of pottery). There were dances, with singing and instrumental
music. The accompaniment to these was provided by four or five large
clarinets, made out of sections of bamboo about four feet in length, at
the top of which was a little bamboo pipe with a simple reed, cut open
at the side and held in place, in the interior of the pipe, with a fibre
ball. The 'master of the fête' ordered the men to see who best could
carry a flute-player on his shoulders—a competition which reminded
me of *mariddo*-lifting among the Bororo and the races which the Gé
ran among themselves, each bearing a log.

Invitations were sent out in advance, so that the participants would have time to collect and cure the little animals—rats, monkeys, squirrels—that they would wear strung round their necks. The wheel-game divided the village into two camps: Elder and Younger. The teams would station themselves at the west end of a circular terrain while two lancers, one from each camp, would take up their positions at the north and south ends, respectively. Each group would then roll towards the other a wheel-like section of tree-trunk. As this passed in front of the lancers, they would try to shoot an arrow into it. Each hit entitled the archer in question to take one of his adversary's arrows. This game is strikingly similar to certain games found in North America.

Next came target-practice, with a doll as the main target. This was not without its risks: any archer whose arrow stuck into the post on which the doll stood was destined for a bad end, magical in its origins —as was also, for that matter, anyone who dared to sculpt a wooden doll in the likeness of a human being, instead of a straw doll or a wooden monkey.

In this way, day after day, I would try to reconstruct from its last fragments a culture which had fascinated Europe, and one which, on the right bank of the upper Machado, might well disappear on the very day of my departure. For on November 7th, 1938, as I stepped aboard our galiot, then just back from Urupa, the natives headed for Pimenta Bueno to join forces with the companions, and with the family, of Abaitara.

It was a melancholy affair, this liquidation of the surviving elements of a dying culture. And yet, towards the end of it, a surprise was in store for me. It was at nightfall, when everyone was taking advantage of the afterglow of the camp-fire to make ready for sleep. Taperahi, the chief, was already stretched out in his hammock. He began to sing, in a distant, hesitant tone which seemed hardly to belong to him. Immediately two men, Walera and Kamini, came and crouched at his feet, while a shiver of excitement ran throughout the little group. Walera called out once or twice: the chief's singing became more exact in intonation, and his voice firmer. Suddenly I realized what was going on: Taperahi was acting a play, or more exactly a musical comedy, with a mingling of singing and speech. He was taking all the parts—a dozen or so—and for each he had a special tone of voice: piercing, high-pitched and squeaky, guttural, organ-like; and for each he had a recurrent musical theme: a veritable leit-motif, in fact. The tunes seemed astonishingly close to Gregorian chant. After the *Sacre du*

Printemps evoked by the Nambikwara flutes, I seemed to be listening to an exotic version of *Les Noces*.

Abaitara was so fascinated by the performance that I had great difficulty in persuading him to tell me what was going on; but eventually I got enough out of him to piece together a vague idea of the subject. We were listening to a farce. The hero was the *japim* bird (an oriole, with black and yellow feathers and a song so modulated as to sound almost human); the other characters were animals—tortoise, jaguar, falcon, ant-eater, tapir, lizard, and so on; utensils, like a stick, or a pestle; and finally spirits, like the supernatural being, Maira. Each expressed himself in a style so nicely adapted to its nature that I was soon able to identify them without prompting. The story hinged on the adventures of the *japim* which, at first menaced by the other animals, managed to outwit them in one way or another and in the end got the better of them all. The performance was held on two successive evenings and lasted some four hours on each occasion. There were moments when Taperahi seemed so carried away by inspiration that speech and song would pour forth from him, while shouts of laughter rang out on every side. At other times he seemed exhausted: his voice grew weak, and though he tried one theme after another he seemed not to pursue any to its conclusion. Then one of the two chorus-men, or both in unison, would come to his rescue, either by calling out again and again, while the main actor took a short rest, or by suggesting to him some musical theme, or by taking one or other of the roles for the time being, so that a passage of dialogue, in our sense, would follow. And then, firmly back in the saddle, Taperahi would proceed with a new episode.

As the night went on we could see that the effort of poetic creation was accompanied by loss of consciousness. The characters were going beyond the performer, as it were, and his different voices took on so strong an individuality that it seemed unbelievable that they all belonged to the same person. At the end of the second evening, Taperahi suddenly got out of his hammock, still singing the while, and began to meander round the camp, calling for *cahouin*. The spirits had taken control of him. All of a sudden he grabbed a knife and pounced upon Kunhatsin, his principal wife, who had the greatest difficulty in getting away from him and escaping into the forest, while the other men held their chief down and forced him back into his hammock. Once there, he immediately fell asleep and in the morning all was back to normal.

32 *Amazonia*

Wʜᴇɴ I got to Urupa, where it becomes possible to proceed by motor-boat, I found my companions installed in a spacious hut made of straw, raised upon stakes, and partitioned off into several little rooms. We had nothing to do but sell off the remains of our equipment to the local population, barter for chickens, milk, or eggs—for there were one or two cows about—luxuriate in idleness and get back our strength until the river, then swollen by the rains, would allow the first motor-boat of the season to get upstream as far as Urupa. This would take three weeks. Each morning, as we mixed our reserves of chocolate into our milk, we would while away the breakfast-hour by watching Vellard taking a bone-splinter or two out of Emydio's hand and putting that hand gradually back into its right shape. The sight was both disgusting and fascinating, and it merged in my mind with the look of the forest, with its multiplicity of threatening shapes. I took my own left hand as a model and began to draw whole landscapes made up of hands emerging from bodies as twisted and convoluted as liana. The dozen or so sketches which I made in this way disappeared during the occupation of Paris, and may for all I know be lying forgotten in some German attic; but it soothed me to make them and before long I went back to the work of observation.

From Urupa to Rio Madeira the telegraph stations are tied to the little hamlets where a group of rubber-tappers gives point to the sporadic population of the river-bank. These stations have not that element of absurdity which marks the stations on the plateau, and the life of those marooned there is less of a nightmare. Or, rather, the nightmare is less uniform. The resources of each particular area give it a character of its own. Kitchen-gardens are full of water-melons, whose melting flesh is the tropics' pinkish, half-warm substitute for snow; and imprisoned in the yard behind the house are edible land-tortoises which ensure that every family has the equivalent of a 'Sunday roast'. On special occasions the family may even enjoy a *gallinha em molho pardo* (chicken in brown sauce), followed by a *bolo podre* (literally a 'rotten cake'), and a *baba de moça* ('maid's saliva': a white cheese mixed with honey). The poisonous juice of manioc, fermented for weeks on end with peppers, provides a powerful, velvety sauce. A land of plenty: '*Aqui so falta o que não tem*'—'The only thing we don't have is what we haven't got.'

All these dishes are spoken of as 'colossally' delicious, for the Amazonian loves his superlatives. Generally speaking a dessert, or a remedy, are good or bad 'as the devil himself'. Every waterfall is 'vertiginous'. Every piece of game is 'monstrously big'. And every exchange of views is rich in peasant deformations. The inversion of phonemes, for instance: *percisa* for *precisa*, *prefeitamente* for *perfeitamente*, *Tribucio* for *Tiburcio*. It is likely also to be marked by long silences with only a solemn interjection or two to break into them: '*Sim, Señhor!*' or '*Disparate!*' These relate to thoughts as dark and confused as the forest itself.

Just occasionally commercial travellers, *regatão* or *mascate*—most of them Syrians or Lebanese who travel by canoe—arrive after a journey of several weeks, bringing with them medicines and ancient newspapers, the one as subject as the other to deterioration from damp. Thus it was that, in a rubber-tapper's hut, I came upon an old newspaper and learnt, four months late, that the Munich agreement had been followed by general mobilization in France. The forest people have a richer imaginative life than their counterparts on the savannah. There are poets among them: in one family, for instance, the father and mother, who were called respectively Sandoval and Maria, made up all their children's names from the six syllables comprised in their own. Thus their daughters were Valma, Valmaria, and Valmarisa, and their sons Sandomar and Marival. The grandsons were Valdomar and Valkimar. Certain pedants christen their sons Aristotle and Newton and delight in the medicines, popular throughout Amazonia, which are called Precious Dye, Oriental Tonic, Gordona Specific, Bristol Pills, English Water, and Heavenly Balm. Unless they take (with fatal results) bichlorhydrate of quinine instead of sulphate of soda, they become so used to their drugs that to quieten a toothache they need to take a whole tube of aspirin at one swallow. In fact I noticed on the lower reaches of the Machado a little warehouse which seemed, in symbolical style, to send two kinds of goods, and two only, upstream: cemetery railings and enemas.

Side by side with these 'scientific' remedies there exists a corpus of popular specifics. These consist of *resguardos*, prohibitions, and *orações*, prayers. A pregnant woman, for instance, can eat whatever she likes. After she has given birth, and for the eight days following, she can eat the flesh of chicken and partridge. Up till the fortieth day after the birth, she can also eat deer-meat and certain fish (*pacu, piava, sardinha*). From the forty-first day onwards she can resume sexual relations and add to her diet wild boar and 'white' fish. For a year, however, she may not touch tapir, tortoise, red deer, *mutum*, or the so-called 'leather' fish: *jetaurama* and *curimata*. And this is what our informants had to say on the subject: '*Isso e mandamento da lei de Deu, isso e do inicio do mundo, a mulher so e purificada depois de cuarenta dias. Si não faz, o fim o triste....* *Depois do tempo da menstruação, a mulher fica immunda, o homem que anda com elle fica immundo tambem, e a lei de Deu para mulher.*' And, as a last explanation: '*E uma cousa muita fina, a mulher.*' Or, in other words: 'As it is laid down by the law of God, which goes back to the beginning of the world, the woman is made pure only after forty days. After menstruation the woman is unclean, and the man who goes with her becomes unclean also. It's a very delicate thing, the woman.'

And now, on the margins of black magic, here is the *Oração do sapo secco*, the Prayer of the Dried Toad, as it appears in a book hawked from hut to hut, the *Livro de São Cypriano*. Take a big toad, a *cururu* or a *sapo leiteiro*, bury him up to its neck on a Friday, and feed him with the embers of a fire. He will swallow them all. Eight days later, go and look for him: he'll have disappeared. But at the spot where he had been left there will be the beginnings of a three-branched and three-coloured tree. The white branch stands for love, the red for despair, the black for mourning. The name of the prayer derives from the fact that a dead toad dries up to such a degree that even the carrion-birds will not touch it. So the person concerned takes the branch that most corresponds to his purpose and keeps it hidden from everyone else: *e cousa muita occulta*. The prayer is declaimed at the time of the toad's burial:

Eu te enterro com palma de chão la dentro
Eu te prende baixo de meus pes ate como for o possivel
Tem que me livras de tudo quanto e perigo
So soltarei voce quando terminar minha missão
Abaixo de São Amaro sera o meu protetor
As undas do mar serão meu livramento
Na polvora do sol sera meu descanso
Anjos da minha guarda sempre me accompanham

E o Satanez não tera força me prender
Na hora chegada no pinga de meio dia
Esta Oração sera ouvida
São Amaro voce e supremes señhores dos animaes crueis
Sera o meu protetor Mariterra (?)
Amen.

I bury you one foot deep in the earth
I take you beneath my feet in so far as I can
You are to deliver me from all that is danger
I shall not release you till I have completed my mission
My protector will be under the invocation of St Amaro
The waves of the sea shall be my deliverance
In the dust of the earth shall be my rest
Accompany me always, my guardian angels,
And Satan will not be strong enough to seize hold of me
When it is noon exactly this prayer will be heard
St Amaro, you and the supreme lords of cruel animals
shall be my protector Mariterra (?)
Amen

The people also resort to the *Oração da fava*, the Prayer of the Bean, and the *Oração do morcego*, the Prayer of the Bat.

Fanatics and inventors are to be found in these parts, where the rivers can be navigated by small motor-boats and civilization, as represented by Manaus, is no longer a three-parts-obliterated memory, but rather a reality to be experienced twice or even thrice in a lifetime. For instance, one head of a station on the telegraph line used to lay out, for himself, his wife, and his two children, plantations of enormous size in the very middle of the forest. He also manufactured gramophones, and eau-de-vie by the gallon. Fate was against him, however: every night his horse was attacked by the so-called vampire-bats. When he fitted out the horse with armour made of tent-canvas, the horse would tear it to pieces on a branch. So he tried smearing the horse with pepper-juice, and then with copper sulphate, but the bats 'wiped it all away with their wings' and went on sucking the poor animal's blood. The only effective method was to disguise the horse as a wild boar with four skins, cut out and sewn together. His ever-fertile imagination helped him to forget a great disappointment: the visit to Manaus, where all his savings vanished into the hands of the doctors who overcharged him, the hotel where he was starved, and his children, who were encouraged by the shopkeepers to ransack every one of their shelves.

I should like to say more of the ways in which these pitiable figures from Amazonian life feed upon their own eccentricity and their own despair. Among them are heroes or saints like Rondon and his companions, who scattered across the unexplored parts of the map names taken from the positivist calendar: some of them allowed themselves to be massacred rather than open fire in reply to the Indians' attacks. There were daredevils, too, who plunged deep into the forest to keep strange rendezvous with tribes known to them alone: sometimes they would loot the natives' humble harvest until an arrow put an end to them. There were dreamers who built an ephemeral empire in some unvisited valley. Maniacs who squandered in solitude the kind of activity which leads others to a vice-regal throne. Victims, finally, of the intoxication which swept away people more powerful than themselves; of the bizarre fate of such people the adventurers to be found on the Rio Machado, on the edge of the forests inhabited by the Mundé and the Tupi-Kawahib, are a living illustration.

One day I cut out of a newspaper a story which, though awkwardly told, is not without a certain grandeur. Here it is:

Extract from *A Pena Evangelica* (1938):

In 1920 the price of rubber fell and the big chief (Colonel Raymundo Pereira Brasil) abandoned the *seringaes* on the edge of the Igarapé São Thomé, so that they remained more or less virgin. Time passed. Ever since I left the Colonel's territories, my adolescent soul had preserved an indelible memory of those fertile forests. I roused myself from the apathy into which I had been thrown by the sudden fall in the price of rubber and, already well trained in, and used to, the Bertholletia Excelsa, I suddenly remembered the *castanhaes* which I used to see at S Thomé.

At the Grand Hotel in Belem-do-Para, I met one day my former chief, Colonel Brasil. He still had signs of his former great wealth. I asked him for permission to go and 'work' his chestnut forests. He was kind enough to accord me this permission. He spoke to me, saying: 'All that has been abandoned. It is a long way off, and the only people still there are those who never managed to get away. I don't know how they live, and I don't care. You can go there if you want to.'

I got a few slender resources together, asked for credit from

Messrs J. Adonias, Adelino G. Bastos, and Gonçalves Pereira & Co., took a ticket on one of the Amazon River steam-boats, and headed for Tapajoz. At Itaituba we joined forces: Rufino Monte Palma, Melentino Telles de Mendonça, and myself. Each of us had fifty men. We banded together, and we won through. Soon we reached the mouth of the Igarapé São Thomé. There we found an entire population foundering in abandonment and despair: old men fit for nothing, women more or less naked, children stunted and fearful. When shelters had been built and everything was ready I assembled all my men and their families and said to them: 'Here is everyone's *boia*—cartridges, salt, flour. In my hut there is neither clock nor calendar. Work will begin when we can see the outlines of our calloused hands, and the hour of rest will come with the night that God has given us. Those who do not accept this will be given nothing to eat. They will have to be content with palm-nut pap and salt made from the buds of the big-headed *anaja* (the buds of this palm-tree yield, after boiling, a bitter and salty residue). We have provisions for sixty days, and we must make the most of them. Not one hour of this precious time can be lost.' My associates followed my example and sixty days later we had 1420 barrels (a barrel held about 130 litres) of chestnuts. We loaded our boats and travelled, with the men we had recruited, to Itaituba. I stayed on with Rufino Monte Palma and the rest of our troop to take the motorboat *Santelmo*, which kept us waiting a good fifteen days. When we got to the port of Pimental we embarked, complete with chestnuts and everything, on the gaiola *Sertanejo*, and at Belem we sold our chestnuts for 47 milreis 500 ($2.30) the hectolitre. Unluckily four men died on the journey. We never went back there. But today, with prices as high as 220 milreis the hectolitre —higher than ever before, according to documents in my possession —this chestnut-work has solid and positive advantages, unlike the underground diamond, where so much is for ever unknown. And that, my friends in Cuiaba, is how people get Para chestnuts in the State of Mato-Grosso.

At least the narrator and his friends earned for their one hundred and fifty or one hundred and seventy men a total, in sixty days, of something like three thousand five hundred dollars. But what are we to say of the rubber-tappers whose last agonies I was able to witness during the final weeks of my stay?

33 *Seringal*

THE principal species of the latex-tree, the *hevea* and the *castilloa*, are called in local parlance respectively *seringa* and *caucha*. The first is the more important of the two: it grows only near river-banks, where the marge itself constitutes an imperfectly defined zone, made over by a vague form of governmental authorization not to landowners but to *patrons*, as they called: these *patrões de seringal* are tenants of food-and-mixed-provision shops. If not, as occasionally happens, 'in business on their own', they hold a concession from an entrepreneur or from the little river-transport company which has the monopoly of navigation on the mainstream of the river and on its tributaries. The rubber-seeker is designated in the first place as a 'client' and is called a *freguez*—i.e. a client of the shop in the zone where he carries on his activities: he binds himself to make at that particular shop all his purchases, including the *aviação* (which has nothing to do with aviation), and also to sell it his entire harvest. In return he gets his working tools and a season's provision of victuals. These are debited to his account. He also gets the concession of an area called the *collocação*: this consists of a series of paths, each of which leads from the hut on the river-bank to the principal rubber-producing trees in the forest nearby. These trees will have been picked out in advance by others of the *patron*'s employees: the *matteiro* and the *ajudante*.

Early each morning (for it is believed to be a good thing to set to work in the dark) the *seringueiro* will set off along one of his paths, armed with his *faca* (a curved knife) and his *coronga* (a lamp that he wears attached to his hat, like a miner). When he makes his incisions in the *seringas*, a considerable delicacy is required: both the types of cut in question (the 'flag' and the 'fishbone' are their names) need to be employed correctly if the tree is neither to remain dry nor to exhaust its supplies prematurely.

By ten in the morning, between one hundred and fifty and one hundred and eighty trees will have been cut. After breakfasting, the *seringueiro* goes back along the same path and collects the latex, which will have been flowing since early morning into small zinc cups attached to the trunk. The contents of these are then poured into a bag, which he makes for himself, of coarse cotton material impregnated with rubber. When he gets back to his hut towards five in the evening, the next phase begins: the 'fattening', that is to say, of the ball-shaped piece of rubber that is in process of formation. The 'milk' is slowly incorporated into the ball, which has been skewered horizontally on a stick of wood and hung over a fire. The smoke coagulates it, in one thin layer after another, and these are evened out by turning the ball slowly on its axis. The ball is considered to be finished when it reaches the standard weight: that weight varies, according to the region concerned, between sixty and a hundred and forty pounds. When the trees are becoming exhausted it may take several weeks to complete a ball. These balls are of many kinds, dependent on the quality of the latex and the method of their construction. When ready, they are taken along the river-bank, where the *patron* comes once a year to collect them. He then takes them to his own warehouse and has them flattened down into *pelles de borracha*, or 'rubber skins'; these he strings together to form rafts which are then launched downstream. At each successive set of rapids the rafts come to pieces, and have to be patiently put together again until at last they get to Manaus or Belem.

And so (I am here simplifying what is often a complicated situation) the *seringueiro* is subject to the *patron*, and the *patron*, in his turn, to the navigation company which controls the main rivers. This system results from the collapse in the price of rubber which dates from the year 1910, when rubber from plantations in Asia began to compete with Brazilian rubber. Only a man who was really in need would now work at the extraction of rubber, but the transportation of that rubber downriver remained lucrative—all the more so as goods fetch about four times the price, on the *seringal*, that is paid for them initially. Those who were in a position to do so gave up the direct handling of rubber and concentrated on its transport. In this way they had all the advantages of the system and ran none of its risks; the *patrão* was doubly at the mercy of the transporter, in that the latter could either raise his tariffs at will or refuse to victual his client. A *patron* whose shop is empty will lose his clients: either they get away without paying their debts or they die of hunger where they are.

The *patron* is in the hands of the transporter, therefore, and the client in those of the *patron*. In 1938 rubber sold at two per cent of the price it commanded at the climax of the great boom. And although things improved for a time during the Second World War they are not much better today. A collector working on the banks of the Machado can count on getting between two hundred and one thousand two hundred kilos of rubber a year, according to the fluctuations of the season. At the very best, in 1938, this would enable him to buy half the goods he really needed: rice, black beans, dried meat, salt, ammunition, paraffin, and cotton cloth. He could not have kept going at all without these things. The difference was made up either by hunting or by running into ever greater debt: a collector's debts began when he first 'set up house' and very often they went on increasing till the day he died.

It may be worth while to set down here the monthly budget of a family of four people, as it was in 1938. Fluctuations in the price of rice make it possible for anyone who wishes to do so to work out the equivalent figures in gold:

	Unit-price in milreis	global price
Two kilos of cooking fat . . .	10·500	42·000
Five kilos of sugar	4·500	22·500
Three kilos of coffee	5·000	15·000
One litre of paraffin	5·000	5·000
Four bars of soap	3·000	12·000
Three kilos of salt (for salting game) .	3·000	9·000
Twenty bullets, cal. ·44 . . .	1·200	24·000
Four pounds of tobacco . . .	8·000	34·000
Five packets of cigarette-paper . .	1·200	6·000
Ten boxes of matches	0·500	5·000
Two knobs of garlic	1·500	3·000
A hundred grammes of pepper (for curing)	3·000	3·000
Four cans of condensed milk . .	5·000	20·000
Five kilos of rice	3·500	17·500
Thirty litres of manioc 'flour' . .	2·500	75·000
Six kilos of *xarque* (dried meat) . .	8·000	48·000
Total	65.400	341.000

To the annual budget there must also be added cotton cloth, of which in 1938 a length was worth from thirty to one hundred and twenty milreis: shoes at from forty to sixty a pair; a hat, at from fifty to sixty; and needles, buttons, thread, and medicines, which last they consumed in flabbergasting quantity. For instance one tablet of quinine (and each member of each family would use a whole tube a day) or of aspirin would cost one milreis. And we must remember at this point that a really good 'season' on the Machado (harvest-time for rubber is from April to September, since the forest cannot be walked in during the rainy season)—a really good season—would bring in two thousand four hundred milreis. (A *fina* fetched in Manaus, in 1936, around four milreis the kilo, of which the producer received half.) Even if the *seringueiro* has no young children, eats nothing but what he gets for himself out hunting and the manioc 'flour' which he grows and manufactures himself, over and above the rest of his work his bills for a bare minimum of food will more than cover his income from even an exceptionally good season.

Whether he is or is not in business on his own, the *patron* lives in terror of bankruptcy. And bankruptcy is never far away if his clients disappear without having repaid his advances. So he employs an armed foreman to keep watch on the river. A few days after I left the Tupi-Kawahib I had a strange encounter on the river, which remained with me as the very image of life on the *seringal*. This is what I wrote in my diary on December 3rd, 1938:

'Towards ten o'clock the weather was grey and soggy. Suddenly we met a little *montaria*, drawn by a thin man, with his wife, a fat mulatto woman with crinkly hair, and a child of about ten. They were exhausted and the woman finished every sentence in tears. They were on their way back from an expedition on the Macha-dinho—eleven *cachoeiras* (falls), and one of them—Jaburu—with a *varação por terra*, where they had to take everything out of the boat and carry it overland. They had been looking for one of their *freguezes* who had run away with his girl-friend, taking with them a boat and all his belongings, after stocking up with *aviação* and leaving a note to say that *a mercadoria e muito cara e não tem coragem pagar a conta* (everything was too dear and he hadn't the courage to pay his bill). The people we met were employees of the Com-padre Gaetano. Appalled at their responsibility, they had gone after the fugitive, meaning to capture him and bring him back to their *patron*. They had a rifle with them.'

The rifle, as they called it, was a carbine, usually a Westminster, calibre .44, which served for hunting and, if need be, for other purposes also.

A few weeks later I noted down the wording of this poster, at the door of the Calama Limitada shop which stood at the confluence of the Machado and the Madeira:

LUXURY GOODS OF VERY SPECIAL QUALITY

comprising fat, butter and milk
will be sold on credit only
on the orders of the patron.
Where no such order has been given
they will be sold only in return for
immediate payment in money
or in exchange for some equivalent article.

Immediately beneath this was another poster:

YOU TOO CAN HAVE SMOOTH HAIR!

Even if you are a person of colour!
However wavy or crinkly your hair may be
it will become smooth and glossy if you
make regular use of the newest preparation

ALISANTE

On sale at 'The Big Bottle'
rue Uruguayana, Manaus.

So used are the *seringueiros* to sickness and poverty that their life is not always as grim as it sounds. Doubtless the time is far distant when the high price of rubber allowed them to build saloons made from wooden planks at points where two rivers met. These turned into rowdy gambling-hells whence the *seringueiros*, having lost in a night the fortunes that they had taken years to build up, would set off in the morning to get their *aviação* on credit from a sympathetic *patron* and begin the whole process all over again. I saw the ruins of one such saloon, the Vatican as it was called: even the name spoke for its vanished splendours. On Sunday the rubber-tappers would arrive there in pyjamas of striped silk, soft hat, and varnished shoes, and listen to virtuosi who 'played' tunes by firing off revolvers of varying sounds and calibres. Silk pyjamas are no longer to be got in the *seringal*. But life there is still given an equivocal charm by the young women who lead a precarious existence as concubines of the *seringueiros*. This concubinage is known as *casar na igreja verde*—'getting married in the green church'. Sometimes the *mulherada*, or 'womenfolk', will band together and organize a dance. Each will give five milreis, or some coffee, or some sugar, or the loan of a hut rather larger than the others, with a lantern well filled for the night. They arrive in flimsy dresses, made-up, and with their hair specially dressed, with a kiss of the hand on arrival for the host and hostess. They use make-up to give themselves the illusion not so much of beauty as of health. Rouge and powder conceal the effects of smallpox, tuberculosis, and malaria. For the rest of the year each lives, unkempt and in rags, with her 'man' in his *barração*: for this one night they arrive, vivid and well got-up, in high-heeled shoes. Even so, they have had to walk a mile or more along muddy forest paths in their ball-dresses. And before dressing they have washed in squalid rivulets and dressed by night: it will have rained all day. There is a terrifying contrast between these fragile attempts at civilization and the monstrous reality which waits for them at the door.

The bodies shown off by their badly cut dresses are characteristically Indian, with the very high breasts lodged almost under the armpits and squeezed tight by the material that has to hold in place the protruding belly. The arms are small, the legs thin and prettily made; hands, wrists, ankles, and feet are all very delicate. The men, in white linen trousers, heavy shoes, and pyjama-tops, will ask their partners for a dance. (As I have already said, these women are not married. They are *companheiras*—sometimes *amaziadas*, or 'fixed up', sometimes *desoccupadas*, 'free, available'.) Each leads the lady of his choice to the middle of the *planqaue* of *babassu* straw, where the scene is lit by a murmurous paraffin-lamp, or *pharol*. For a few moments they wait for the downbeat, which will be given by the *caracacha*, a box of nails shaken by a dancer not, for the moment, on the floor; and then off they go: one, two-three, one, two-three, and so on, with their feet dragging noisily on a plank floor mounted on stakes.

The dances are those of an earlier day. Above all, the *desfeitera*, made up of endless repetitions, between which the music of the accordion (to the accompaniment at times of the *violão* and the *cavaquinho*) stops to allow all the dancers to improvise, each in turn, a distich charged with overtones of passion or teasing. To these the ladies must, in turn, reply in similar style. This is not easy for them, for they feel shy, *com vergonha*: some run away and hide their blushes, others rattle off an unintelligible couplet, like schoolgirls who have learnt something by heart. Here is the distich which was improvised about ourselves, one evening at Urupa:

> Um e medico, outro professor, outro fiscal do Museu,
> Escolhe entr'es três qual e o seu.

(One is a doctor, the other a professor, the other an Inspector from the Museum: choose which of the three shall be yours.)

Luckily the poor girl to whom this was addressed had no idea what to say in reply.

When the ball goes on for several days, as it sometimes does, the women put on a fresh dress each evening.

If the Nambikwara had taken me back to the stone age, and the Tupi-Kawahib to the sixteenth century, I now felt myself, by contrast, in the eighteenth century, such as it might have been in some small Caribbean harbour or along the coast of the mainland. I had crossed a whole continent. But the now-imminent end of my travels was first made manifest in this return-journey from the depths of time.

PART IX

The Return

34 *The Apotheosis of Augustus*

O NE stage in the journey had been particularly discouraging: Campos Novos. Separated from my companions by the epidemic which was immobilizing them some fifty-odd miles farther back, I could do nothing but wait on the far edge of the station where a handful of people were dying of malaria, hookworm disease, and, above all, hunger. The Paressi woman whom I had engaged to do my washing insisted that she be given not merely soap, but a meal, before she would get down to work; without it, she explained, she would be too weak to do anything. And she was right: these people had lost all aptitude for life. Too weak and too ill to struggle, they aimed merely to do less and need less; what they sought was that state of torpor which would demand from them a minimum of physical effort and at the same time make them less conscious of their wretchedness.

The Indians contributed in quite another way to this dismal state of affairs. I was by no means popular with either of the two bands which had met up at Campos Novos and were constantly on the point of leaping at each other's throats. I had to be continually on the watch, and it was practically impossible to carry on with my work. Field-work is taxing enough even in normal conditions: the anthropologist must get up at first light and remain alert until the last of the natives has gone to sleep (even then he sometimes has to watch over their slumber). He must try to pass unnoticed, and yet always be at hand. He must see everything, remember everything, take note of everything. He must be ready to make the most of a humiliating indiscretion, to go to some snotty-nosed urchin and beg for information, and keep himself ever in readiness to profit by a moment of complaisance or free-and-easiness. Or, it may well be, for days together a fit of ill humour among the natives will compel him to shut down on his curiosity and simulate a sombre reserve. The investigator eats his heart out in the exercise of his profession: he has abandoned, after all, his environment, his friends, and his habits, spent a considerable amount of money and time, and compromised his health. And the only apparent result is that his presence is forgiven by a handful of wretched people who will soon, in any case, be extinct; whose main occupations are sleeping and picking their lice; and whose whim can decide the success or the failure of his whole enterprise. When the natives are frankly hostile, as they were at Campos Novos, the situation deteriorates: the Indians, un-willing even to be looked at, will disappear without warning for days on end, hunting or collecting. The investigator still hopes to resume the neighbourly relations for which he has paid so dearly, and so he hangs about endlessly, marks time, turns aimlessly round and round, rereading his old notes, making a fair copy of them, attempting an 'interpretation'. Or else he sets himself some pointless and minutely detailed task, a caricature of his professional activity; measuring, for instance, the distance between one fire-site and the next, or count-ing, one by one, the branches which make up the now-deserted shelters.

It is a time, above all, of self-interrogation. Why did he come to such a place? With what hopes? And to what end? What *is*, in point of fact, an anthropological investigation? Is it the exercise of a profession like any other, differentiated only by the fact that home and office-laboratory are several thousand miles apart? Or does it follow upon some more radical decision—one that calls in question the system within which one was born and has come to manhood? In my case I had been almost five years away from France. I had given up my academic career. The more astute among my classmates were climbing their ladders, rung after rung. Those whose leanings were towards politics, as my own had once been, were already Members of Parlia-ment and would soon be Ministers, whereas I was roaming the desert, hunting down the outcasts of humanity. Who or what had provoked me to blow sky-high the normal progressions of my life? Was it all a ruse, a well-judged detour which would allow me eventually to resume my career with certain extra advantages of which due note would be taken? Or did my decision bespeak a profound incapacity to live on good terms with my own social group? Was I destined, in fact, to live in ever greater isolation from my fellows? The strange paradox was that, so far from making me free of a 'new world', my life of adventure tended rather to thrust me back into my old one, while the world to which I had laid claim slipped through my fingers. No

sooner had I mastered the men and the landscapes which I had travelled
so far to see than they lost the meaning which I had hoped to find in
them; and in the place of these disappointing, though immediately
present, images I found myself haunted by others which had remained
in reserve from my past. Never, when they were a part of the reality
around me, had I set any value upon them. But when I was travelling
in areas which few had set eyes upon, and sharing the existence of
peoples whose wretchedness was the price—paid by them, of course—
of my investigation into the distant past, I found that neither people nor
landscape stood in the foreground of my mind. This was occupied,
rather, by fugitive visions of the French countryside from which I had
cut myself off, or fragments of music and poetry which were the
perfectly conventional expression of a civilization against which I had
taken my stand: such, at any rate, was how I must interpret my actions,
if my life were to retain any sense of purpose. For weeks on end, on
that plateau of the western Mato Grosso, I was obsessed not by my
surroundings, which I should never see again, but by a hackneyed tune
that my memory deformed still further: the third of Chopin's Etudes,
op. 10, which seemed to me—and I well knew how bitter was the irony
of it—to summarize all that I had left behind me.

Why Chopin, to whom I had never been especially drawn?
Brought up to admire Wagner above all things, I had only lately
discovered Debussy—even after I had been persuaded by the
second or third performance of *Les Noces* that the world of
Stravinsky was more real and more valid than the savannah of central
Brazil: had swept away, in fact, my previous notion of music. But at
the moment when I left France it was *Pelléas* that gave me the spiritual
nourishment which I needed; so why was it that Chopin, and the most
banal of his works, should have had such a hold upon me in the desert?
More concerned with this problem than with the observations which
would have given point to my existence, I told myself that the progress
implicit in passing from Chopin to Debussy might well be amplified
when the passage was made in the opposite direction. I was now
experiencing in Chopin the marvels which had made me prefer
Debussy: in Chopin they were implicit merely, and uncertain, and so
discreet that I, not at first discerning them, had hurried rather towards
the music in which they were plainly manifest. I was advancing on
both fronts: deeper knowledge of the older composer had led me to
recognize beauties destined to remain hidden from those who had not
first come to know Debussy. Some people love Chopin because they

know nothing of the subsequent evolution of music; but where they love by default, I loved by excess. There was also the fact that, when I wished to encourage the apparition of certain emotions within myself, I no longer needed an explicit stimulus; a hint, an allusion, a premonition of certain forms, and I was well away.

For mile after mile the same melodic phrase rose up in my memory. I simply couldn't get free of it. Each time it had a new fascination for me. Initially imprecise in outline, it seemed to become more and more intricately woven, as if to conceal from the listener how eventually it would end. This weaving and re-weaving became so complicated that one wondered how it could possibly be unravelled; and then suddenly one note would resolve the whole problem, and the solution would seem yet more audacious than the procedures which had preceded, called for, and made possible its arrival; when it was heard, all that had gone before took on a new meaning, and the quest, which had seemed arbitrary, was seen to have prepared the way for this undreamed-of solution. Was that what travel meant? An exploration of the deserts of memory, rather than of those around me? One afternoon, when the overwhelming heat sent a hush of sleep over the encampment, I was squatting in my hammock, protected from the 'pests', as they are called over there, by the mosquito-net whose narrow weave made it even more difficult to breathe. Suddenly I realized that the problems which tormented me would make a good subject for a play. I imagined it as clearly as if it had already been written. The Indians had disappeared; for six days I wrote from morning till night on the backs of sheets covered with lists of words, and sketches, and genealogies. After which my inspiration left me in the very middle of my work. It has never returned, and when I reread what I had scribbled down I don't think it was much to be sorry about.

My play was called *The Apotheosis of Augustus* and was, in effect, a new version of Corneille's *Cinna*. In it I put on the stage two men who had been friends in childhood and re-met at a moment of crisis in both their very different careers. The one had opted, as he thought, against civilization, only to find that he was heading back towards it by a very complicated route and had destroyed, in so doing, the sense and the value of the alternative which he had supposed to be his concern. The other had been marked out from birth for the world and its honours, only to find that all his efforts had tended towards the abolition of that world and those honours. Each sought, therefore, to destroy the other, and in so doing to save, even at the price of his own death, the significance of what had gone before.

The action began at the moment when the Senate, wishing to confer on Augustus a rank higher even than that of Emperor, voted for his apotheosis and made ready to admit him, in his own lifetime, to the ranks of the gods. In the palace gardens two guards talk over the day's news and try to foresee how it will affect them. Surely the policeman will become a thing of the past? How could they 'protect' a god whose privilege it is to turn himself into an insect, or even to become invisible and paralyse whomever he pleases? They ought to strike, perhaps; in any case they deserve a rise in pay.

The chief of police appears and explains their mistake. The mission of the police does not mark them off from those whom they serve. Ends are not their concern: the police force is indistinguishable from the person and the interests of its master; they shine with his glory. When the Head of the State becomes a god, his police have a share in the godhead. For them, as for him, all things become possible. The force fulfils its true nature and could take as its device the motto of the private detective agencies: itself unseen, it sees and hears all.

The stage then fills with people who have come from the meeting of the Senate and have much to say of what has gone on there. Many and various are the interpretations of Augustus' passage from manhood to divinity. Those with 'great interests' in their charge see in it new ways of making money, while Augustus, Emperor to his fingers' ends, thinks only of the confirmation of his own power and, as a consequence, of his new immunity from plotting and intrigue. His wife Livia sees the apotheosis as the natural summit of his career: 'No one could have deserved it more'—the Académie Française, in fact. . . . Camille, Augustus' young sister, is in love with Cinna, and she brings Augustus the news that Cinna is back in Rome after ten years' adventurous absence. She hopes that Augustus will receive Cinna and that Cinna, capricious and poetical as ever, will perhaps dissuade the Emperor from going over irrevocably to the Establishment. Livia dislikes the idea: Cinna the madcap, only been happy among savages, has always brought an element of disorder into Augustus' career. Augustus is tempted to take her part, but successive delegations of priests, painters, and poets begin to make him hesitate. All conceive the divinity of Augustus as an essentially other-worldly measure. The priests, for instance, take it for granted that the temporal power will pass into their hands, since they are the authorized mediators between gods and men. The artists want Augustus to be seen henceforward as an idea, rather than as a person, thereby outraging the Imperial couple; instead of what they had in mind—marble statues, larger than life and substantially more beautiful—Augustus and Livia find themselves being presented in the likeness of whirlwinds or polyhedra. And the confusion grows all the greater when a troupe of light women—Leda, Europa, Alkmene, and Diana—offer to share with the Emperor their experience of commerce with divinity.

Augustus, left alone on the stage, finds himself faced with an eagle: not the conventional eagle, divinity's attribute, but a wild creature, evil-smelling and lukewarm to the touch. It is, none the less, Jupiter's eagle; the same who carried off Ganymede after a bloody combat in which the boy struggled in vain. Augustus can hardly believe his ears when the bird explains to him that his divinity will consist simply in immunity to the feeling of repulsion which overcomes him, as a man, when the eagle draws near. He will know that he is a god not because of any sensation of inner radiance or any capacity to work miracles, but because he will endure without disgust the nearness of a wild creature which will smell disgustingly and cover him with its droppings. Carrion, decay, and cloacal secretions will come to seem his natural accompaniment: 'Butterflies will copulate on the nape of your neck. Any patch of ground will seem to you good enough to lie on: you will not think of it, as you do now, as prickly, swarming with insects, and certainly infectious. . . .'

In the second act we find that the eagle has made Augustus ponder the problem of the relation between Nature and Society. He decides to see Cinna; Cinna who once chose Nature, as against Society, while Augustus, by opting for Society against Nature, set out on the path that led to the throne. It is a discouraged Cinna who answers his summons. During his ten adventurous years away the thought of Camille had dominated all others. Camille was the sister of his boyhood friend, and had he wanted to marry her he had only to ask. Augustus would have given her to him gladly. But he could not have borne to win her within Society's rules; he wanted to bear her off in the teeth of its disapproval. Whence his quest for an unorthodox prestige that would enable him to force Society's hand and wrest from it what, in point of fact, it was only too ready to give.

Cinna had returned home loaded with marvels. Every hostess in Rome had put him at the top of her list. Only he knew, meanwhile, that the celebrity he had paid for so dearly was based on a lie. The experiences with which he was credited were a myth; the journey a deception; but all seemed true enough to those who had seen only its shadow. Cinna, jealous of Augustus' destiny, had coveted an ever greater Empire: 'I said to myself that no one in the world, not even Plato himself, can imagine the infinite diversity of leaves and flowers that are to be found in the world. I would be the first to count those leaves and those flowers, one by one. I would learn in my own body the meaning of fear and cold and hunger and exhaustion—things beyond the imagining of you who live in comfortable houses with a well-filled granary to hand. I've lived on lizards and snakes and grasshoppers— things of which the very idea would turn your stomach—and I ate them with the ardour of a neophyte, convinced that I was forging a new bond between myself and the universe.' But Cinna's efforts were all in vain: 'I lost everything,' he said. 'Even what was most human became inhuman to me. To while away the interminable days I took to reciting lines from Aeschylus and Sophocles; and I so soaked myself in some of them that now when I hear them in the theatre their beauty means nothing to me. Every phrase reminds me of powdering foot-paths, and burnt grass, and eyes reddened by the sands.'

In the later scenes of the second act Augustus, Cinna, and Camille stand revealed in the full extent of their predicaments. Camille has eyes only for her explorer, who tries in vain to make her see how false are his stories. 'I did my best to explain the emptiness and futility of all that had happened, but no sooner were these transformed as "a travel-ler's tale" than she was dazzled and all adream. Yet there was nothing to it: the earth was like any other earth, and the tufts of grass like that meadow over there.' Finally Camille revolted against his attitude, for she knew that she was not exempt from her lover's general loss of interest in life. It was not as a person that he loved her, but as a symbol of the only possible remaining link between himself and Society. As for Augustus he recognized with horror that Cinna was speaking with the eagle's voice. But he could not turn back. Too many political interests were involved in his apotheosis, and he rebelled, above all, against the idea that there was not, for the man of action, a point at which he would find at once his rest and his reward.

The third act opens in an atmosphere of crisis. On the eve of the ceremony of apotheosis, all Rome is invaded by divinity. The Imperial palace cracks open and animals and plants run wild inside it. The city returns to a state of Nature, as if a cataclysm had overwhelmed it. Camille has broken with Cinna, and the break gives him the final proof that he has reached a point of total frustration. Augustus becomes the main object of his rancour. The relaxed ways of Nature now seem to him quite pointless beside the organized delights of humane society; but he clings to his uniqueness, none the less: 'It's nothing, I know, but a nothing that is still dear to me, because I chose it.' He cannot bear to think that both Nature and Society have been granted to Augustus, and that instead of winning Nature at the cost of a great renunciation Augustus had acquired it over and above Society as a kind of bonus. He will kill Augustus, thus proving that choice is, after all, ineluctable.

At this moment Augustus calls on Cinna to help him. He is no longer in control of events. How can he, without stepping out of character, resubmit them to his will? In a moment of high excitement they agree that the solution is for Cinna to carry out his plan and murder Augustus. Each then would gain the immortality he had dreamed of: Augustus official immortality as the historian, the sculptor, and the priest conceive it; and Cinna the dark immortality of the regicide, which would allow him to rejoin Society and yet continue to deny it.

I'm not really quite sure how it all ended. (The last scenes remained unfinished.) I fancy that Camille involuntarily brought things to a close: reverting to her original sentiments she persuaded Augustus that he had misread the situation and that Cinna, rather than the eagle, was the emissary of the gods. Augustus then devised a political solution. If he could manage to hoodwink Cinna he would also hoodwink the gods. He and Cinna had agreed that he would dismiss his bodyguard and offer no defence to Cinna's dagger; but when the time actually came he would double the guard and make sure that Cinna never got near him. Their respective careers would remain perfectly in character: Augustus would bring off the last of his great ventures; he would be a god, but a god among men, and he would pardon Cinna; for Cinna it would be just one more failure.

35 A Little Glass of Rum

THE foregoing fable has only one excuse: that it illustrates the disordered state of mind into which one is plunged by the prolonged abnormality of the traveller's way of life. But the problem has still to be solved: how can the anthropologist get free of the contradiction implicit in the circumstances of his choice? Under his very nose, and at his disposition, he has a society: his own. Why does he decide to disdain it, reserving for societies distant and different from his own the patience and devotion which he has deliberately withheld from his fellow-citizens? It is not by chance that the anthropologist is rarely on terms of neutrality with his own social group. Where he is a missionary or an administrator, he can be presumed to have identified himself so entirely with a certain order that all his energies are now given to its propagation. And when his professional activity takes place on the scientific or higher academic level, objective factors in his past can very probably be adduced to prove that he is ill- or unsuited to the society into which he was born. He has, in fact, become an anthropologist for one of two reasons: either he finds it a practical method of reconciling his membership of a group with his severely qualified acceptance of it—or, more simply, he wishes to turn to advantage an initial attitude of detachment which has already brought him, as we say, 'half-way to meet' societies unlike his own.

But if he tries to think straight, he will have to ask himself whether he is really justified in setting such great store by exotic societies (and the more exotic they are, the more he will prize them). Is this not rather a function of the disdain, not to say the hostility, which he feels for the customs of his own milieu? At home, the anthropologist may be a natural subversive, a convinced opponent of traditional usage: but no sooner has he in focus a society different from his own than he becomes respectful of even the most conservative practices. Nor is this mere perversity: I have known anthropologists who were also conformists.

381

But their conformism is derived retrospectively and at second hand, as a result of their having already assimilated their own society into the societies they were investigating. It is to the latter that they owe allegiance, and, if they have thought better of their initial revolt against their own society, it is because they have made an additional concession to the others: that of treating their own society as they would wish all others to be treated. The dilemma is inescapable: either the anthropologist clings to the norms of his own group, in which case the others can only inspire in him an ephemeral curiosity in which there is always an element of disapproval; or he makes himself over completely to the objects of his studies, in which case he can never be perfectly objective, because in giving himself to all societies he cannot but refuse himself, wittingly or not, to one among them. He commits, that is to say, the sin with which he reproaches those who question the privileged status of his vocation.

I first began to worry seriously about this at the time of the enforced sojourn in the Antilles which I have described in my opening chapters. In Martinique I went over certain rusticated, half-abandoned rum-distilleries where neither methods nor apparatus had been changed since the eighteenth century. In Porto Rico, by contrast, the factories of the company which enjoys a quasi-monopoly of cane-sugar were agleam with white-enamelled tanks and chromium-plated faucets. And yet in Martinique, where the ancient wooden barrels are silted up with sediment, the rum was like velvet on the palate and had a delicious scent: in Porto Rico it was brutal and vulgar. Can it be that the finesse of the Martiniquais rums was due to impurities which archaic methods of manufacture do nothing to disturb? The contrast illustrated, to my way of thinking, the paradox of civilization: we know that its magic derives from the presence within it of certain impurities, and yet we can never resist the impulse to clean up precisely those elements which give it its charm. We are doubly right but that very rightness proves us wrong. For we are right to wish to increase our production and cut manufacturing costs. But we are also right when we treasure some of the imperfections which we are doing our best to eliminate. Society sets itself, in short, to destroy precisely those things which give it most flavour. This contradiction does not seem to apply so directly to societies unlike our own. For as we are ourselves implicated in the evolution of our own society, we are to some extent in the dock with the accused. Our situation compels us to take certain courses of action towards certain ends, and there is nothing we can do to prevent this.

But when another society comes under scrutiny, all is changed: objectivity, out of the question before, is ours for the asking. Where we had been agents in the transformations in progress, we become mere spectators, all the more able to estimate the situation in that the balance of future and past, which had been present to us as a moral dilemma, can now be a pretext for aesthetic contemplation and disinterested meditation.

In thus thinking the matter out, I may have shown just where the contradiction lies. I may have shown where it began, and how we managed to come to terms with it. But I have certainly not put an end to it. Must we therefore conclude that it is with us for ever? People have sometimes said so, and inferred from this that our work was quite pointless. Our vocation expressed itself, they said, in a liking for societies and cultures very different from our own. It caused us, in fact, to overestimate the one at the expense of the other. Surely this pointed to a basic inconsistency? How could we announce that these societies were 'important', if our judgment were not based on the values of the society which inspired us to begin our researches? We ourselves were the products of certain inescapable norms; and if we claimed to be able to estimate one form of society in its relation to another we were merely claiming, in a shamefaced and roundabout way, that our society was superior to all the others.

Behind the arguments of these worthy spokesmen there was nothing but an execrable play upon words: they pretended that mystification (which they themselves so often practise) is the contrary of mysticism (with which they, quite wrongly, reproach us). The enquiries of archaeology and anthropology show that certain civilizations —some of them now vanished, others still with us—have known quite well how best to solve problems with which we are still struggling. To take one instance only: it is now only a few years since we discovered the physical and physiological principles on which are based the Eskimoes' costume and manner of life. If they can exist in these conditions, it is not from long conditioning, or from an exceptional physical constitution, but from their discovery of scientific principles of which we had until lately no idea at all. So true was this that it also exploded the pretensions of those explorers who had claimed to have 'improved upon' Eskimo costume: the results were the opposite of those that had been hoped for. The Eskimoes had already arrived at the perfect solution: all that we needed, to be convinced of this, was to grasp the theory which lay beneath it.

The difficulty does not lie there. Certain social groups must be adjudged superior to ourselves, if the comparison rests upon their success in reaching objectives comparable to our own; but, in the same instant, we earn the right to pass judgment upon them, and therefore to condemn all those other objectives which do not coincide with our own. Implicitly we claim for our own society, for its customs, and for its norms, a position of privilege, since an observer from a different social group would pass different verdicts upon those same examples. This being so, how can we claim for our studies the rank of a science? If we are to get back to a position of objectivity, we should abstain from all judgments of this sort. We have to admit that human societies can choose among a gamut of possibilities. These choices cannot be compared with each other: one is as good as another. But then there arises a new problem; for if, in the first instance, we are threatened by obscurantism, in the form of a blind rejection of anything that is not our own, there is also an alternative danger: that of an eclecticism which bids us reject nothing at all, when faced with an alien culture. Even if that society should itself protest against the cruelty, the injustice, and the poverty which characterize it, we must not pass judgment. But as these abuses also exist among ourselves, how shall we have the right to fight them at home if, when they appear elsewhere, we make no move to protest?

The anthropologist who is critic at home and conformist elsewhere is therefore in a contradictory position. But beneath this contradiction is another, from which it is even less easy to escape. If he wishes to contribute to the improvement of his own social system he cannot but condemn, wherever he comes upon them, conditions analogous to those which he deplores at home. He loses, in so doing, all claim to be objective and impartial. Conversely the detachment enjoined upon him by moral scruples, and by the rigorous methods of science, will prevent him from finding fault with his own society, once it is taken for granted that his business is to know, not to pass judgment. The man who takes action in his own country cannot hope to understand the world outside: the man who takes all knowledge for his ambition must give up the idea of ever changing anything at home.

If the contradiction were insurmountable the anthropologist would be wrong to hesitate over the alternatives which are open to him. He is what he has chosen to be: an anthropologist; therefore he must accept the mutilated condition which is the price of his vocation. He has chosen and must accept the consequences of his choice: his place lies with 'the others', and his role is to understand them. Never can he act in their name, for their very otherness prevents him from thinking or willing in their place: to do so would be tantamount to identifying himself with them. He must also resign himself to taking no action in his own society, for fear of adopting a partisan's position in respect of values which may recur in other societies: such a position could not but then prejudice his judgment. His initial choice alone will remain, and he will make no attempt to justify that choice. It is a pure, a motiveless act: or, if motivated at all, will derive from external considerations, borrowed from the history or the character of each one of us.

Luckily we have not yet reached that point. We are on the edge of the abyss, and we have peeped into it, but we can still look for a way out. And get out we can, provided that we are not too extreme in our judgments and are willing to phase the difficulty in two stages.

No society is perfect. Each has within itself, by nature, an impurity incompatible with the norms to which it lays claim: this impurity finds outlet in elements of injustice, cruelty, and insensitivity. How are we to evaluate those elements? Anthropological enquiry can provide the answer. For while the comparison of a small number of societies will make them seem very different from one another, these differences will seem smaller and smaller as the field of investigation is enlarged. It will eventually become plain that no human society is fundamentally good: but neither is any of them fundamentally bad; all offer their members certain advantages, though we must bear in mind a residue of iniquity, apparently more or less constant in its importance, which may correspond to a specific inertia which offers resistance, on the level of social life, to all attempts at organization.

This may surprise the habitual reader of travel-books, who delights in hearing of the 'barbarous' customs of this people or that. But these superficial reactions are soon put in their place, once the facts have been correctly interpreted and re-established in a wider perspective. Take the case of cannibalism, which is of all savage practices the one we find the most horrible and disgusting. We must set aside those cases in which people eat one another for lack of any other meat—as was the case in certain parts of Polynesia. No society is proof, morally speaking, against the demands of hunger. In times of starvation men will eat literally anything, as we lately saw in the Nazi extermination-camps.

There remain to be considered what we may call the positive forms of cannibalism—those whose origins are mystical, magical, or religious. By eating part of the body of an ancestor, or a fragment of an enemy corpse, the cannibal hoped to acquire the virtues, or perhaps to neutralize the power, of the dead man. Such rites were often observed with great discretion, the vital mouthful being made up of a small quantity of pulverized organic matter mixed, on occasion, with other forms of food. And even when the element of cannibalism was more openly avowed, we must acknowledge that to condemn such customs on moral grounds implies either belief in a bodily resurrection, which would be compromised by the material destruction of the corpse, or the affirmation of a link between body and spirit, and of the resulting dualism. These convictions are of the same nature as those in the name of which ritual cannibalism is practised, and we have no good reason for preferring the one to the other—all the more so as the disregard for the sanctity of death, with which we reproach the cannibal, is certainly no greater, and indeed arguably much less, than that which we tolerate in our European 'anatomy lessons'.

But above all we must realize that certain of our own usages, if investigated by an observer from a different society, would seem to him similar in kind to the cannibalism which we consider 'uncivilized'. I am thinking here of our judicial and penitentiary customs. If we were to look at them from outside it would be tempting to distinguish two opposing types of society: those which practise cannibalism—who believe, that is to say, that the only way to neutralize people who are the repositories of certain redoubtable powers, and even to turn them to one's own advantage, is to absorb them into one's own body. Second would come those which, like our own, adopt what might be called anthropoemia (from the Greek *emein*, to vomit). Faced with the same problem, they have chosen the opposite solution. They expel these formidable beings from the body public by isolating them for a time, or for ever, denying them all contact with humanity, in establishments devised for that express purpose. In most of the societies which we would call primitive this custom would inspire the profoundest horror: we should seem to them barbarian in the same degree as we impute to them on the ground of their no-more-than-symmetrical customs.

Societies which seem to us ferocious may turn out, when examined from another point of view, to have their humane and benevolent sides. Take the Plains Indians of North America: they are doubly significant—first because some of them practised a moderated form of cannibalism, and second because they are one of the few primitive peoples who were endowed with an organized police force. This force, which also had to mete out justice, would never have imagined that the punishments accorded to the guilty could take the form of a severance of social links. An Indian who broke the laws of his tribe would be sentenced to the destruction of all his belongings—his tent and his horses. But at the same time the police became indebted to him and were required, in fact, to compensate him for the harm he had been made to suffer. This restitution put the criminal, once again, in debt to the group, and he was obliged to acknowledge this by a series of gifts which the entire community—including the police—would help him to get together. These reciprocities continued, by way of gifts and counter-gifts, until the initial disorder created by the crime and its punishment had been completely smoothed over and order was once again complete. Not only are such customs more humane than our own, but they are more coherent, even if we are to formulate the problem in terms of modern psychology. It would seem logical that in return for the 'infantilization' of the guilty man which is implied in the notion of punishment, we should also acknowledge that he is entitled to a gratification of some sort. If this is not done, the initial step loses its effectiveness and may even bring about results directly contrary to those hoped for in the first place. The summit of absurdity in this context is to do as we do and treat the guilty simultaneously as children, in that they are meet for punishment, and as grown-ups, in that we refuse them all subsequent consolation. It is grotesque to believe that we have made a 'great spiritual advance' simply because, instead of eating our fellow human beings, we prefer to mutilate them, both physically and morally.

If analyses of this sort are sincerely and methodically conducted they have two results. First, they encourage us to take a level-headed and unbiassed view of customs and ways of life remote from our own —without, however, attributing to them absolute merits such as no society can claim to possess. Second, they dissuade us from taking for granted the 'rightness' or 'naturalness' of our own customs, as can easily be the case if we know of no others, or know of them only partly and with bias. Anthropological analysis tends, admittedly, to enhance the prestige of other societies and diminish that of our own: in that respect its action is contradictory. But reflection will show, I think, that this contradiction is more apparent than real.

It has sometimes been said that only in western society have anthropologists been produced. Therein, it was said, lay its greatness;

anthropology might question all its other merits, but here at least was one before which we could not but bow our heads, since, but for that, we ourselves would not exist. But the contrary argument could also be sustained: that if the West has produced anthropologists, it is because it was so tormented by remorse that it had to compare its own image with that of other societies, in the hope that they would either display the same shortcomings or help the West to explain how these defects could have come into being. But even if it is true that the comparison of our own society with all others, present or past, will lead to the collapse of the foundations on which it rests—even so, others will meet the same fate. The general average of which I spoke earlier throws into relief the existence of a few sociological ogres, among whom we ourselves must be numbered. Nor is this an accident: if it were not that we deserved, and for that matter still deserve, first prize in this grim competition, anthropology would never have come into being; we should have felt no need of it. If anthropology cannot take a detached view of our civilization, or declare itself not responsible for that civilization's evils, it is because its very existence is unintelligible unless we regard it as an attempt to redeem it. Yet other societies have shared in the same original sin, though they are doubtless few in number, and fewer still as we descend the ladder of progress. I need cite one instance only: that open wound on the flank of Americanism, the Aztecs. Their maniacal obsession with blood and torture is a universal trait, but comparison allows us to define it in their case as excessive, even if it can be explained in terms of the necessity of taming the fear of death. That obsession puts them on a par with ourselves; for, if they were not alone in their iniquity, they nevertheless stand, as we ourselves stand in other respects, on the side of immoderation.

And yet this self-inflicted self-condemnation does not mean that we award a first prize for excellence to this or that society, present or past, localized at a determinable point in space or time. That would be a great injustice: for we should be failing to realize that if we had been members of that prize-winning society we might have found it intolerable and condemned it, just as we condemn the one to which we belong today. Is it then the case that anthropology tends to condemn *all* forms of social order, whatever they may be, and to glorify a condition of Nature which can only be corrupted by the establishment of social order? 'Don't trust the man who comes to put things in order,' said Diderot, whose position has just been stated. For him the history of our race could be summed up as follows: 'Once there was natural

Man. Within that natural Man, an artificial Man was later introduced. Between the two, war broke out, and will go on raging till life comes to an end.' This conception is absurd. Whoever says 'Man', says 'Language', and whoever says 'Language', says 'Society'. The Polynesians visited by Bougainville (and it was in the 'Supplement' to Bougainville's travels that Diderot put forward his theory) lived in society every bit as much as we do. Anyone who questions this is moving counter to the direction in which anthropological analysis would have us go.

Turning over these problems in my mind, I become convinced that Rousseau's is the only answer to them. Rousseau is much decried these days; never has his work been so little known; and he has to face, above all, the absurd accusation that he glorified the 'state of Nature' for its own sake. (That may have been Diderot's error, but it was never Rousseau's.) What Rousseau said was the exact contrary; and he remains the only man who shows us how to get clear of the contradictions into which his adversaries have led us. Rousseau, of all the *philosophes*, came nearest to being an anthropologist. He never travelled in distant countries, certainly; but his documentation was as complete as it could be at that time and, unlike Voltaire, he brought his knowledge alive by the keenness of his interest in peasant customs and popular thought. Rousseau is our master and our brother, great as has been our ingratitude towards him; and every page of this book could have been dedicated to him, had the object thus proffered not been unworthy of his great memory. For there is only one way in which we can escape the contradiction inherent in the notion of position of the anthropologist, and that is by reformulating, on our own account, the intellectual procedures which allowed Rousseau to move forward from the ruins left by the *Discours sur l'Origine de l'Inegalité* to the ample design of the *Social Contract*, of which *Emile* reveals the secret. He it is who showed us how, after we have destroyed every existing order, we can still discover the principles which allow us to erect a new order in their stead.

Never did Rousseau make Diderot's mistake—that of exalting the 'natural Man'. There is no risk of his confusing the state of Nature with the state of Society; he knows that the latter is inherent in mankind, but that it brings evils with it, and that the question to be solved is whether or not these evils are themselves inherent in that state. We must go beyond the evidence of the injustices of abuses to which the social order gives rise and discover the unshakable basis of human society.

There are two ways in which anthropology contributes to this quest. It shows that that base cannot be found in our own civilization: of all the societies we can examine ours is indeed perhaps the one furthest from it. Secondly, by enabling us to distinguish the characteristics common to the majority of human societies, it helps us to constitute a model, to which no society corresponds exactly, but which defines closely the direction in which our investigations should be oriented. Rousseau thought that the image nearest to it, for experimental purposes, was what we now call the neolithic age. I am inclined to think that he was right. In the neolithic age, Man had already made most of the inventions which are indispensable to his security. We have seen why writing need not be included among these; to say that writing is a double-edged weapon is not a mark of 'primitivism'; the cyberneticians of our own day have rediscovered that truth. During the neolithic age, Man put himself beyond the reach of cold and hunger; he acquired leisure to think; and although he was more or less at the mercy of disease it is not certain that our advances in the field of hygiene have done more than transfer to other mechanisms the responsibility of maintaining a certain measure of demographic equilibrium: the epidemics which contributed to that equilibrium were no more dreadful than the famines and wars of extermination which later took their place.

In that myth-minded age, Man was no more free than he is today; but it was his humanness alone which kept him enslaved. As he had only a very restricted control over Nature, he was protected, and to a certain degree emancipated, by the protective cushion of his dreams. As and when these dreams turned into knowledge, so did Man's power increase; this gave us, if I may so put it, the 'upper hand' over the universe, and we still take an immense pride in it. But what is it, in reality, if not the subjective awareness that humanity is being progressively more and more sundered from the physical universe? The great determining factors in that universe are no longer acting upon us as redoubtable strangers; rather is their operation not now through the intermediacy of thought, as they colonize us in the interests of the silent world whose agents we have now become?

Rousseau was probably right when he held that it would have been better for our happiness if humanity had kept to 'the middle ground between the indolence of the primitive state and the questing activity to which we are prompted by our *amour-propre*'. That middle state was, he said, 'the best for Man'; and only some 'ill-boding turn of events' could have caused us to leave it. That turn of events was found in the development of mechanical civilizations—a phenomenon doubly exceptional in that it was first, unique, and second, belated. And yet it remains clear that the middle state of which Rousseau wrote is in no way a primitive condition. It presupposes and tolerates a certain degree of progress; and although no society as yet described corresponds to its privileged image, even if 'the example of the savages, who have almost always been found at this point of development, seems to confirm that mankind was designed to remain at it for ever'.

The study of these savages does not reveal a Utopian state of Nature; nor does it make us aware of a perfect society hidden deep in the forests. It helps us to construct a theoretical model of a society which corresponds to none that can be observed in reality, but will help us to disentangle 'what in the present nature of Man is original, and what is artificial'. It also helps us 'to know closely a state which no longer exists, which may never have existed, which probably never will exist, and of which we must, none the less, have an exact notion if we are to judge our present situation correctly'. I have already quoted this in order to bring out the significance of my observations among the Nambikwara; for Rousseau's thought, ever in advance of his time, does not dissociate theoretical sociology from those researches in the laboratory, or in the field, which he knew to be necessary. 'Natural Man' does not pre-date Society; nor is he outside it. Our task is to re-discover the 'natural Man' in his relation to the social state outside of which our human condition cannot be imagined; the anthropologist must draw up, therefore, the programme of the experiments which 'are necessary if we are to understand natural Man'; and he must 'determine the best way of making these experiments within Society itself'.

But this model—and here lies Rousseau's solution—is eternal and universal. Other societies may not be better than our own; even if we believe them to be so we have no way of proving it. But knowing them better does none the less help us to detach ourselves from our own society. It is not that our society is absolutely evil, or that others are not evil also; but merely that ours is the only society from which we *have* to disentangle ourselves. In doing so, we put ourselves in a position to attempt the second phase of our undertaking: that in which, while not clinging to elements from any one particular society, we make use of one and all of them in order to distinguish those principles of social life which may be applied to the reform of our own customs, and not of those of societies foreign to our own. In relation to our own society, that is to say, we stand in a position of privilege which is exactly contrary to that which I have just described; for our own society is the only one which we can transform and yet not destroy, since the changes which we should introduce would come from within.

There is a risk, certainly, in placing beyond space and time the model from which we take our inspiration: the risk of underestimating the reality of progress. Our argument is, in brief, that men have always and everywhere undertaken the same task, and assigned to themselves the same object; all that has differed is the means employed. I must own that this attitude does not at all disturb me; it seems the closest to the facts, as they are revealed to us by history and anthropology; and above all it seems to me to yield results. The zealots of progress run the risk of underestimating, and thus of knowing too little about, the immense riches which our race has accumulated to one side and the other of the narrow furrow on which they keep their eyes fixed. By overvaluing the importance of what has been done in the past, they depreciate what still remains to be done. If our race has concentrated on one task, and one alone—that of building a society in which Man can live—then the sources of strength on which our remote ancestors drew are present also in ourselves. All the stakes are still on the board, and we can take them up at any time we please. Whatever was done, and done badly, can be begun all over again: 'The golden age which blind superstition situated behind or ahead of us is *in us*.' Human brotherhood acquires a palpable significance when we find our image of it confirmed in the poorest of tribes, and when that tribe offers us an experience which, when joined with many hundreds of others, has a lesson to teach us. That lesson may even come to us with a milleniary freshness; for, knowing as we do that for thousands of years past mankind has done nothing but repeat itself, we shall attain that noble cast of thought which, transcending all that has been done and redone, assigns as the starting-point of our reflections that indefinable grandeur which is the mark of true beginnings. To be a man means, for each of us, member-ship of a class, a society, a country, a continent, and a civilization. For those of us who are earth-bound Europeans, our adventurings into the heart of the New World have a lesson to teach us: that the New World was not ours to destroy, and yet we destroyed it; and that no other will be vouchsafed to us. In grasping these truths we come face to face with ourselves. Let us, at any rate, set them out as they first appeared to us, in that place, and at that moment in time, when our world lost the chance that was still open to it: that of choosing between its missions.

36 Conclusion

IT WAS in Asia, many years later, that—for myself, at
any rate—the problems suggested by this book were to find their
solution. In September 1950 I was in a Mogh village in the Chittagong
hill tracts. For some days I had been watching the women as they went
each morning to the temple with food for the bonzes. During the
siesta hours I listened to the strokes on the gong which punctuated the
prayers, and to the children's voices softly intoning the Burmese
alphabet. The *kyong* stood at the edge of the village on the top of a
little wooded hillock like those with which Tibetan painters like to
garnish their far distances. At its foot was the *jédi*, or pagoda. In that
poor village it was no more than a circular earthen construction which
rose from the ground in seven concentric stages, rising step by step, in a
square enclosure trellised with bamboo. We took off our shoes before
climbing up, and the moistened surface of the clay was very agreeable
to the feet. Here and there on the steep little slope we could see the
stalks of pineapples that had been wrenched off the day before by
people from the village who felt it to be improper that their priests,
whose needs were looked to by the lay population, should also allow
themselves to grow fruit. The top of the hillock looked like a tiny
town-square surrounded on three sides by straw hangars, beneath
which were sheltering large objects made of bamboo and hung with
many-coloured paper. These kite-like creations were made for use in
local processions. On the fourth side stood the temple itself; it stood on
stakes like the houses of the village, and differed from them only in that
it was bigger and that a thatch-roofed square feature dominated the
main part of the building. After our upward scramble through the mud,
the ritual ablutions came quite naturally and seemed to have no
religious significance. We went into the temple. There was no light
but that which came down from the top of the lantern formed by the
hollow cage in the centre, just above where the altar was bedecked with

393

standards of rag or matting. Certain glimmers also penetrated the thatch of the walls. About fifty brass statues stood about on the altar and beside it was hung a gong. On the walls we could see one or two pious chromolithographs and the skull of a stag. The floor was made up of large sections of bamboo, split down the middle and plaited together. Shiny from the continual movement of bare feet, it yielded to the touch as softly as any carpet. A peaceful barn-like atmosphere prevailed and there was a smell of hay. The simple, spacious room might have been an abandoned hay-loft; and when combined with the courtesy of the two bonzes, erect, with their two straw pallets on bedsteads, and with the touching care and devotion which had been lavished on the assemblage or manufacture of all the accessories of worship, all this brought me nearer than ever before to having some idea of the meaning of a sanctuary. 'You need not do as I do,' said my companion as he prostrated himself four times before the altar: and I, respecting his opinion, remained motionless. This was rather from discretion than from *amour-propre*: he knew that I did not subscribe to his faith, and I should have been afraid of abusing the ritual gestures had I given him to believe that I thought them no more than conventions. And yet, for once, I should have felt no embarrassment had I followed his example. Between that form of worship and myself there was no misunderstanding to get in the way. It was not a question of bowing down to idols, or of adoring a supposedly supernatural order of things, but simply of paying homage to decisive reflections which had been formed twenty-five centuries earlier by a thinker, or by the society which created his legend. To those reflections my civilization could contribute only by confirming them.

For what, after all, have I learnt from the masters I have listened to, the philosophers I have read, the societies I have investigated, and that very Science in which the West takes such a pride? Simply a fragmentary lesson or two which, if laid end to end, would reconstitute the meditations of the Sage at the foot of his tree. When we make an effort to understand, we destroy the object of our attachment, substituting another whose nature is quite different. That other object requires of us another effort, which in its turn destroys the second object and substitutes a third—and so on until we reach the only enduring Presence, which is that in which all distinction between meaning and the absence of meaning disappears: and it is from that Presence that we started in the first place. It is now two thousand five hundred years since men discovered and formulated these truths. Since then we have discovered nothing new—unless it be that whenever we investigated what seemed to be a way out, we met with a further proof of the conclusions from which we had tried to escape.

Of course I am also aware of the dangers of a state of resignation that has been arrived at too hastily. This great religion of not-knowing-ness is not based upon our incapacity to understand. It bears witness, rather, to our natural gifts, raising us to the point at which we discover truth in the guise of the mutual exclusiveness of being and knowing. And, by a further audacity, it has achieved something that, elsewhere, only Marxism has brought off: it has reconciled the problem of meta-physics with the problem of human behaviour. Its schism appeared on the sociological level, in that the fundamental point of difference between the Great and the Little Vehicles is whether or not we should believe that the salvation of any one individual depends on the salvation of humanity as a whole.

And yet the historical solutions of Buddhist morality lead to a chilling alternative: either Man must answer 'Yes' to the question I have just outlined, in which case he must enter a monastery; or he thinks differently and gets off lightly with the practice of a virtuous egoism.

But injustice, poverty, and suffering exist: and, by existing, provide an intermediary solution. We are not alone, and it is not within our control either to remain deaf and blind to the rest of mankind, or to plead guilty, in ourselves, for all humanity. Buddhism can remain perfectly coherent and, at the same time, respond to appeals from without. Perhaps even, in a vast section of the world, it has found the missing link in the chain. For if the last moment in the dialectical process which leads to enlightenment is of value, so also are all those moments which precede and are similar to it. The absolute 'No' to meaning is the last of a series of stages which leads from a lesser to a greater meaning. The last step needs, and at the same time validates, all those which went before it. In its own way, and on its own level, each of them corresponds to a truth. Between Marxist criticism which sets Man free from his first chains, and Buddhist criticism, which completes that liberation, there is neither opposition nor contradiction. (The Marxist teaches that the apparent significance of Man's condition will vanish the moment he agrees to enlarge the object that he has under consideration.) Marxism and Buddhism are doing the same thing, but at different levels. The passage between the two extremes is guaranteed by all those advances in knowledge that our race has accomplished in the last two thousand years, thanks to an indissoluble movement of thought which runs from East to West and, perhaps only to confirm its origin, has removed from one to the other. Just as beliefs and superstitions dissolve when we try to fix clearly in our minds the truth about human relations, so does morality give way to history, and fluid forms give way to constructions, and creation give way to nothingness. We have only to turn the initial move back upon itself to discover its symmetry; its parts can be superimposed one upon the other, and the stages through which we have already passed are not cancelled, but rather confirmed, by those which succeed them.

As he moves forward within his environment, Man takes with him all the positions that he has occupied in the past, and all those that he will occupy in the future. He is everywhere at the same time, a crowd which, in the act of moving forward, yet recapitulates at every instant every step that it has ever taken in the past. For we live in several worlds, each more true than the one within it, and each false in relation to that within which it is itself enveloped. Some of these worlds may be apprehended in action, others exist because we have them in our thoughts: but the apparent contradictoriness of their co-existence is resolved by the fact that we are constrained to accord meaning to those worlds which are nearer to us, and to refuse it to those more distant. Truth lies rather in the progressive expansion of meaning: but an expansion conducted inwards from without and pushed home to explosion-point.

As an anthropologist I am no longer, therefore, the only person to suffer from a contradiction which is proper to humanity as a whole and bears within itself the reason for its existence. Only when I isolate the two extremes does the contradiction still persist: for what is the use of action, if the thinking which guides that action leads to the discovery of meaninglessness? But that discovery cannot be made immediately: it must be thought, and I cannot think it all at once. There may be twelve stages, as in the Boddhi; but whether they are fewer, or more numerous, they exist as a single whole, and if I am to get to the end of them, I shall be called upon continually to live through situations, each of which demands something of me: I owe myself to mankind, just as much as to knowledge. History, politics, the social and economic universe, the physical world, even the sky—all surround me in concentric circles, and I can only escape from those circles in thought if I concede to each of them some part of my being. Like the pebble which marks the surface of the wave with circles as it passes through it, I must throw myself into the water if I am to plumb the depths.

The world began without the human race and it will end without it. The institutions, manners, and customs which I shall have spent my life in cataloguing and trying to understand are an ephemeral efflorescence of a creative process in relation to which they are meaningless, unless it be that they allow humanity to play its destined role. That role does not, however, assign to our race a position of independence. Nor, even if Man himself is condemned, are his vain efforts directed towards the arresting of a universal process of decline. Far from it: his role is itself a machine, brought perhaps to a greater point of perfection than any other, whose activity hastens the disintegration of an initial order and precipitates a powerfully organized Matter towards a condition of inertia which grows ever greater and will one day prove definitive. From the day when he first learned how to breathe and how to keep himself alive, through the discovery of fire and right up to the invention of the atomic and thermonuclear devices of the present day, Man has never—save only when he reproduces himself—done other than cheerfully dismantle million upon million of structures and reduce their elements to a state in which they can no longer be reintegrated. No doubt he has built cities and brought the soil to fruition; but if we examine these activities closely we shall find that they also are inertia-producing machines, whose scale and speed of action are infinitely greater than the amount of organization implied in them. As for the creations of the human mind, they are meaningful only in relation to that mind and will fall into nothingness as soon as it ceases to exist. Taken as a whole, therefore, civilization can be described as a prodigiously complicated mechanism: tempting as it would be to regard it as our universe's best hope of survival, its true function is to produce what physicists call entropy: inertia, that is to say. Every scrap of conversation, every line set up in type, establishes a communication between two interlocutors, levelling what had previously existed on two different planes and had had, for that reason, a greater degree of organization. 'Entropology', not anthropology, should be the word for the discipline that devotes itself to the study of this process of disintegration in its most highly evolved forms.

And yet I exist. Not in any way, admittedly, as an individual: for what am I, in that respect, but a constantly renewed stake in the struggle between the society, formed by the several million nerve-cells which take shelter in the anthill of the brain, and my body, which serves that society as a robot? Neither psychology, nor metaphysics, nor art can provide me with a refuge; for one and all are myths subject, within and without, to that new kind of sociology which will arise one day and treat them as severely as has our earlier one. Not merely is the first person singular detestable: there is no room for it between 'ourselves' and 'nothing'. And if, in the end, I opt for 'ourselves', although it is no more than an appearance, it is because unless I destroy myself—an act which would wipe out the conditions of the decision I have to make— there is really only one choice to be made: between that appearance and nothing. But no sooner have I chosen than, by that very choice, I take on myself, unreservedly, my condition as a man. Thus liberated from an intellectual pride whose futility is only equalled by that of its object, I also agree to subordinate its claims to the objective will-to-emancipa- tion of that multitude of human beings who are still denied the means of choosing their own destiny.

Man is not alone in the universe, any more than the individual is alone in the group, or any one society alone among other societies. Even if the rainbow of human cultures should go down for ever into the abyss which we are so insanely creating, there will still remain open to us—provided we are alive and the world is in existence—a precarious arch that points towards the inaccessible. The road which it indicates to us is one that leads directly away from our present serfdom: and even if we cannot set off along it, merely to contemplate it will procure us the only grace that we know how to deserve. The grace to call a halt, that is to say: to check the impulse which prompts Man always to block up, one after another, such fissures as may be open in the blank wall of necessity and to round off his achievement by slamming shut the doors of his own prison. This is the grace for which every society longs, irrespective of its beliefs, its political regime, its level of civilization. It stands, in every case, for leisure, and recreation, and freedom, and peace of body and mind. On this opportunity, this chance of for once detaching oneself from the implacable process, life itself depends. Farewell to savages, then, farewell to journeying! And instead, during the brief intervals in which humanity can bear to interrupt its hive-like labours, let us grasp the essence of what our species has been and still is, beyond thought and beneath society: an essence that may be vouchsafed to us in a mineral more beautiful than any work of Man; in the scent, more subtly evolved than our books, that lingers in the heart of a lily; or in the wink of an eye, heavy with patience, serenity, and mutual forgiveness, that sometimes, through an involuntary understanding, one can exchange with a cat.

Bibliography

Handbook of South American Indians, ed. by J. Stewart, Smithsonian Institution, Washington, D.C., 6 vols., 1946–50.

P. GAFFAREL, *Histoire du Brésil français au 16ᵉ siècle*, Paris, 1878.

J. DE LÉRY, *Histoire d'un voyage faict en la terre du Brésil*, new edition (by P. Gaffarel), Paris, 1880, 2 vols.

A. THEVET, 'Le Brésil et les Brésiliens', in *Les classiques de la colonization*, 2; selected and annotated by Suzanne Lussagnet, Paris, 1953.

Y. D'ÉVREUX, *Voyage dans le Nord du Brésil fait durant les années 1613–14*, Leipzig and Paris, 1864.

L. A. DE BOUGAINVILLE, *Voyage autour du monde*, Paris, 1771.

P. MONBEIG, *Pionniers et planteurs de São Paulo*, Paris, 1952.

J. SANCHEZ-LABRADOR, *El Paraguay Catolico*, 3 vols. Buenos Aires, 1910–17.

G. BOGGIANI, *Viaggi d'un artista nell'America Meridionale*, Rome, 1895.

D. RIBEIRO, *A arte dos indios Kadiuéu*, Rio de Janeiro, undated (1950).

K. VON DEN STEINEN, (*a*) *Durch Zentral-Brasilien*, Leipzig, 1886.

(*b*) *Unter den Naturvölkern Zentral-Brasiliens*, Berlin, 1894.

A. COLBACCHINI, *I Bororos orientali*, Turin, 1925.

C. LÉVI-STRAUSS, 'Contribution à l'étude de l'organization sociale des Indiens Bororo', *Journal de la Société des Américanistes*, new series, vol. 28, 1936.

C. LÉVI-STRAUSS, *La Vie familiale et sociale des Indiens Nambikwara*, Société des Américanistes, Paris, 1948.

C. LÉVI-STRAUSS, 'Le syncrétisme religieux d'un village mogh du territoire de Chittagong (Pakistan)', *Revue de l'Histoire des religions*, 1952.

C. NIMUENDAJU (*a*) *The Apinayé*, Anthropological Series, Catholic University of America, No. 8, 1939. (*b*) *The Serente*, Los Angeles, 1942.

E. ROQUETTE-PINTO, *Rondonia*, Rio de Janeiro, 1912.

C. M. DA SILVA RONDON, *Lectures Delivered by*, Publications of the Rondon Commission, No. 43, Rio de Janeiro, 1916.

THEODORE ROOSEVELT, *Through the Brazilian Wilderness*, New York, 1914.

K. OBERG, *Indian Tribes of Northern Mato Grosso, Brazil*, Smithsonian Institution, Institute of Social Anthropology, Publication, No. 15, Washington, D.C., 1953.

JULIO C. TELLO: (*a*) 'Wira Kocha, Inca', vol. 1, 1923; (*b*) 'Discovery of the Chavin culture in Peru', *American Antiquity*, vol. 9, 1943.

Index

A

Ailly, Pierre d', 80
Amazonian forest, character of, 336, 339
Amazonian forest-peoples, imaginative qualities of, 358; magical and medical devices, 358–9, chestnut-workings, 361
America, first penetration of, 240 ff.
American hybrid, sub-species of, 246
Anthropology, role of adventure in, 17; ambiguities of, 58 ff.; self-interrogatory aspect of, 374; fundamental dilemma of, 382 ff.; contradictions involved in, 384; a by-product of remorse?, 388; and bases of society, 389–90; and progress, 392
Arawaks, the, 239
Aztecs, the, 388

B

Barão de Melgaço, sojourn at, 315–16
Barra dos Bugres, bonesetter at, 257
Bernier, François, 44
Boas, Franz, 63
Boggiani, Guido, 135
Bororo, 198–231 passim; hierarchical structure of, 178 ff.; lay-out of villages, 203 ff.; moieties, function of, among, 205 ff.; clan structure, 206; material equipment of, 210;

accessories of dress, 210; baitemannageo, function of, 214 ff.; attitude to the dead, 218 ff., 228 ff.; sorcerers, role of among, 220 ff.; evening roll-call, 225; Tugaré clans, dances of, 226 ff.;
Bougainville, Louis Antoine de, 44, 94 ff., 389
Bouglé, Celestin, 49 ff.
Brazil, author's first notion of, 49; character of interior, 123
Breton, André, 26
Buddhism, morality of, 395 ff.

C

Caduveo, 141 ff., 149 ff.; capital of, 151 ff.; pottery, jewellery, and statuettes among, 155 ff.; face- and body-paintings of, 161 ff., 173 ff.; hierarchical structure of, 179
Campos Novos, 373 ff.
Cellini, Benvenuto, 332
Chapadão, the, 191
Chittagong hill tracts, the, 393 ff.
Chopin, Frédéric, author and, 375
Cities westward drive in, 125 ff.
Colonialism, early character of, 79 ff.
Columbus, 77 ff., 80 ff.
Corneille, author's version of, 376–80
Corumba, 183 ff.
Courtin, René, 121
Cousin, Jean, 86

401